what!

INTERACTIONS

Western Canadian Edition

JACK HOPE

MARIAN SMALL

Consultants

Valeen Chow
Ralph Connelly
Larry Elchuck
Peggy Hill
Alexander Norrie
Deborah Tempest
Sheila Tossell

ESL Consultant

Wendy McDonell

Prentice Hall Ginn Canada

INTERACTIONS 6

Canadian Cataloguing in Publication Data

Main entry under title:
Hope, Jack
Interactions 6

Rev. ed.
Includes index.
ISBN 0-13-858523-7

1. Mathematics - Juvenile literature. I. Small, Marian.
II. Title.

QA107. H676 1997 510 C96-932600-9

ISBN 0-13-858523-7

Prentice Hall, Inc., Englewood Cliffs, New Jersey
Prentice Hall International, Inc., London
Prentice Hall of Australia, Pty., Ltd., Sydney
Prentice Hall of India Pvt., Ltd., New Delhi
Prentice Hall of Japan, Inc., Tokyo
Prentice Hall of Southeast Asia (PTE) Ltd., Singapore
Editora Prentice Hall do Brasil Ltda., Rio de Janeiro
Prentice Hall Hispanoamericana, S.A., Mexico

PUBLISHER MaryLynne Meschino

MANAGING EDITOR Bonnie Di Malta

EDITORS Shirley Barrett, Brenda McLoughlin, Dianne Brassolotto

ART/DESIGN Sandi Meland Cherun/Word & Image Design Studio, ArtPlus Limited Design Consultants

Printed and bound in Canada

A B C D E F G – ML – 01 00 99 98 97

Contents

Unit 1 Investigating Our Community 1

Collecting and Interpreting Data

Who Lives in Our Community? 2-3
Reading histograms, strip graphs and circle graphs, and drawing histograms and strip graphs

Sampling and Bias

What Are Our Community's Favorites? 4-5
Understanding bias, random sampling, and populations

Interpreting First-and Second-Hand Data

How Does Our Weather Compare? 6-7
Using first-hand and second-hand data to draw graphs

Reading, Writing, and Modelling Numbers

How Many People Live in Our Community? 8-9
Reading, writing, and estimating numerals to a million

Reading and Writing Decimals

Who Lives in a Global Village? 10-11
Reading and writing decimals to thousandths

Measuring and Calculating

How Crowded Is Our Community? 12-13
Calculating population density

I Wonder ... ? 14

Thinking Back 15

Unit 2 Examining Number Patterns 16-17

Representing Numbers

Reading the Paper 18-19
Representing whole numbers

Exchanging Currency 20-21
Reading and writing numbers to thousandths

Comparing Baseball Performances 22-23
Comparing decimals

Covering the Hexagon 24-25
Modelling fractions and mixed numbers

Covering the Circle 26-27
Finding equivalent mixed numbers and improper fractions

Comparing the Cards 28-29
Ordering fractions, mixed numbers, and decimals

Riding the Elevator 30
Modelling integers

Comparing Temperatures 31
Comparing integers

Take Your Pick 32

Using Place Value Patterns

Buying Inventory 33
Multiplying and dividing by powers of ten

Examining Measurements 34-35
Renaming measurements

Estimating Germs 36
Estimating large quantities

Take Your Pick 37

Problem Solving Focus

Solving a Problem by Making an Organized List 38

Practising What You've Learned 39

Playing Games for Practice 40

Take Your Pick 41

Showing What You Know 42

Thinking Back 43

Unit 3 Exploring Angles 44-45

Measuring Angles

Comparing Slices 46-47
Comparing by superimposing

Dining Out 48-49
Comparing by rotating

Estimating Signal Flag Angles 50-51
Comparing angles to 90° and 180°

Measuring Letter Angles 52
Using degrees

Measuring Clock Angles 53
Estimating and measuring angles

Drawing Angles 54
Sketching and drawing angles of a given measure

Take Your Pick 55

Exploring Angle Relationships

Examining Triangles 56-57
Classifying triangles by the measure of their angles

Identifying Angles Around Us 58
Comparing angles in the environment

Take Your Pick 59

Problem Solving Focus

Solving a Problem by Drawing a Diagram 60

Practising What You've Learned 61

Playing Games for Practice 62

Take You Pick 63

Showing What You Know 64

Thinking Back 65

Unit 4 Introducing Ratio and Percent 66-67

Using Ratio

Making Punch 68-69
Describing ratio situations

Describing Yields 70-71
Renaming ratios

Take Your Pick 72

Using Percent

Examining Our Planet 73
Recognizing percent

Describing Hockey Players 74-75
Reading percent graphs

Take Your Pick 76

Problem Solving Focus

Solving a Problem by Doing an Experiment 77

Practising What You've Learned 78

Playing Games for Practice 79

Take Your Pick 80

Showing What you Know 81

Thinking Back 82

Unit 5 Investigating Transportation 83

Using Measurements

How Much Can We Take? 84-85
Estimating mass and volume

Using Maps and Schedules

How Do We Read Schedules? 86-87
Interpreting schedules

Approximating Cost and Time

How Should We Go? 88-89
Estimating approximate cost and time

I Wonder ... ? 90

Thinking Back 91

Unit 6 Extending Multiplication and Division 92-93

Estimating Products and Quotients

Estimating Winks and Blinks 94-95
Using approximate numbers

Recycling Phone Books 96
Rearranging to estimate products/quotients

Take Your Pick 97

Extending Multiplication Procedures

Keeping in Shape 98-99
Using informal methods to multiply

Examining Maps 100-101
Using a multiplication algorithm

Making Lunches 102-103
Multiplying decimals and whole numbers

You'll Never Be Stuck Multiplying Decimals 104

Take Your Pick 105

Extending Division Procedures

Comparing Animals 106-107
Dividing by 2-digit divisors

Earning Money 108-109
Interpreting decimal remainders

Comparing Prizes 110-111
Dividing Decimals by Whole Numbers

You'll Never Be Stuck Dividing Decimals 112

Take Your Pick 113

Problem Solving Focus

Solving a Problem by Guessing and Testing 114

Practising What You've Learned 115

Playing Games for Practice 116

Take Your Pick 117

Showing What You Know 118

Thinking Back 119

Unit 7 Examining Motion Geometry 120-121

Using Motions to Create Congruent Shapes

Plotting Diagrams 122-123
Sliding shapes

Drawing Solids and Skeletons 124-125
Using slides to sketch 3-D shapes

Comparing Opposite Places 126-127
Flipping shapes

Examining Line Symmetry 128-129
Applying flips to line symmetry in polygons

Looking at Illusions 130-131
Examining congruent shapes

Plotting Designs 132-133
Combining motions on a coordinate grid

Take Your Pick 134

Problem Solving Focus

Solving a Problem by Working Backward 135

Practising What You've Learned 136

Playing Games For Practice 137

Showing What You Know 138

Thinking Back 139

Unit 8 Examining Number Theory 140-141

Examining Factors and Multiples

Creating Equal Groups 142-143
Finding factors

Lining Up Insects 144-145
Finding multiples and the least common multiple

Cutting Squares 146
Determining common factors and the greatest common factor

Take Your Pick 147

Classifying Numbers

Stretching Objects 148-149
Identifying prime numbers

Sorting Numbers 150-151
Using prime factorization to sort groups of numbers

Arranging Cards 152
Relating number and geometry patterns

Take Your Pick 153

Representing Algebraic Expressions

Generalizing Patterns 154-155
Describing relationships and creating expressions

Balancing Objects 156-157
Understanding equality by balancing objects

Modelling Equality 158-159
Explaining equality using models and diagrams

Finding Unknowns 160
Using pre-algebra strategies to solve single-variable equations

Take Your Pick 161

Problem Solving Focus

Solving a Problem by Finding and Extending a Pattern 162

Practising What You've Learned 163

Playing Games for Practice 164

Take Your Pick 165

Showing What You Know 166

Thinking Back 167

Unit 9 Exploring Probability and Statistics 168-169

Determining and Interpreting Probabilities and Statistics

Sampling Socks 170-171
Predicting by sampling

Describing Families 172-173
Simulating outcomes

Playing Games 174-175
Comparing theoretical and experimental probabilities

Using Different Dice 176-177
Relating the number of faces on a die to probability

Reading Survey Results 178-179
Displaying data in various ways

Comparing Lengths of Movies 180-181
Using stem-and-leaf plots

Take Your Pick 182

Problem Solving Focus

Solving a Problem by Finding Relevant Information 183

Practising What You've Learned 184

Playing Games for Practice 185

Take Your Pick 186

Showing What You Know 187

Thinking Back 188

Unit 10 Investigating Sports 189

Using Numbers

What Are Some Highlights in Sports 190-191
Using numerical data to solve and create problems

Using Measurements

How Can We Measure Sports Balls? 192-193
Estimating and measuring lengths and mass

Using Probability and Statistics

What Can We Learn About Hockey Statistics? 194-195
Using probability and statistics

I Wonder ... ? 196

Thinking Back 197

Unit 11 Exploring Measurement Shortcuts 198-199

Exploring Linear and Area Relationships

Racing Around 200-201
Relating side lengths and perimeters of polygons

Considering Polygons 202-203
Using expressions to find the perimeter of polygons

Measuring Labels 204-205
Relating dimensions and areas of rectangles

Considering Rectangles 206-207
Using expressions to find the area of rectangles

Examining Boxes 208
Determining surface area of right, rectangular prisms

Take Your Pick 209

Exploring Volume and Capacity Relationships

Digging Up Artifacts 210-211
Relating dimensions and volumes of rectangular prisms

Considering Prisms 212-213
Using rules to find volume of right rectangular prisms

Making Stone Soup 214-215
Finding the volumes of irregular solids

Take Your Pick 216

Problem Solving Focus

Solving a Problem by Making a Model 217

Practising What You've Learned 218

Playing Games for Practice 219

Take Your Pick 220

Showing What You Know 221

Thinking Back 222

Unit 12 Investigating the Environment 223

Measuring

How Do We Use Water? 224-225
Relating capacity to volume, using percent

Graphing

How Many Mosquitoes Surround Us? 226-227
Making, comparing different types of graphs

Calculating

What's Happening to Our Forests? 228-229
Using millions, fractions, ratios, areas and estimating percents and area

I Wonder ... ? 230

Thinking Back 231

Index 233-234

UNIT 1

Investigating Our Community

What do you consider to be your community?

Do more people live in Malvern or in your community?
How many more?

About how many times as large is the larger community?

What might be true about 0.5 of the people in Malvern?
in your community?

Use another decimal less than 1.0 to describe your community.

WHO Lives in Our Community?

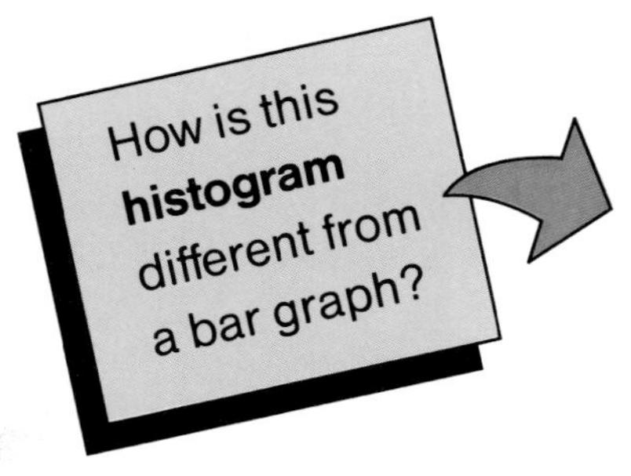

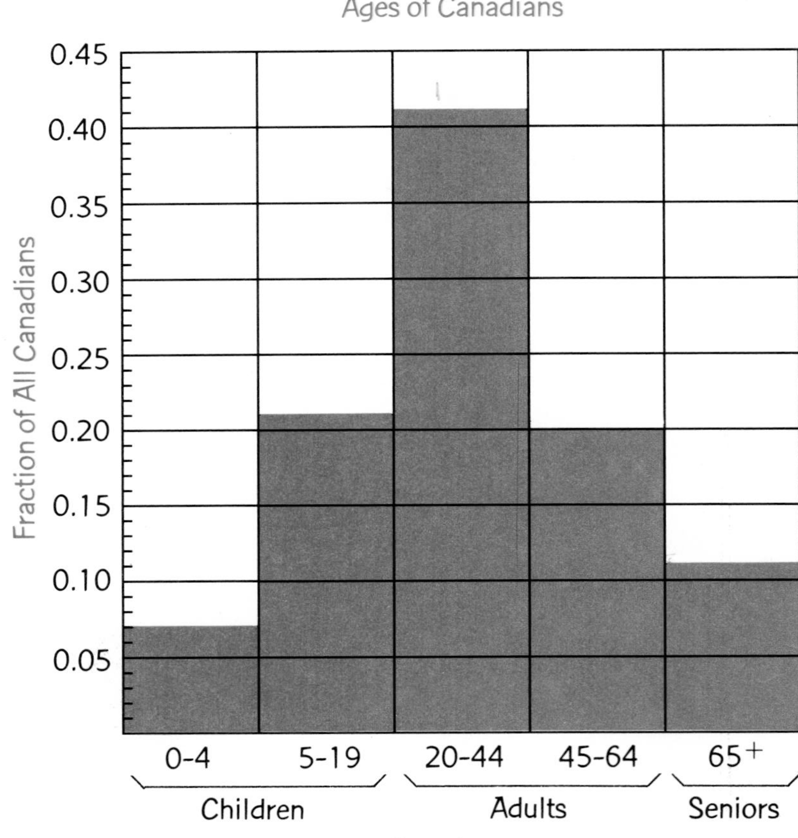

About how many times as many people are represented by the second bar as by the first bar? by the third bar as by the second bar? Why might this be?

1. What decimal tells the portion of Canadians who are seniors? not seniors? adults?

2. About how many adults would there be in 100 people? 1000 people? 12 000 people?

3. Assuming that the Canadian graph represents your community, about how many children live in your community?

4. What do you think *Other* in this **strip graph** includes? In what type of home do most people live? About how many times as many people live in that type as in Other?

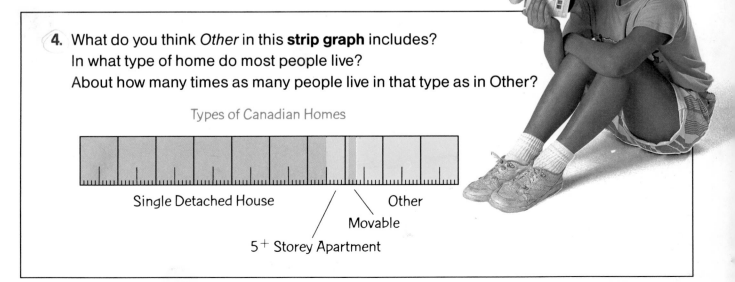

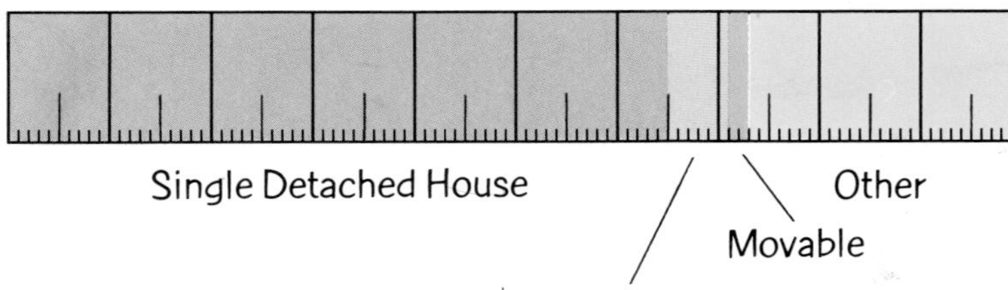

5. Investigate why a graph of the types of homes in your community might be different from the one for all Canadians. What are some key questions to ask in your investigation? Predict the result.

6. Assuming that the Canadian graph represents your community, how many people in your community would live in apartment buildings over 5 storeys high?

7. Show the ages of Canadians in a strip graph. Show the types of homes in a histogram. Which type of graph do you prefer? Tell why.

Occupations of Working Canadians

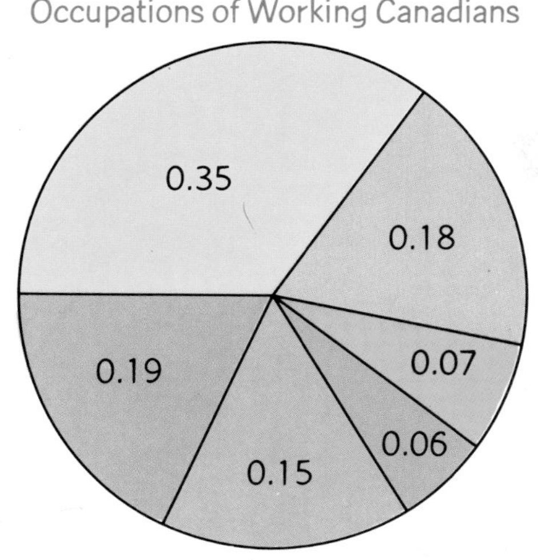

- Service
- Sales and Marketing
- Government
- Farming, Fishing, Forestry, Mining
- Manufacturing
- Other

8. Are there any reasons why a **circle graph** of the occupations for your community would be different from this one for all Canadians? If so, what are they?

9. Choose a topic in your community for which you can design and carry out an experiment in which you collect data by observation.

10. Design a questionnaire and use it to survey a sample of your community. Find out 2 things such as
    - type of housing
    - occupation
    - number of people living in home
    - number of years in present home

    Graph your results. How well do you think your sample represents your entire community? Explain.

11. Use an electronic network to collect data on a topic of interest in your community. Present a report to your class.

Did You Know...?

About 0.9 of the people in Sherbrooke, Québec, are bilingual.

▶ What two languages do you think are spoken there? What languages are spoken in your community? What fraction of your community might speak two or more languages?

WHAT Are Our Community's Favorites?

A TV rating company telephones a **random sample** of people in each urban Canadian area to find out what programs and commercials are watched most.

Then the results of the survey are used to determine the viewing habits and preferences of all the viewers in that area.

1. Why do you think a sample is selected instead of collecting the data from the entire population?

2. Why must a sample be random to be a good sample?

3. Would the results be biased if the TV rating company only sampled Grade 6 students in your area? Explain.

4. What would be the bias if they only sampled different age groups of males in your area?

How to Choose A Good Sample

- must represent the entire population
- must be large enough to give reliable results
- must be as unbiased as possible so it doesn't favor part of the population over another

Suppose you want to know the favorite TV program of Grade 6 students in your school.

5. What is the population for this investigation?

6. Is a random sample of 1 student's opinion large enough to be representative of all the Grade 6 students' opinions? Explain.

7. Would a random sample of 10 students' opinions be more representative of the population? Explain.

8. How would you select the students so that the results are as unbiased as possible?

9. Conduct the investigation. Then use your results to predict which is the favorite program of your school's Grade 6 population.

10. Melissa and Kurt designed and handed out 100 questionnaires to people going into the community library. One question they asked was:

What is your favorite leisure activity? Choose one.

❏ reading ❏ playing sports ❏ watching TV ❏ shopping

50 questionnaires were returned. Here are the results:

	Male	Female
Reading	𝍸 II	𝍸 𝍸 II
Playing sports	𝍸 𝍸	𝍸 I
Watching TV	𝍸 I	𝍸 II
Shopping		II

Melissa and Kurt concluded that most people in the community would rather read books than do anything else in their spare time.

Tell if you agree with each of the following, and describe what else Melissa and Kurt might have done.

- the wording of their question
- the method of gathering data
- the sample they chose to survey
- the conclusion they reached

11. Identify the bias in these statements.

- A school mathematics committee of 4 consisted of 3 females and 1 male.
- An Ontario company was hired by a mountain climbing magazine to determine the type of climbing gear preferred by mountain climbers. The company randomly surveyed 1000 people from Ontario.
- Teenagers from 13-17 years were randomly surveyed to determine the type of music that Canadians like best.

12. Describe an investigation about your community where the random sample would be chosen from

- people 65 years of age and older
- teenagers only
- households with children 3 years old and younger
- different age groups of females (or males)

Did You Know...?

The Gallup poll identifies trends in Canada. For a national survey, a random sample of 1000 Canadians who are 18 years or older are chosen to represent the 18 million people in Canadian who are 18 or older.

▶ If 800 people are randomly surveyed at shopping malls across Canada, is this a representative sample? Explain.

HOW Does Our Weather Compare?

Chris and Rajit collected weather data for their community. They plotted the ordered pairs for time and temperature on a grid, then joined the points to make a **broken-line graph**.

Oct. 3 Temperatures at School

Time	Temperature (°C)	Ordered pair
08:00	2	(08:00, 2)
09:00	4	(09:00, 4)
10:00	6	(10:00, 6)
11:00	11	(11:00, 11)
12:00	17	(12:00, 17)
13:00	22	(13:00, 22)
14:00	20	(14:00, 20)
15:00	18	(15:00, 18)
16:00	17	(16:00, 17)
17:00	15	(17:00, 15)

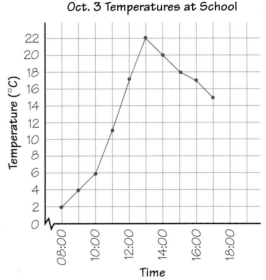

Oct. 3 Temperatures at School

Temperature (°C)

22 20 18 16 14 12 10 8 6 4 2 0

08:00 10:00 12:00 14:00 16:00 18:00

Time

Data that is collected personally is called **first-hand data**.

1. Collect your own first-hand data by measuring the outside temperature every hour during the day.
   Compare it with Chris and Rajit's data. What conclusions can you make?

2. How does the high temperature you recorded compare with that reported in the newspaper? Why might there be a difference?

Data published in a newspaper can be reused by other people, so it is called **second-hand data**.

3. What other general sources can you use to find second-hand data?

The following second-hand data was obtained from Environment Canada.
This, as well as much other weather information, is stored in their computer database.

Average Monthly Temperatures (°C) in the Provincial Capital Cities												
	Jan.	Feb.	Mar.	Apr.	May	June	July	Aug.	Sept.	Oct.	Nov.	Dec.
Victoria	3.4	4.8	6.1	8.4	11.4	14.3	16.2	16.2	13.8	9.7	6.0	3.8
Edmonton	-14.2	-10.8	-5.4	3.7	10.3	14.2	16.0	15.0	9.9	4.6	-5.7	-12.2
Regina	-16.5	-12.9	-6.0	4.1	11.4	16.4	19.1	18.1	11.6	5.1	-5.1	-13.6
Winnipeg	-18.3	-15.1	-7.0	3.8	11.6	16.9	19.8	18.3	12.4	5.7	-4.7	-14.6
Toronto	-6.7	-6.1	-0.8	6.0	12.3	17.4	20.5	19.5	15.2	8.9	3.2	-3.5
Quebec	-12.4	-11.0	-4.6	3.3	10.8	16.3	19.1	17.6	12.5	6.5	-0.5	-9.1
Fredericton	-9.6	-8.5	-2.5	4.0	10.8	16.2	19.3	18.3	13.0	7.3	1.2	-6.6
Halifax	-5.8	-6.0	-1.7	3.6	9.4	14.7	18.3	18.1	13.8	-8.5	3.2	-3.0
Charlottetown	-7.7	-8.0	-3.4	2.3	5.8	14.4	18.4	18.0	13.4	8.0	2.5	-4.1
St. John's	-4.3	-5.0	-2.5	1.3	5.8	10.9	15.4	15.3	11.6	7.0	3.1	-1.7

Average Monthly Precipitation (mm) in the Provincial Capital Cities												
	Jan.	Feb.	Mar.	Apr.	May	June	July	Aug.	Sept.	Oct.	Nov.	Dec.
Victoria	141.1	99.3	71.9	41.9	33.4	27.3	17.6	23.7	36.6	74.4	138.2	151.6
Edmonton	22.9	15.5	15.9	21.8	42.6	76.1	101.0	69.5	47.5	17.7	16.0	19.2
Regina	14.7	13.0	16.5	20.4	50.8	67.3	58.9	40.0	34.4	20.3	11.7	15.9
Winnipeg	19.3	14.8	23.1	35.9	59.8	83.3	72.0	75.3	51.3	29.5	21.2	18.6
Toronto	45.6	45.5	56.9	64.0	66.0	68.9	76.6	84.2	74.2	63.0	70.3	65.5
Quebec	90.0	74.4	85.0	75.5	99.9	110.2	118.5	119.6	123.7	96.0	106.1	108.9
Fredericton	93.3	84.3	90.4	83.4	94.0	86.9	84.5	99.4	92.3	93.1	110.7	118.8
Halifax	146.9	119.1	122.6	124.4	110.5	98.4	96.8	109.6	94.9	126.9	154.4	167.0
Charlottetown	106.3	91.5	92.2	91.8	96.8	91.1	81.5	88.6	94.1	111.7	121.9	133.2
St. John's	147.8	133.6	126.7	110.4	100.9	96.9	77.9	121.8	125.0	151.7	144.7	144.2

4. Plot precipitation (or temperature) in a bar graph for each of 2 provincial capital cities. Round the data to the nearest whole number.
Which city had the least variation in precipitation (or temperature)? the greatest variation? Explain.

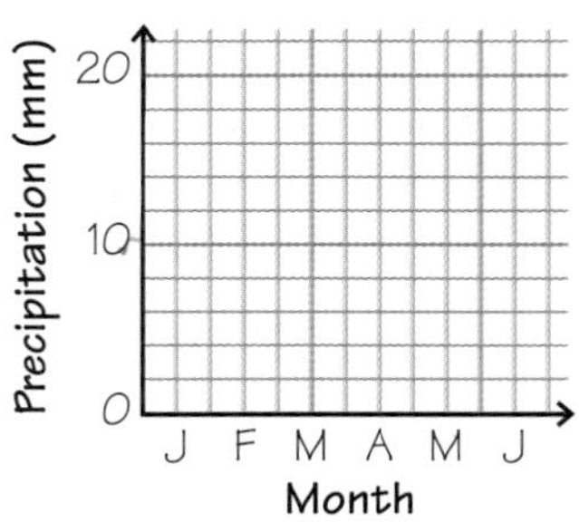

5. Research data for your community and compare it with that for other cities.
Write a report that answers questions like these:

- At what time of year does the weather change the most?
- In what month(s) do we get the most rainfall? the most snowfall?
- How does the height of the land, or distance from an ocean or lake affect the temperature?

Environment Canada has weather records dating back to 1840.

▶ How many years worth of data could you use if you wanted to?
Do you think the weather has changed in your community since then?
If so, how?

HOW Many People Live in Our Community?

The population of Mississauga, Ontario is read four hundred eighty-two thousand, one hundred.

MISSISSAUGA
Population 482 100

The numeral can be written in a place value chart and modelled using counters.

Thousands					
hundreds	tens	ones	hundreds	tens	ones
4	8	2	1	0	0

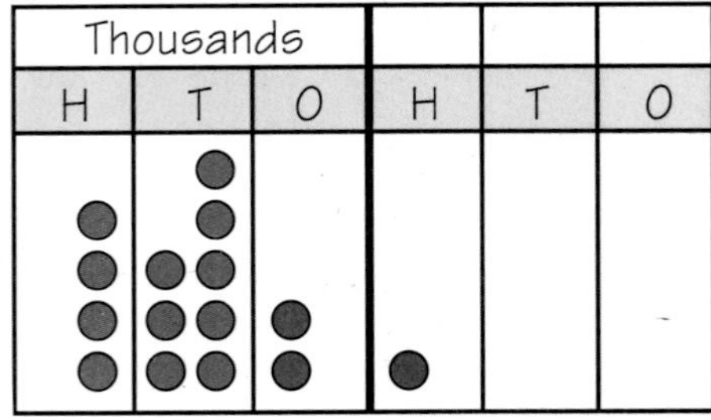

Use a place value chart.

1. How would you show an increase of ten people? a hundred people? a thousand people?

2. How would you show a decrease of a hundred people? ten people? one person?

3. How would you model a population of 999 999? How would you show an increase of 1 more person?
   What is another name for 1000 thousands?

4. What is the population of your community? Write it as a numeral and in words.

The Eight Largest Cities in Canada

City	Population
Calgary, AB	723 300
Edmonton, AB	827 700
Montréal, PQ	3 068 100
Ottawa, ON	651 900
Québec, PQ	622 200
Toronto, ON	3 751 700
Winnipeg, MB	647 100
Vancouver, BC	1 547 000

5. The populations of the 3 largest cities in Canada are over a million. List the cities and their populations in order from greatest to least. Explain your thinking.

6. The populations of the 5 other cities listed are less than a million. List these cities and their populations in order from greatest to least. Did you find some comparisons easier than others? Explain.

7. Which cities' populations would be rounded up when rounded to the nearest hundred thousand?
Round each population to the nearest hundred thousand.

8. The population of Hamilton, ON is five hundred ninety-four thousand, six hundred. Where do you think it ranks? Why?

9. Do you think that the populations are exact numbers? Explain.

10. The population of Oakville, ON is 127 000, rounded to the nearest hundred. What could the greatest and least exact numbers be?

11. Choose one of the cities you listed in question 6. How does its population compare with the population of your community?

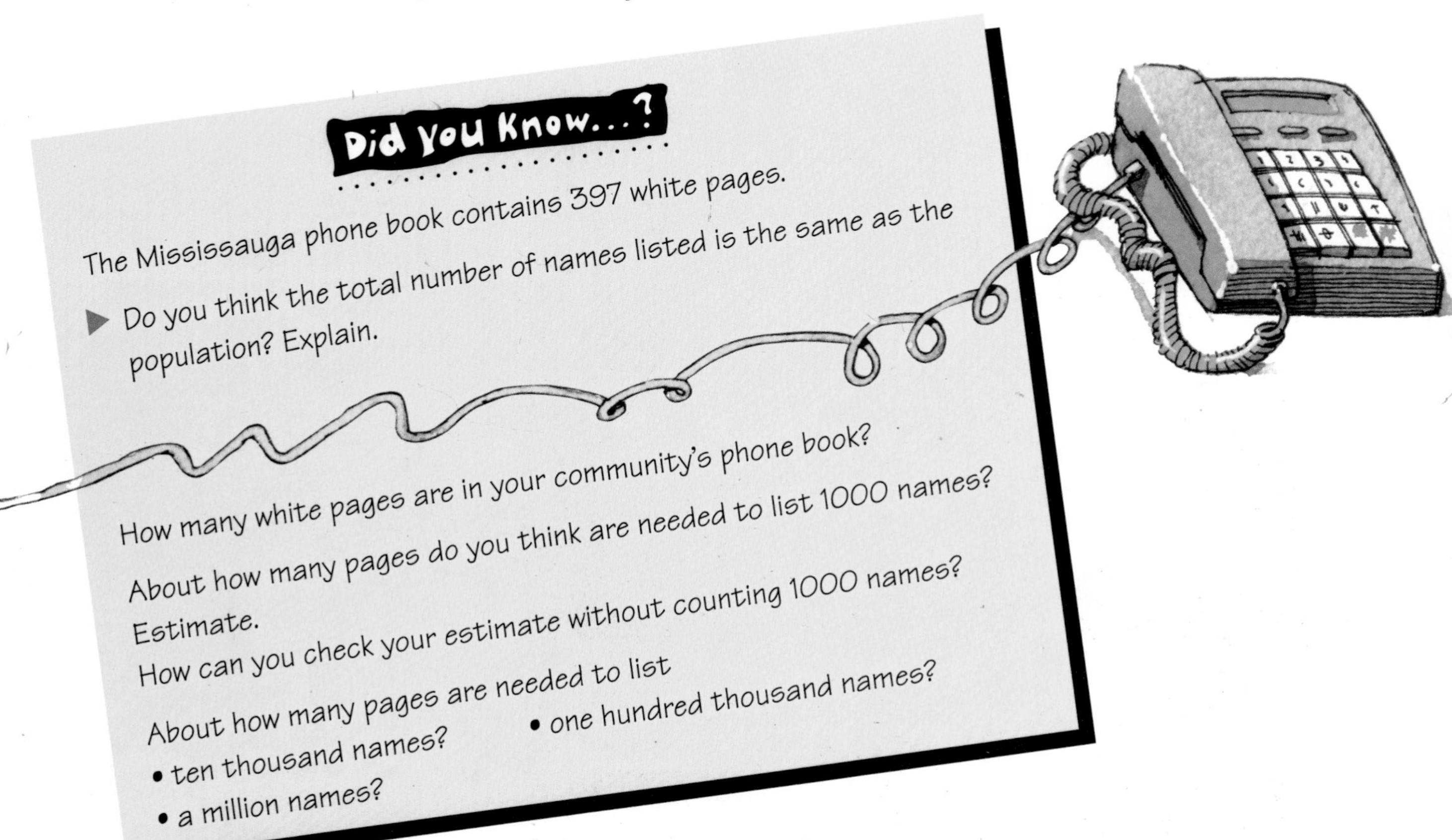

Did You Know...?
The Mississauga phone book contains 397 white pages.
▶ Do you think the total number of names listed is the same as the population? Explain.
How many white pages are in your community's phone book?
About how many pages do you think are needed to list 1000 names? Estimate.
How can you check your estimate without counting 1000 names?
About how many pages are needed to list
• ten thousand names?
• one hundred thousand names?
• a million names?

WHO Lives in a Global Village?

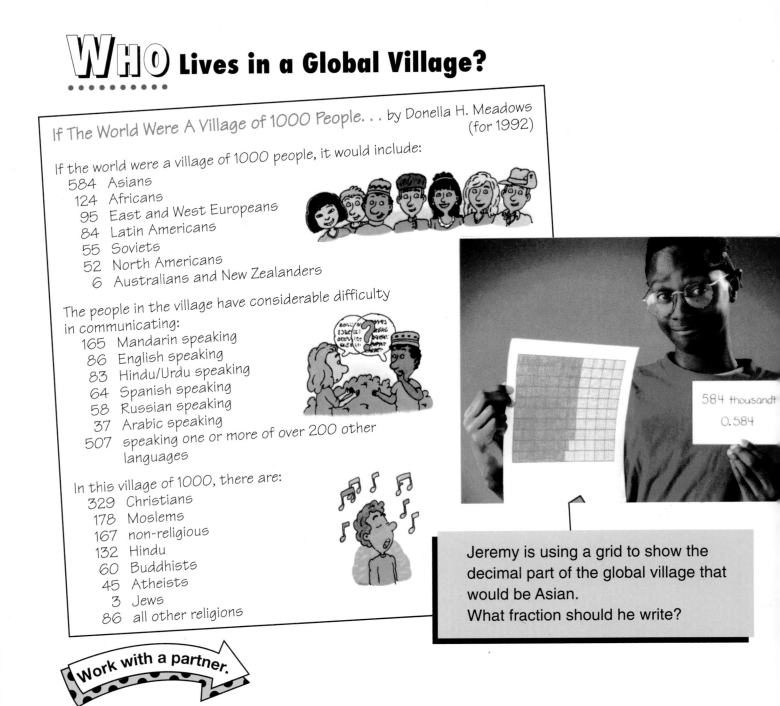

If The World Were A Village of 1000 People. . . by Donella H. Meadows (for 1992)

If the world were a village of 1000 people, it would include:

584 Asians
124 Africans
95 East and West Europeans
84 Latin Americans
55 Soviets
52 North Americans
6 Australians and New Zealanders

The people in the village have considerable difficulty in communicating:

165 Mandarin speaking
86 English speaking
83 Hindu/Urdu speaking
64 Spanish speaking
58 Russian speaking
37 Arabic speaking
507 speaking one or more of over 200 other languages

In this village of 1000, there are:

329 Christians
178 Moslems
167 non-religious
132 Hindu
60 Buddhists
45 Atheists
3 Jews
86 all other religions

Jeremy is using a grid to show the decimal part of the global village that would be Asian.
What fraction should he write?

1. Write a decimal for each group of villagers. Show each decimal on a thousandths grid.
   - Africans
   - non-Africans
   - Christians
   - Moslems
   - non-religious

2. Which describes the North Americans — 0.52 or 0.052? Explain.
   Show the decimal that describes the North Americans on a thousandths grid.

3. Write a decimal to describe the portion of the village that speaks each language. Show three of these facts on a thousandths grid.

4. Write a decimal for each of these facts about the global village.
   - 60 people are over 65 years old.
   - One third of the people are children.
   - Half of the children have received shots for diseases like measles and polio.
   - 70 people own one or more automobiles.
   - Seven people are teachers.
   - One person is a doctor.

5. If the article was about a village of 100 people, then the number of Asians would be 58.

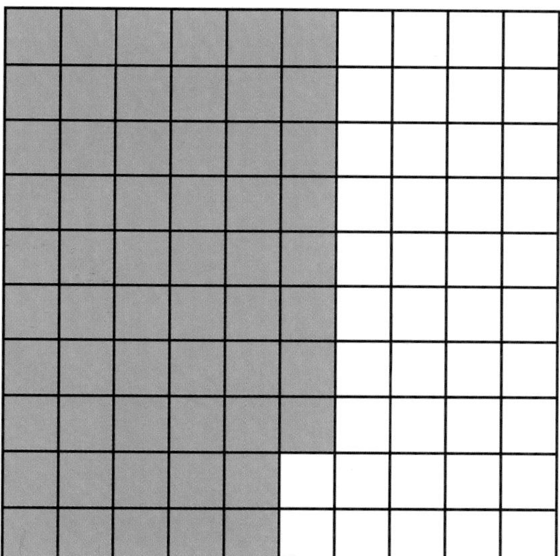

What decimal would describe the Asians now?
Compare this grid with the one showing the Asians in the village of 1000. How do the grids help you to see why 0.584 is 58 hundredths + 4 thousandths?

6. What decimals would describe the people of other nationalities in both villages of 1000 and 100? Show one on both grids.

7. Tell how you might use a thousandths grid to show facts about your community.

Did You Know...?

In the village of 1000 people, 28 babies are born during the year, and 10 people die during the year.

▶ At the end of the year what is the population of the global village? Why can you write the fractions for these facts as $\frac{28}{1000}$ and $\frac{10}{1000}$?

HOW Crowded Is Our Community?

FREDERICTON
POPULATION
46 666

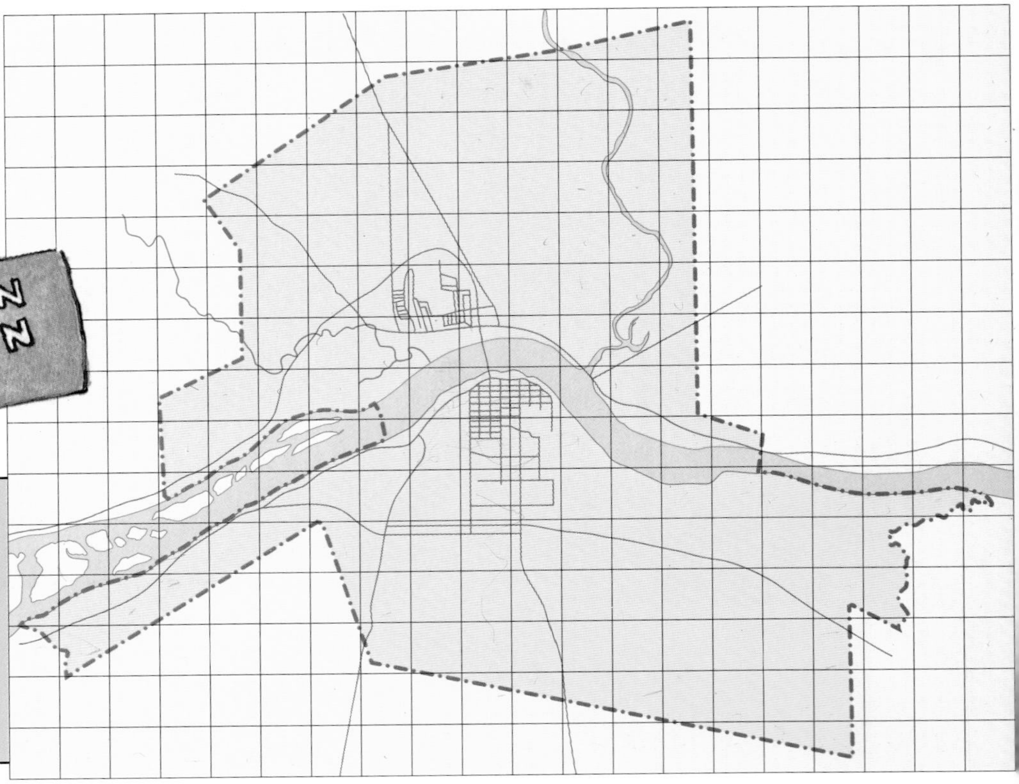

What is the area of the grid in squares? How many square kilometres does it represent?

Scale 1 square represents 1 km^2

If 1000 people lived in 5 km^2, the population density would be 200 people km^2.

1. Estimate the area of
   - all of Fredericton
   - the part of Fredericton north of the river
   - the part of Fredericton south of the river

2. Population density is the number of people who would live in 1 km^2 if the population were distributed equally. Explain.

3. About the same number of people in Fredericton live on the north side of the river as live on the south side. Which side has the greater population density? Explain.

4. Fredericton's area is 130 km^2. How close was your estimate? Estimate and then calculate its population density.

5. Population density is really not the same for every part of the city. What parts would have a higher population density? a lower population density?

6. What would Fredericton's population density be if
   - half the people moved to a different home in Fredericton?
   - half the people moved away from Fredericton?
   - 46 666 more people moved to Fredericton?
   - the area of Fredericton became 10 times as large?

7. Which community has the greatest population density? the least? How did you decide?

Community	Population	Area (km^2)
Happy Valley-Goose Bay, NF	8 610	306
Kingston, ON	56 597	30
Banff, AB	5 688	5
Prince George, BC	69 653	316

8. Without any data, which do you think has the greatest population density? the least? Why?
   - Morden, MB
   - Toronto, ON
   - Canada as a whole

9. Find the population and the area of
   - your community
   - a nearby town

   Calculate each population density.

10. Besides being more crowded, in what ways do you think a more densely populated community is different from one less densely populated?

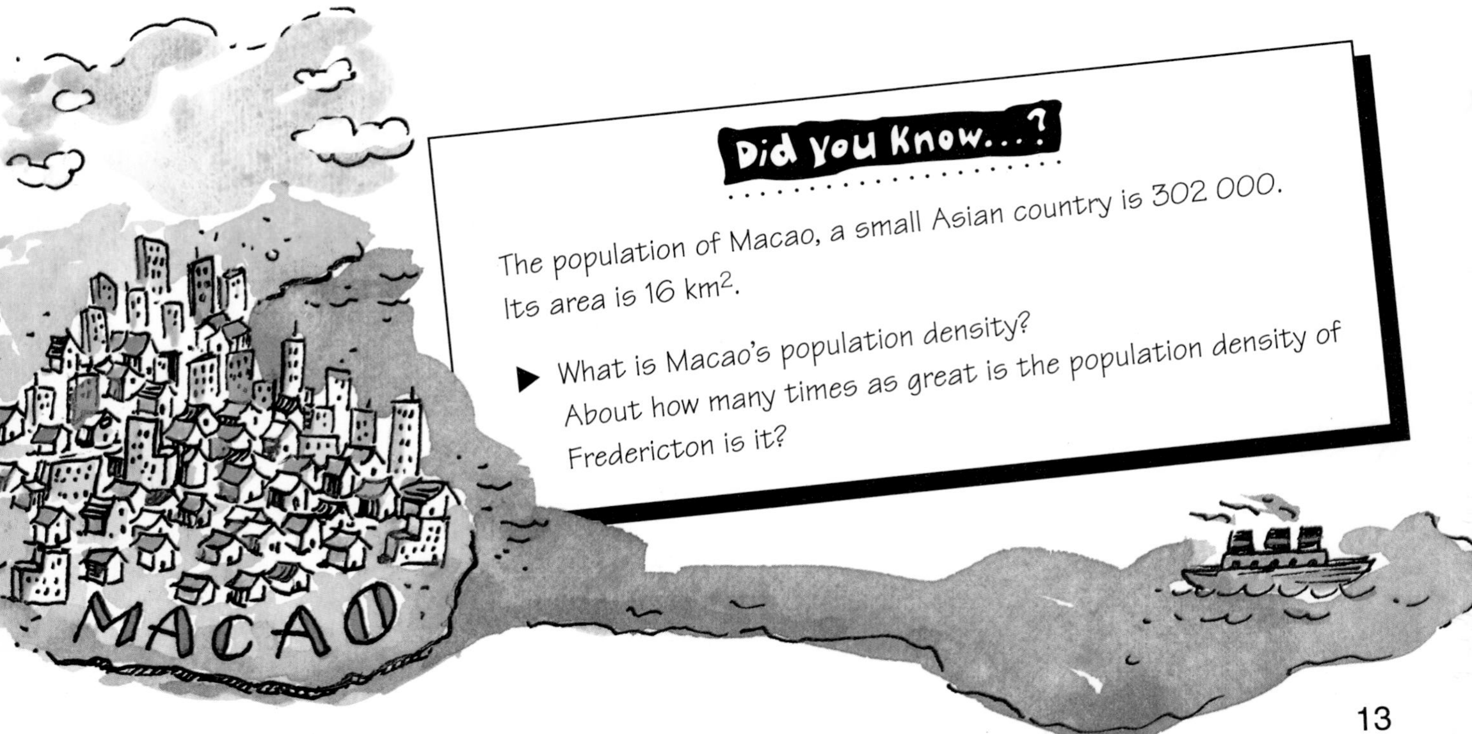

Did you Know...?

The population of Macao, a small Asian country is 302 000. Its area is 16 km^2.

▶ What is Macao's population density? About how many times as great is the population density of Fredericton is it?

? I Wonder... ?

MOVIES

Where do people in your community go to the movies?
About how many people go to the movies there each week? each year?

NEWCOMERS OR NOT

Survey a sample of your community.
About how many people have lived in the community their entire lives?
less than two years?
How well do you think your sample represents your entire community?
Explain.

PER 1000

Choose at least 5 of the following.
Then find the number per 1000 people in your community.

police officers	fire trucks	hospital beds
doctors	dentists	library books
postal outlets	skating rinks	swimming pools
ball diamonds	soccer fields	tennis courts

PHONE NUMBERS

Use the white pages of a phone book.
About how many different phone numbers are listed for your community?
How many different phone exchanges (the first three digits) does your community have?
Would you have predicted this?

GROWING POPULATIONS

The population of Canada almost doubled between 1951 and 1991.
Has the population of your community doubled?
If so, between what years did it double?

Make up your OWN investigation. Then post it on the bulletin board for others to try.

Thinking Back . . .

These are Canadian cities.

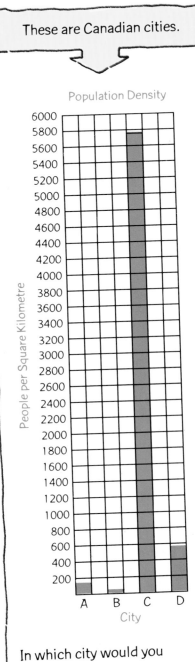

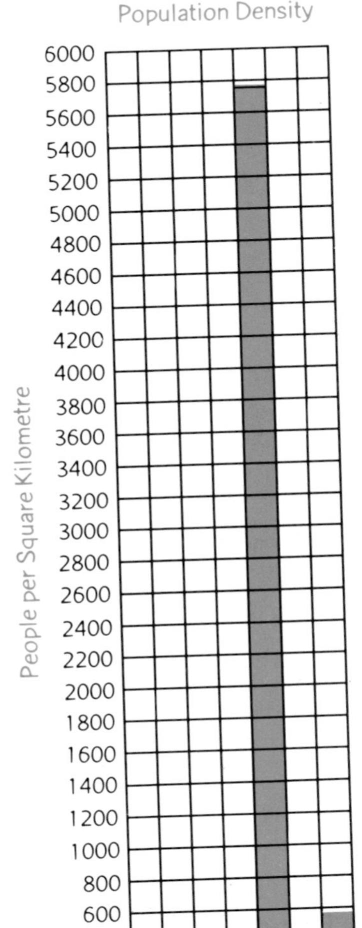

In which city would you like to live? Why?
What other information would you like to have to help you be certain?
Show these population densities on a different type of graph.

Write a letter about your community to someone who has never visited it.
What numbers can you use to describe your community?

Which community grew more?

Population in	1981	1991
Ajax, ON	25 474	57 350
Vancouver, BC	414 281	471 844

How can Kirsten and Angelo both be right?

Tell why it might be useful to know the area of a community.

What else would you like to know about your community? Tell what you would do to find out.

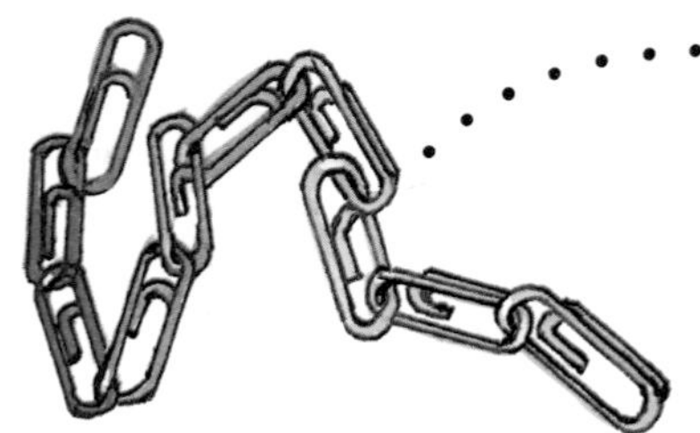

Examining

▼ About how long would a chain of 100 paper clips be? a chain of 10 000 paper clips? 1 paper clip?

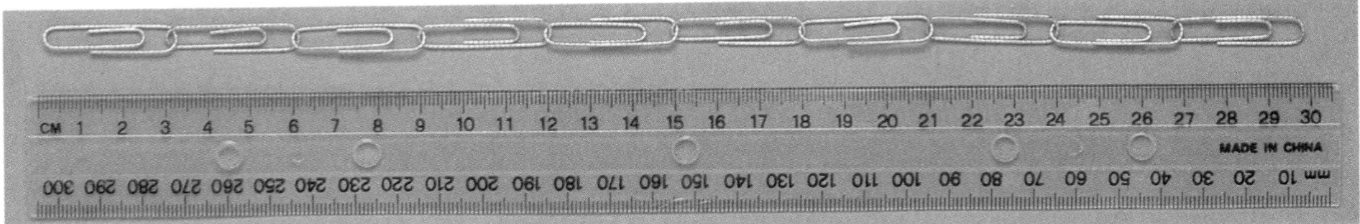

▶ This shows 4004. How do you read 4004? What number would be shown by 40 of each cube? by 400 of each? by 4000 of each?

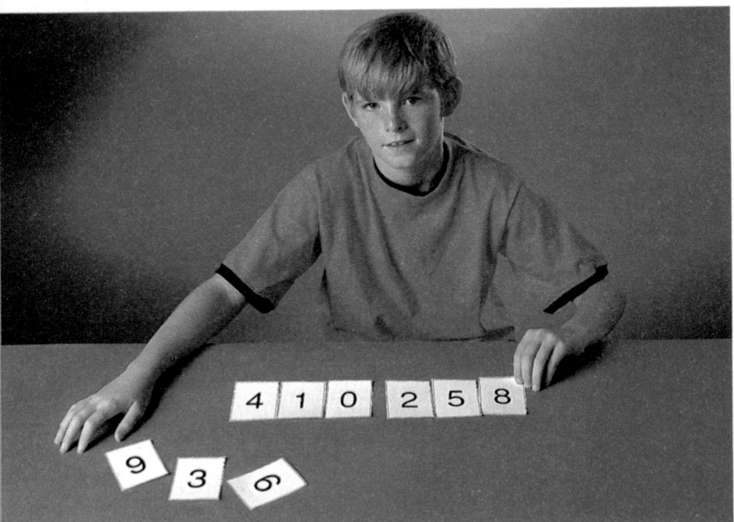

◀ Arrange any of the digits to create three other 6-digit numbers, each of which has

- 5 in the tens place
- the hundred thousands digit four greater than the thousands digit
- the ten thousands digit one less than the hundreds digit

Read your numbers.
Order them from greatest to least.

▶ This shows 1.099. How do you read 1.099? What number would be shown if one more small rectangle is colored? one more small square?

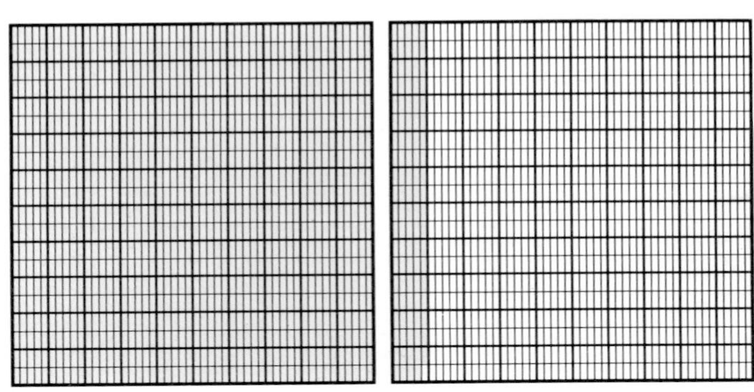

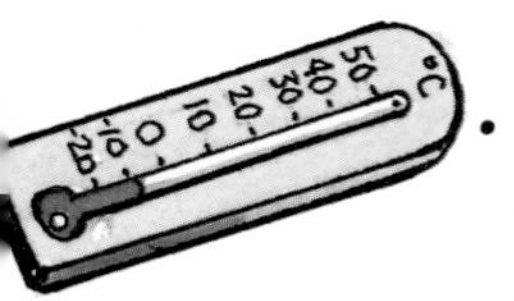

Number Patterns

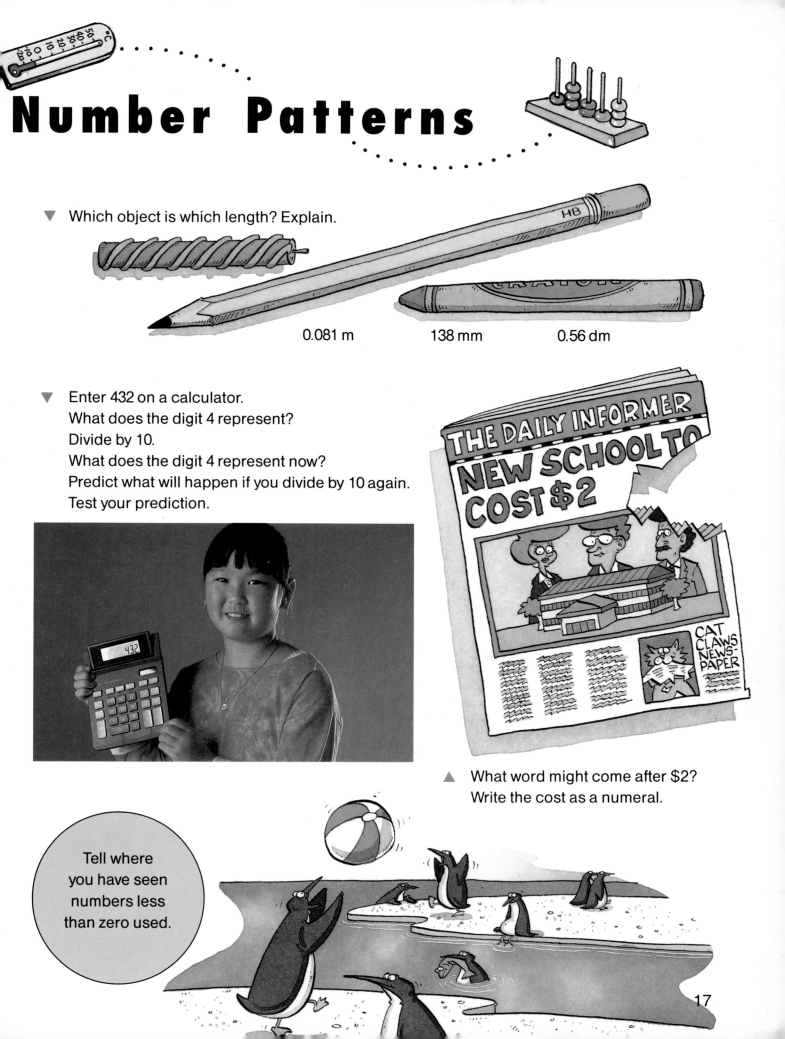

▼ Which object is which length? Explain.

0.081 m   138 mm   0.56 dm

▼ Enter 432 on a calculator.
What does the digit 4 represent?
Divide by 10.
What does the digit 4 represent now?
Predict what will happen if you divide by 10 again.
Test your prediction.

▲ What word might come after $2?
Write the cost as a numeral.

Tell where you have seen numbers less than zero used.

You can only travel on the lines of the grid.
Label points that are as far from A as from B.

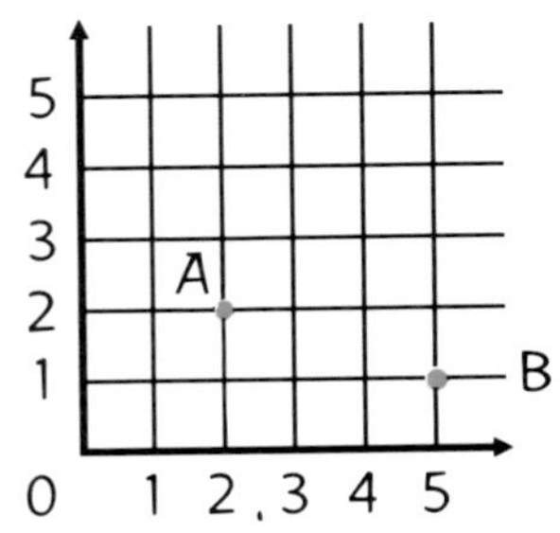

Reading the Paper

Representing whole numbers

Weekday Circulation	
The Edmonton Journal	166 910
The Globe and Mail (Toronto)	305 723
La Presse (Montréal)	194 958
The Vancouver Province	173 928
The Winnipeg Free Press	164 041

The circulation of The Edmonton Journal is one hundred sixty-six thousand nine hundred ten.

What does circulation mean?

Which other circulation also starts one hundred sixty? Model it.
Explain how you know which of the 2 papers has the greater circulation.

Use a place value mat.

1. Model the circulations of the other 3 papers.
   Order all 5 circulations from greatest to least.
   Explain how you decided the order.

2. The weekday circulation of The Ottawa Citizen is between that of The Edmonton Journal and The Vancouver Province.
   It is about 1000 copies different from The Vancouver Province's. What might it be?

3. Match each paper with its circulation. Make a chart.

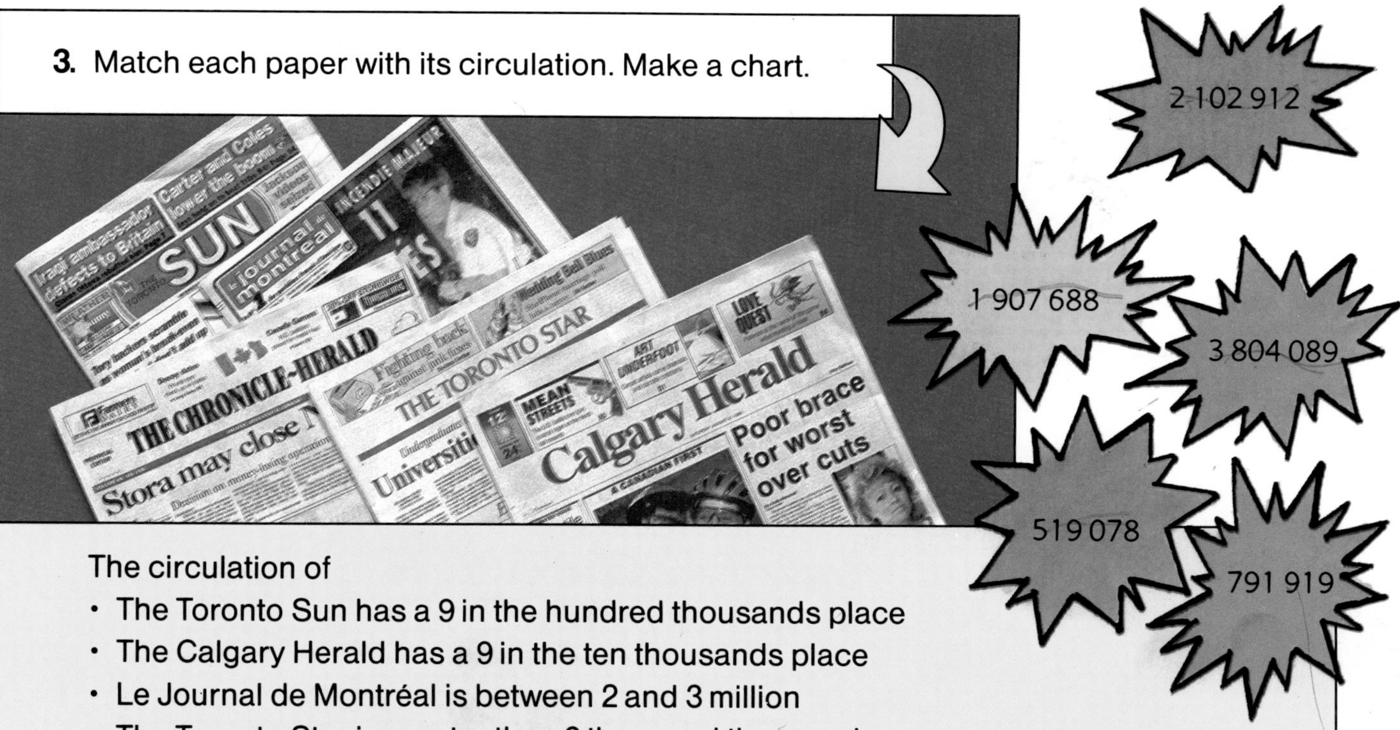

The circulation of

- The Toronto Sun has a 9 in the hundred thousands place
- The Calgary Herald has a 9 in the ten thousands place
- Le Journal de Montréal is between 2 and 3 million
- The Toronto Star is greater than 3 thousand thousands
- The Halifax Chronicle Herald has a 0 in the hundreds place

4. Make up different clues for two of the weekly circulations. Give them to another group to figure out.

5. Model each weekly circulation. Order them from greatest to least. Explain how you decided the order.

6. Round each circulation to the nearest hundred thousand. Tell how you rounded.

7. Round each circulation to the nearest million. Which circulations round to the same number of millions?

8. Why might we write 3.8 million to describe the circulation of The Toronto Star? Write the circulation for The Toronto Sun and Le Journal de Montréal in this way. Could you write the circulation for The Calgary Herald using the word million? If so, how?

9. Which paper sells about 10 000 000 copies in 20 weeks? About how many weeks would it take each of the other papers to sell 10 000 000 copies?

10. The Wall Street Journal sells about 1 800 000 copies each day. Find the circulations of three papers in your province. About how many weeks would it take each of those papers to sell that many copies?

You have 20 counters.
All of the purple squares must hold the same number.
No square can have more than 6 counters.
What different ways could you arrange the counters?

Exchanging Currency

Reading and writing numbers to thousandths

The first Canadian $1 coin was a silver dollar, introduced in 1935. Our current $1 coin, the loonie, replaced the Canadian $1 bill in 1987. Our Canadian dime has looked the same since 1937.

1. What fraction of a dollar is a dime? Write the fraction as a decimal.

   What fraction of a dollar is a penny? a quarter? Write the fractions as decimals.

   Show the value of a penny, dime, and quarter on a hundredths grid.

When money from other countries is compared to Canadian money, it is usually written as a decimal in thousandths. Exchange rates can be obtained from a bank or a newspaper. For example:

Currency	Value in Canadian Dollars
French franc	0.245
German mark	0.825
Japanese yen	0.012
Mexican peso	0.457

2. Is each currency above worth more or less than a dollar? How do you know?

3. Model the value of two of the currencies on a thousandths grid. Then express each decimal as a fraction.

4. Round each Canadian value to the nearest hundredth. How many pennies is each currency worth?

   Round each value to the nearest tenth. How many dimes is each currency worth?

5. Which currency is worth the most? the least?

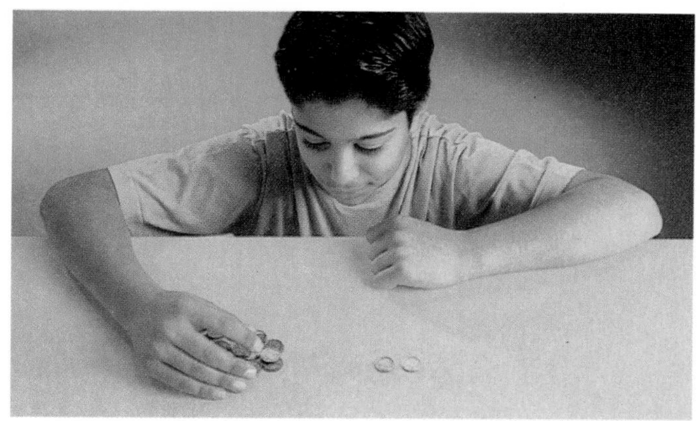

6. Which currency is worth almost half a dollar?
   Which currency is worth about 1 quarter?

7. Write the exchange rate for an imaginary country that would be worth $\frac{3}{4}$ of a dollar.

8. Reid said, "If you exchanged 10 French francs, you should receive $2.45 Canadian." Do you agree with him? Why or why not?

   How much would you receive if you exchanged 100 francs? 1000 francs? 10 000 francs?

9. How much would you receive if you exchanged 1000 German marks? 1000 Mexican pesos?

10. Tara wondered how much this flight would cost if you were paying with Japanese yen. She reasoned:

    1000 Japanese yen = $12
    So 10 000 yen = $120
    20 000 yen = $240
    40 000 yen = $480
    41 000 yen = $480 + $12
    42 000 yen = $480 + $24
    = $504

    Do you agree with Tara's solution? Explain.

11. Think of something you'd like to buy in Canada. How much would you need if you were paying with a foreign currency?

How could you multiply 99 and 38 in your head?

Comparing Baseball Performances

Comparing decimals

One of the greatest baseball players was Ted Williams of the Boston Red Sox.

In 1941, his batting average was .406 or 406 hits in 1000 times at bat.

About how many hits did he have in 100 times at bat? 10 times at bat?

How does this decimal appear different from the way we normally write decimals?

Baseball fans say four-oh-six. How do we say it?

American League Batting Champions

1988	Wade Boggs	Boston	.366
1989	Kirby Puckett	Minnesota	.339
1990	George Brett	Kansas City	.329
1991	Julio Franco	Texas	.342
1992	Edgar Martinez	Seattle	.343
1993	John Olerud	Toronto	.363

1. Model these batting averages. Then order them from best to poorest.

2. How many of the batting champions hit more than 35 hits in 100 times at bat? How do you know?

3. Round each average to the nearest hundredth. Does the order change? Why do you think averages are given in thousandths?

4. Batting Averages of Top Hitters
1992 World Champion Toronto Blue Jays

Player	Average
Roberto Alomar	.310
Joe Carter	.264
Candy Maldonado	.272
John Olerud	.284
Dave Winfield	.290

Model the best and the poorest of these batting averages.

Which average is closest to $\frac{1}{3}$? $\frac{1}{4}$? $\frac{3}{10}$?

5. About how many more hits than the poorest hitter would the best hitter likely get in 1000 times at bat?

6. In 1992, Maldonado had 3 more hits than Olerud. But Olerud had a better batting average. Explain how this can be.

7. Would you expect the Blue Jay team batting average to be more or less than .300? Explain.

8. Would you ever see a batting average of 1.000 in a season? What would it mean?

9. Another baseball statistic is the earned run average or ERA. It tells the average number of runs the pitchers allowed the other team to score in each game. Which team in the 1992 World Series— Atlanta with 3.14 or Toronto with 3.91— had the higher ERA? Which had the better ERA? Explain.

10. Order these ERAs from greatest to least and then from best to poorest.

Montreal	3.25	New York	3.66
Boston	3.58	Texas	4.09

What do you notice about the lists?

11. Find out how decimals are used to compare performances in other sports.

What fraction of a hexagon is a triangle?
a trapezoid? a blue rhombus?
Why is it difficult to write the fraction of a hexagon covered by an orange square?
a tan rhombus?

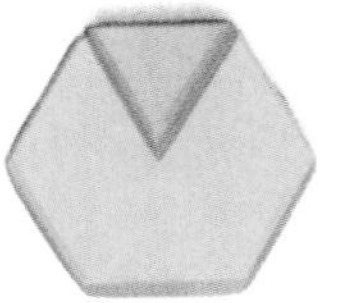

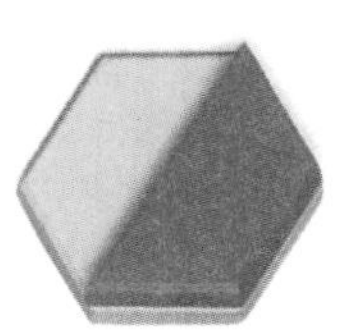

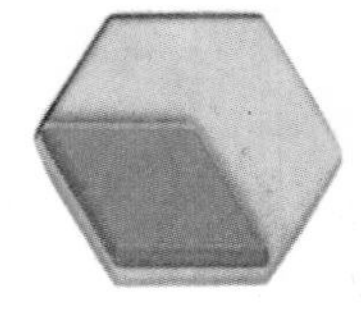

Covering the Hexagon

Modelling fractions and mixed numbers

Suppose the hexagon is 1 whole.

Work with a partner.

Use the yellow, red, blue, and green pattern blocks.

1. Model each fraction. Then record your models on triangle dot paper.

$\frac{2}{3}$ $\frac{5}{6}$ $\frac{4}{3}$ $\frac{7}{6}$

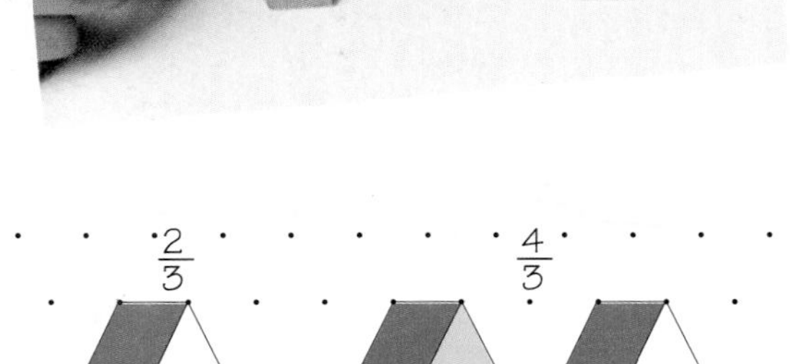
2/3
4/3

Fractions less than 1 are called **proper fractions**. Fractions greater than 1 are called **improper fractions**.

2. Use the pattern blocks to show 2 halves. What fraction can you write? What whole number?

3. Use pattern blocks that are all of one color. Find other fraction names for 1. Then find other names for 2, 3, and 4.

4. Is Marlene right? Why or why not?

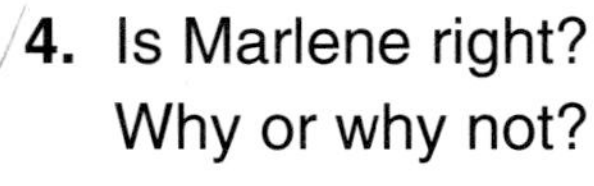

My right hand has $1\frac{1}{2}$.
My left hand has $\frac{3}{2}$.
Which is more?
I think three halves is more.

$1\frac{1}{2}$ and $\frac{3}{2}$ are equivalent. $1\frac{1}{2}$ is a **mixed number**. Why do you think it is called mixed?

5. Cover hexagons using these pieces. Find two names for each covered amount. Then record your models on triangle dot paper.

- 5 red
- 7 blue
- 6 red
- 8 green
- 6 blue
- 12 green

6. Use yellow pieces and pieces of one other color to show these amounts. How many pieces do you need? Write the mixed numbers.

$\frac{8}{3}$ $\frac{16}{6}$ $\frac{10}{2}$

7. Use pieces that are all of one color to find the improper fraction for each mixed number.

$2\frac{1}{6}$ $3\frac{2}{3}$ $4\frac{1}{2}$

8. The yellow and red design is named $3\frac{3}{2}$. If it is covered with all red pieces, what is its new name?

Make the same design using yellow and green pieces. Write the number. If it is covered with all green pieces, what is its new name?

9. Find three different number names for each design.

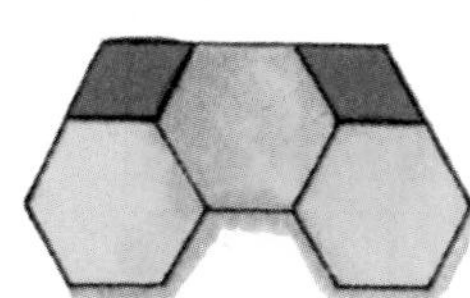

Make your own design and write its number name. Try to name it another way.

10. This design has a value of $\frac{11}{6}$. Rearrange the pieces to show $\frac{11}{6}$ as a mixed number.

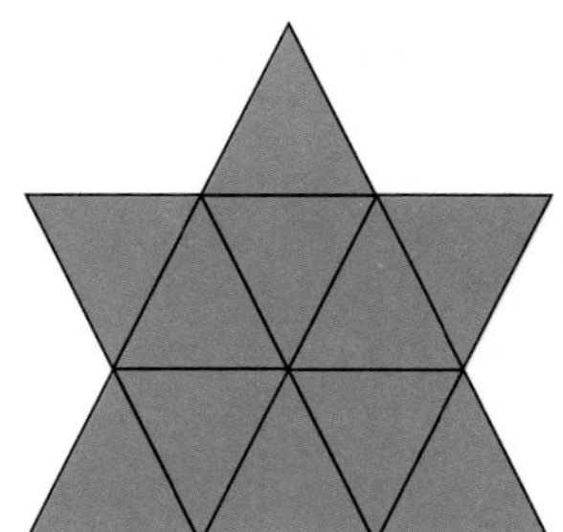

11. What is the value of this design?

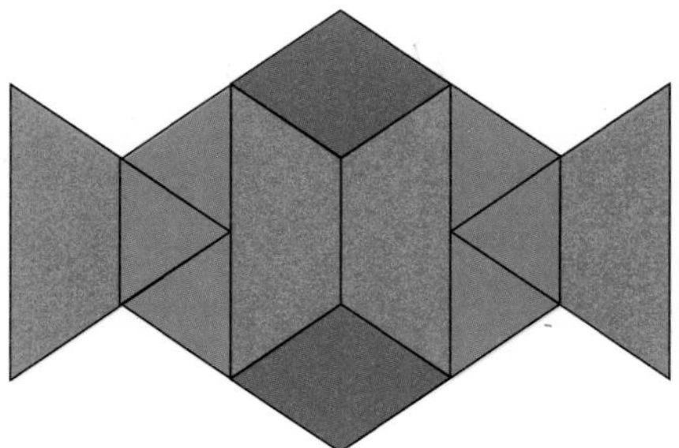

Choose any 3 digit number where the digits are different.
Reverse the digits.
Subtract the lesser number from the greater one.
Keep going. What happens?
Try it several times.
375
573
– 375

Covering the Circle

Finding equivalent mixed numbers and improper fractions

Suppose the circle is 1 whole.

1. What mixed number is represented in each diagram?

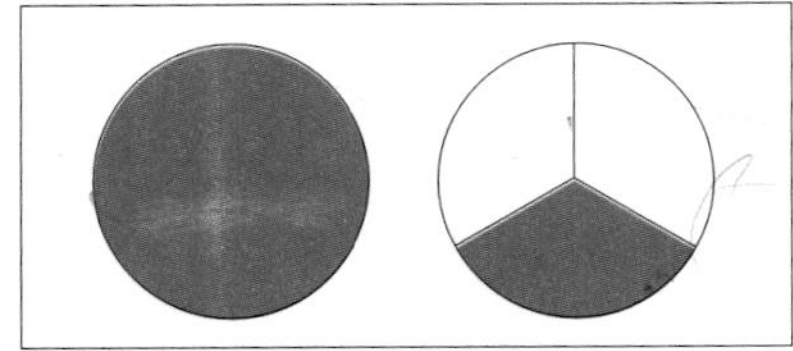

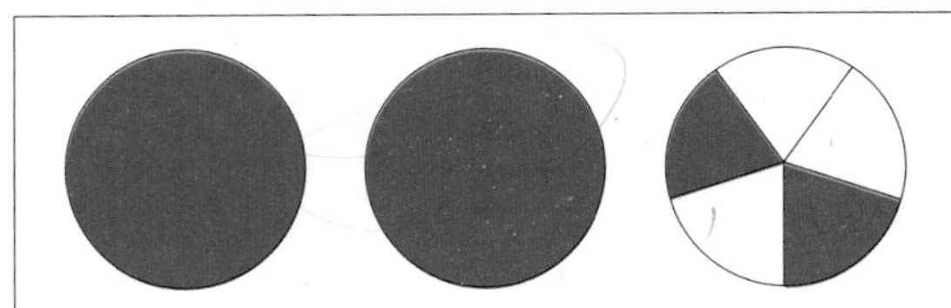

How can you divide each whole to show the improper fraction?

Jamie wrote these statements: $1\frac{1}{3} = \frac{3}{3}$ and $\frac{1}{3} = \frac{4}{3}$ and $2\frac{2}{5} = \frac{10}{5}$ and $\frac{2}{5} = \frac{12}{5}$

He noticed: If you multiply the whole number by the denominator and add the numerator, you get the numerator of the improper fraction. Explain why the rule works.

2. Use Jamie's rule to decide if these pairs of mixed numbers and improper fractions are equivalent. Use fraction circles to check.
   - $1\frac{1}{2}$ and $\frac{3}{2}$
   - $1\frac{1}{3}$ and $\frac{5}{3}$
   - 2 and $\frac{8}{4}$
   - $1\frac{4}{5}$ and $\frac{9}{5}$
   - $\frac{6}{5}$ and $1\frac{1}{5}$
   - $\frac{15}{7}$ and $2\frac{2}{7}$
   - $\frac{13}{4}$ and $12\frac{1}{4}$
   - $\frac{18}{6}$ and 3

3. Use Jamie's rule to write the equivalent improper fraction for each mixed number. Use fraction circles to check.

   $2\frac{1}{3}$ $1\frac{3}{10}$ $4\frac{1}{2}$ $3\frac{3}{8}$ $7\frac{4}{5}$ $10\frac{7}{8}$

4. Is this statement true?
   $\frac{3}{2} = \frac{6}{4}$ Explain.

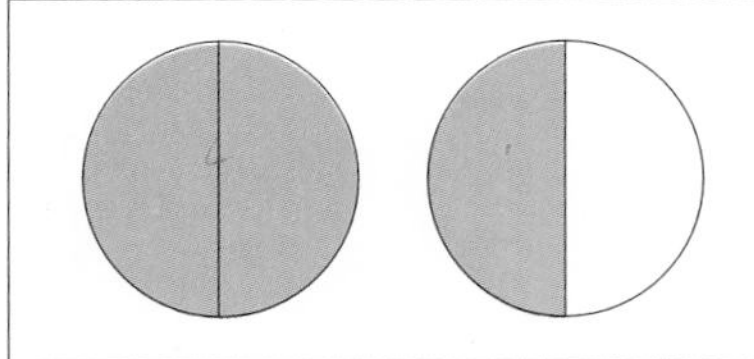

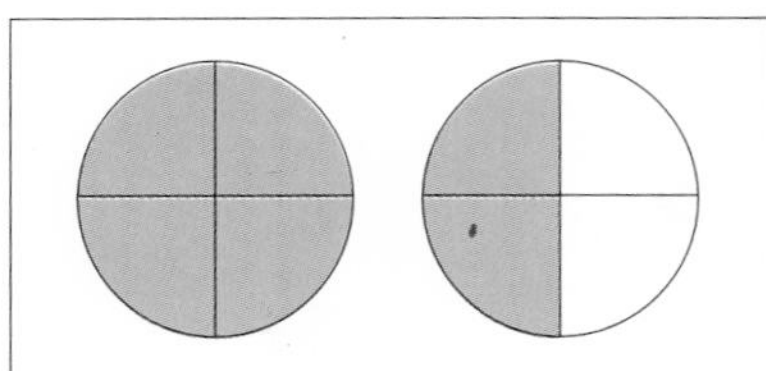

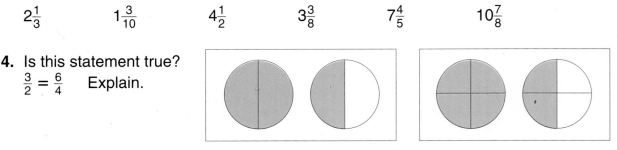

5. Draw the fraction circles that represent the improper fractions in question 1. Then divide each piece in half. Write the new improper fraction. Is it equivalent to the original?

6. Is this statement true?

$\frac{9}{6} = \frac{3}{2}$ Explain.

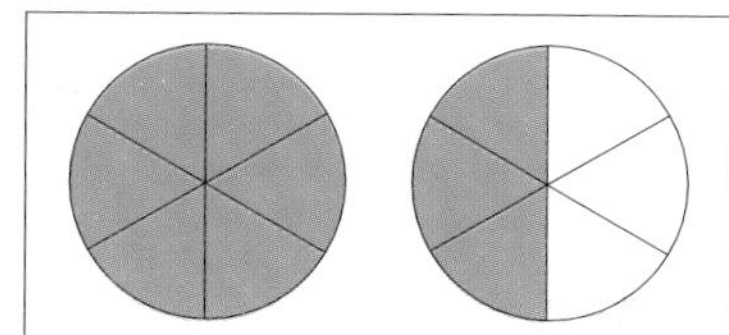

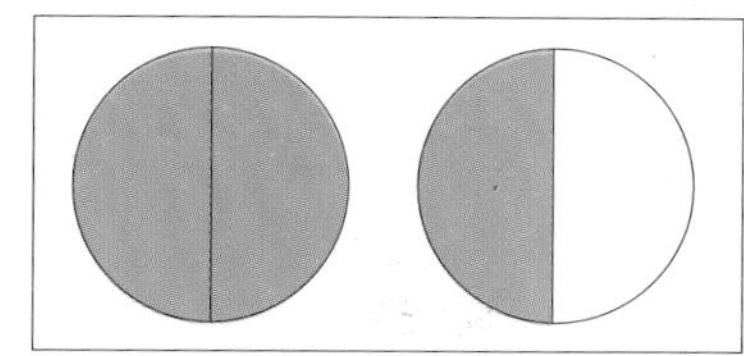

Helen wrote the statements from Problems 4 and 6 like this: $\frac{3}{2} = \frac{6}{4}$ (×2, ×2) and $\frac{9}{6} = \frac{3}{2}$ (÷3, ÷3)

She noticed: You can write different equivalent fractions by multiplying or dividing both the numerator and the denominator by the same whole number. Do you agree? Draw fraction circles to justify your answer.

7. Is each pair of improper fractions equivalent? If so, write the number sentence. If not, write a true number sentence.

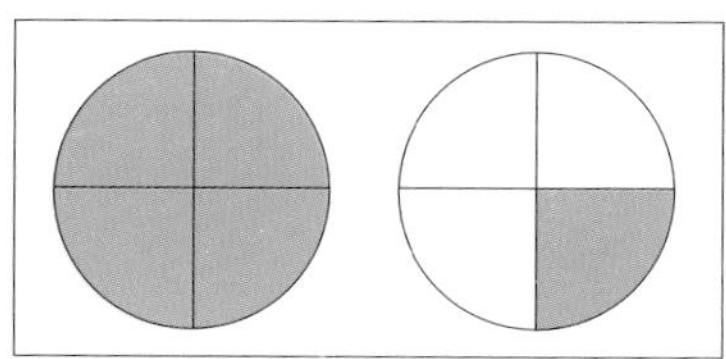

and

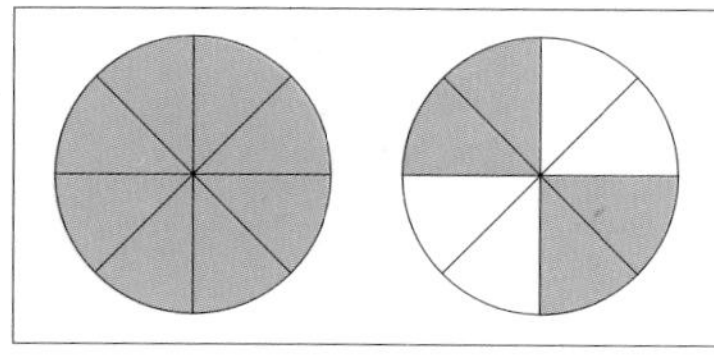

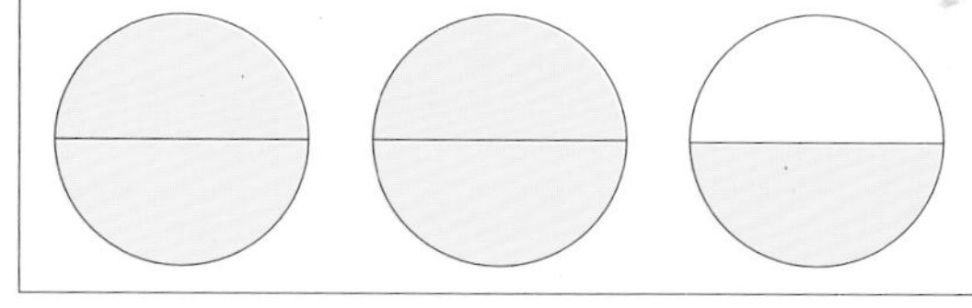

and

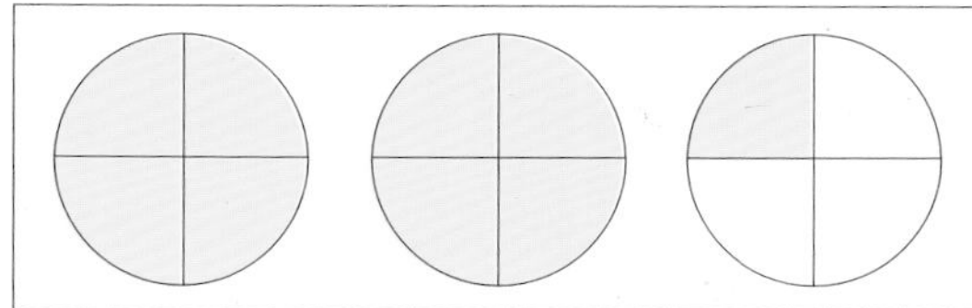

8. Multiply each numerator and denominator by the whole numbers 4 and 5 to produce two new equivalent fractions.

$\frac{7}{2}$ $\frac{9}{3}$ $\frac{11}{4}$ $\frac{13}{5}$

9. Divide each numerator and denominator by the whole numbers 2 and 3 to produce two new equivalent fractions.

$\frac{12}{6}$ $\frac{24}{18}$ $\frac{36}{30}$ $\frac{72}{48}$

10. Why can you write $\frac{2}{2} = \frac{1}{1}$?

$\frac{9}{8} = \frac{1125}{1000}$? $\frac{7}{5} = 1\frac{4}{10}$?

11. Find the missing number.

$\frac{125}{100} = \frac{25}{?}$ $\frac{7}{4} = \frac{?}{100}$

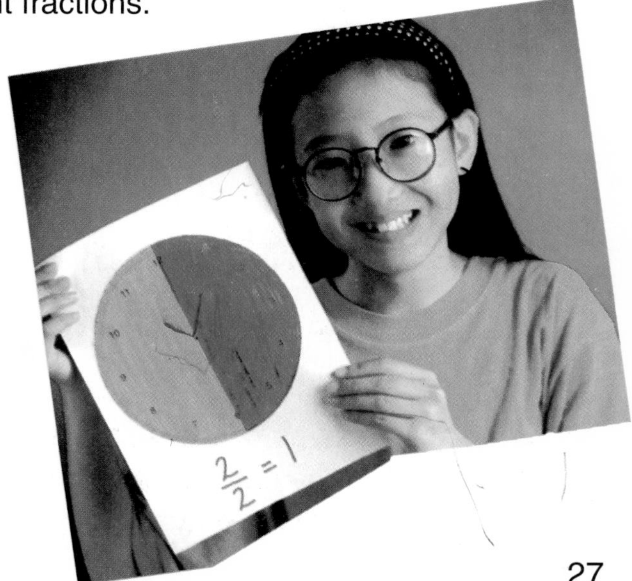

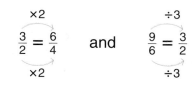

When you divide a number by 3, 5, or 7, the remainder is 2. What could the number be?

Comparing the Cards

Ordering fractions, mixed numbers, and decimals

To play this game you'll need a deck of blank cards to write on. It would be helpful to have a calculator too.

- To start the game, all the cards are dealt face down, and the dealer says either "Greatest" or "Least."
- Then each player turns over the top card. The player whose card shows the greatest (or least) value takes the set of face-up cards.
- The player with the most sets of cards wins.

1. Which of the cards in each set is greatest? Explain how you know.

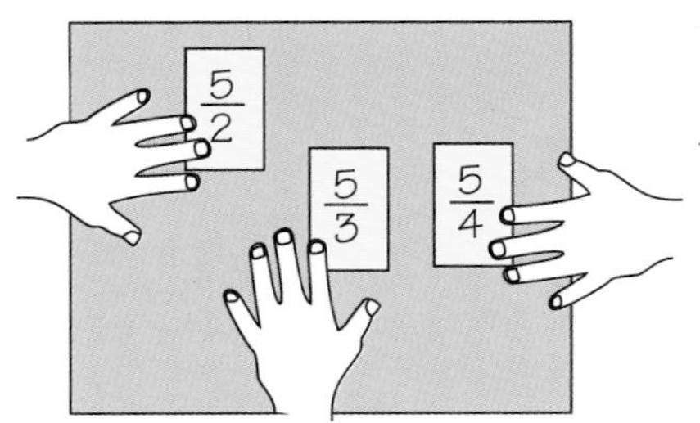

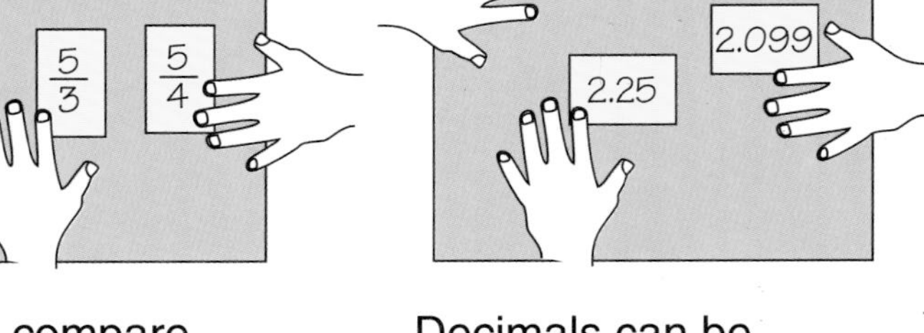

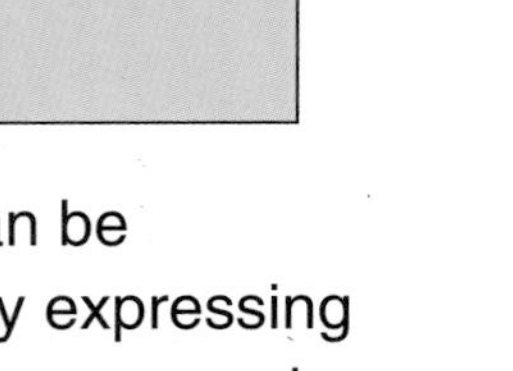

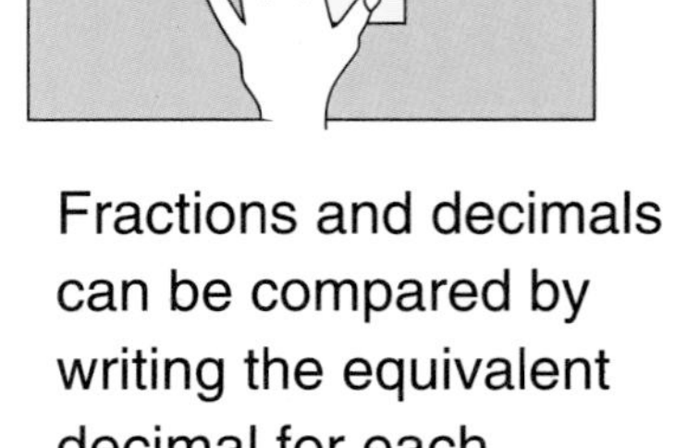

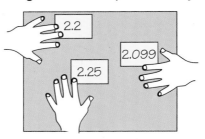

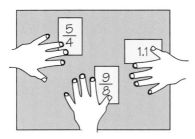

One way to compare fractions is by writing equivalent fractions with the same denominator.

$\frac{5}{2} = \frac{30}{12}$ (×6) $\frac{5}{3} = \frac{?}{12}$

$\frac{5}{4} = \frac{?}{12}$

Decimals can be compared by expressing each to the same number of decimal places.

$2.2 = 2\frac{200}{1000} = 2.200$

$2.25 = 2\frac{250}{1000} = ?$

$2.099 = ?$

Fractions and decimals can be compared by writing the equivalent decimal for each fraction. Use a calculator to divide.

$\frac{5}{4}$ means $5 \div 4$

for $\frac{9}{8}$, $8\overline{)9.000}$

$5 \div 4 = ?$

2. What is another way to compare the set of three fraction cards above?

3. Make a different set of three cards using any of the cards shown above. Which has the least value? Why? Compare the equivalent decimal numbers to check.

4. Order the set of cards in each row from greatest to least.

0.502	0.52	0.25	0.205	0.5
1.778	1.787	1.877	1.87	1.78
3.81	3.108	3.18	3.018	3.1
10.008	10.08	10	10.8	10.085

5. Write the decimal equivalent for each number.

6. Write the set of numbers shown by each dot on the number line in order from greatest to least.

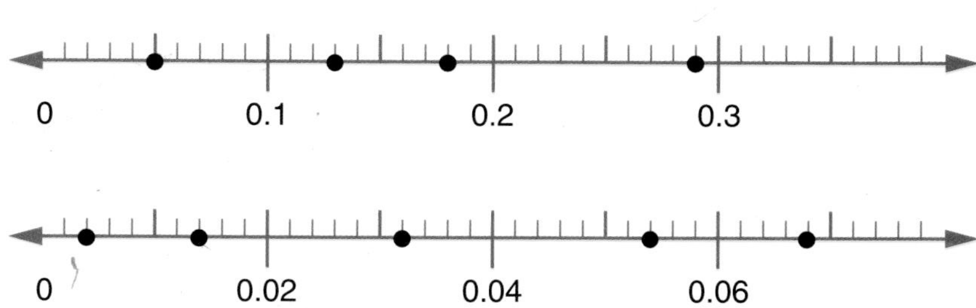

7. Order the set of cards in each row from greatest to least.

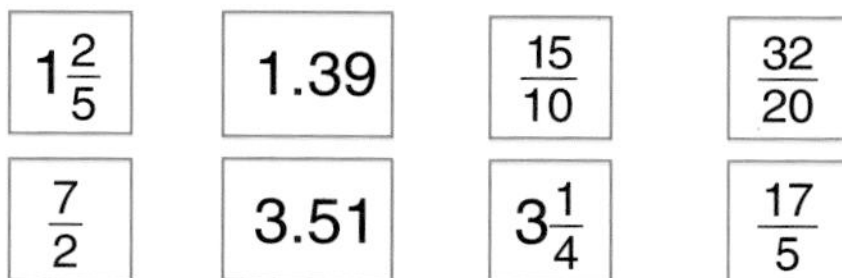

8. How would you decide which of these two cards is greater? $\frac{4}{3}$ $\frac{11}{8}$

9. Order the cards in each row from least to greatest.

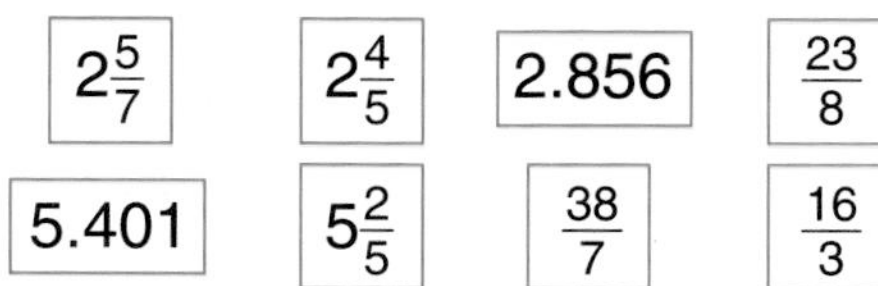

10. Play a rounding number game with a partner.

When my number is rounded to the nearest hundredth, it's 6.53. What's my number?
It must be in the range from 6.525 to 6.534.

A structure made from centimetre cubes has a volume of 30 cm^3. What might it look like?

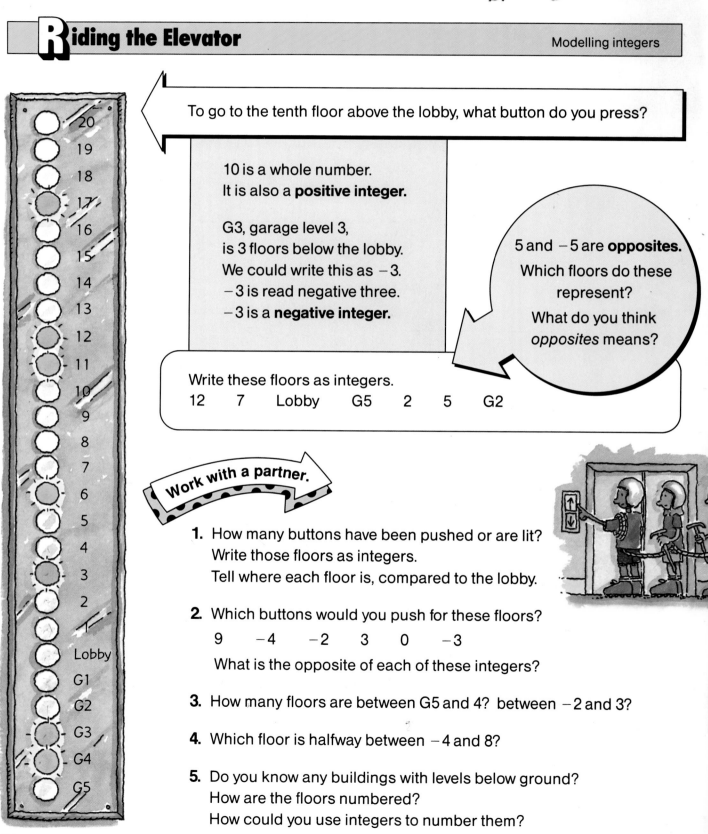

Riding the Elevator

Modelling integers

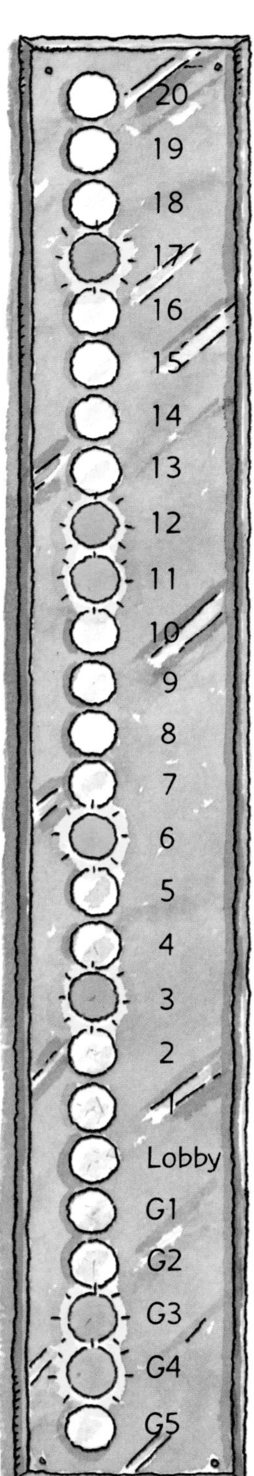

To go to the tenth floor above the lobby, what button do you press?

10 is a whole number.
It is also a **positive integer.**

G3, garage level 3,
is 3 floors below the lobby.
We could write this as −3.
−3 is read negative three.
−3 is a **negative integer.**

5 and −5 are **opposites.**
Which floors do these represent?
What do you think *opposites* means?

Write these floors as integers.

12   7   Lobby   G5   2   5   G2

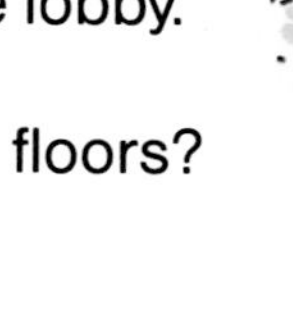

1. How many buttons have been pushed or are lit?
   Write those floors as integers.
   Tell where each floor is, compared to the lobby.

2. Which buttons would you push for these floors?
   9   −4   −2   3   0   −3
   What is the opposite of each of these integers?

3. How many floors are between G5 and 4? between −2 and 3?

4. Which floor is halfway between −4 and 8?

5. Do you know any buildings with levels below ground?
   How are the floors numbered?
   How could you use integers to number them?

Explain how to use $4 \times 50 = 200$ to find the sum of $47 + 49 + 53 + 54$.

Comparing Temperatures

Comparing integers

Average January Temperatures (°C)

City	Early Morning	Midafternoon
Calgary, AB	−18	−6
Churchill, MB	−31	−24
Regina, SK	−23	−13
Vancouver, BC	0	5
Windsor, ON	−9	−1
Winnipeg, MB	−24	−14

Is the midafternoon usually warmer or cooler than the early morning?

Is 5°C warmer than 0°C?
Is −6°C warmer than −18°C?

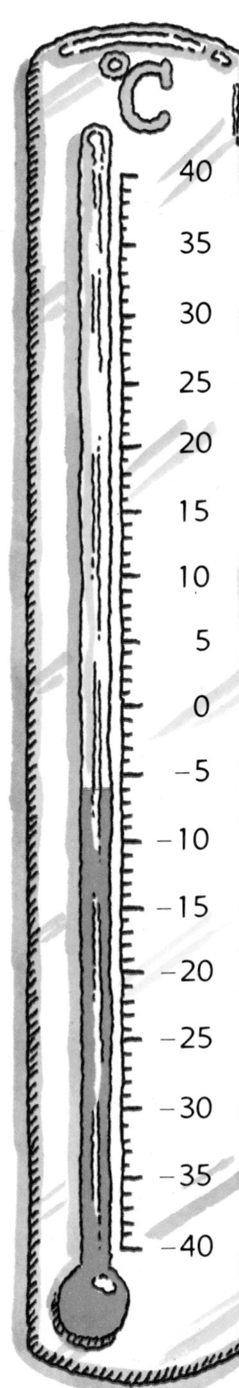

How does a thermometer show which temperatures are warmer?

Compare a thermometer to a number line.

1. Which temperatures are warmer than −10°C?
2. Order the cities from coldest to warmest using the morning temperatures.
   Does the order change if you use the afternoon temperatures?
3. Which cities have temperature changes of 10°C or more?
4. The temperatures in Whitehorse, YK, are usually 2°C colder than those in Winnipeg. What would they be?
5. The temperatures in Edmonton, AB, are slightly warmer than those in Regina. What might they be?
6. What are the January temperatures where you live?
   What are some factors that affect temperature?

Take Your Pick

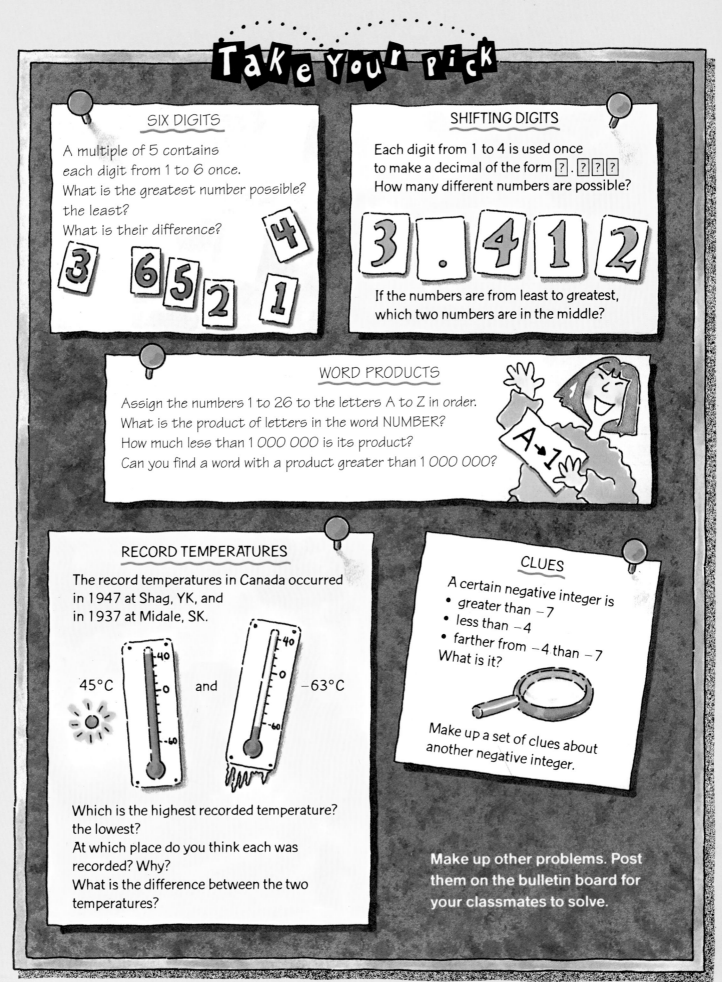

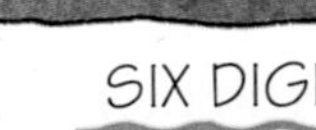

SIX DIGITS

A multiple of 5 contains each digit from 1 to 6 once.
What is the greatest number possible? the least?
What is their difference?

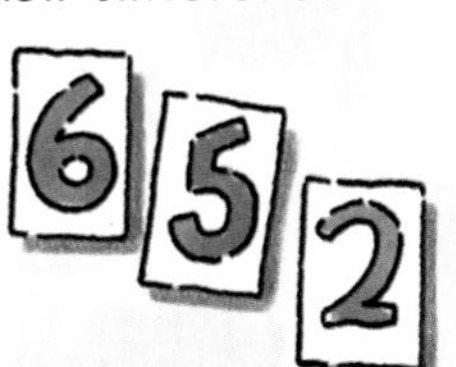

SHIFTING DIGITS

Each digit from 1 to 4 is used once to make a decimal of the form ? . ? ? ?
How many different numbers are possible?

If the numbers are from least to greatest, which two numbers are in the middle?

WORD PRODUCTS

Assign the numbers 1 to 26 to the letters A to Z in order.
What is the product of letters in the word NUMBER?
How much less than 1 000 000 is its product?
Can you find a word with a product greater than 1 000 000?

RECORD TEMPERATURES

The record temperatures in Canada occurred in 1947 at Shag, YK, and in 1937 at Midale, SK.

45°C and −63°C

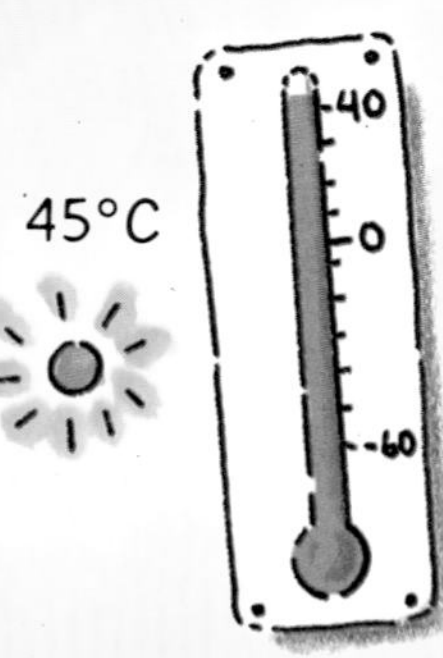

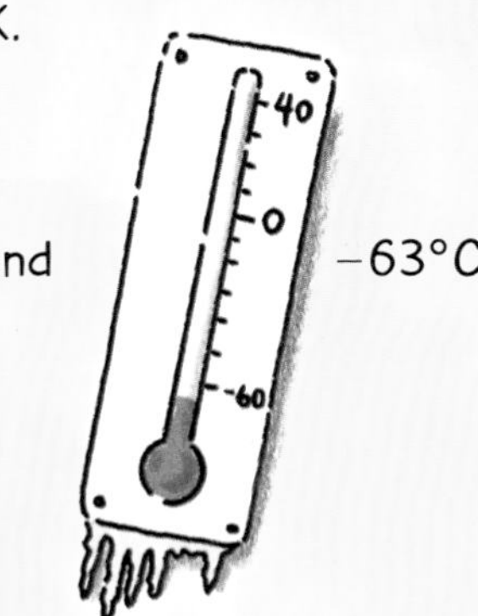

Which is the highest recorded temperature? the lowest?
At which place do you think each was recorded? Why?
What is the difference between the two temperatures?

CLUES

A certain negative integer is

- greater than −7
- less than −4
- farther from −4 than −7

What is it?

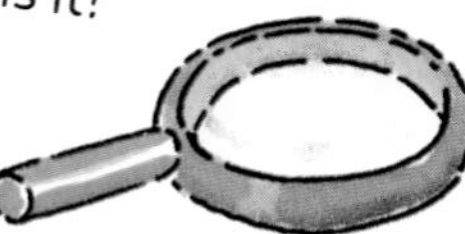

Make up a set of clues about another negative integer.

Make up other problems. Post them on the bulletin board for your classmates to solve.

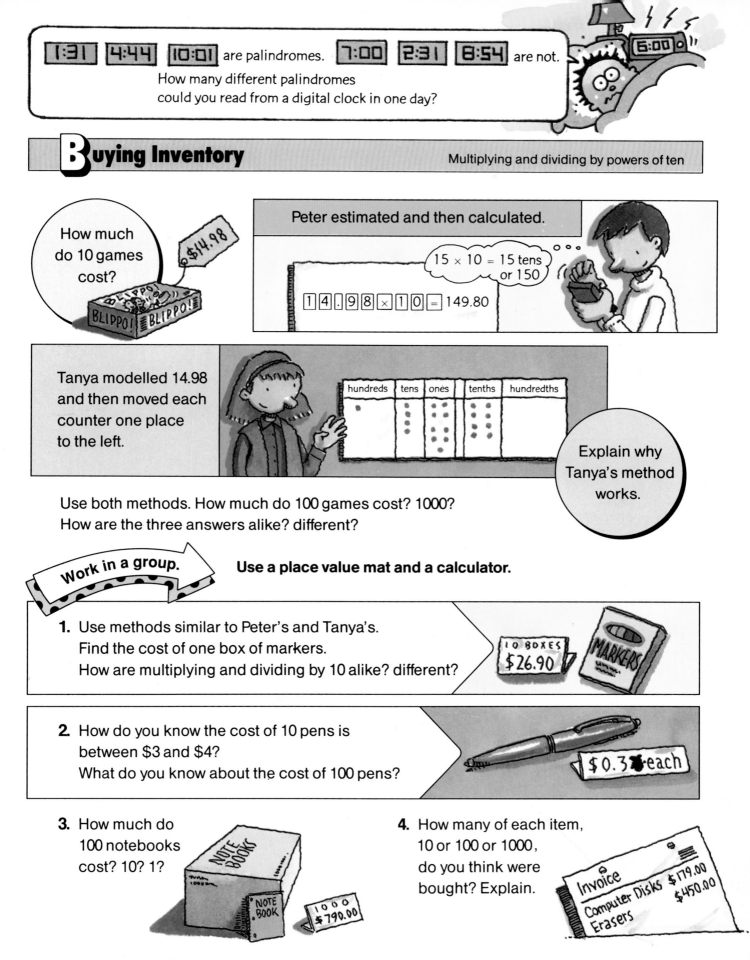

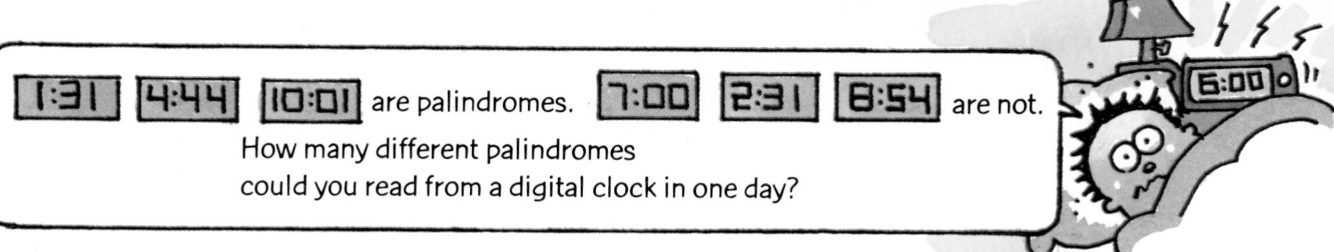

1:31 4:44 10:01 are palindromes. 7:00 2:31 8:54 are not.

How many different palindromes could you read from a digital clock in one day?

Buying Inventory

Multiplying and dividing by powers of ten

How much do 10 games cost?

Peter estimated and then calculated.

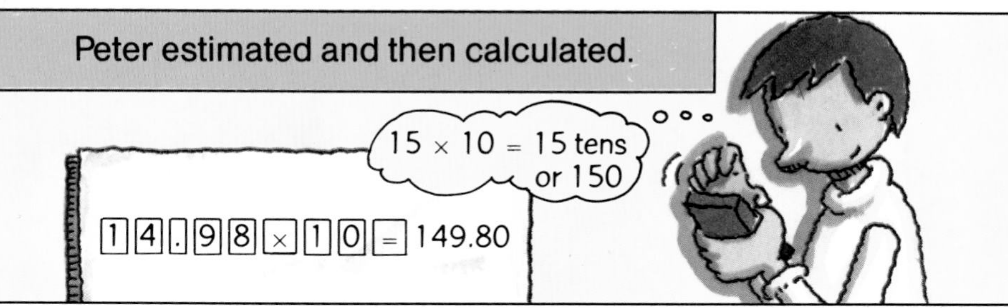

Tanya modelled 14.98 and then moved each counter one place to the left.

Explain why Tanya's method works.

Use both methods. How much do 100 games cost? 1000?
How are the three answers alike? different?

Use a place value mat and a calculator.

1. Use methods similar to Peter's and Tanya's.
   Find the cost of one box of markers.
   How are multiplying and dividing by 10 alike? different?

2. How do you know the cost of 10 pens is between $3 and $4?
   What do you know about the cost of 100 pens?

3. How much do 100 notebooks cost? 10? 1?

NOTE BOOKS
NOTE BOOK
1000
$790.00

4. How many of each item, 10 or 100 or 1000, do you think were bought? Explain.

Invoice
Computer Disks $179.00
Erasers $450.00

5. Tell how to multiply and divide by 10, 100, and 1000 in your head.

How are these shapes alike? different?

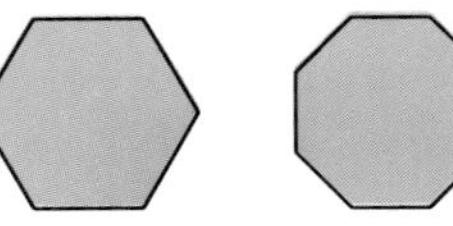

Examining Measurements

Renaming measurements

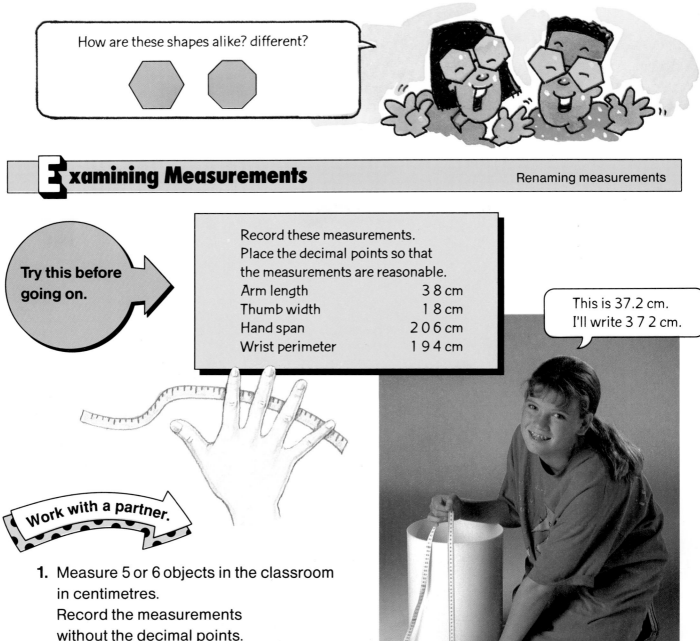

Try this before going on.

Record these measurements.
Place the decimal points so that
the measurements are reasonable.

Arm length	3 8 cm
Thumb width	1 8 cm
Hand span	2 0 6 cm
Wrist perimeter	1 9 4 cm

This is 37.2 cm.
I'll write 3 7 2 cm.

Work with a partner.

1. Measure 5 or 6 objects in the classroom in centimetres.
   Record the measurements without the decimal points.
   Trade them with your partner.
   Place the decimal points in each other's measurements.
   Check each other's work.

2. If you rewrite the body measurements above as millimetres, will the new numbers be greater or less? Tell why. Rewrite them. How are centimetres and millimetres related?

   How are the two pairs of numbers related?

3. If you rewrite the body measurements above as metres, will the new numbers be greater or less? Tell why. Rewrite them. How are centimetres and metres related?

   How are the two pairs of numbers related?

4. Would you ever record body measurements in kilometres? Explain.

5. By what number would you multiply or divide measurements in centimetres to change them to decimetres? What other unit changes involve the same computation?

6. The lengths of these unusual animals are recorded without decimal points. But they are correct because of the units used. What could you do to determine which is longest and which is shortest? Do it.

Komodo monitor	225 cm
Southern elephant seal	5 m
Harvest mouse	135 mm
Least storm petrel	14 cm

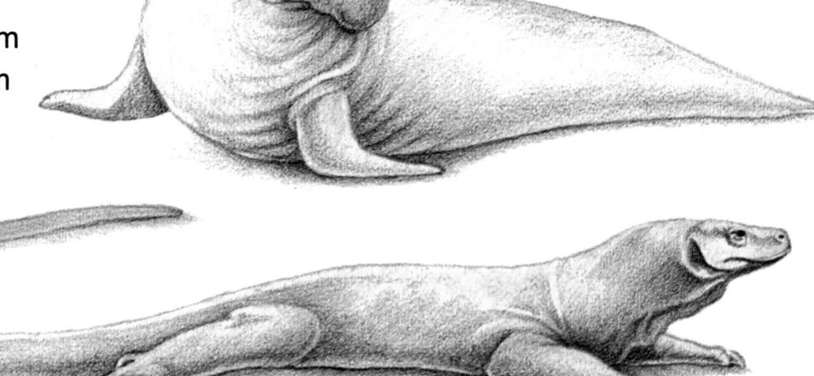

7. Complete each statement.

1 km = ? m	1 m = ? dm	1 dm = ? cm
1 cm = ? mm	1 m = ? cm	1 m = ? mm

8. Would another unit be more appropriate, or just as appropriate, for any of these measurements? Explain and make those changes.

Tallest Lego tower	181.5 dm
Longest zipper	76.2 dm
Largest paper clip	700 cm
Longest railway run	9438 km
Longest sofa	3740 mm
Tallest orchid	7620 mm
Longest stuffed toy	0.83 km

9. What do the prefixes *milli, centi, deci,* and *kilo* mean?

10. How is changing from one unit to another related to using place value?

11. Do you think there are units longer than metres but shorter than kilometres? Try to find other metric units of length. Why do you think they are rarely used?

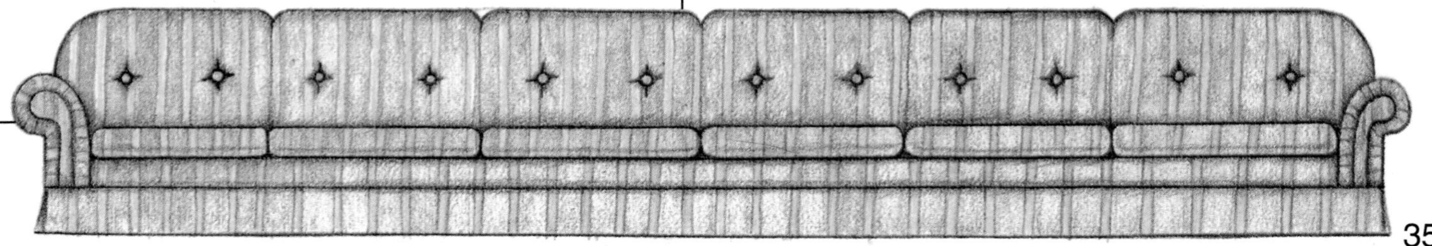

45 × 67 and 546 × 7 are two pairs of factors that use the digits 4, 5, 6, and 7. Predict which product will be greater. Check using a calculator. Rearrange the digits to make the greatest possible product.

Estimating Germs

Estimating large quantities

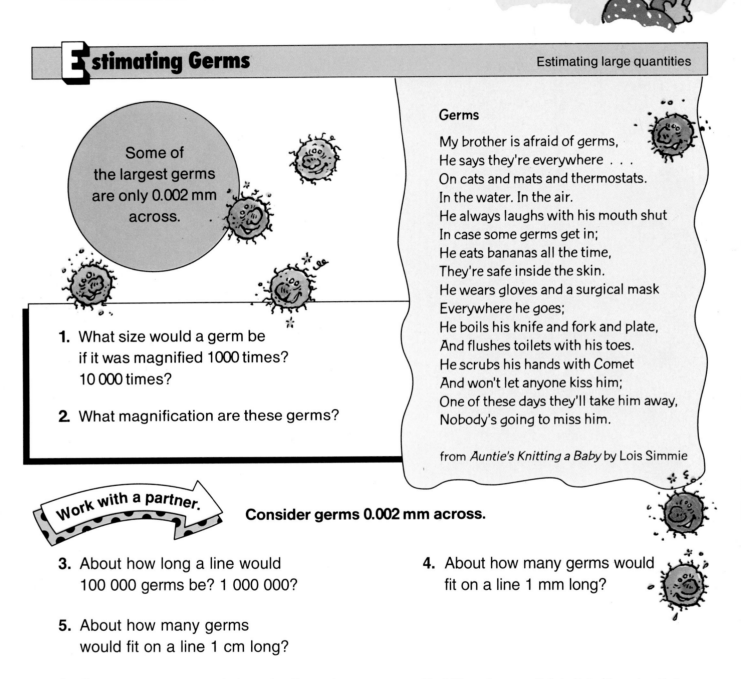

Some of the largest germs are only 0.002 mm across.

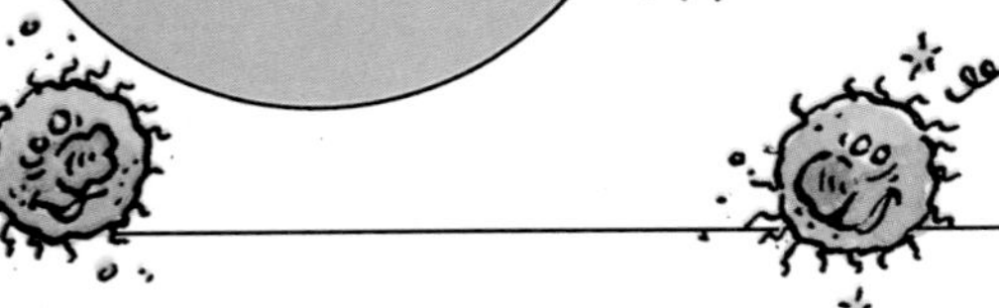

1. What size would a germ be if it was magnified 1000 times? 10 000 times?

2. What magnification are these germs?

Germs

My brother is afraid of germs,
He says they're everywhere . . .
On cats and mats and thermostats.
In the water. In the air.
He always laughs with his mouth shut
In case some germs get in;
He eats bananas all the time,
They're safe inside the skin.
He wears gloves and a surgical mask
Everywhere he goes;
He boils his knife and fork and plate,
And flushes toilets with his toes.
He scrubs his hands with Comet
And won't let anyone kiss him;
One of these days they'll take him away,
Nobody's going to miss him.

from *Auntie's Knitting a Baby* by Lois Simmie

Consider germs 0.002 mm across.

3. About how long a line would 100 000 germs be? 1 000 000?

4. About how many germs would fit on a line 1 mm long?

5. About how many germs would fit on a line 1 cm long?

6. Some germs are only one tenth as large. Will there be more or fewer germs in a 1 mm line? Explain.

7. Why do you think it took scientists a long time to find out about germs?

Take Your Pick

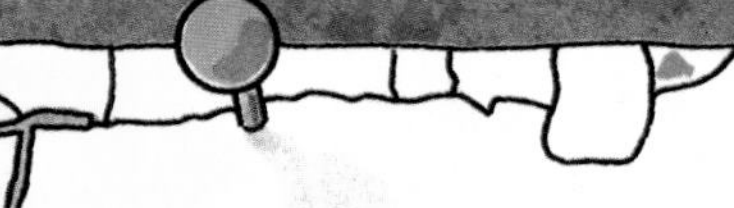

SCALES

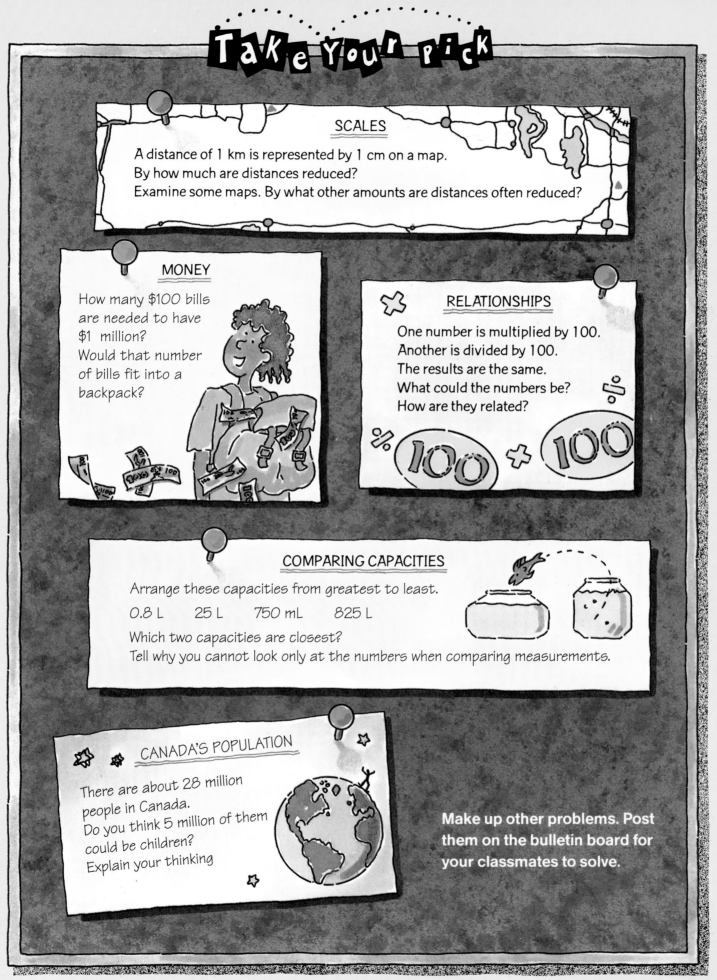

A distance of 1 km is represented by 1 cm on a map.
By how much are distances reduced?
Examine some maps. By what other amounts are distances often reduced?

MONEY

How many $100 bills are needed to have $1 million?
Would that number of bills fit into a backpack?

RELATIONSHIPS

One number is multiplied by 100.
Another is divided by 100.
The results are the same.
What could the numbers be?
How are they related?

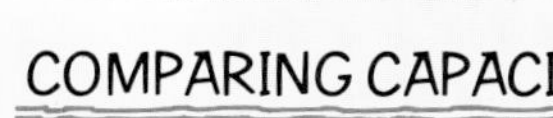

COMPARING CAPACITIES

Arrange these capacities from greatest to least.

0.8 L 25 L 750 mL 825 L

Which two capacities are closest?
Tell why you cannot look only at the numbers when comparing measurements.

CANADA'S POPULATION

There are about 28 million people in Canada.
Do you think 5 million of them could be children?
Explain your thinking

Make up other problems. Post them on the bulletin board for your classmates to solve.

Solving a Problem By Making an Organized List

Try this before going on.
FOUR DIGITS
How many 4-digit even numbers can you create using each of these digits once?
2
3
4
5

Marc's group solved the problem by making a list.

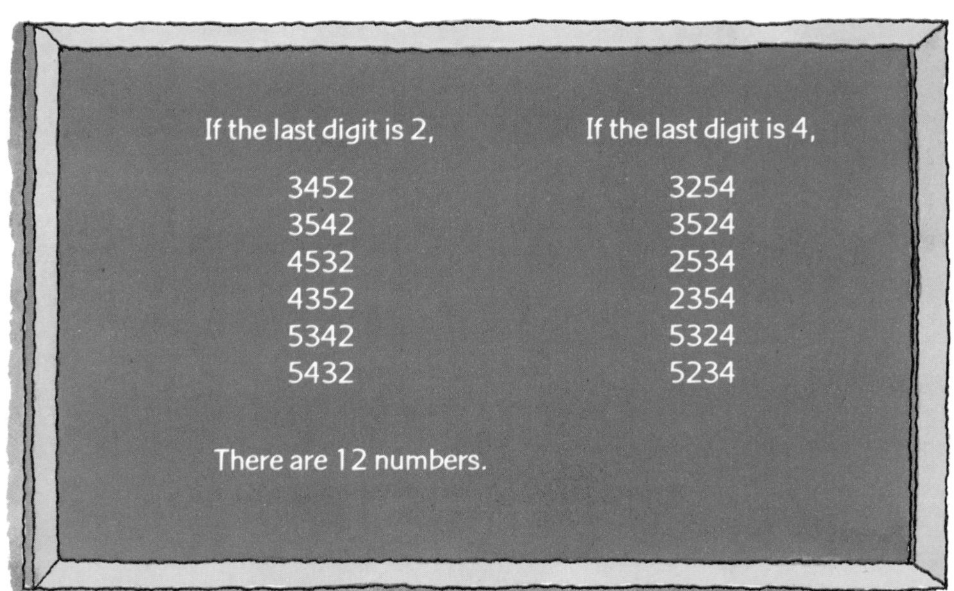

If the last digit is 2,

If the last digit is 4,

There are 12 numbers.

Solve each problem by making an organized list.

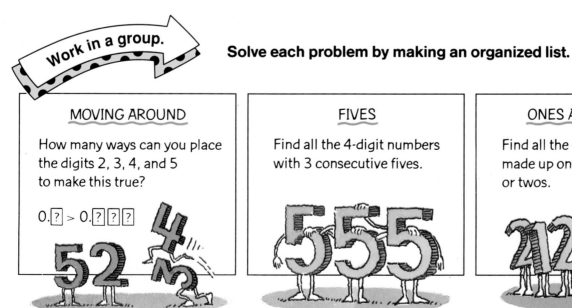

MOVING AROUND

How many ways can you place the digits 2, 3, 4, and 5 to make this true?

0.[?] > 0.[?][?][?]

FIVES

Find all the 4-digit numbers with 3 consecutive fives.

ONES AND TWOS

Find all the 4-digit numbers made up only of ones or twos.

Practising What You've Learned

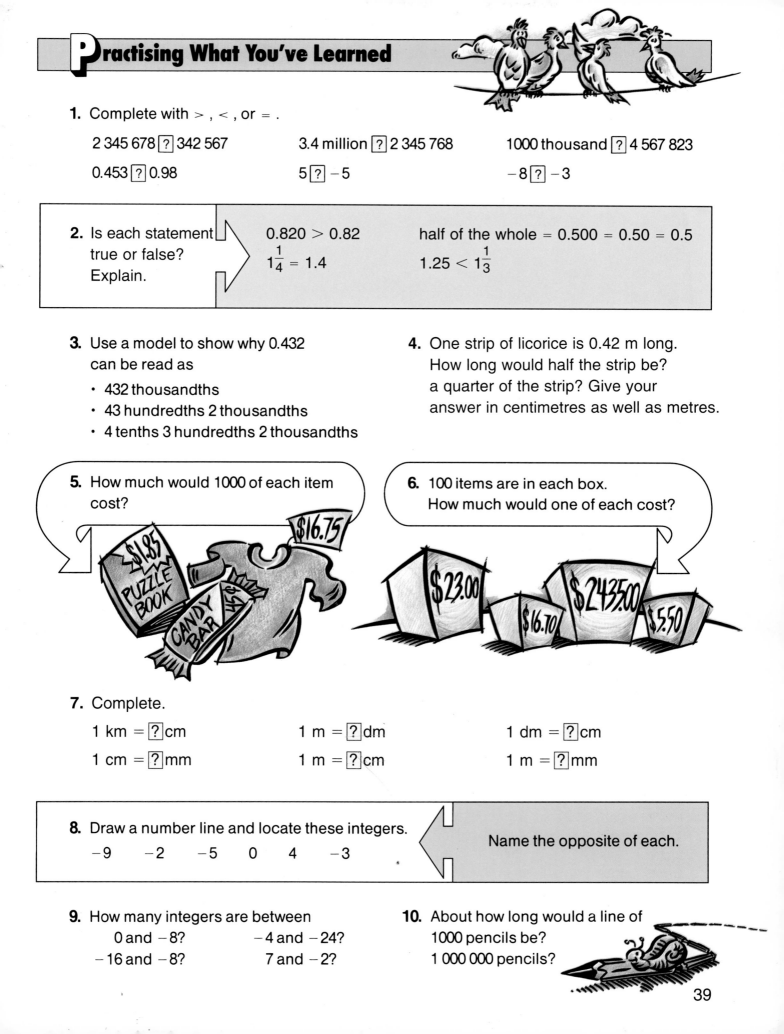

1. Complete with $>$, $<$, or $=$.

   2 345 678 ? 342 567   3.4 million ? 2 345 768   1000 thousand ? 4 567 823

   0.453 ? 0.98   5 ? −5   −8 ? −3

2. Is each statement true or false? Explain.

   $0.820 > 0.82$ half of the whole $= 0.500 = 0.50 = 0.5$

   $1\frac{1}{4} = 1.4$ $1.25 < 1\frac{1}{3}$

3. Use a model to show why 0.432 can be read as
   - 432 thousandths
   - 43 hundredths 2 thousandths
   - 4 tenths 3 hundredths 2 thousandths

4. One strip of licorice is 0.42 m long. How long would half the strip be? a quarter of the strip? Give your answer in centimetres as well as metres.

5. How much would 1000 of each item cost?

6. 100 items are in each box. How much would one of each cost?

7. Complete.

   1 km = ? cm   1 m = ? dm   1 dm = ? cm

   1 cm = ? mm   1 m = ? cm   1 m = ? mm

8. Draw a number line and locate these integers.

   −9   −2   −5   0   4   −3

   Name the opposite of each.

9. How many integers are between

   0 and −8?   −4 and −24?

   −16 and −8?   7 and −2?

10. About how long would a line of 1000 pencils be? 1 000 000 pencils?

Playing Games for Practice

Play each game in a group of 2, 3, or 4.

Four Spins

- In turn roll two dice and form the greater 2-digit number possible.
- Spin the spinner and multiply or divide your number.
- Spin 3 more times.
- Score 1 point for a final number less than 100
  2 points for a final number between 100 and 10 000
  3 points for a final number greater than 10 000
- Continue until one player has 15 points.

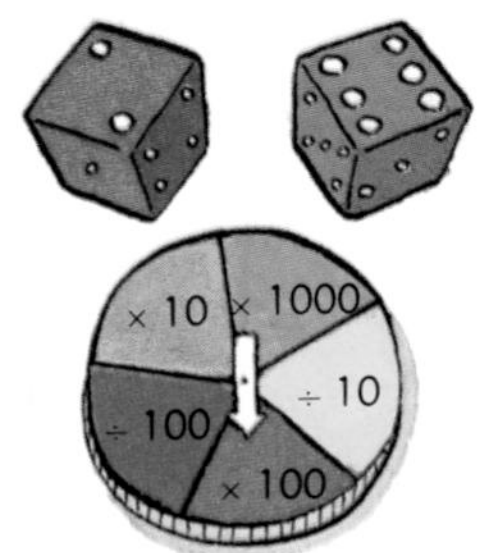

43
43 000
430
4.3
0.430
Score 1 point.

Over and Under

- Remove the face cards and tens from a deck of playing cards.
- Shuffle the deck and deal each player 6 cards.
- Take turns drawing a card from the top of the deck, placing the cards in a row in the order drawn until a 6-digit target number is created.
- Arrange your 6 cards to create a 6-digit number as close as possible to the target number.
- The player with the closest number scores 1.
- Continue until one player has 10 points.

Example

Target number

Closer
Score 1 point.

Variation: Arrange your 6 cards to create a 6-digit number as different in value as possible from the target number.

Take Your Pick

MEASURING HAIR

A human hair is about 0.007 cm wide. About how many hairs placed side-by-side would measure 1 cm? 1 m?

NEGATIVE FIVE

Tell as many things as you can that are true about the number -5.

COMPARING FRACTIONS

Ann compared $\frac{9}{10}$ and $\frac{10}{11}$. "$\frac{10}{11}$ must be greater than $\frac{9}{10}$ because $\frac{10}{11}$ is only $\frac{1}{11}$ less than 1 and $\frac{9}{10}$ is $\frac{1}{10}$ less than 1."
Use Ann's method to compare these fractions:

- $\frac{2}{3}$ and $\frac{4}{5}$
- $\frac{99}{100}$ and $\frac{100}{101}$
- $\frac{499}{500}$ and $\frac{999}{1000}$

$\frac{4}{5}$ $\frac{99}{100}$

HOW-MANY?

Use only the digits 1 and 2. How many numbers like this can you create that are greater than 1 200 000?

WRAP IT UP

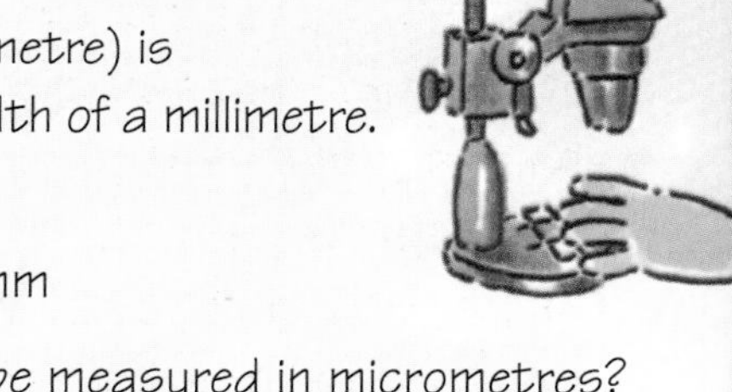

1 μ m (micrometre) is one thousandth of a millimetre. Complete.

1 μ m = ? mm

What might be measured in micrometres?

Make up other problems. Post them on the bulletin board for your classmates to solve.

Showing What You Know

1. Use each of the digits 2 and 4 once and 0 as many times as you need to create a number between
   - 24, and 24 hundredths
   - 1 and 7 tenths, and 17 thousandths

2. Write a number between
   - 38 hundred thousand and 4 million
   - 435 thousandths and 22 hundredths

3. Order the numbers $3\frac{7}{9}$, $3\frac{3}{4}$, 3.777, $\frac{37}{10}$ from least to greatest.

   Explain what you did.

4. You have 5 tickets for a draw. Only 1000 tickets are sold. What fraction and decimal show your chance of winning the draw?

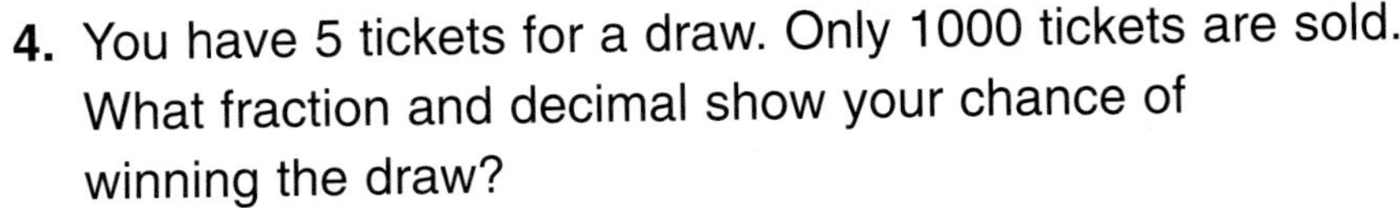

5. What do you multiply or divide the first number by to get the second number?

   - 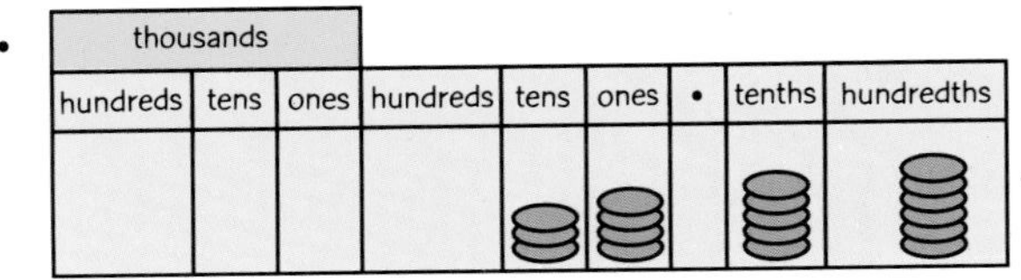

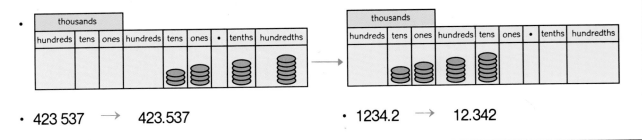

→

thousands								
hundreds	tens	ones	hundreds	tens	ones	•	tenths	hundredths

   - 423 537 → 423.537
   - 1234.2 → 12.342

6. The time is 10:55. What time will it be in
   - 2 and a half hours?
   - $\frac{5}{4}$ hours?
   - 1.1 hours?
   - $1\frac{1}{3}$ hours?

7. A CD costs $33.00. How much will 10 cost? 100? 1000?

8. In what place will the 3 be if 673.8 is
   - multiplied by 100?
   - multiplied by 1000?
   - divided by 100?
   - divided by 1000?

9. The temperature at Halifax was −5°C at 8 a.m.
   It rose 8°C by 1 p.m.
   What was the temperature at 1 p.m.?

10. Two negative integers are 6 apart. One is twice as far from 0 on a number line as the other. What are the integers?

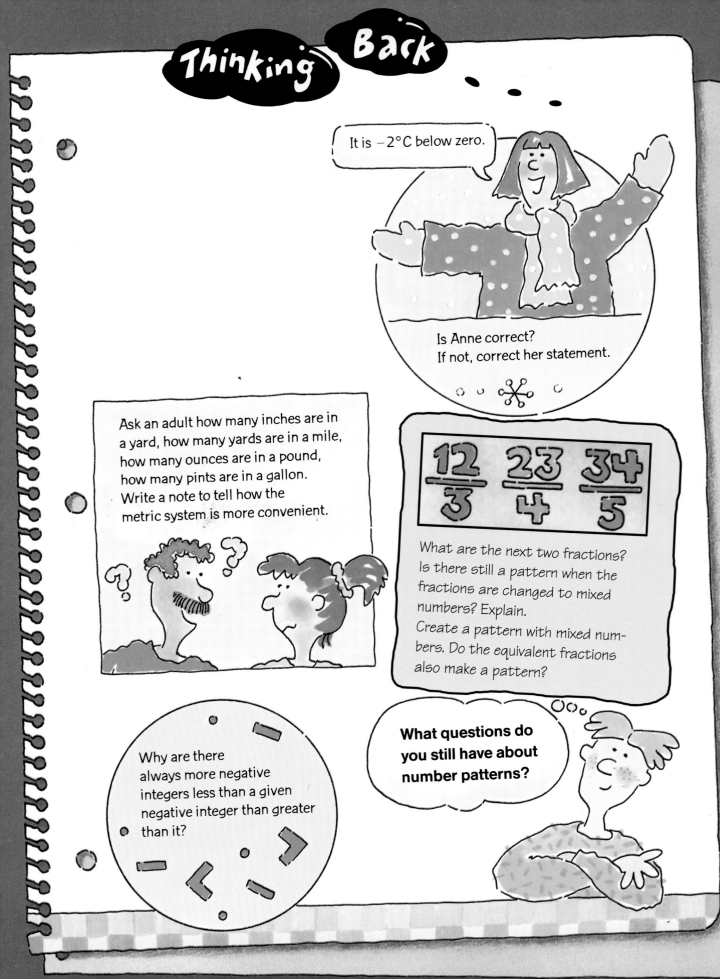

Thinking Back

Is Anne correct?
If not, correct her statement.

Ask an adult how many inches are in a yard, how many yards are in a mile, how many ounces are in a pound, how many pints are in a gallon. Write a note to tell how the metric system is more convenient.

$\frac{12}{3}$ $\frac{23}{4}$ $\frac{34}{5}$

What are the next two fractions? Is there still a pattern when the fractions are changed to mixed numbers? Explain.
Create a pattern with mixed numbers. Do the equivalent fractions also make a pattern?

Why are there always more negative integers less than a given negative integer than greater than it?

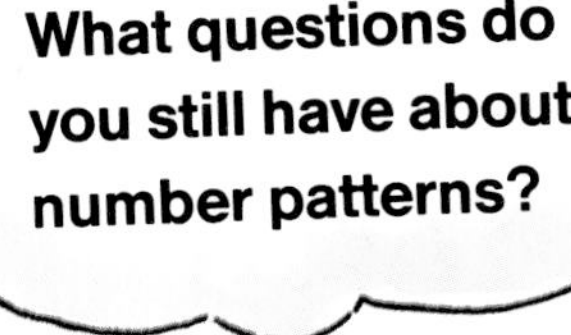

What questions do you still have about number patterns?

Exploring

▼ Which pair of scissors is open the greatest amount?

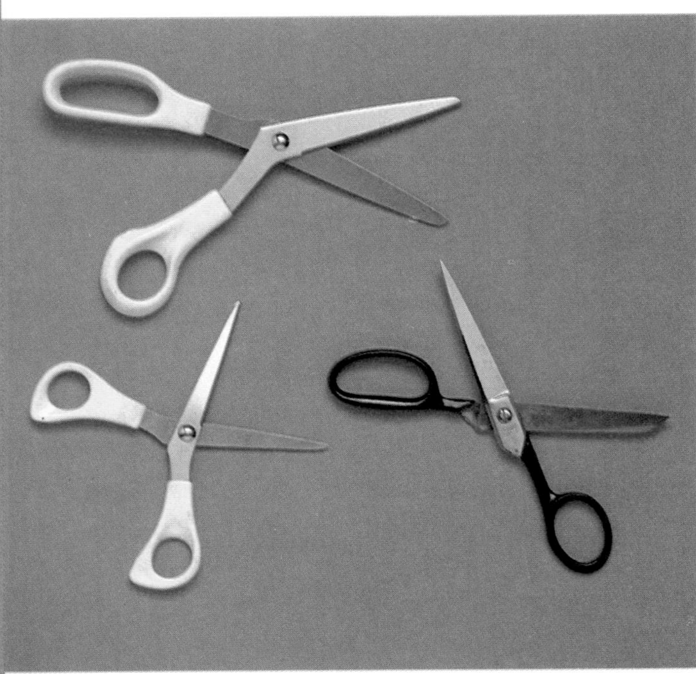

▼ Compare the corners of pattern blocks. Tell what you notice.

▼ Which pair of geostrips is open the greatest amount? the least?

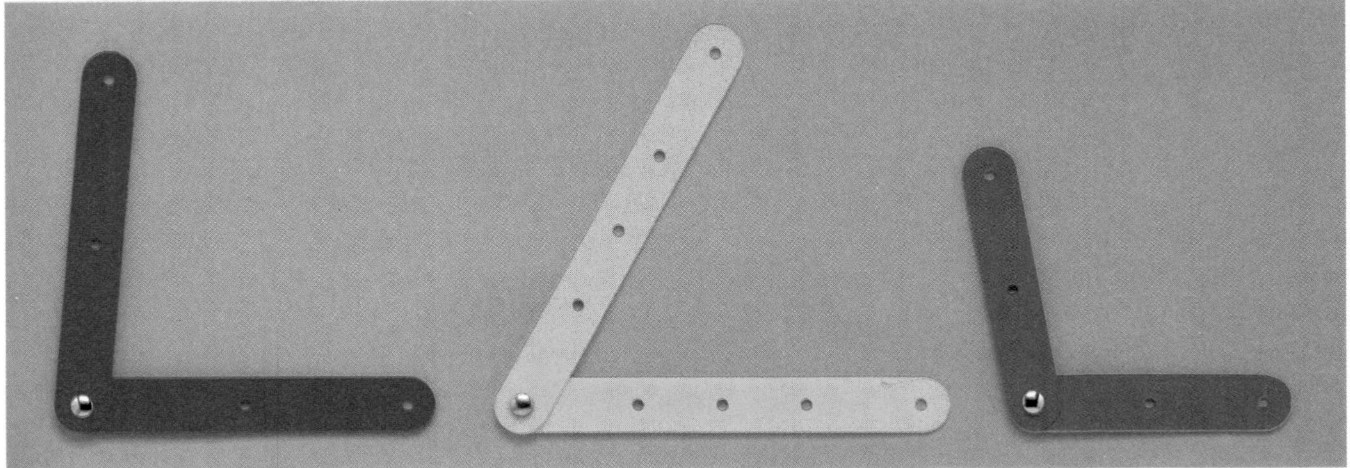

Use a pair of geostrips to form another opening between the greatest and the least openings.

Angles

▶ What time is shown?
Name a time in the hour when the hands are
- farther apart (a greater angle)
- closer together (a lesser angle)

▼ What appears to be true about the angles formed by crossing two straws?
How could the straws be crossed to form four equal angles?

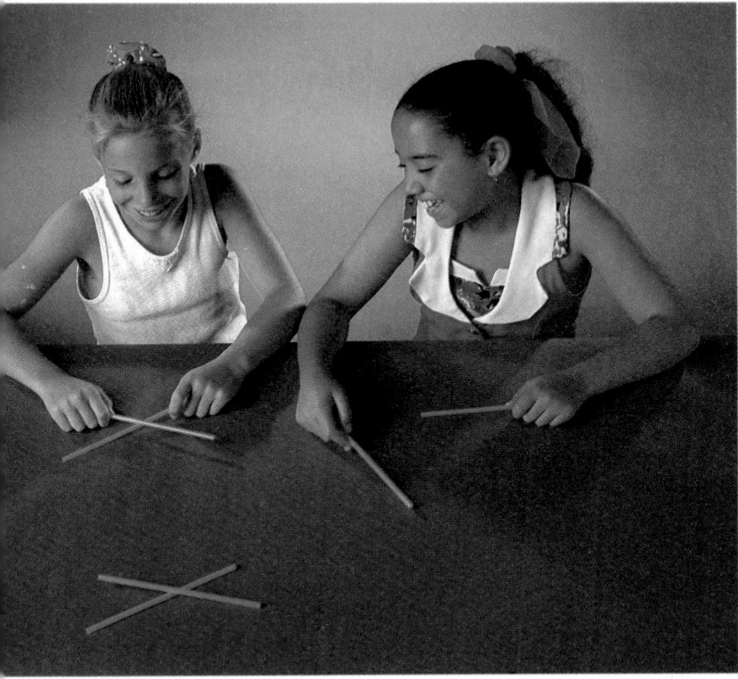

▼ Fold a piece of paper to show four equal angles.
Explain what you did.

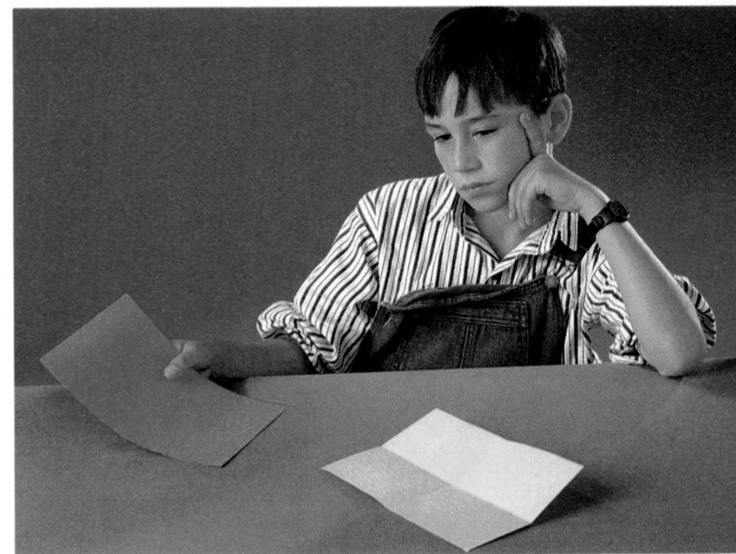

How would you explain what an angle is?
What examples would you show?

It costs 1.25 ¢ to make one penny.
How much more than their value does it cost to make $1000 worth of pennies?

Comparing Slices

Comparing by superimposing

An **angle** has a vertex and two arms.
Point out the vertex and arms for the angle of one of the pizza slices.

You can compare the sizes of angles by comparing the amount of spread between the arms of each angle.

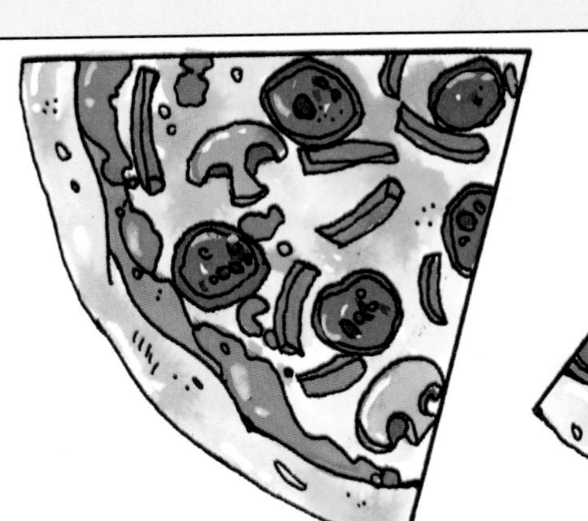

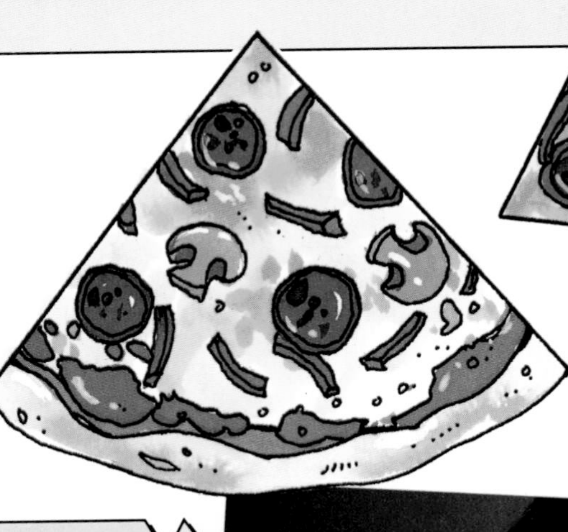

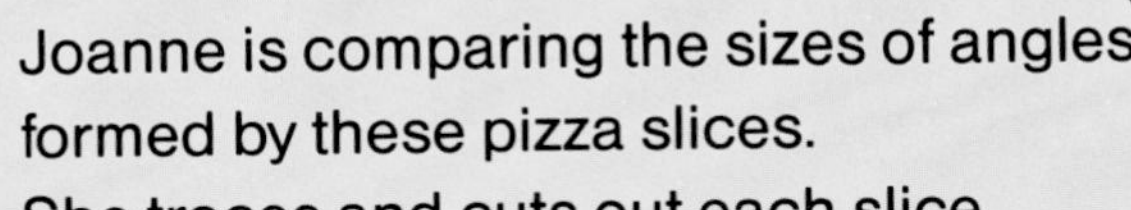

Joanne is comparing the sizes of angles formed by these pizza slices.
She traces and cuts out each slice.

Show how to use cut-out slices to compare the sizes of the angles.

Trace and cut out each slice.

1. Which pie slice shows the greatest angle? the least angle?

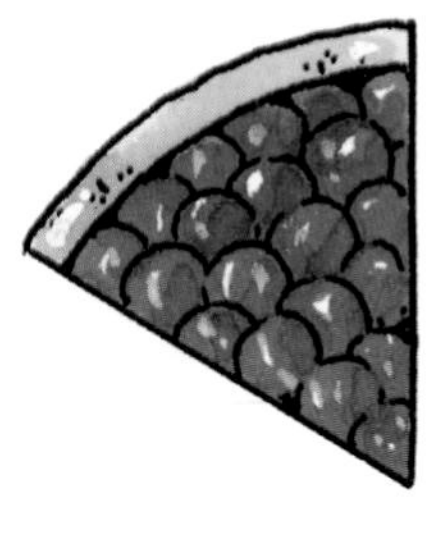

2. Make a slice whose angle is between the size of these two. Explain what you did.

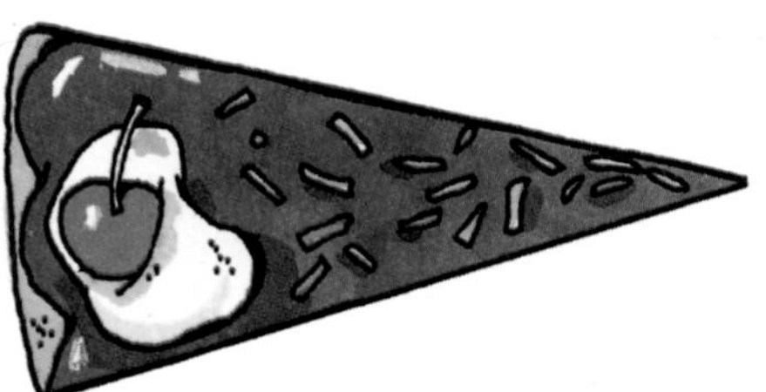

3. Make a slice with an angle
   - half as great as this one
   - twice as great as this one

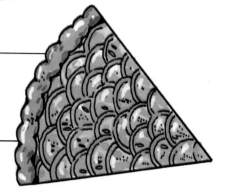

4. Put these two slices together to form a larger slice. Tell what you notice about the new angle.

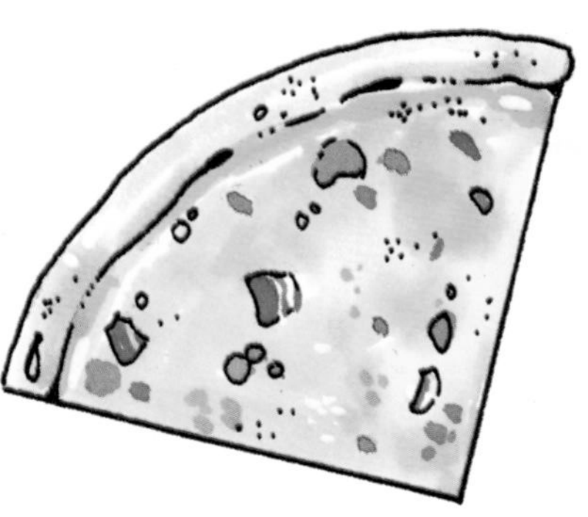

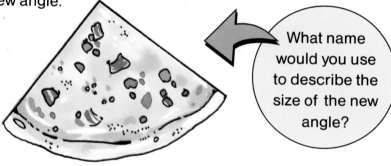

What name would you use to describe the size of the new angle?

5. Explain how to cut a cake into 8 equal slices. How does the size of each angle compare to a square corner?

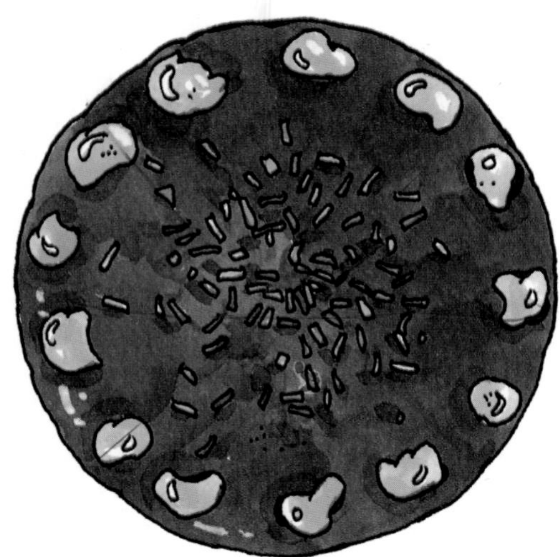

6. Explain the difference between comparing the sizes of angles formed by slices and comparing the areas of slices.

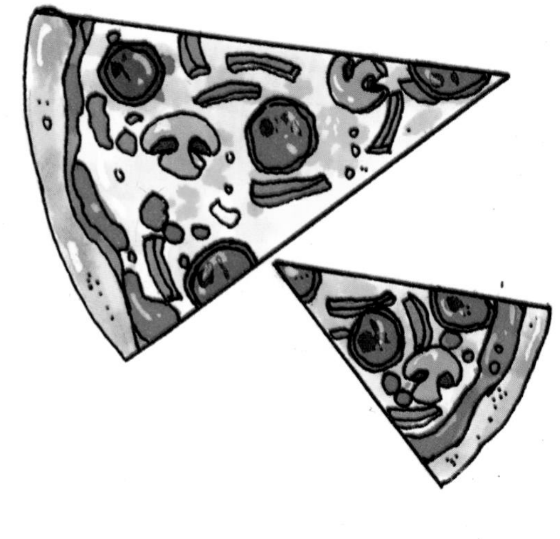

You are coloring the edges of a cube.
You want edges that meet to be different colors.
What is the least number of colors you need to use?

Dining Out

Comparing by rotating

You can also compare the sizes of angles by comparing the amount of turn from one arm to the other in each angle.

This is a revolving restaurant.
Which group of diners turned through the greater angle between having their orders taken and receiving their food?

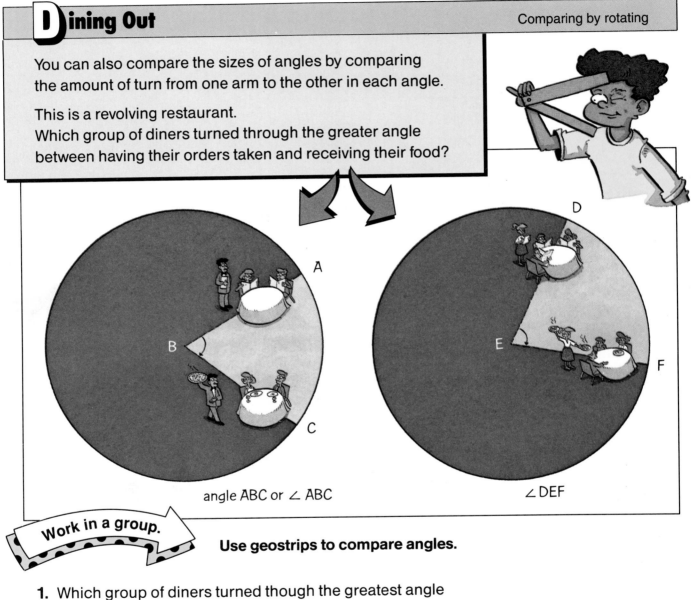

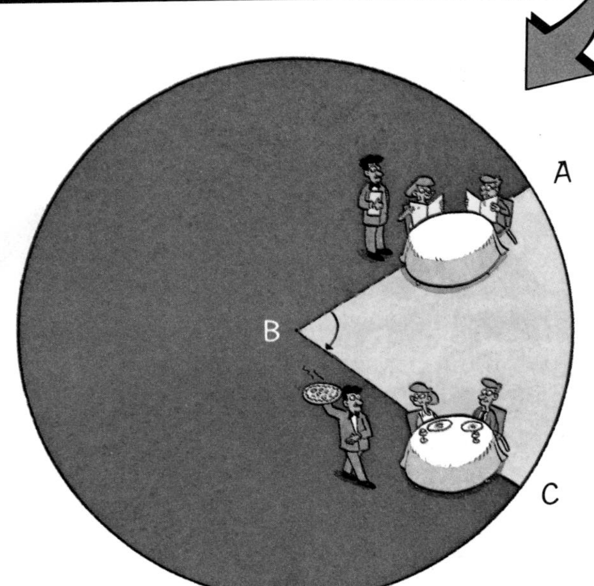

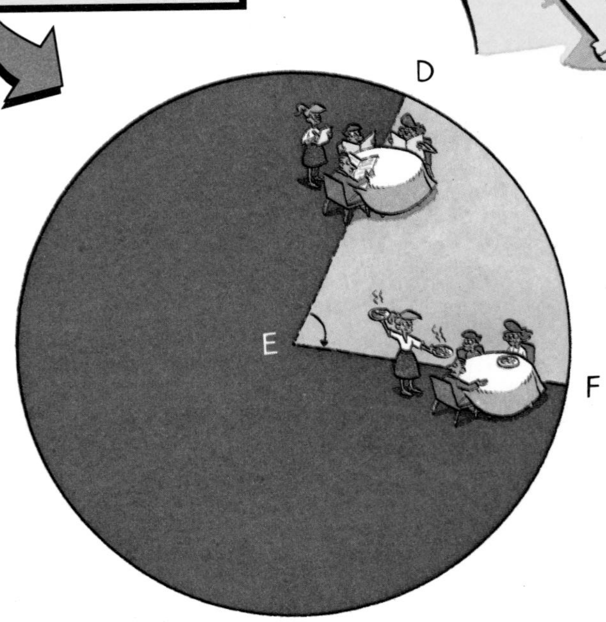

Use geostrips to compare angles.

1. Which group of diners turned though the greatest angle between receiving their food and having their table cleared?

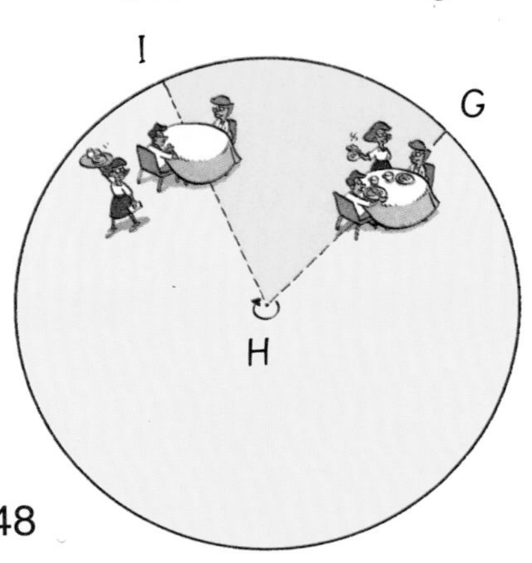

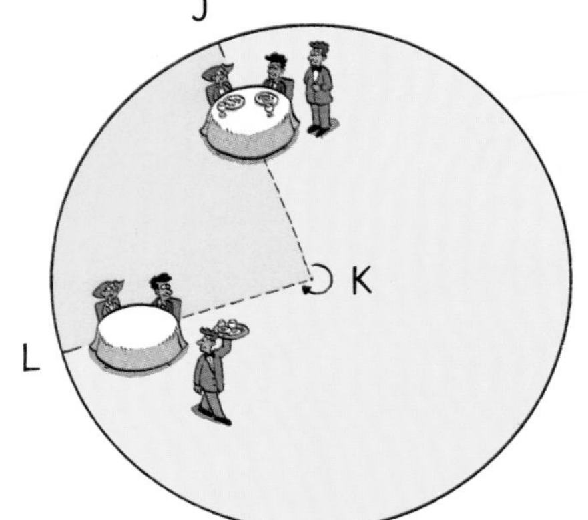

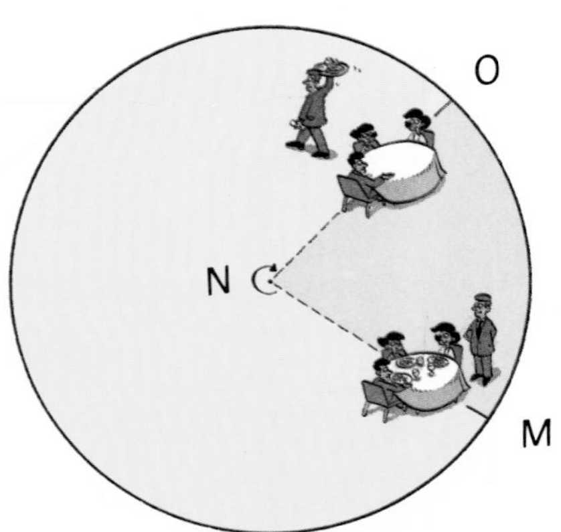

2. After a $\frac{1}{4}$ turn clockwise, table 1 will be at position 7. At which position will
   - table 1 be after a $\frac{1}{2}$ turn?
   - table 13 be after an $\frac{1}{8}$ turn?
   - table 23 be after a $\frac{3}{4}$ turn?
   - table 6 be after $1\frac{1}{2}$ turns?

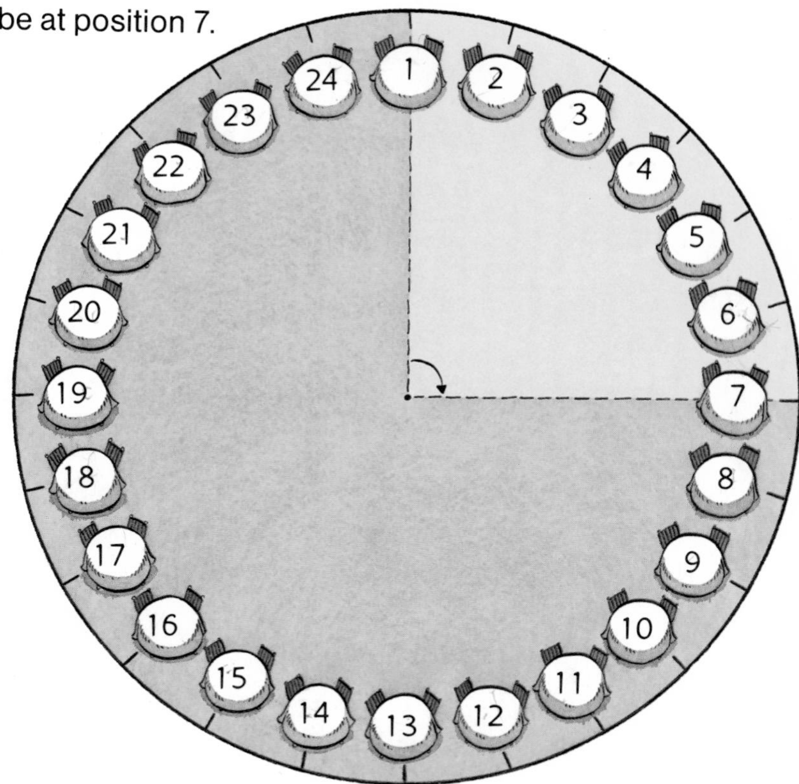

3. What is the position of table 6 after
   - a $\frac{1}{4}$ turn clockwise?
   - $1\frac{1}{4}$ turns clockwise?
   - $2\frac{1}{4}$ turns clockwise?
   - $3\frac{1}{4}$ turns clockwise?

   Tell what you notice.

4. What clockwise turn moves
   - table 1 to 19?
   - table 6 to 9?
   - table 17 to 14?

   Find more than one answer for each.

5. The restaurant rotates one complete turn every hour. About how many minutes will it take for each turn below? How can the first two answers help you find the third?

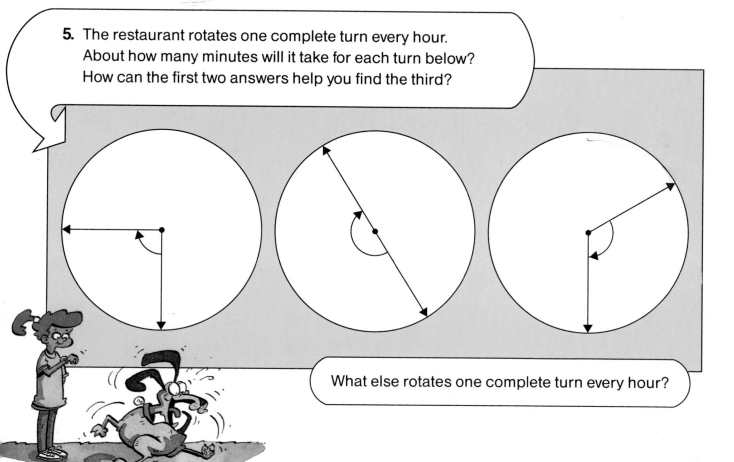

What else rotates one complete turn every hour?

Roll a pair of dice. Multiply the numbers. Record the ones digit. Repeat 20 times. Make a bar graph showing the 20 ones digits. What do you notice?

Estimating Signal Flag Angles

Comparing angles to 90° and 180°

Signal flags held at different angles can be used to send messages.

What is this message?

The Semaphore Alphabet

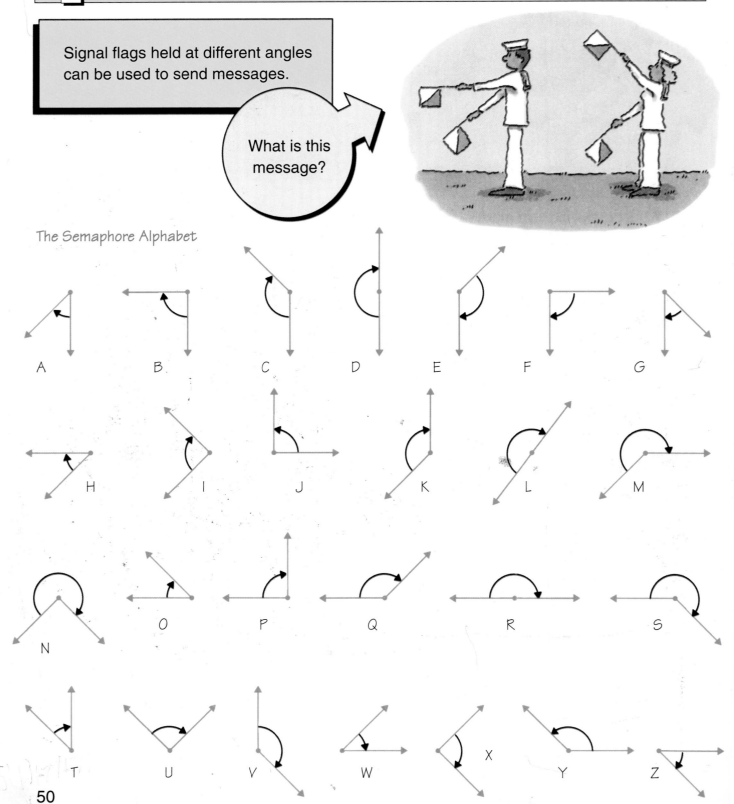

A B C D E F G

H I J K L M

N O P Q R S

T U V W X Y Z

A square corner of a piece of paper can be used to measure a **right angle**, which is 90° (read 90 degrees).

The straight edge of the paper can be used to measure a **straight angle**, which is 180°.

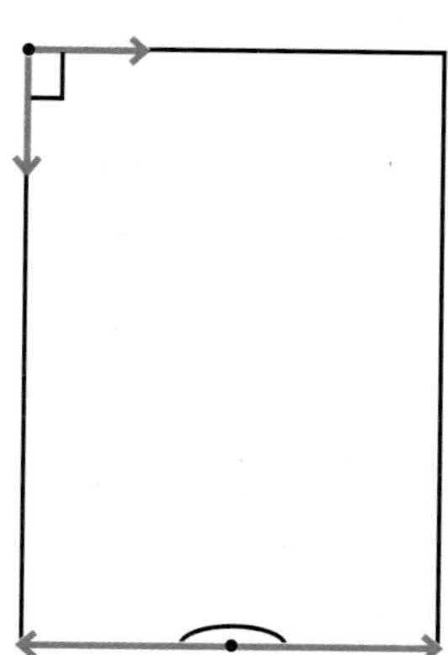

Use your paper angle tester to check.

1. Which letters of the Semaphore Alphabet have angles
   - equal to 90°?
   - equal to 180°?
   - less than 90°?
   - greater than 90° but less than 180°?
   - greater than 180° but less than 360°?

2. Which of the semaphore letters show a counterclockwise turn? Which of these angles is greatest?

3. What letter is signalled when
   - the upper flag in H is moved 90° clockwise?
   - both flags in B are moved 90° clockwise?
   - both flags in D are moved 90° clockwise?
   - the upper flag in I is moved 90° clockwise?

4. How much less than 360° is the angle for the letter N? L?

5. Is the sum of the angles greater than 180°, equal to 180°, or less than 180° but greater than 90°?
   - for the letters A and B?
   - for B and C?
   - for E and G?
   - for EGG?

6. What is the sum of the angles for CUE?

7. How many of each letter would you need to have angle measures equal to 360°?
   - A
   - B
   - D

8. Signal a word for your partner to decipher that contains only letters with angles
   - less than 90°
   - equal to 90°
   - greater than 90° but less than 180°

A strip of paper is cut into three pieces.
The longest one is double the length of the middle-sized one, which is double the length of the shortest one.
What fraction of the strip is each piece?

Measuring Letter Angles

Using degrees

My snake, with neither pad nor pen,
delineates a splendid N,
an agile H, a supple L,
an X with little parallel,

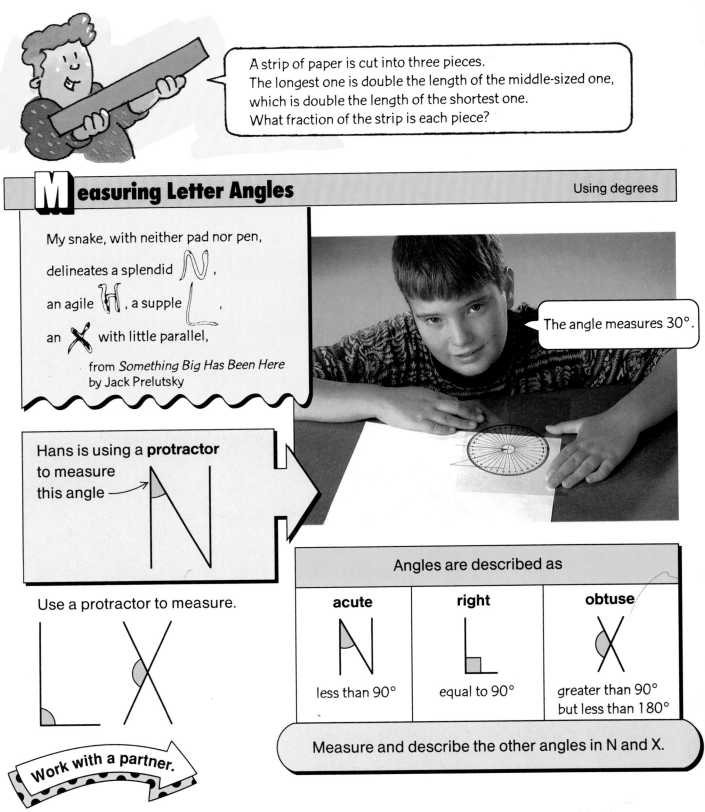

from *Something Big Has Been Here*
by Jack Prelutsky

Hans is using a **protractor** to measure this angle

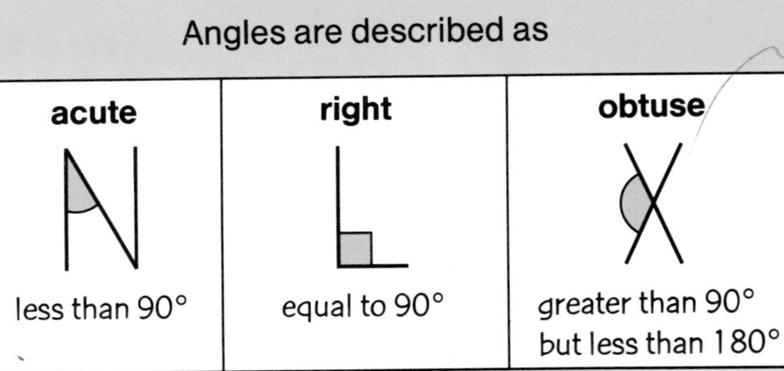

The angle measures 30°.

Angles are described as		
acute	**right**	**obtuse**
less than 90°	equal to 90°	greater than 90° but less than 180°

Use a protractor to measure.

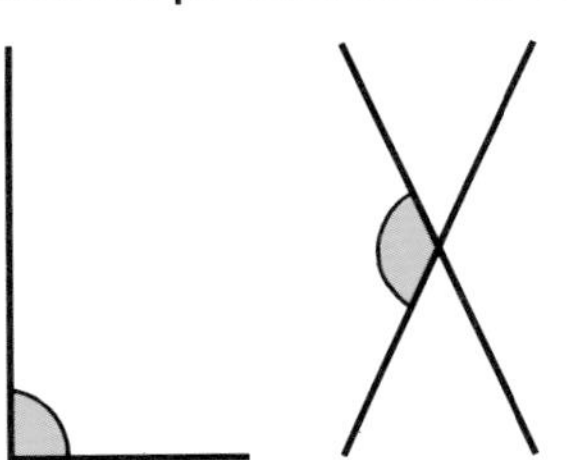

Measure and describe the other angles in N and X.

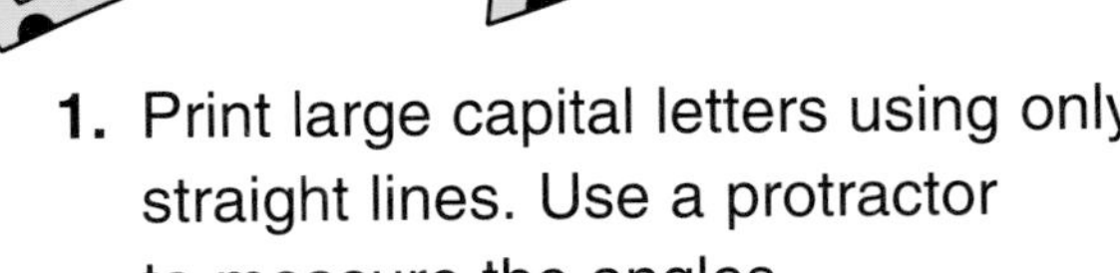

Work with a partner.

1. Print large capital letters using only straight lines. Use a protractor to measure the angles.
2. Record the letters in a table. Mark the angles you measured.

Acute	N X
Right	L
Obtuse	X

3. Estimate the letter of the alphabet that shows the greatest angle; the smallest angle; the greatest number of equal angles. Use a protractor to check.

Each letter represents a different digit.
Why is there no solution?
FIVE + SEVEN = TWELVE

Measuring Clock Angles

Estimating and measuring angles

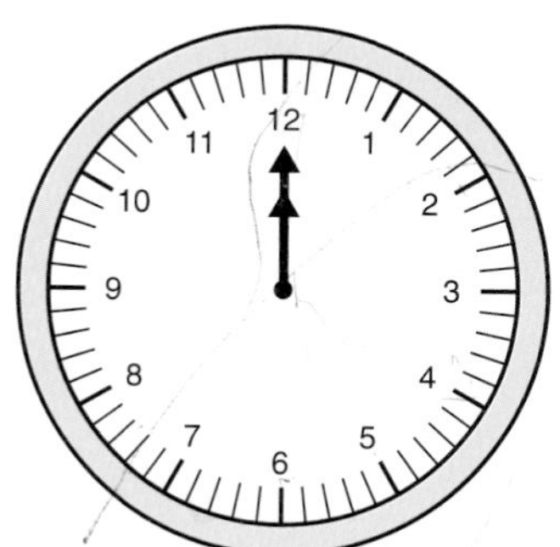

On the face of a clock the hour hand goes through one complete rotation (360°) from noon to midnight.
The face is divided into 12 sections so each section measures $360° \div 12 = 30°$.

1. At what hour does the clock show an angle of 30°? 60°? 90°? 120°? 180°? 210°?
2. Which of the above angles are acute? obtuse?

Angles that are greater than 180° but less than 360° are **reflex angles**.

3. Is the angle of the hands at 11:00 an acute angle or a reflex angle? Explain.
4. Make a chart showing each hour. Classify the angle as acute, right, obtuse, straight, or reflex.

Time	Measure of angle	Type of angle
1:00	30°	acute
2:00		

5. Classify each of these angles. Then estimate the size.

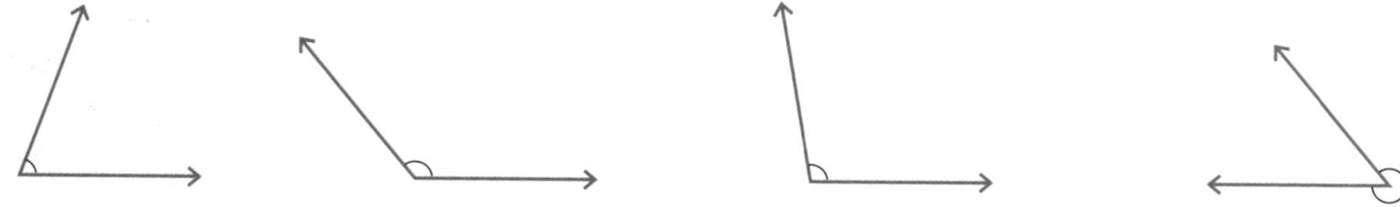

6. Trace the angles in question 5 and extend the arms. Measure each angle with a circular protractor, and record the measure to the nearest degree.
7. What are the approximate and exact measures of the angle between the hour hand and the minute hand when the clock reads 1:15? 13:15?

Describe and continue this pattern.
3×4
33×34
333×334

Drawing Angles

Sketching and drawing angles of a given measure

Use a circular protractor.

1. Demonstrate to your partner how to draw an acute angle of 45˚.

2. What is the measure of the related reflex angle?

45°

3. Estimate, then measure the size of each angle. Determine the size of the other related angle.

4. Before you draw an angle accurately, it is helpful to sketch it first. Why might this be?

5. Sketch the following angles. Then draw an accurate angle using a protractor. Classify the angles.

   10˚ 33˚ 49˚ 62˚ 96˚ 160˚ 175˚

6. Sketch the following reflex angles. Then draw an accurate angle using a protractor.

   185˚ 192˚ 221˚ 248˚ 269˚ 328˚ 340˚

7. How can you accurately draw an angle measuring 396˚?

Take Your Pick

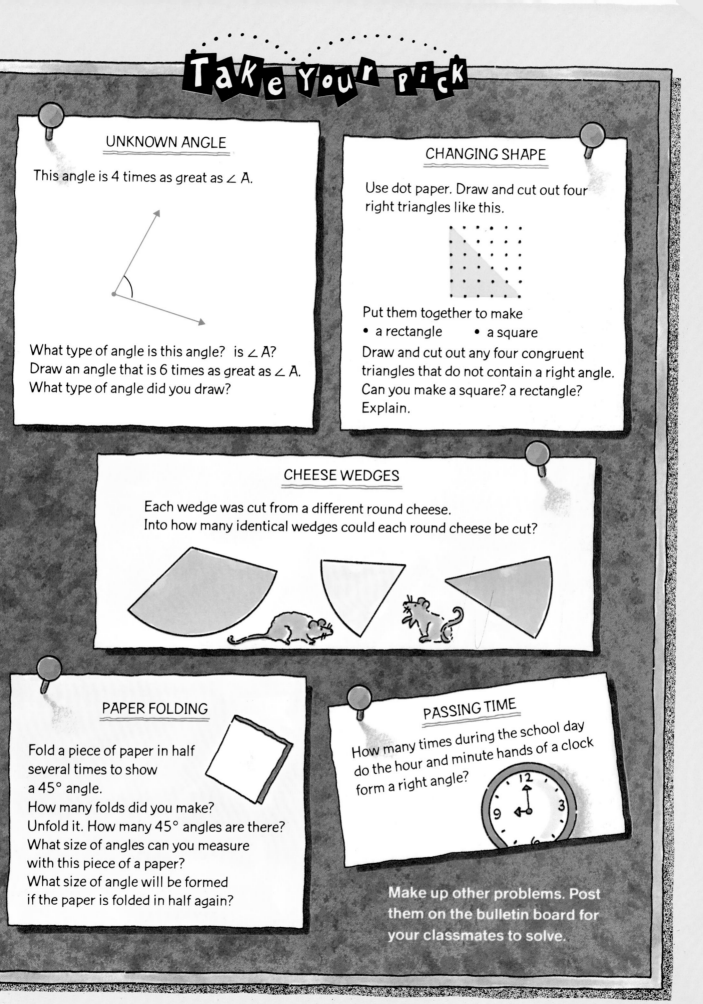

UNKNOWN ANGLE

This angle is 4 times as great as ∠ A.

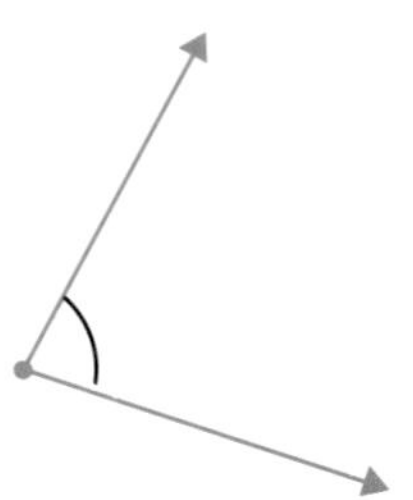

What type of angle is this angle? is ∠ A?
Draw an angle that is 6 times as great as ∠ A.
What type of angle did you draw?

CHANGING SHAPE

Use dot paper. Draw and cut out four right triangles like this.

Put them together to make
- a rectangle
- a square

Draw and cut out any four congruent triangles that do not contain a right angle. Can you make a square? a rectangle? Explain.

CHEESE WEDGES

Each wedge was cut from a different round cheese.
Into how many identical wedges could each round cheese be cut?

PAPER FOLDING

Fold a piece of paper in half several times to show a 45° angle.
How many folds did you make?
Unfold it. How many 45° angles are there?
What size of angles can you measure with this piece of a paper?
What size of angle will be formed if the paper is folded in half again?

PASSING TIME

How many times during the school day do the hour and minute hands of a clock form a right angle?

Make up other problems. Post them on the bulletin board for your classmates to solve.

A computer printer prints 192 characters in a second.
About how many characters does it print in 1 h?
Estimate how long it would take to print one of your favourite books.

Examining Triangles

Classifying triangles by the measure of their angles

Triangles can be classified by the type(s) of angles they contain.

- acute-angled triangle
- right-angled triangle
- obtuse-angled triangle

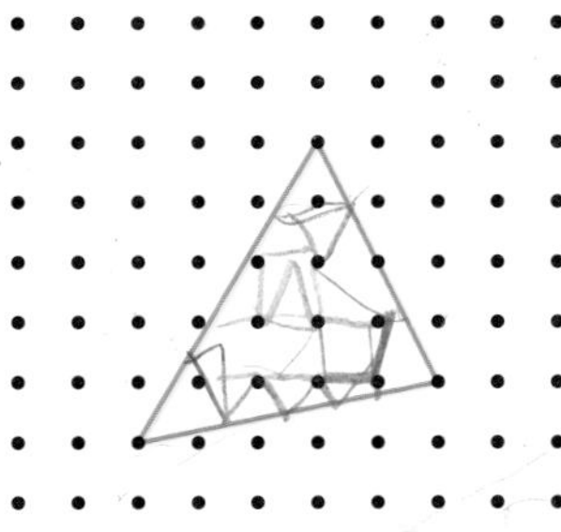

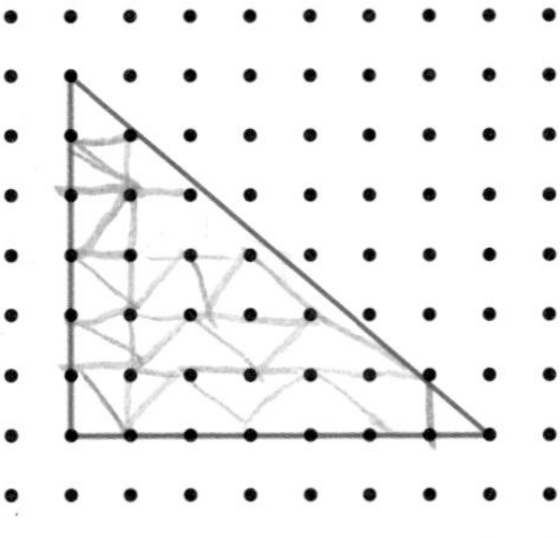

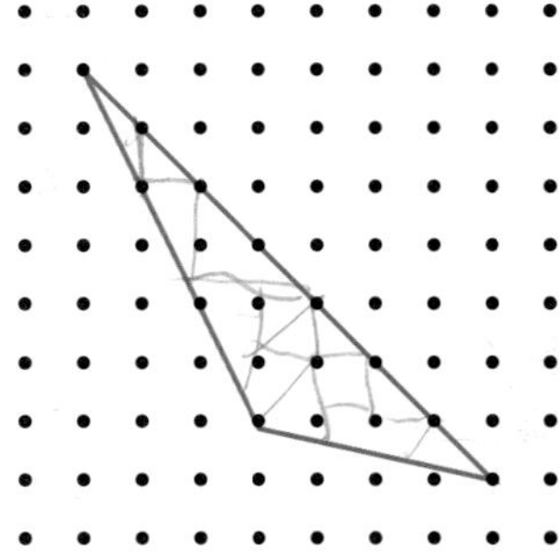

1. How can you classify each of the angles in the first triangle?

2. What are the two different types of angles contained in the second triangle? Which name best describes this triangle?

3. What are the two different types of angles contained in the third triangle? Which name best describes this triangle?

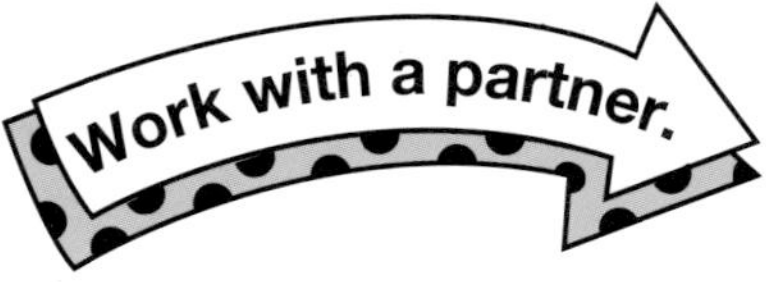

Use a circular protractor and a ruler.

4. Create 10 or more different triangles on a geoboard. Draw the triangles on dot paper. Measure the angles and record the degrees.

5. What is the sum of the angles in each triangle?

6. Why can a triangle never contain two right angles?

7. Why can a triangle never contain two obtuse angles?

8. Classify all the triangles you made as acute-angled, right-angled, or obtuse-angled.

9. Use what you noticed about the sum of the angles to find the unknown angles. Measure to check your answer. Then classify the triangles.

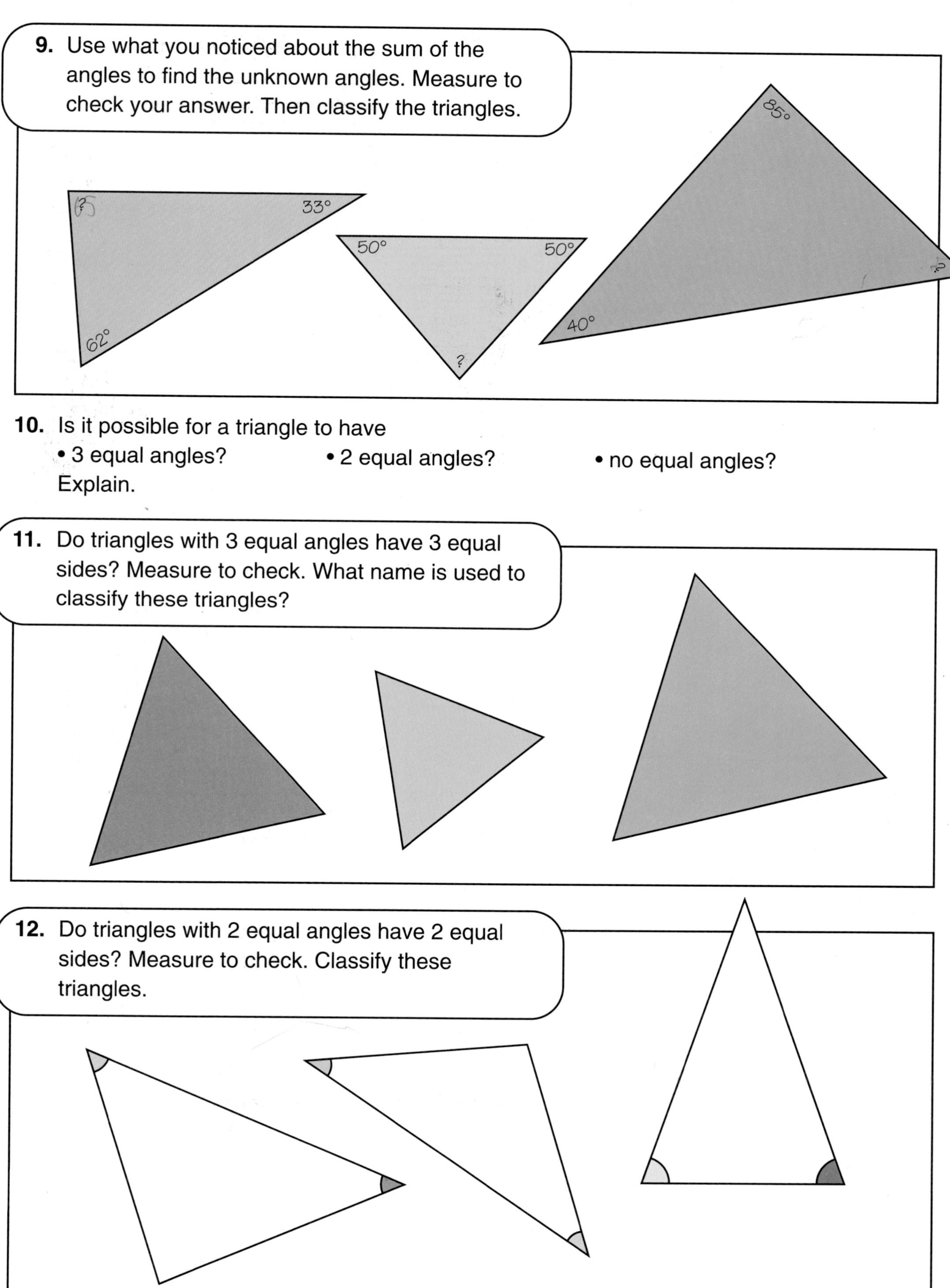

10. Is it possible for a triangle to have

- 3 equal angles?
- 2 equal angles?
- no equal angles?

Explain.

11. Do triangles with 3 equal angles have 3 equal sides? Measure to check. What name is used to classify these triangles?

12. Do triangles with 2 equal angles have 2 equal sides? Measure to check. Classify these triangles.

To find a dog's age in human years, count its first year as 15, its second as 10, and each year after that as 5.
How old in human years would a dog born in 1988 be?

Identifying Angles Around Us

Comparing angles in the environment

Angles are everywhere.

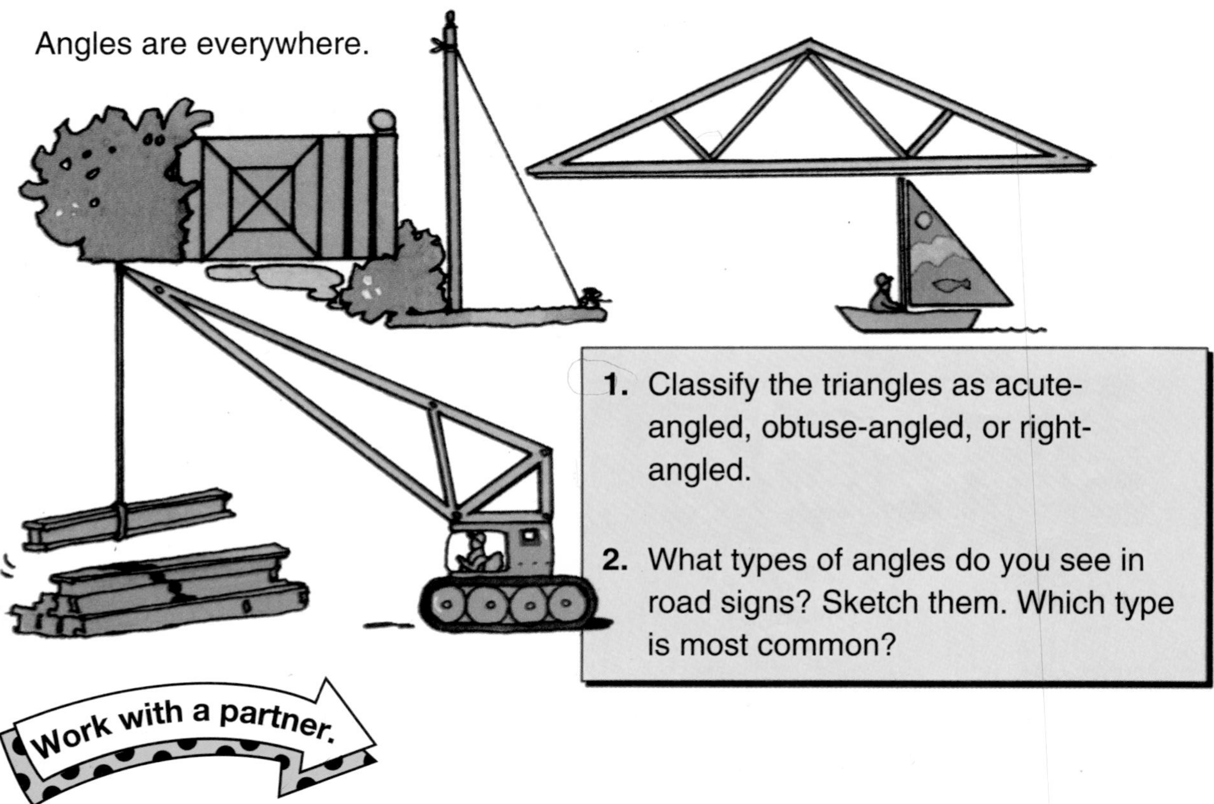

1. Classify the triangles as acute-angled, obtuse-angled, or right-angled.

2. What types of angles do you see in road signs? Sketch them. Which type is most common?

Work with a partner.

3. Classify the angles in each object. Estimate the size of each angle.

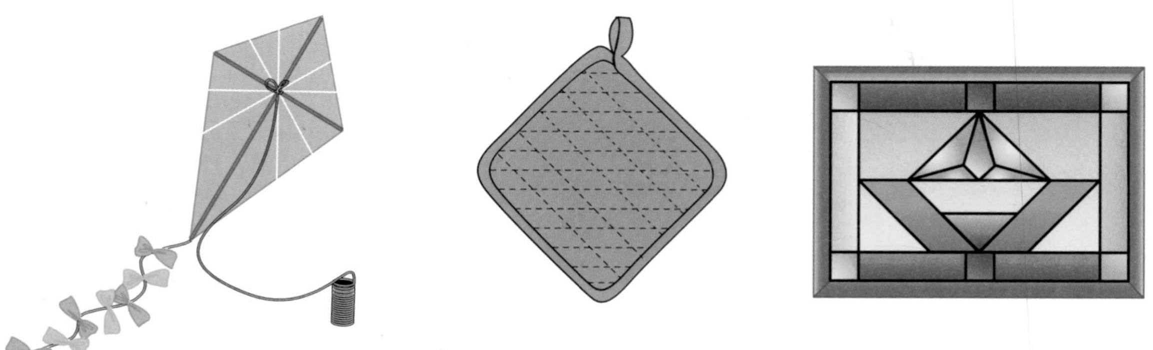

4. Look for angles used in business signs, logos, flags, quilts, and wallpaper designs.
   Classify the angles used. Is one type more common than the others?
   How common is it to see triangles in these creations? Classify the triangles.
   Is one type more common than the others?

Take Your Pick

DIVIDING LINES

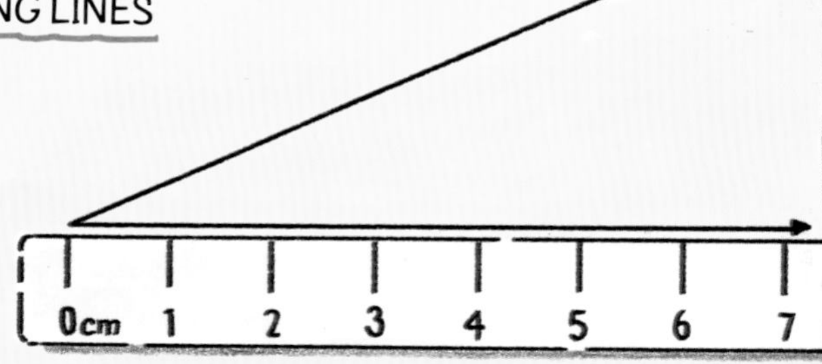

Draw any acute angle.
Mark off every centimetre from the vertex on the bottom arm.
Draw a 60° angle at each mark.
What do you notice about the lengths the top arm is divided into?
What happens if you use an angle other than 60°?

CAN YOU DO IT?

Can you draw a quadrilateral with 4 obtuse angles?
3? 2? 1? 0? Explain.

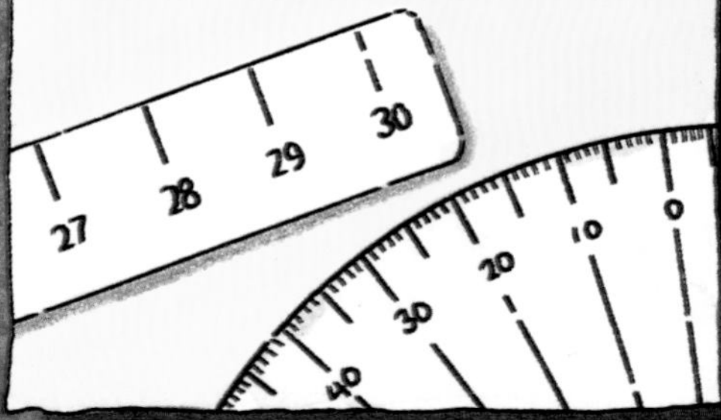

PATTERN BLOCK ANGLES

What type of interior angle is found in each set of these pattern blocks?
Set 1 : hexagon, trapezoid, blue and tan rhombuses
Set 2: triangle, trapezoid, blue and tan rhombuses

Trace and label new angles formed by combining

- 2 blocks to form an acute angle
- 2 blocks to form an obtuse angle
- 3 blocks to form a right angle
- 5 blocks to form a straight angle

Measure and record the degrees in each angle.
How many blocks do you need for a reflex angle?

CONNECTING MIDPOINTS

Draw a rectangle on dot paper.
Mark the midpoints of each side.

P is the midpoint of side CD.
It is the same distance from C as from D.

Connect the midpoints.
What shape do you get?
What do you notice about the angles in the new shape?

QUADRILATERAL ANGLES

Draw any quadrilateral.
Measure each angle.
What do you notice about the sum of the angles?
Do other quadrilaterals have the same angle sum?

Make up other problems. Post them on the bulletin board for your classmates to solve.

Solving a Problem by Drawing a Diagram

HOCKEY PUCK

A hockey puck crosses three parallel lines.
Its straight-line path forms a 60° angle with the first line.
What other angles are formed as the puck crosses each line?

David's group solved the problem by drawing a diagram.

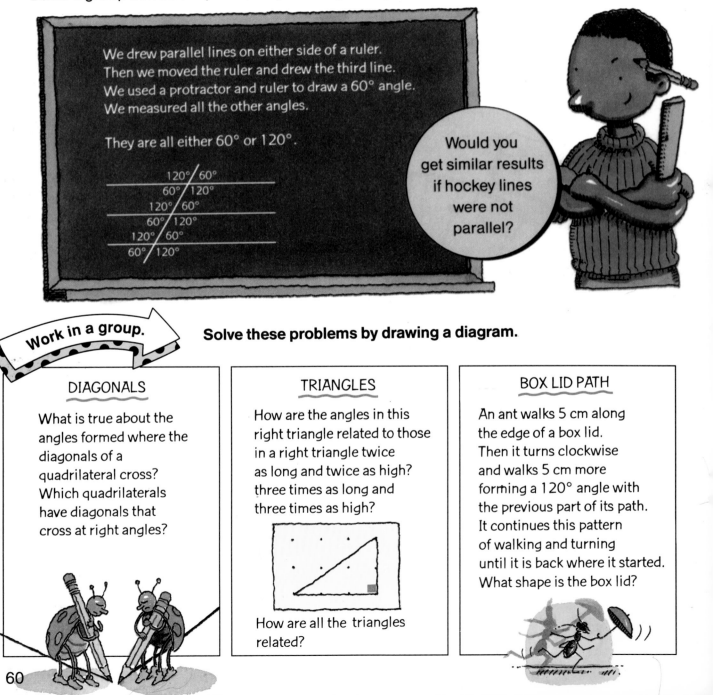

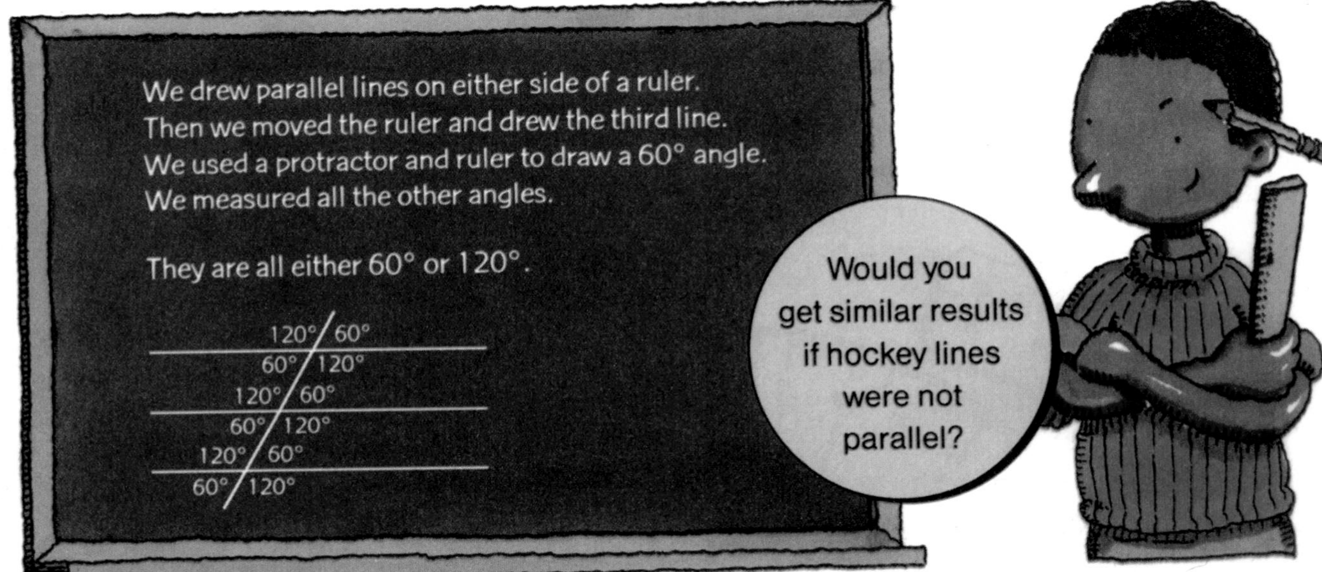

We drew parallel lines on either side of a ruler.
Then we moved the ruler and drew the third line.
We used a protractor and ruler to draw a 60° angle.
We measured all the other angles.
They are all either 60° or 120°.
120° 60°
60° 120°
120° 60°
60° 120°
120° 60°
60° 120°
Would you get similar results if hockey lines were not parallel?

Work in a group.

Solve these problems by drawing a diagram.

DIAGONALS

What is true about the angles formed where the diagonals of a quadrilateral cross?
Which quadrilaterals have diagonals that cross at right angles?

TRIANGLES

How are the angles in this right triangle related to those in a right triangle twice as long and twice as high? three times as long and three times as high?

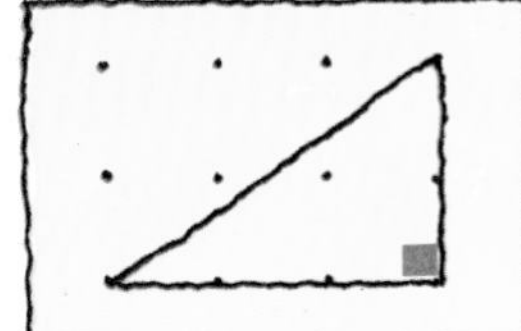

How are all the triangles related?

BOX LID PATH

An ant walks 5 cm along the edge of a box lid.
Then it turns clockwise and walks 5 cm more forming a 120° angle with the previous part of its path.
It continues this pattern of walking and turning until it is back where it started.
What shape is the box lid?

Practising What You've Learned

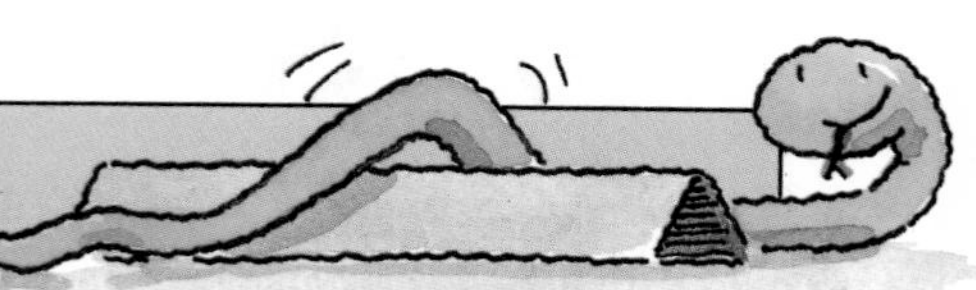

1. Explain how you know that ∠ ABD must be greater than ∠ CBD.

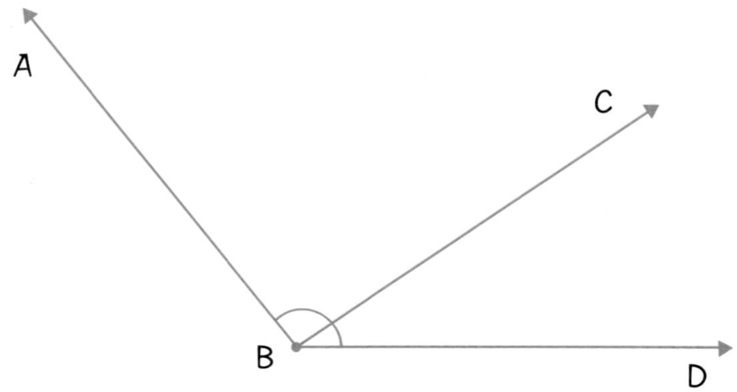

2. Use a square corner. Which crackers have angles less than a right angle? greater than? equal to?

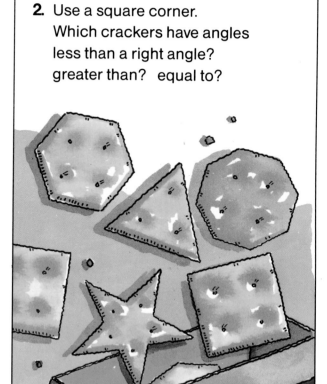

3. List two examples of each type of angle— acute, right, and obtuse— seen in your classroom.

4. How many colored sections would it take to form an acute angle? a right angle? an obtuse angle? a straight angle? a reflex angle?

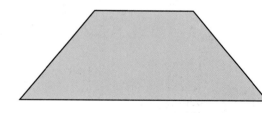

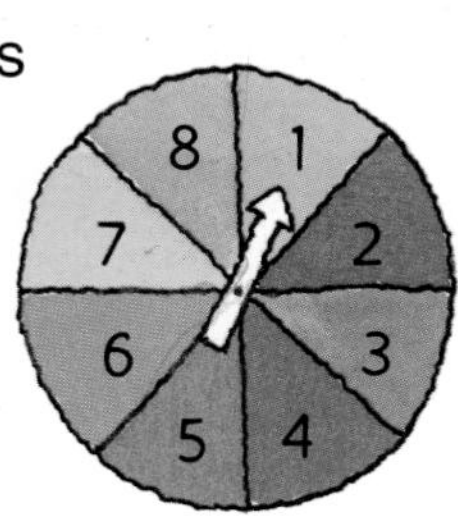

5. Estimate and then measure each angle.

6. What angle does a minute hand on a clock turn through every 20 min?

7. Find the unknown angle without measuring. Explain what you did.

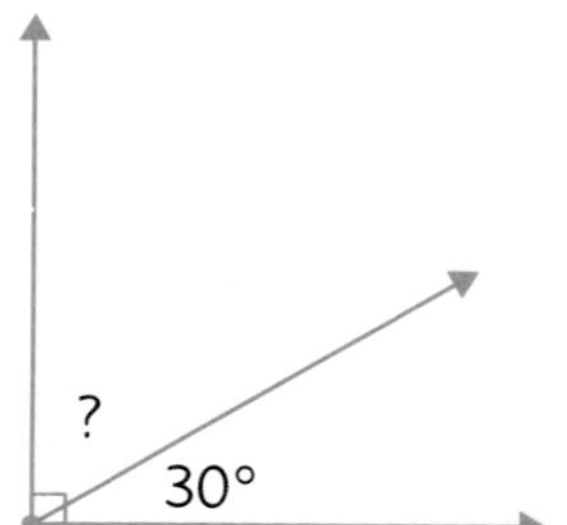

Playing Games for Practice

Play each game in a group of 2, 3, or 4.

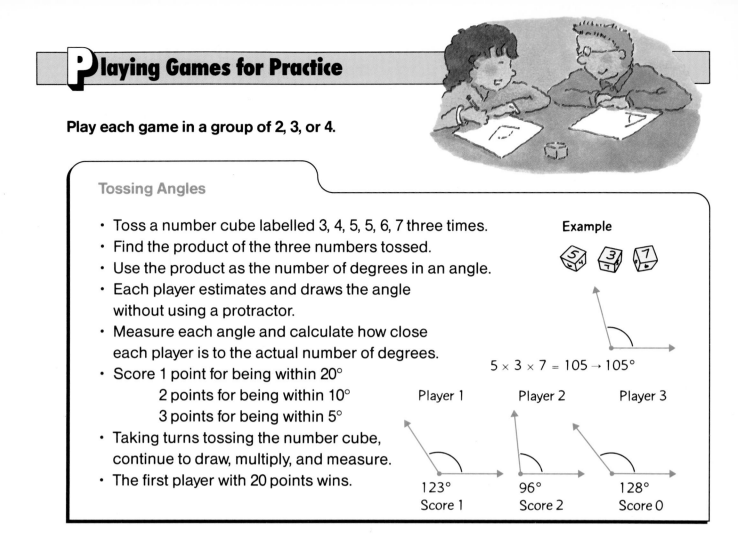

Tossing Angles

- Toss a number cube labelled 3, 4, 5, 5, 6, 7 three times.
- Find the product of the three numbers tossed.
- Use the product as the number of degrees in an angle.
- Each player estimates and draws the angle without using a protractor.
- Measure each angle and calculate how close each player is to the actual number of degrees.
- Score 1 point for being within 20°
  2 points for being within 10°
  3 points for being within 5°
- Taking turns tossing the number cube, continue to draw, multiply, and measure.
- The first player with 20 points wins.

Example

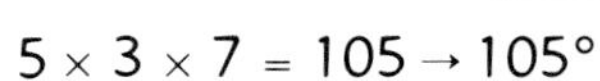

Player 1 Player 2 Player 3

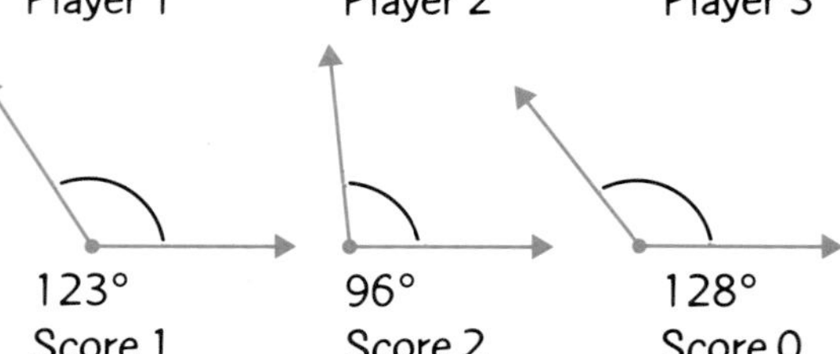

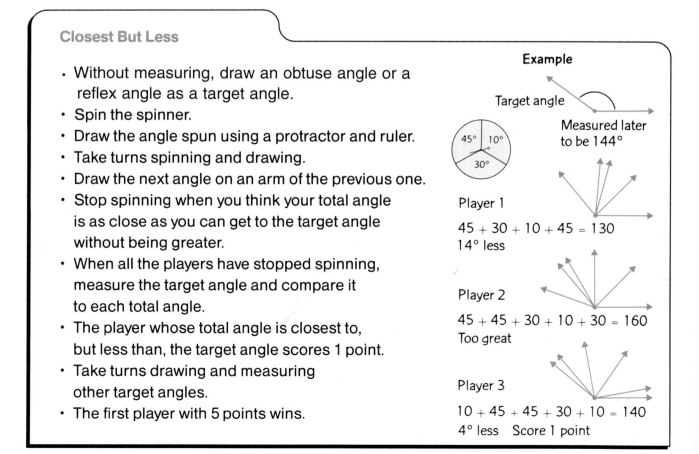

Closest But Less

- Without measuring, draw an obtuse angle or a reflex angle as a target angle.
- Spin the spinner.
- Draw the angle spun using a protractor and ruler.
- Take turns spinning and drawing.
- Draw the next angle on an arm of the previous one.
- Stop spinning when you think your total angle is as close as you can get to the target angle without being greater.
- When all the players have stopped spinning, measure the target angle and compare it to each total angle.
- The player whose total angle is closest to, but less than, the target angle scores 1 point.
- Take turns drawing and measuring other target angles.
- The first player with 5 points wins.

Example

Target angle

Measured later to be 144°

45° 10° 30°

Player 1

45 + 30 + 10 + 45 = 130
14° less

Player 2

45 + 45 + 30 + 10 + 30 = 160
Too great

Player 3

10 + 45 + 45 + 30 + 10 = 140
4° less Score 1 point

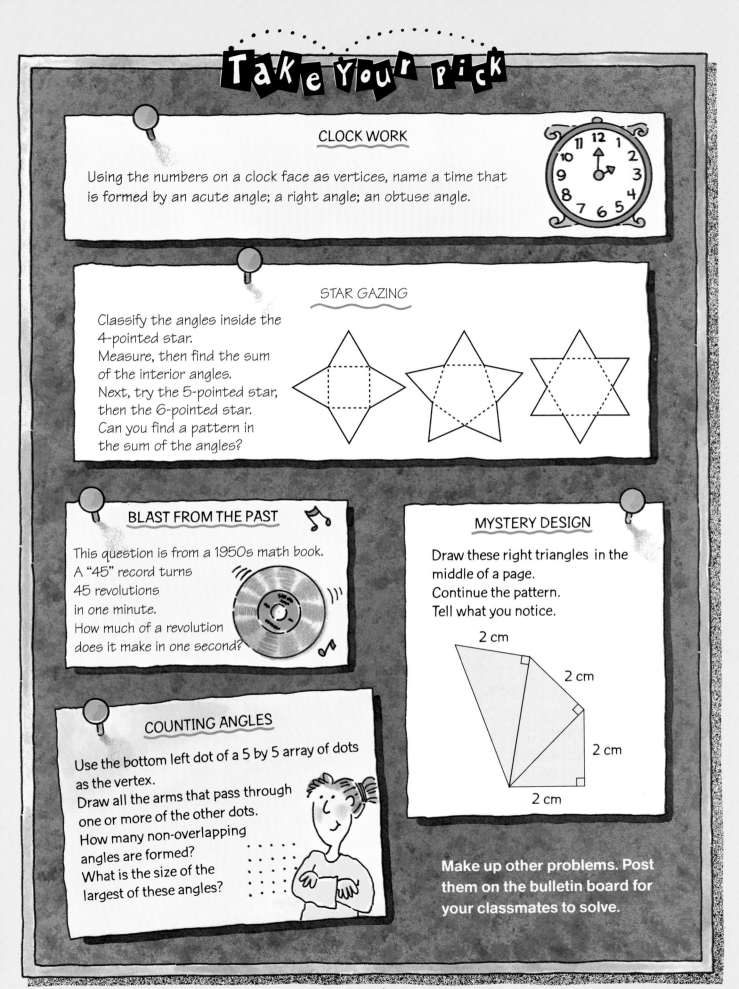

Take Your Pick

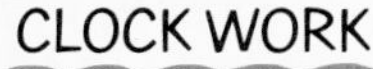

CLOCK WORK

Using the numbers on a clock face as vertices, name a time that is formed by an acute angle; a right angle; an obtuse angle.

STAR GAZING

Classify the angles inside the 4-pointed star.
Measure, then find the sum of the interior angles.
Next, try the 5-pointed star, then the 6-pointed star.
Can you find a pattern in the sum of the angles?

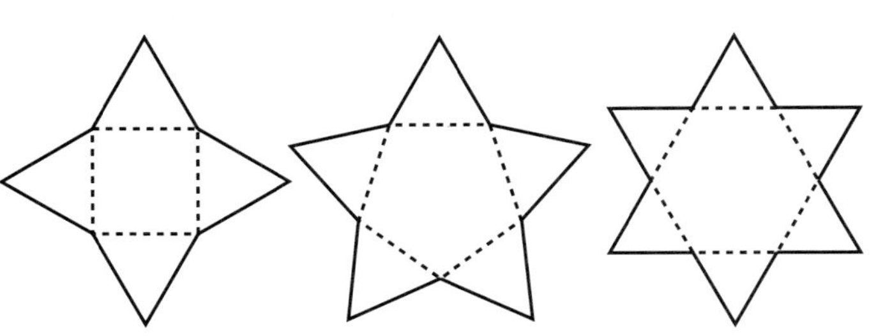

BLAST FROM THE PAST

This question is from a 1950s math book.
A "45" record turns 45 revolutions in one minute.
How much of a revolution does it make in one second?

MYSTERY DESIGN

Draw these right triangles in the middle of a page.
Continue the pattern.
Tell what you notice.

2 cm
2 cm
2 cm
2 cm

COUNTING ANGLES

Use the bottom left dot of a 5 by 5 array of dots as the vertex.
Draw all the arms that pass through one or more of the other dots.
How many non-overlapping angles are formed?
What is the size of the largest of these angles?

Make up other problems. Post them on the bulletin board for your classmates to solve.

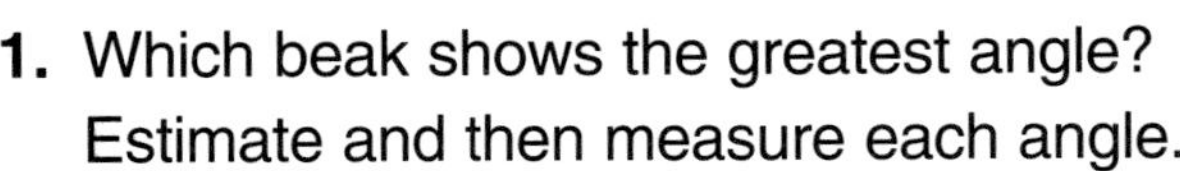

Showing What You Know

1. Which beak shows the greatest angle? Estimate and then measure each angle.

2. Use a protractor and ruler to draw a triangle with 30°, 60°, and 90° angles.

3. Draw an angle between 45° and 60° without using a protractor. Then measure it to check.

4. All slices are equal. Find the angle of each without measuring. Explain.

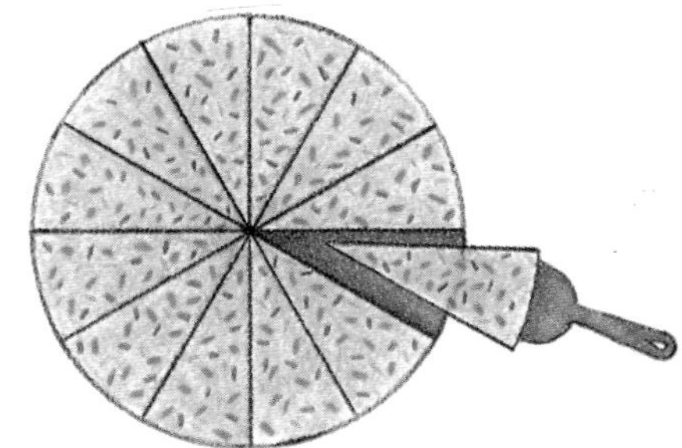

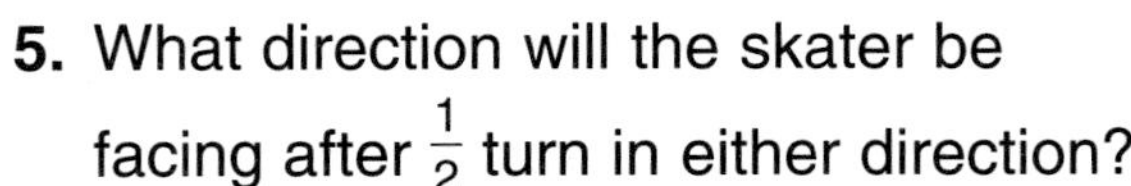

5. What direction will the skater be facing after $\frac{1}{2}$ turn in either direction?

6. Find the unknown angle without measuring.

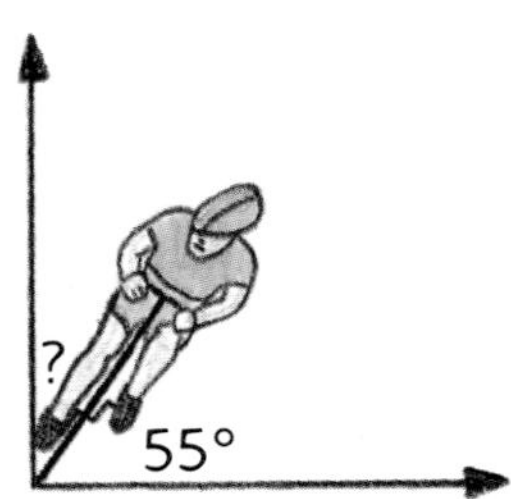

7. What time will the clock show when the minute hand has made a $\frac{1}{4}$ turn? a $\frac{1}{2}$ turn? a $\frac{3}{4}$ turn?

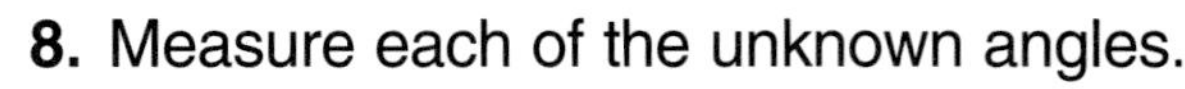

8. Measure each of the unknown angles.

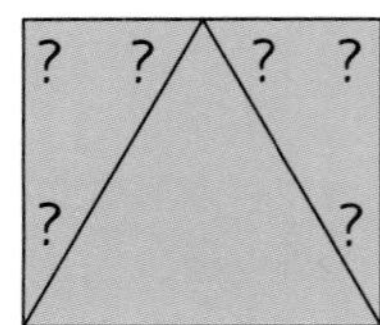

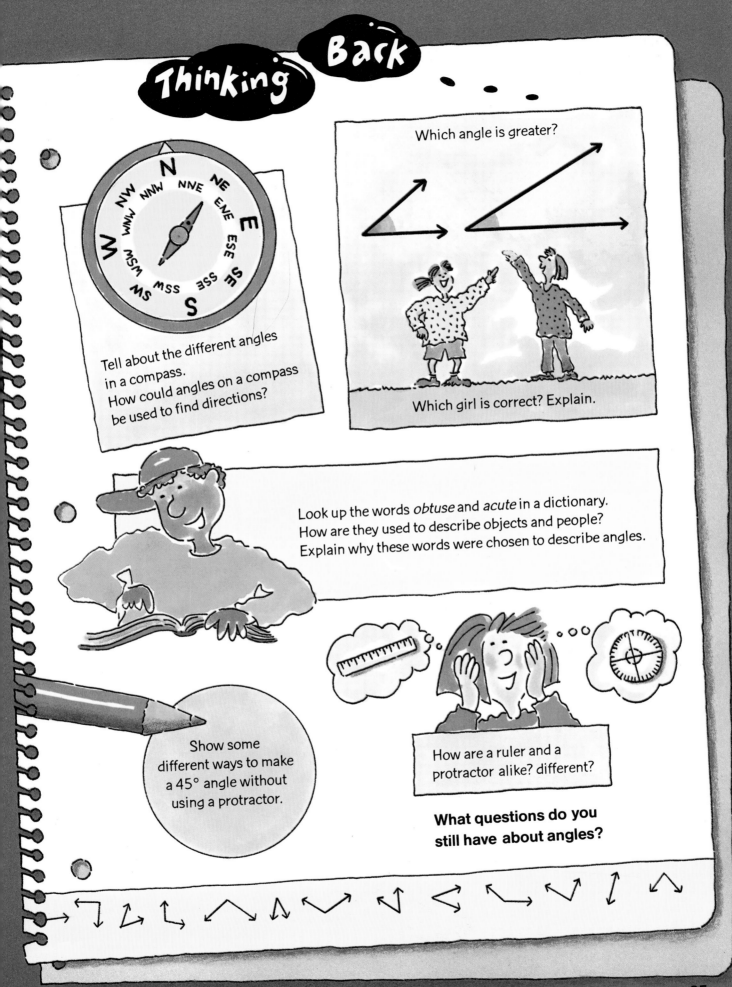

Thinking Back . . .

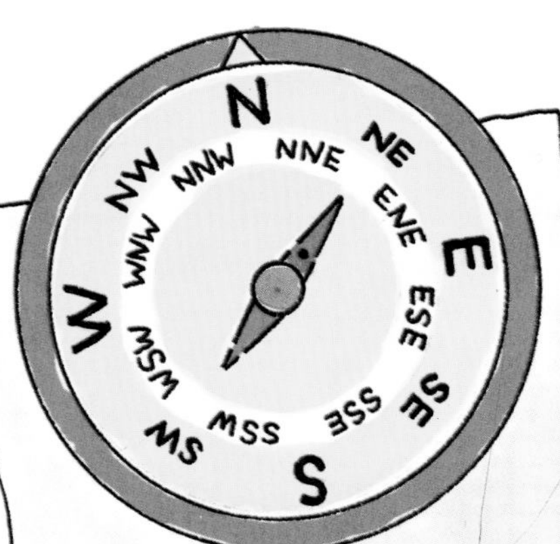

Tell about the different angles in a compass.
How could angles on a compass be used to find directions?

Which angle is greater?

Which girl is correct? Explain.

Look up the words *obtuse* and *acute* in a dictionary.
How are they used to describe objects and people?
Explain why these words were chosen to describe angles.

Show some different ways to make a 45° angle without using a protractor.

How are a ruler and a protractor alike? different?

What questions do you still have about angles?

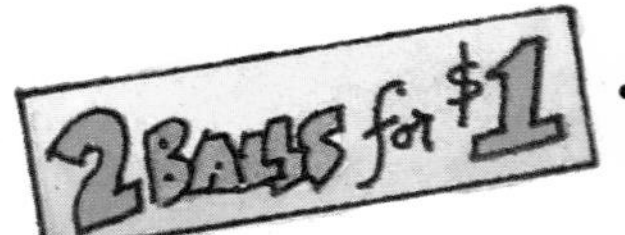

Introducing

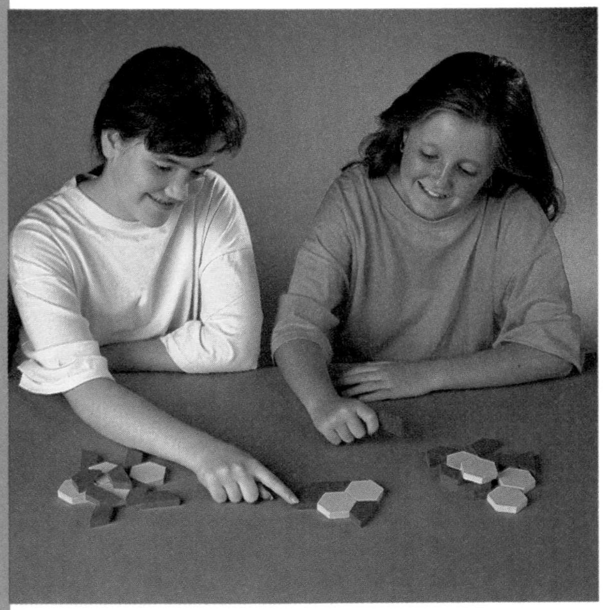

◀ Use red and yellow pattern blocks to make a pattern.
Use twice as many red as yellow.
How many red blocks did you use? yellow?
How many blocks did you use in all?

Try this two more times using different numbers of red and yellow blocks, but still twice as many red as yellow.

What do you notice about the three numbers of red blocks? of all the blocks?

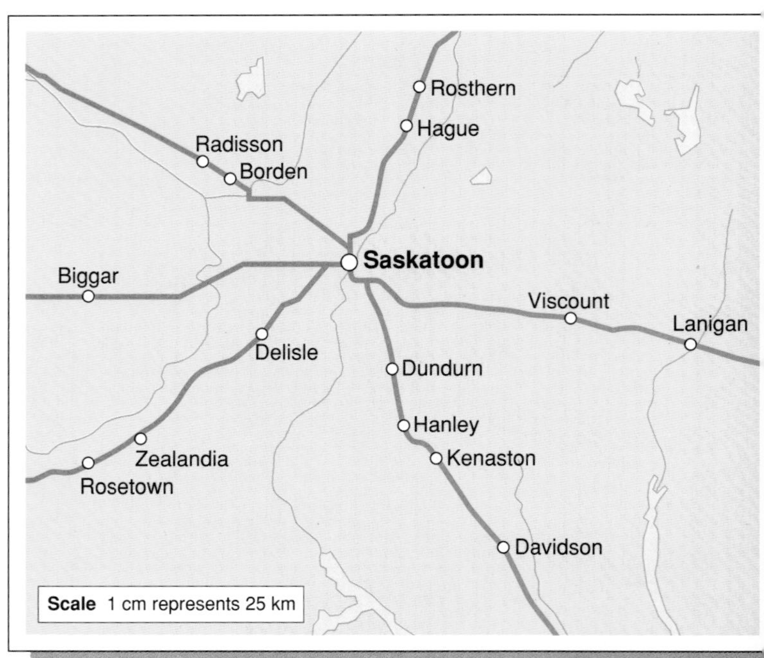

▶ About how many kilometres is Viscount from Saskatoon?
Which communities are almost 100 km from Saskatoon?
Use a ruler to measure each distance to the nearest tenth of a centimetre. Then multiply by 25.

▼ How much would you expect to pay for 8 items?
2 items? 6 items?

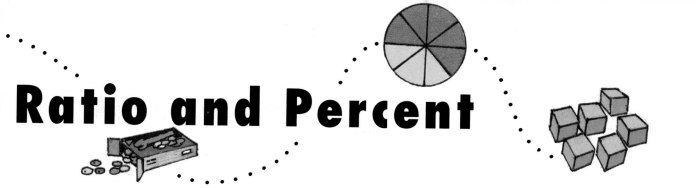

Ratio and Percent

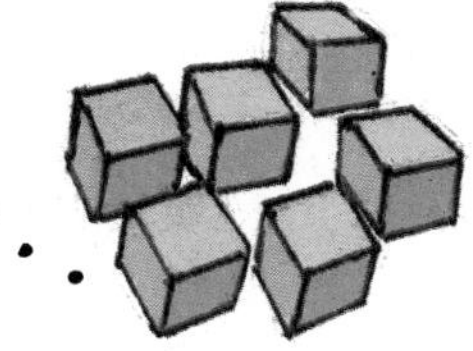

▼ What fraction of the cubes are green?

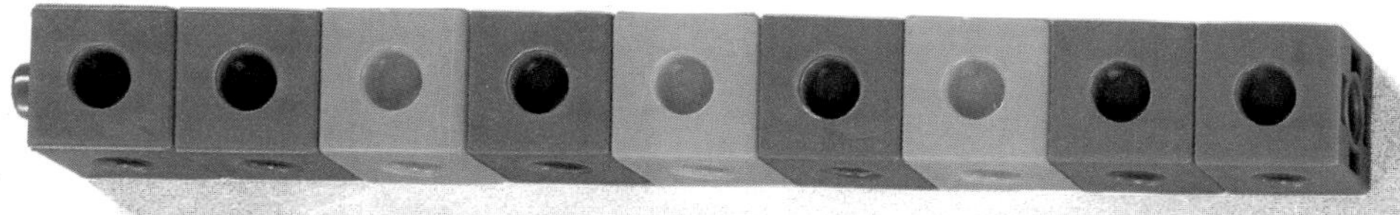

Do you agree that there are 2 green cubes for each pink cube? Explain.

Use pink and green cubes. Link 10 cubes so that $\frac{4}{5}$ of them are green.
How many green cubes are there for each pink one?

▼ Commercial construction is about 4 times as much as which other types of construction?
About what fraction of new construction is housing?
Why do you think there is so much more housing construction than other types of construction?

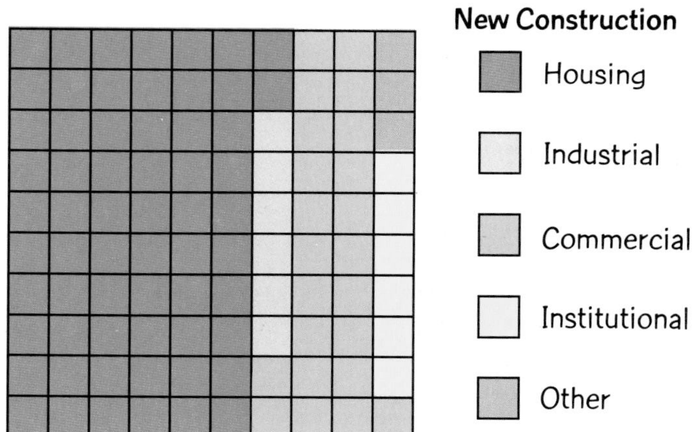

▼ Which statements are reasonable? Explain.

- All babies born in Canada are Canadian.
- About one-half of all 11-year olds are boys.
- About one-half of the time the sun sets in the West.

Write two other statements that are reasonable.
Use *all* in one and *one-half* in the other.

I bought 100 pens. They cost $100 before taxes.
How many of each type did I buy?

Making Punch

Describing ratio situations

Lise is making orange-grapefruit punch.

The **ratio** 4 to 1 tells the number of cartons of orange juice for each carton of grapefruit juice.

It can also be written 4 : 1 and $\frac{4}{1}$.

It is always read 4 to 1.

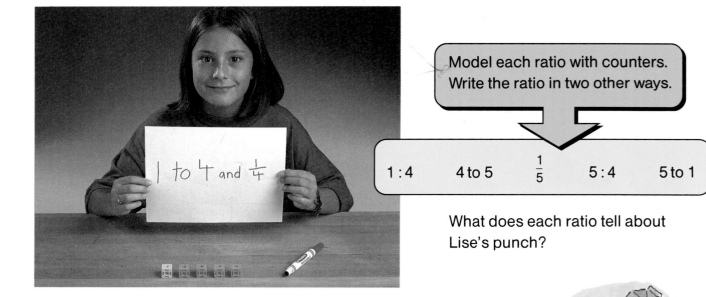

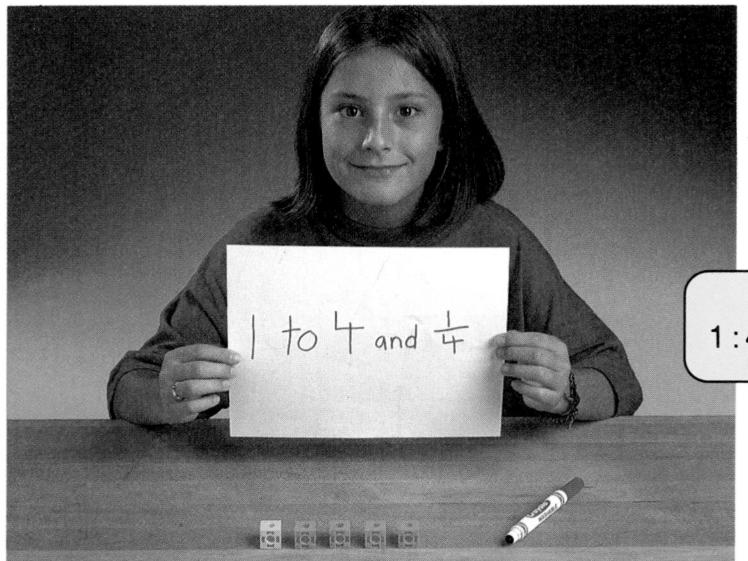

Model each ratio with counters.
Write the ratio in two other ways.

1 : 4 4 to 5 $\frac{1}{5}$ 5 : 4 5 to 1

What does each ratio tell about Lise's punch?

Use counters to model the ratios.

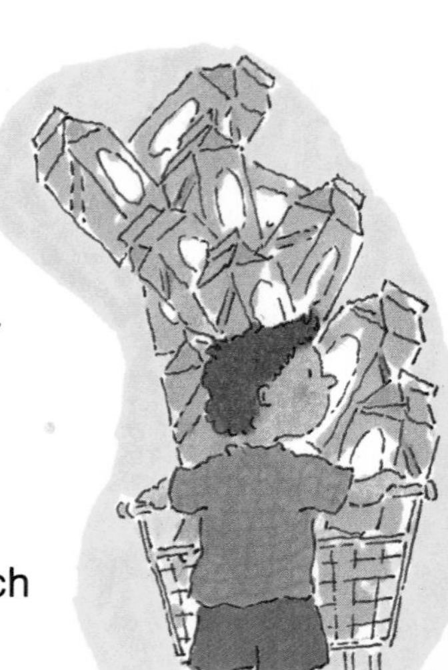

1. Ali uses 3 cartons of orange juice for each carton of grapefruit juice.
   What ratio compares the orange juice to the grapefruit juice?
   What does 1 : 4 tell about Ali's punch?
   Is Ali's punch more or less orange-tasting than Lise's?

2. Write a ratio of orange juice to grapefruit juice that describes a punch
   - less orange-tasting than Ali's
   - more orange-tasting than Lise's

3. Jean and Kirk are making a cranberry-pineapple punch.

The ratio is 1 to 1.
The ratio is 2 to 2.

Which ratio is correct? Explain.
Write a ratio of cranberry juice to pineapple juice that describes a punch with

- twice as much cranberry as pineapple juice
- twice as much pineapple as cranberry juice
- very little cranberry
- very little pineapple

4. Catie makes a punch using 4 L of papaya juice and 2 L of limeade.
What is the ratio of papaya juice to limeade?
Then she adds one more litre of each juice.
Is the ratio the same? Explain.
If not, how many litres of each could she add to return the punch to the original taste?

5.

Punch
5 L orange juice
4 L peach juice
2 L ginger ale

What does each ratio describe about the punch?

4 : 5   5 to 11 $\frac{9}{2}$

How could you change the ratio of the ingredients to make it more bubbly?
less bubbly?

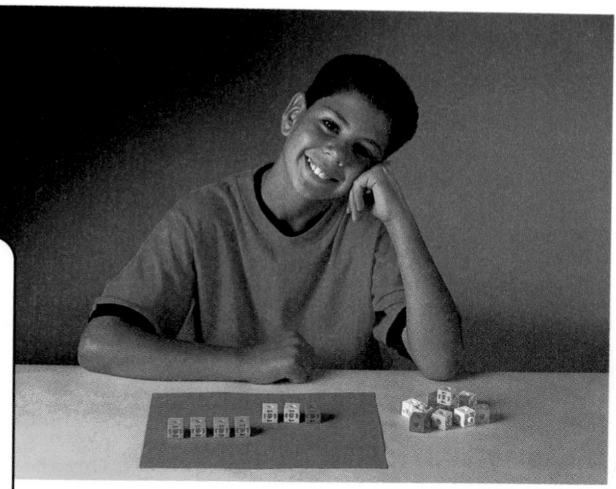

6. A punch contains orange juice, lemonade, raspberry juice, and ginger ale.
Lemonade to raspberry juice is 2 : 1.
Orange juice to lemonade is 4 : 2.
Ginger ale to raspberry juice is 2 : 1.
What is the ratio of orange juice to raspberry juice?
ginger ale to orange juice?
lemonade to the total amount of punch?

7. Make up a punch recipe and some ratio problems about it for another group to solve.

8. Investigate other mixtures that involve ratios.

Which whole numbers less than 100 meet each condition? meet all three conditions?

- an even number
- a multiple of 5
- sum of digits is 9

Describing Yields

Renaming ratios

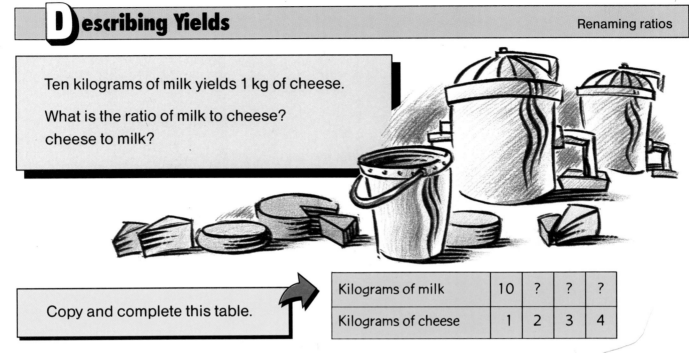

Ten kilograms of milk yields 1 kg of cheese.

What is the ratio of milk to cheese? cheese to milk?

Copy and complete this table.

Kilograms of milk	10	?	?	?
Kilograms of cheese	1	2	3	4

Write the other milk to cheese ratios suggested by the table.
All four ratios are **equivalent**. Why?

Jerid made this graph. He plotted the 4 points (milk, cheese) from the table. Then he drew a line through them.

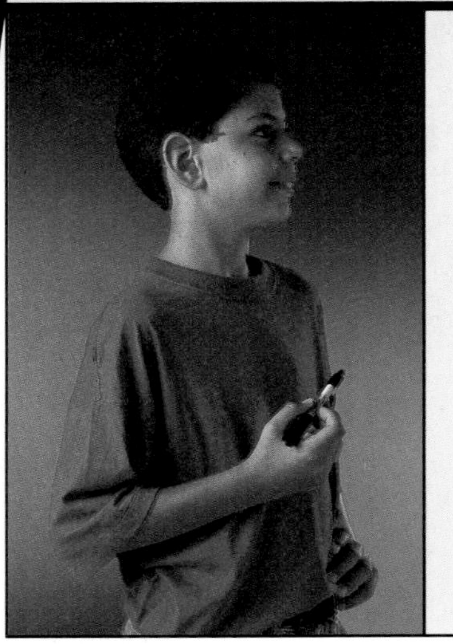

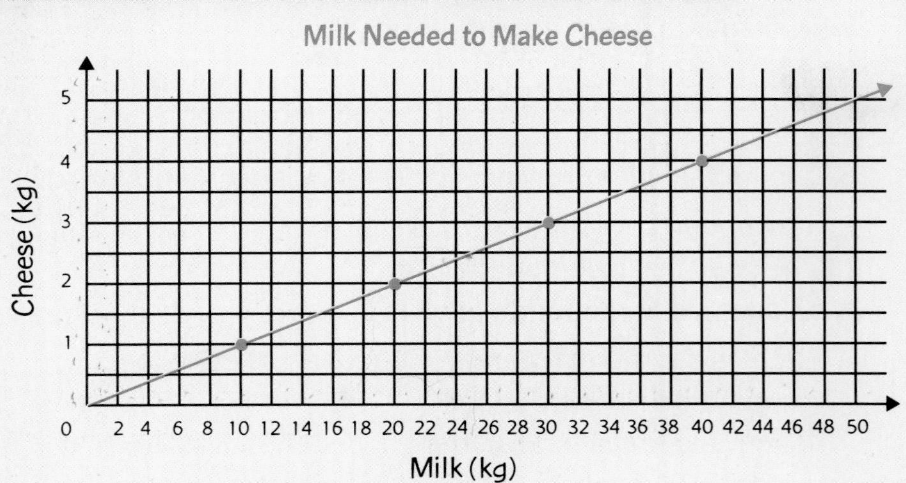

1. Use the graph.
   How much cheese does 25 kg of milk yield? 50 kg?
   Write three other milk to cheese ratios.

2. One kilogram of butter requires 21 kg of milk. What is the ratio of milk to butter?
Make a table to show the amount of milk needed for 2 kg, 3 kg, and 4 kg of butter. Then draw a graph.
What are three other milk to butter ratios?

3. It takes about 160 L of maple sap to make 4 L of maple syrup.
Write the ratio of sap to syrup as [?] : 1.
To graph this, what scale would you use for the sap? the syrup? Why?
Make a table and then draw a graph.
How much sap does it take to yield 2.5 L of syrup?
How much syrup does 60 L of sap yield?

4. One cup of uncooked rice yields 2 cups of cooked rice.
Write the ratio of uncooked to cooked rice.
How is this yield different from the earlier ones?

5. It takes 2 kg of soybeans to make 5 kg of tofu.
Find three equivalent ratios of soybeans to tofu.
How many kilograms of soybeans does it take to make 400 kg of tofu?
How much tofu is made from 100 kg of soybeans?

6. One cup of unpopped corn yields from 34 cups to 44 cups of popped corn depending on the quality of the corn.
What are the ratios of unpopped to popped corn?
How many cups of unpopped corn are needed to make 352 cups of popped corn using the best quality corn? the poorest quality corn?

7. Investigate some other yields such as cooking pasta, drying fruit, cooking beans, making fresh juice.
Which yield less and which yield more?

Take Your Pick

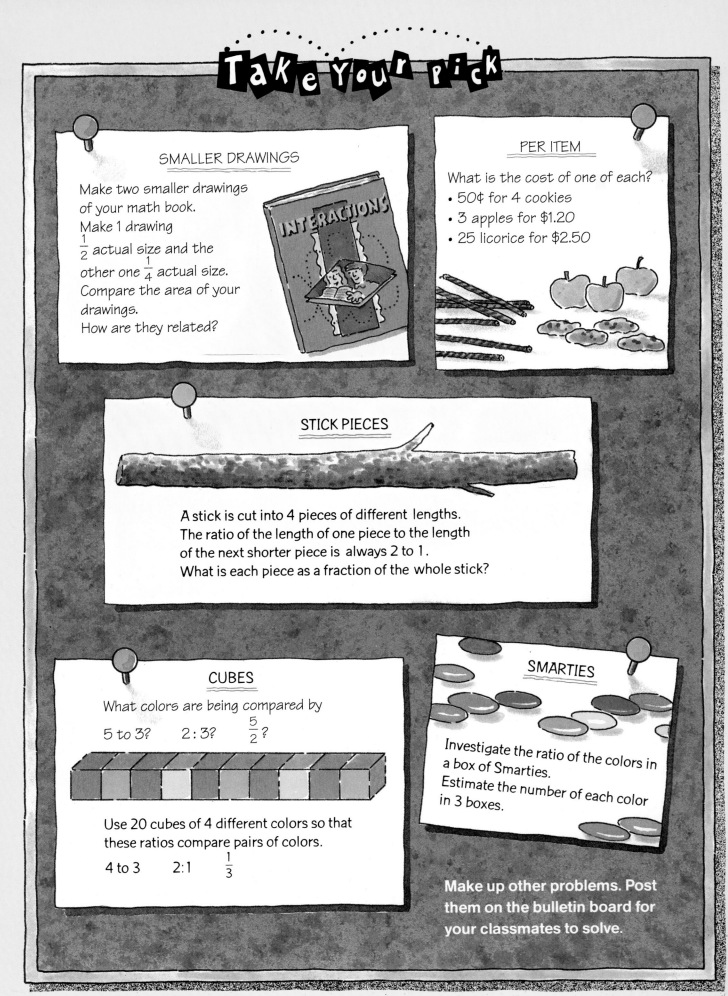

SMALLER DRAWINGS

Make two smaller drawings of your math book.
Make 1 drawing $\frac{1}{2}$ actual size and the other one $\frac{1}{4}$ actual size.
Compare the area of your drawings.
How are they related?

PER ITEM

What is the cost of one of each?

- 50¢ for 4 cookies
- 3 apples for $1.20
- 25 licorice for $2.50

STICK PIECES

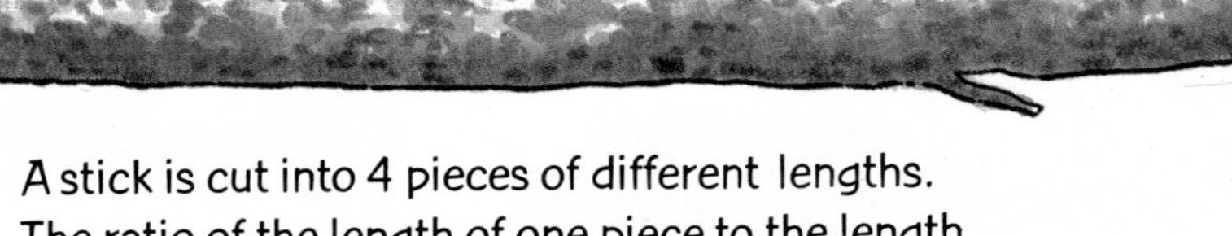

A stick is cut into 4 pieces of different lengths.
The ratio of the length of one piece to the length of the next shorter piece is always 2 to 1.
What is each piece as a fraction of the whole stick?

CUBES

What colors are being compared by

5 to 3? 2 : 3? $\frac{5}{2}$?

Use 20 cubes of 4 different colors so that these ratios compare pairs of colors.

4 to 3 2:1 $\frac{1}{3}$

SMARTIES

Investigate the ratio of the colors in a box of Smarties.
Estimate the number of each color in 3 boxes.

Make up other problems. Post them on the bulletin board for your classmates to solve.

If March 13 is a Friday,
when is the next Friday the 13th?

FRI
13

Examining Our Planet

Recognizing percent

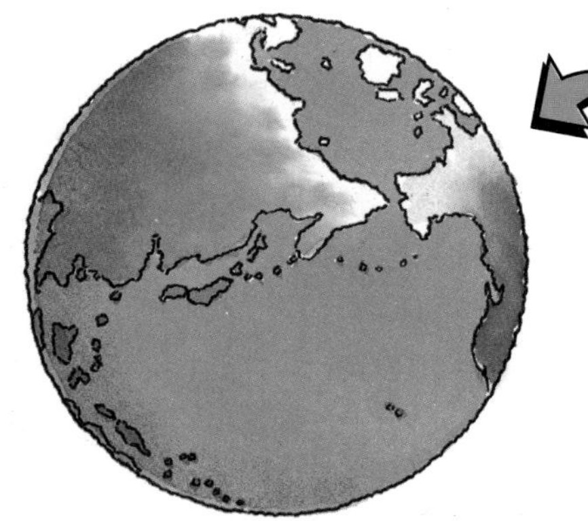

Water covers about 70 km^2 out of every 100 km^2 of the earth's total surface.

Ratios out of 100, like $\frac{70}{100}$, are called **percents**.

$\frac{70}{100}$ can be written 70%.

Show 70% on a hundredths grid.
What is 70% as a fraction? as a decimal?
What percent of the earth's total surface must be land?

Work with a partner.

Show each percent on a hundredths grid.

1. Deserts cover about 14% of the earth's land surface.
   What is this as a fraction? as a decimal?
   Is this more or less than $\frac{1}{5}$?

2. Rain forests cover about half as much land as deserts.
   What percent is this?

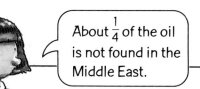

3. About 64% of the earth's oil is found in the Middle East.
   Which student is more accurate? Why?

About $\frac{1}{4}$ of the oil is not found in the Middle East.

No, about $\frac{1}{3}$ is not.

4. The Pacific Ocean covers about 32% of the earth's total surface.
   What is this percent as a fraction? as a decimal?
   Why can we say the Pacific is about 50% of the earth's water surface?

5. The Atlantic Ocean covers about half as much as the Pacific.
   About what percent is this of the earth's total surface?
   of the earth's water surface?

6. Find out two other facts about the earth that can be expressed as percents.
   Make up a problem for another pair to solve.

Use the dots in a 4 by 4 array as vertices. Create a shape with as many sides as possible.

Describing Hockey Players

Reading percent graphs

What percent of the players in the 1991–92 season were born in British Columbia? Eastern Canada? Western Canada? outside of Canada?

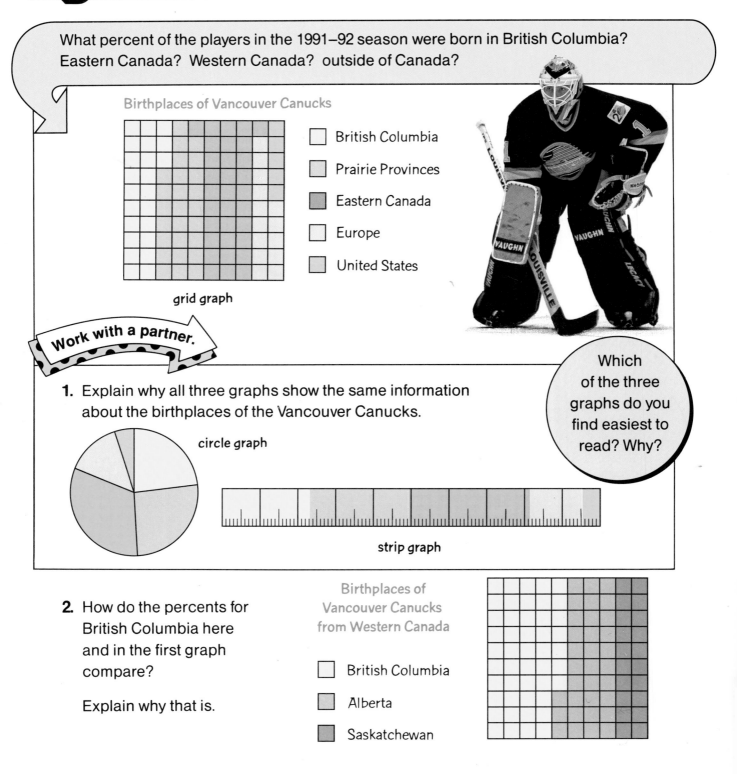

Birthplaces of Vancouver Canucks

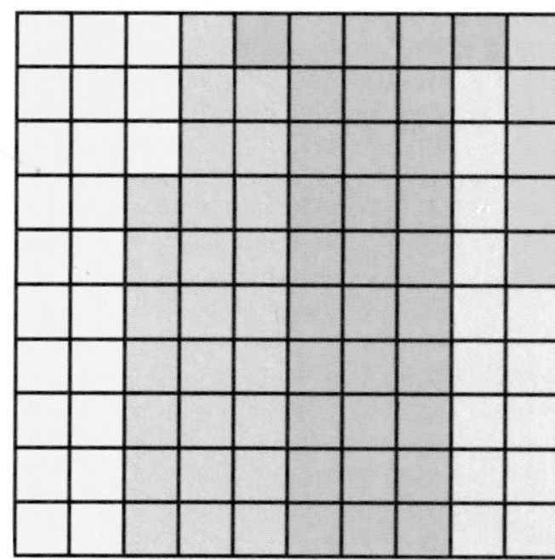

grid graph

1. Explain why all three graphs show the same information about the birthplaces of the Vancouver Canucks.

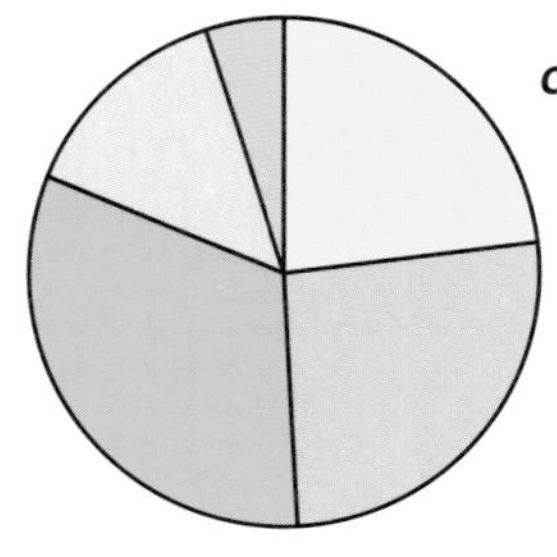

circle graph

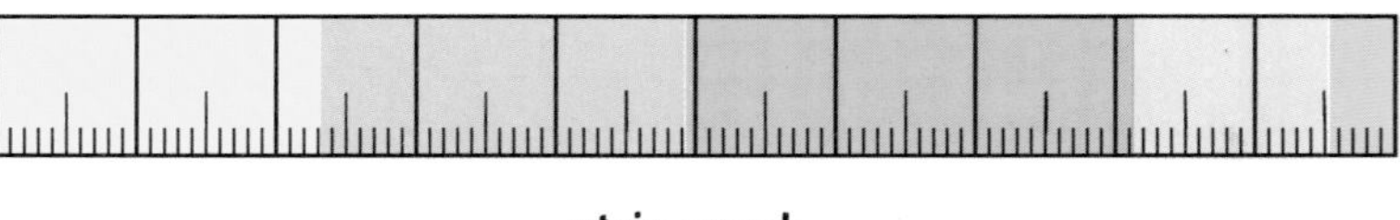

strip graph

Which of the three graphs do you find easiest to read? Why?

2. How do the percents for British Columbia here and in the first graph compare?

   Explain why that is.

Birthplaces of Vancouver Canucks from Western Canada

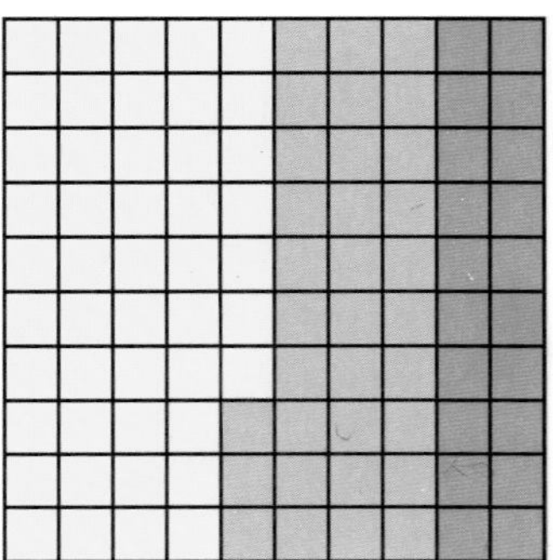

3. What are the unknown percents?
About what fraction of each circle graph is the largest section?

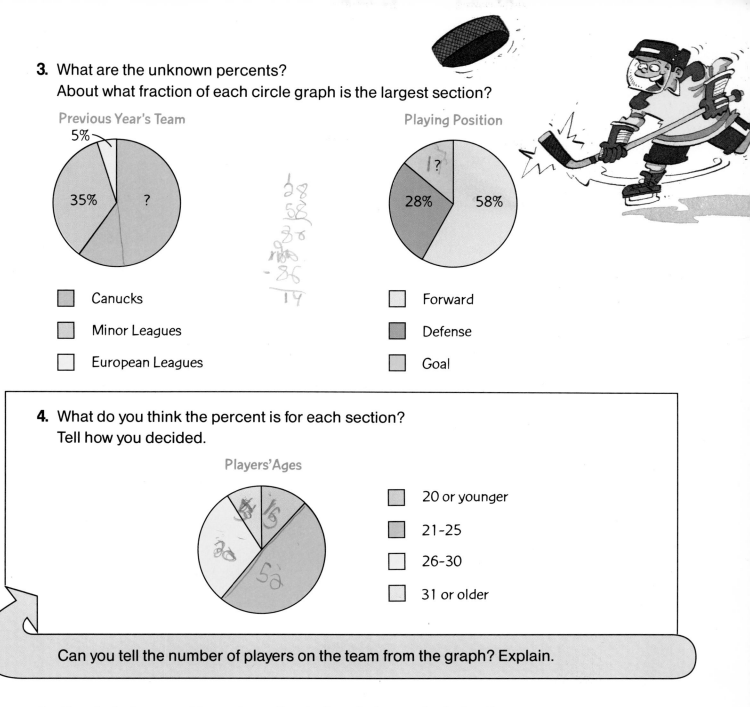

Previous Year's Team

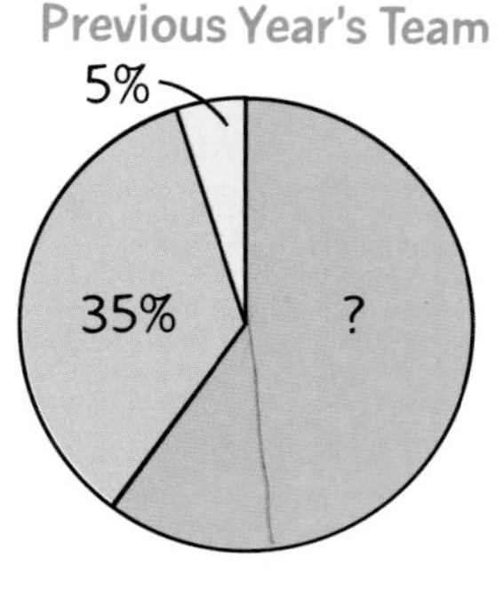

Canucks

Minor Leagues

European Leagues

Playing Position

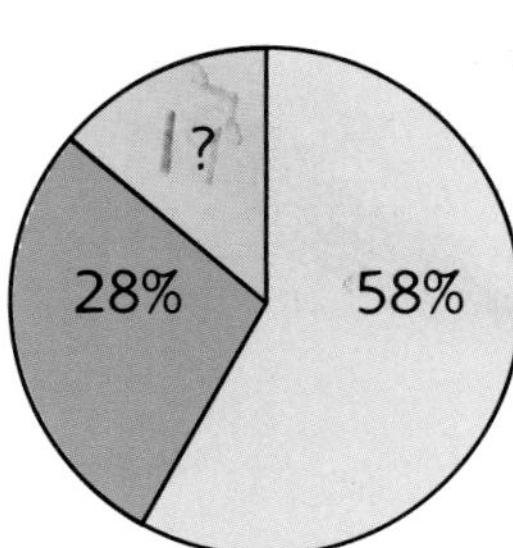

Forward

Defense

Goal

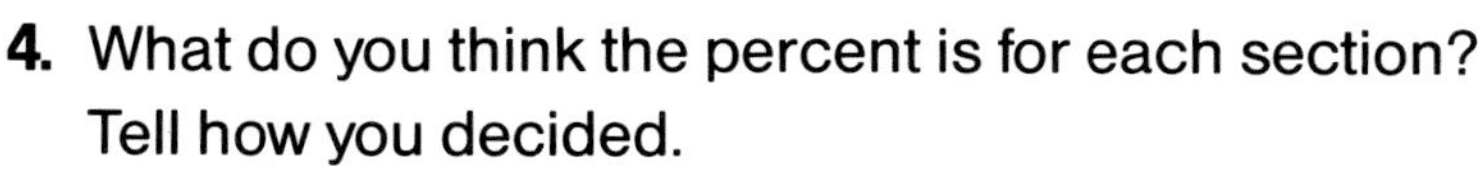

4. What do you think the percent is for each section?
Tell how you decided.

Players' Ages

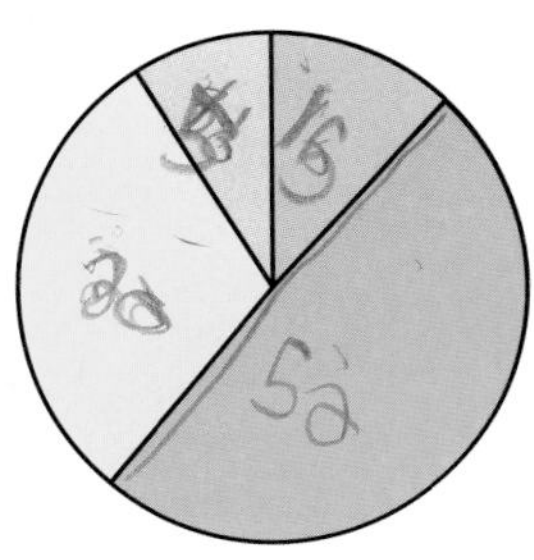

20 or younger

21-25

26-30

31 or older

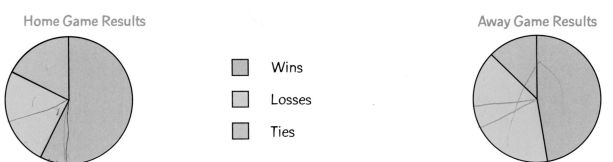

Can you tell the number of players on the team from the graph? Explain.

5. About what percent is each section in the circle graphs below?
Where was the greater percent of games won? lost? tied?
About what percent greater?

Home Game Results

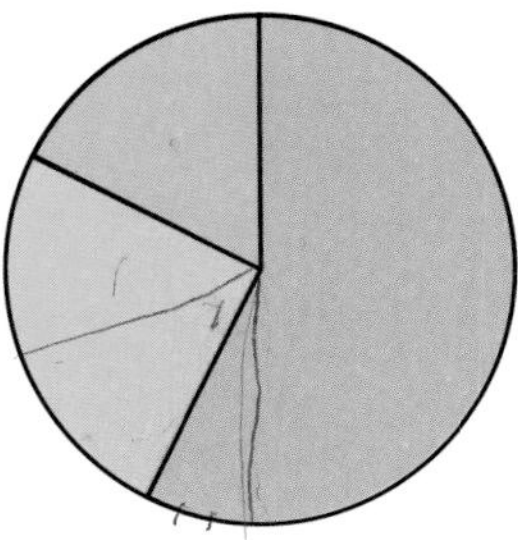

Wins

Losses

Ties

Away Game Results

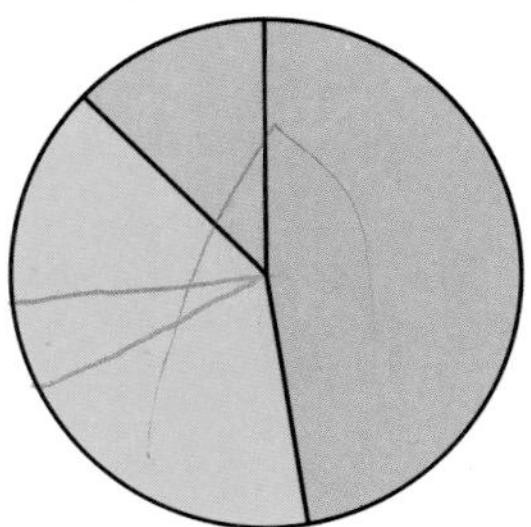

6. Find out about another NHL team. For which data do you think a graph would be least similar to the Canucks? most similar?

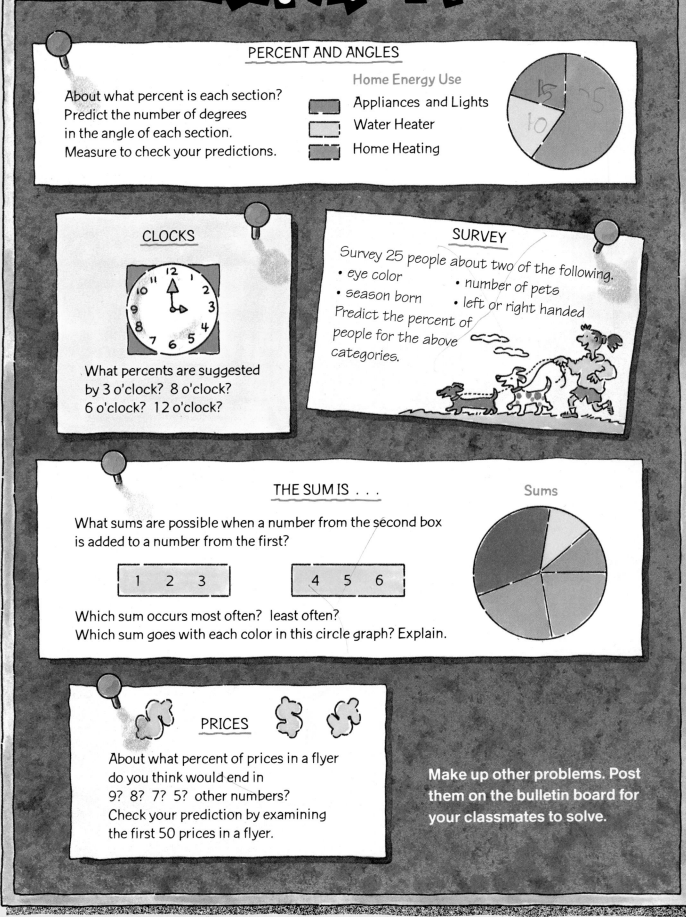

PERCENT AND ANGLES

About what percent is each section?
Predict the number of degrees in the angle of each section.
Measure to check your predictions.

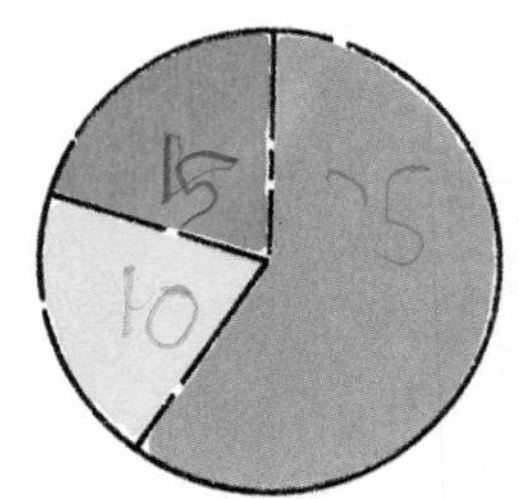

CLOCKS

What percents are suggested by 3 o'clock? 8 o'clock? 6 o'clock? 12 o'clock?

SURVEY

Survey 25 people about two of the following.

- eye color
- number of pets
- season born
- left or right handed

Predict the percent of people for the above categories.

THE SUM IS . . .

What sums are possible when a number from the second box is added to a number from the first?

1 2 3		4 5 6

Which sum occurs most often? least often?
Which sum goes with each color in this circle graph? Explain.

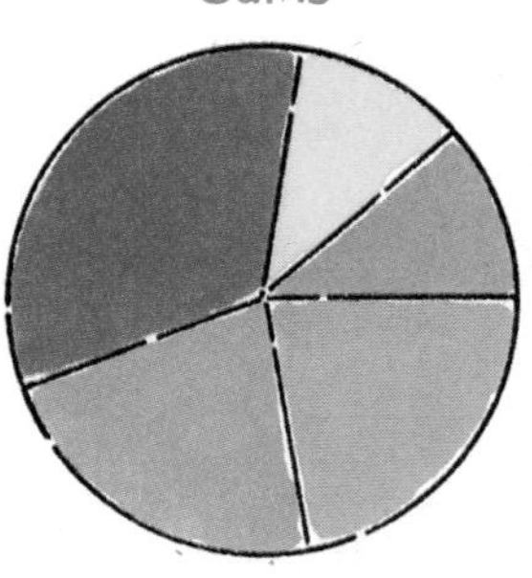

PRICES

About what percent of prices in a flyer do you think would end in 9? 8? 7? 5? other numbers?
Check your prediction by examining the first 50 prices in a flyer.

Make up other problems. Post them on the bulletin board for your classmates to solve.

Solving a Problem by Doing an Experiment

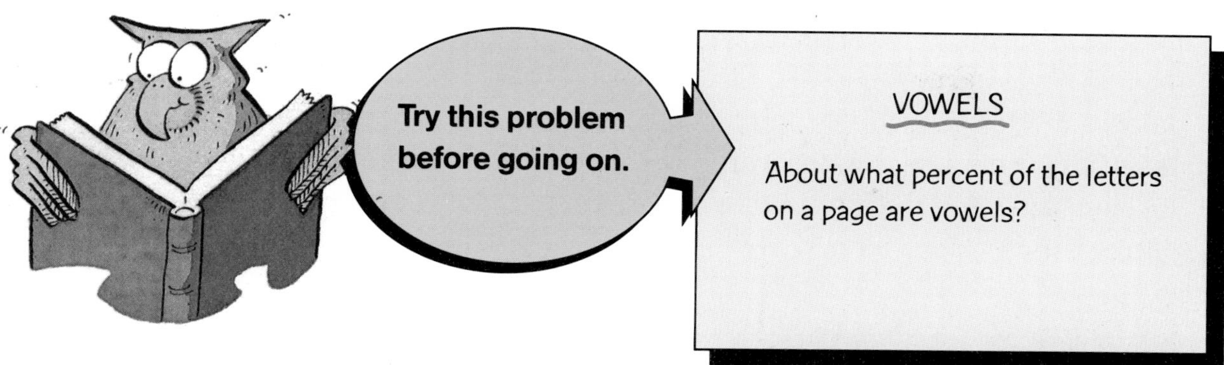

VOWELS

About what percent of the letters on a page are vowels?

Shauna's group solved the problem by planning and doing an experiment.

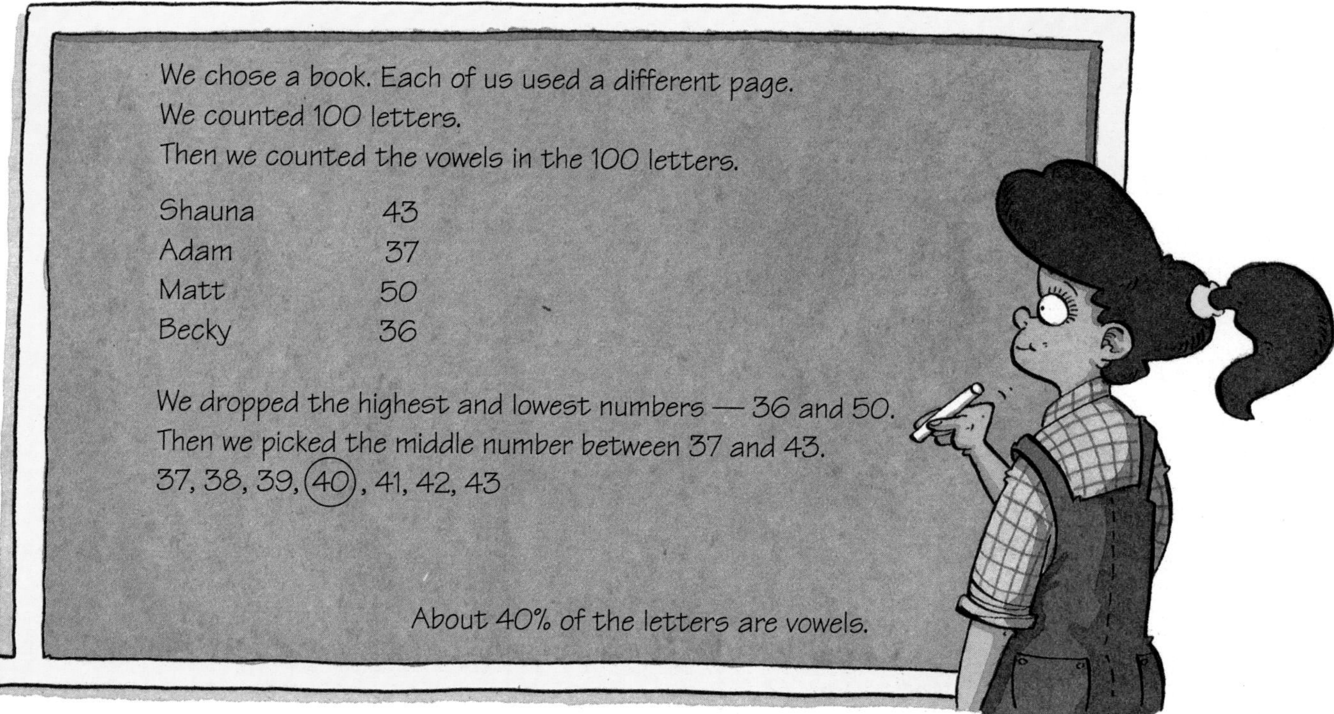

We chose a book. Each of us used a different page.
We counted 100 letters.
Then we counted the vowels in the 100 letters.

Shauna	43
Adam	37
Matt	50
Becky	36

We dropped the highest and lowest numbers — 36 and 50.
Then we picked the middle number between 37 and 43.
37, 38, 39, (40), 41, 42, 43

About 40% of the letters are vowels.

About what percent of the alphabet are the vowels?
Why do you think the two percents are so different?

Solve these problems by planning and doing an experiment.

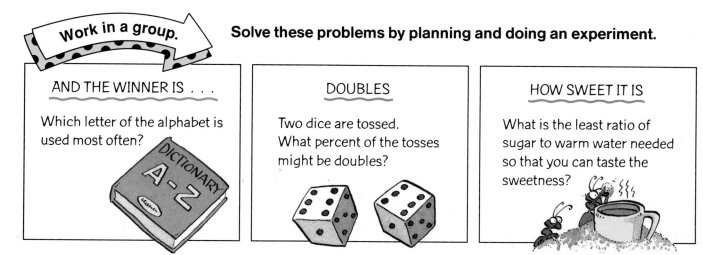

AND THE WINNER IS . . .

Which letter of the alphabet is used most often?

DOUBLES

Two dice are tossed.
What percent of the tosses might be doubles?

HOW SWEET IT IS

What is the least ratio of sugar to warm water needed so that you can taste the sweetness?

Practising What You've Learned

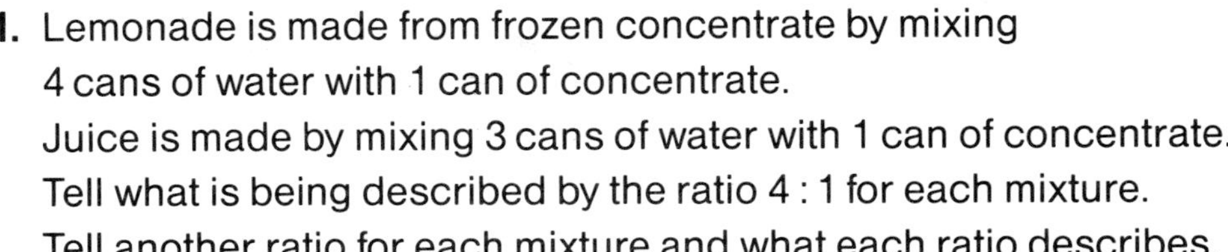

1. Lemonade is made from frozen concentrate by mixing 4 cans of water with 1 can of concentrate.
   Juice is made by mixing 3 cans of water with 1 can of concentrate.
   Tell what is being described by the ratio 4 : 1 for each mixture.
   Tell another ratio for each mixture and what each ratio describes.

2. Use colored cubes to show that these ratios are equivalent.
   1 : 3 2 to 6 $\frac{3}{9}$

3. 35% of a hundredths grid is colored. What other percent is shown on the grid?

4. Draw a rectangle on dot paper. Then draw another rectangle that is twice as long and twice as wide. What ratio compares the length of the first one to the length of the second one? What ratio compares the widths? the areas?

5. Use hundredths grids to show $\frac{3}{10}$, $\frac{1}{4}$, and $\frac{1}{5}$. Write each as a percent.

6. About what percent of each is colored?

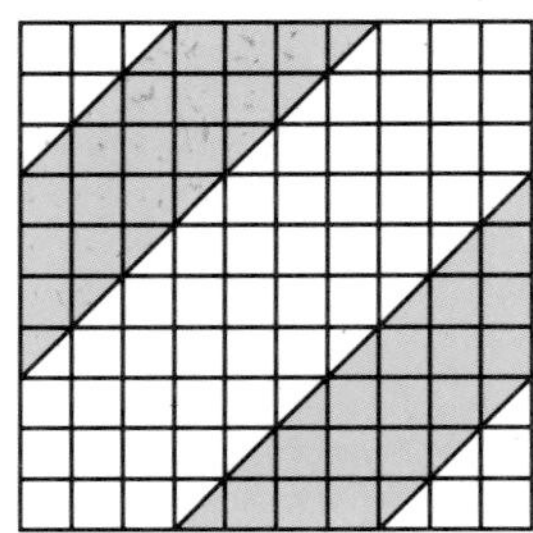

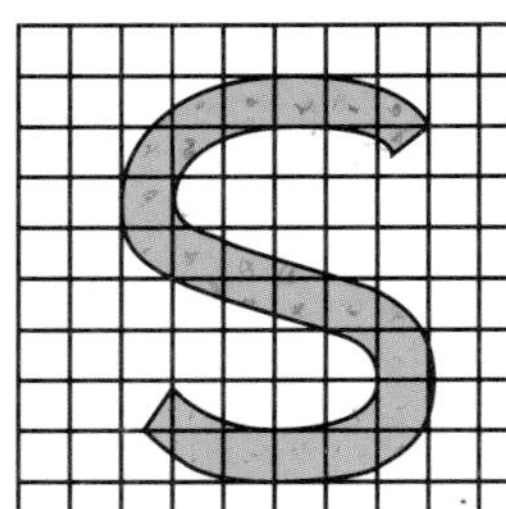

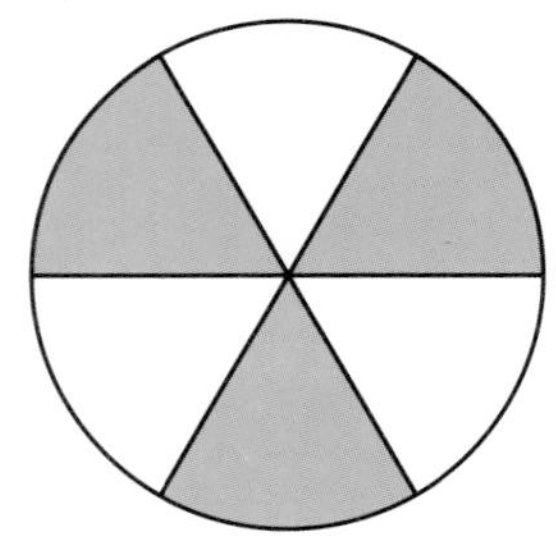

7. What is the approximate percent for each part of Canada?

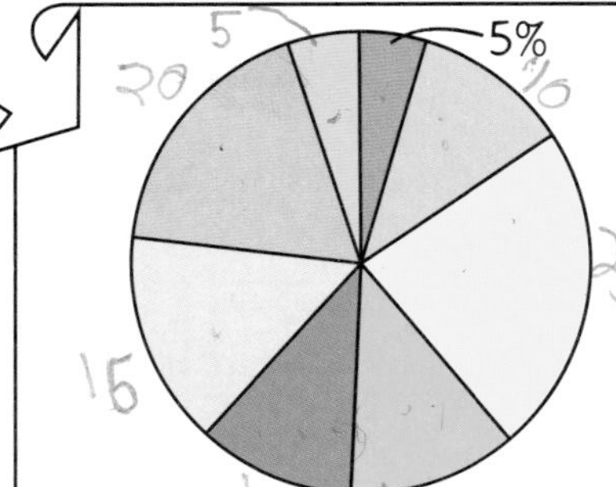

Native Population in Canada (1986)

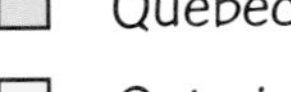

- Atlantic Provinces
- Québec
- Ontario
- Manitoba
- Saskatchewan
- Alberta
- British Columbia
- Territories

8. Which is the best price for kiwi fruit?
   - 2 for 95¢
   - 4 for $1.80
   - 3 for $1.50

Playing Games for Practice

Play each game in a group of 2, 3, or 4.

Ratio Concentration

- Shuffle the cards and place them face down in a 6 by 5 array.
- Turn over two cards.
- If the cards show equivalent ratios, keep them and take another turn.
- If the cards do not show equivalent ratios, turn them face down again.
- Take turns until all matches have been made.
- The player with the greatest number of cards wins.

Example

1 : 3   80%

Turn face down again.

4 : 10 $\frac{2}{5}$

Keep these.

In a Row

- Shuffle the cards.
- Deal each player 4 cards which are placed face up in a row in the order dealt.
- Take a card from the top of the deck and place it on one of your 4 cards.
- Take turns until one player has a row of 4 cards in order from least to greatest.
- That player scores 1 point.
- Continue playing.
- The first player with 5 points wins.

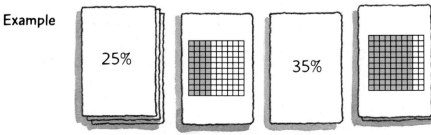

Example

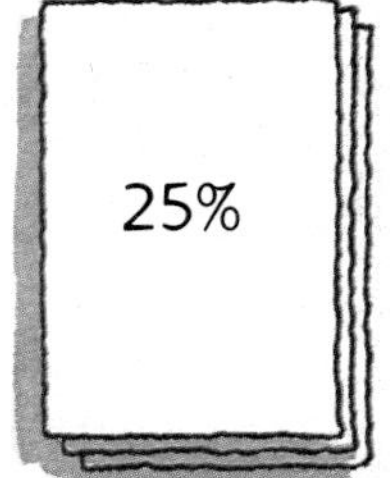

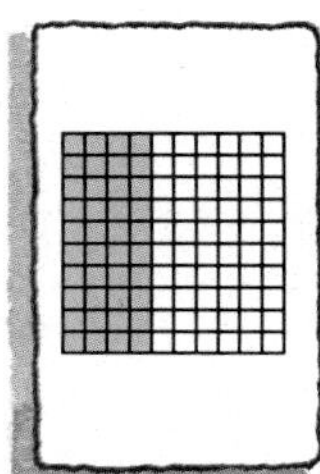

35%

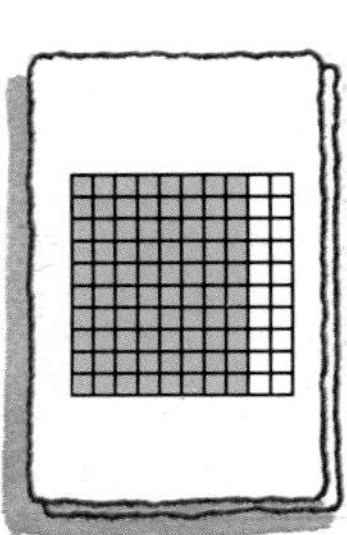

Need a card between 25% and 35% or between 40% and 80%

Take Your Pick

ONE TO THREE

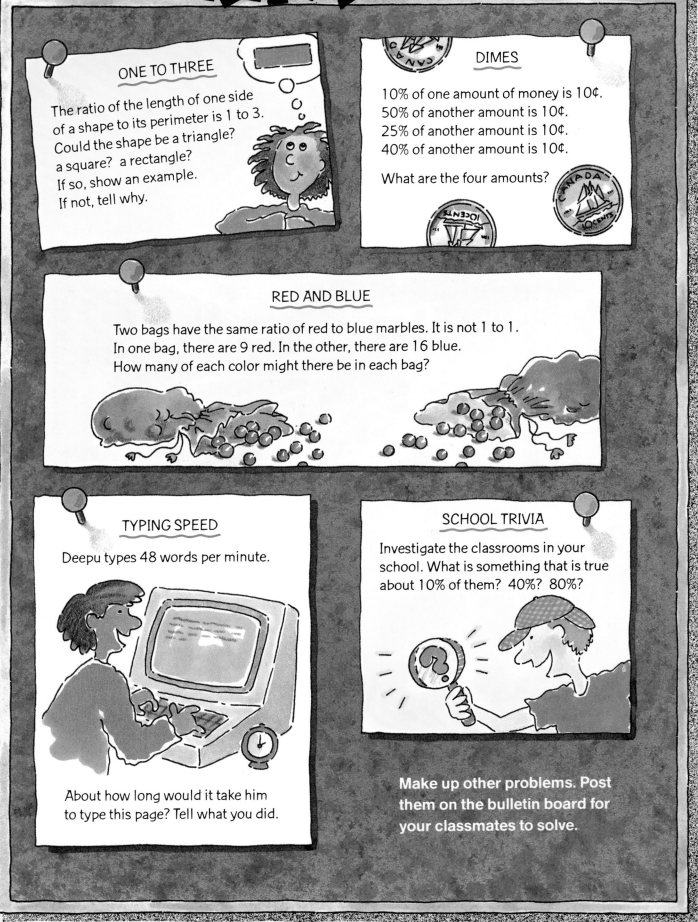

The ratio of the length of one side of a shape to its perimeter is 1 to 3. Could the shape be a triangle? a square? a rectangle? If so, show an example. If not, tell why.

DIMES

10% of one amount of money is 10¢.
50% of another amount is 10¢.
25% of another amount is 10¢.
40% of another amount is 10¢.

What are the four amounts?

RED AND BLUE

Two bags have the same ratio of red to blue marbles. It is not 1 to 1. In one bag, there are 9 red. In the other, there are 16 blue. How many of each color might there be in each bag?

TYPING SPEED

Deepu types 48 words per minute.

About how long would it take him to type this page? Tell what you did.

SCHOOL TRIVIA

Investigate the classrooms in your school. What is something that is true about 10% of them? 40%? 80%?

Make up other problems. Post them on the bulletin board for your classmates to solve.

Showing What You Know

1. $\frac{3}{5}$ of a class are boys. What does the ratio 2 : 3 tell about the class?

2. What are two ratios equivalent to ten : ten thousand?

3. Use 12 cubes of only 2 colors to show each ratio.
   Tell what each ratio describes.
   $\frac{2}{4}$ 3 to 1 8 : 4 1 to 11

4. What percent might you use to describe hardly any? almost all? a little over half? just less than a quarter?

5. An angle is halved. One half is halved. This process is repeated one more time. What is the ratio of the smallest angle to the original angle?

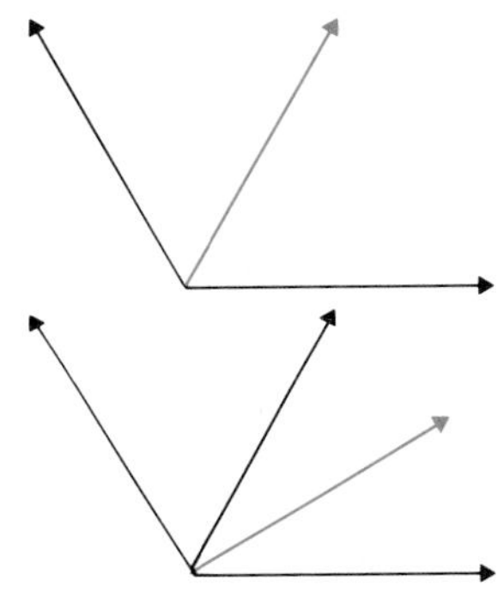

6. What is the ratio of Jennifer's present height to her height at age 7? How much has her height increased?

7. What is the ratio of the number of complete turns the hour hand of a clock makes to the number of complete turns the minute hand makes in the same amount of time?

8. Compared to garden watering, which water use is
   - about the same?
   - triple?
   - ten times as great?

   About what percent is the purple section?

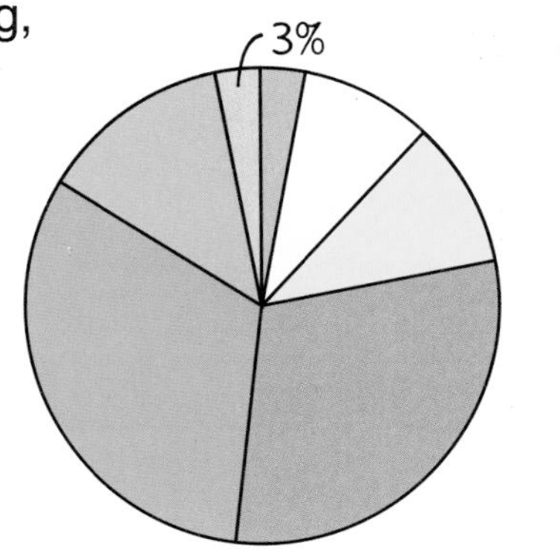

9. Which is the best deal? Why?

10. What percent of the numbers from 1 to 100 are and are not multiples of 3?

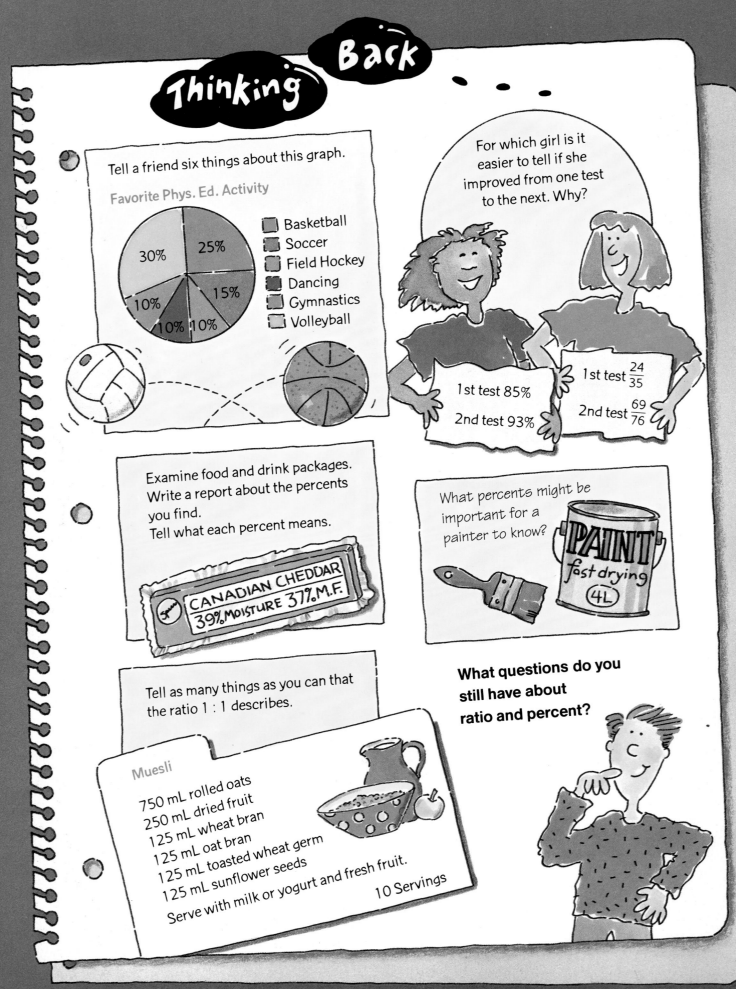

Thinking Back . . .

Tell a friend six things about this graph.

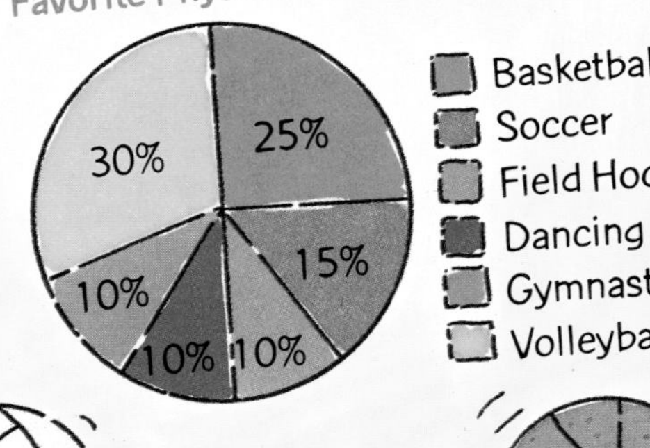

For which girl is it easier to tell if she improved from one test to the next. Why?

Examine food and drink packages. Write a report about the percents you find. Tell what each percent means.

What percents might be important for a painter to know?

Tell as many things as you can that the ratio 1 : 1 describes.

Muesli

750 mL rolled oats
250 mL dried fruit
125 mL wheat bran
125 mL oat bran
125 mL toasted wheat germ
125 mL sunflower seeds
Serve with milk or yogurt and fresh fruit.

10 Servings

What questions do you still have about ratio and percent?

UNIT 5

Investigating Transportation

Truro Trip Expenses
2 buses at $1200.00 each
motel rooms at $55.50 each

The 57 students in the Connaught Street School Band are travelling from Fredericton, NB, to Truro, NS, to perform.
What might be the total cost for buses and motel rooms?
What other costs might there be?
How would you estimate the cost for each student?
What fundraising activities might be used to raise the money needed?

HOW Much Can We Take?

Make a model of this suitcase.
What is the volume of your model? of the suitcase?
About how long is the strap around the suitcase?

Work in a group.

Model your solutions.

1. Another piece of luggage holds only about half as much. What might its dimensions be?

2. How would you arrange suitcases the size of the one shown above to get the greatest number of them
   - into a car trunk 10 dm by 10 dm by 3 dm?
   - into a minivan storage area 12 dm by 6 dm by 6 dm?
   - into a roof carrier 13 dm by 10 dm by 6 dm?

   What is the greatest number of suitcases you can get in each trunk?
   What is the volume of each trunk?

3. How could you find the volume of a small suitcase? a medium suitcase? a large suitcase? What size would you say an average suitcase is?

4. The cargo compartment of a 47-seat bus holds 75 average suitcases.
Use your average. What is the approximate volume of a cargo compartment?

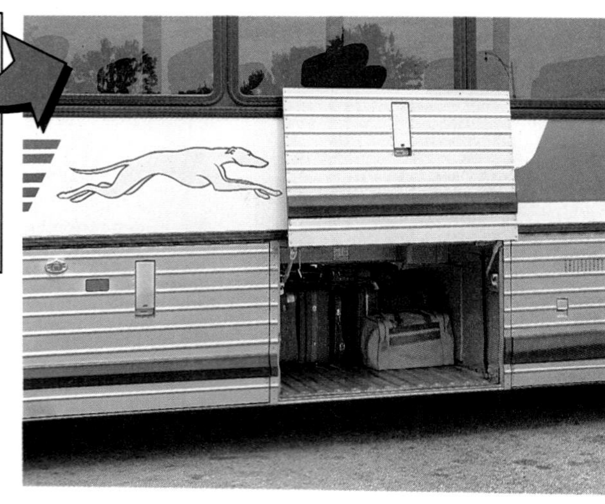

5. A DC-9 plane carries 92 passengers. Airlines plan that the ratio of checked luggage to passengers will be 6 to 5. How many pieces of checked luggage would you expect on a full DC-9 plane?

6. The maximum mass for a piece of luggage allowed on North American flights is 34 kg.
The average mass of a piece of checked luggage is about 12 kg.
Compare the two masses in different ways.

7. Find the mass of a packed suitcase. Do you think the average mass for a piece of checked luggage is reasonable?

8. Estimate the total mass of checked luggage on a full DC-9 plane using
   - maximum mass
   - average mass

   What is the difference?

9. Why do you think that planes and buses have mass instead of volume restrictions for luggage?

Did You Know...?

About 22 000 pieces of luggage are unclaimed or missing at Toronto's International Airport each year.

▶ About how many is that per day?
If 55 000 passengers use the airport each day, about what fraction of the luggage is unclaimed or missing?

HOW Do We Read Schedules?

How do you read this bus schedule to follow the route
- from the Atlantic Provinces to Québec?
- from Québec to the Atlantic Provinces?

What does ET mean? AT? Ar? Lv?

Which place has two Ar times for the route from Québec? Why?

Where is the Daily 20 bus at 8 a.m.? 11:30 a.m.? 1 p.m.?

RIVIÈRE DU LOUP–EDMUNDSTON–MONCTON–AMHERST

READ DOWN **AM–BLACK** PM–RED **READ UP**

	Daily 20 ▼	Daily 22 ▼	Daily 24 ▼	Daily 26 ▼	↓	Route 2	↑	Daily 25 ▲	Daily 27 ▲
	4:15		3:30	8:15	Lv	RIVIÈRE DU LOUP	Ar	12:35	
	↓		↓	↓	Lv	RIVIÈRE VERTE JCT	Lv	12:25	
			4:05	8:45	Lv	ST. HONORÉ	Lv	11:55	
			4:15	9:00	Lv	ST. LOUIS DU HA HA	Lv	11:40	
ET			4:25	9:10	Lv	CABANO	Lv	11:30	
			4:37	9:22	Lv	NOTRE DAME DU LAC	Lv	11:18	
			4:50	9:35	Lv	VILLE DÉGELIS	Lv	11:05	
	5:50		5:20	10:05	Ar	EDMUNDSTON (ET)	Lv	10:35	
	6:50		6:20	11:05	Ar	EDMUNDSTON (AT)	Lv	11:35	
	7:15	12:40			Lv		Ar	10:15	
	7:45	1:10			Lv	ST. LEONARD	Lv	9:35	
	8:05	1:30			Lv	GRAND FALLS	Lv	9:15	
	8:40	2:05			Lv	PERTH ANDOVER	Lv	8:45	
	9:10	2:35			Lv	FLORENCEVILLE	Lv	8:10	
	9:25	2:50			Lv	HARTLAND	Lv	7:45	
	9:45	3:10			Ar	WOODSTOCK	Lv	7:30	
	9:55	3:20			Lv		Ar	7:15	
	10:10	3:35			Lv	MEDUCTIC	Lv	7:00	
	10:25	3:50			Lv	POKIOK	Lv	6:45	
AT	11:15	4:40			Ar	FREDERICTON	Lv	6:00	
	12:00	5:30			Lv		Ar	4:15	8:05
	12:25	↓			Lv	OROMOCTO	Lv	↑	↑
	12:55	6:25			Lv	MILL COVE	Lv	3:20	
	1:30	7:05			Ar	SUSSEX	Lv	2:45	
	1:35	7:10			Lv		Ar	2:35	
	↓	7:35			Lv	PETITCODIAC	Lv	2:10	
	2:10	7:50			Lv	SALISBURY	Lv	1:55	
	2:45	8:15			Ar	MONCTON	Lv	1:30	5:55
	3:00				Lv		Ar	1:00	5:30
	3:40				Lv	SACKVILLE	Lv	12:20	4:50
	4:00				Ar	AMHERST	Lv	12:00	4:30

Use the bus schedule.

1. How long does it take to go by bus from Rivière du Loup to Amherst? How long does the opposite trip take?

2. What is the shortest time between stops on the route of the Daily 20 bus? How often is the time between stops that short?

3. For the Daily 20 bus, how much time is spent at scheduled stops? How much time is spent driving?

4. The distance between Rivière du Loup and Amherst is 664 km. What is the average speed of the bus? How long would it take to drive that distance in a car? Explain the difference.

Use the airline schedule.

Days	Dep	Arr	Flight(s)	Stop
LETHBRIDGE				
CALGARY				
X67	0645	0725	AC1726	-
	1015	1055	AC1730	-
X6	1240	1325	AC1734	-
	1455	1535	AC1732	-
X6	1705	1745	AC1736	-
X6	1910	1950	AC1728	-
EDMONTON				
X67	0645	0840	AC1726–AC1702	1
X6	1015	1230	AC1730–AC1504	1
6	1015	1225	AC1730–AC1629	1
X6	1240	1440	AC1734–AC1712	1
X6	1455	1640	AC1732–AC1716	1
6	1455	1655	AC1732–AC1510	1
X6	1705	1840	AC1736–AC1720	1
X6	1910	2050	AC1728–AC1604	1
CALGARY				
EDMONTON				
X67	0610	0700	AC1685	-
X67	0700	0740	AC1700	-
X67	0800	0840	AC1702	-
6	0830	0910	AC1704	-
X67	0900	0940	AC1704	-
7	1000	1050	AC1708	-
6	1135	1225	AC1629	-
X6	1140	1230	AC1504	-
X67	1220	1300	AC8953	-
X6	1400	1440	AC1712	-
X6	1500	1540	AC1714	-
6	1540	1620	AC1716	-
X6	1600	1640	AC1716	-
67	1600	1640	AC8955	-
6	1605	1655	AC1510	-
X67	1700	1740	AC1718	-
	1800	1840	AC1720	-
X6	2010	2050	AC1604	-
X6	2015	2100	AC133	-
6	2020	2110	AC1604	-
6	2310	2355	AC160	-

5. What does Dep mean?
   Arr? Stop?

   Monday is day 1.
   In the Day column, X6 means every day except Saturday.
   What does 6 mean?
   X67? no entry?

6. How many flights are there from Lethbridge to Calgary on weekdays? on weekends?

7. Times from 1 o'clock in the afternoon to midnight are recorded as 1300, 1301, 1302, . . ., 2358, 2359, 0000. This refers to the 24 hour clock. Use the 12 hour clock and a.m. and p.m. to tell the departure times from Lethbridge to Calgary.

8. How long is a flight from Lethbridge to Calgary? Are the flights direct? How can you tell?

9. Are there any direct flights from Lethbridge to Edmonton? How long is flight AC1730–AC1504? How long is the stop in Calgary?

10. The distance from Lethbridge to Edmonton is about 450 km. Estimate the average flying speed. About how much less time would a direct flight be than flight AC1730–AC1504?

11. Choose a destination and a train, bus, or airline schedule. On a given day, how many ways could you get to your destination? How long would it take?

Vancouver International Airport handles about 25 000 travellers a day on about 525 flights.

▶ About how many passengers are there per flight?

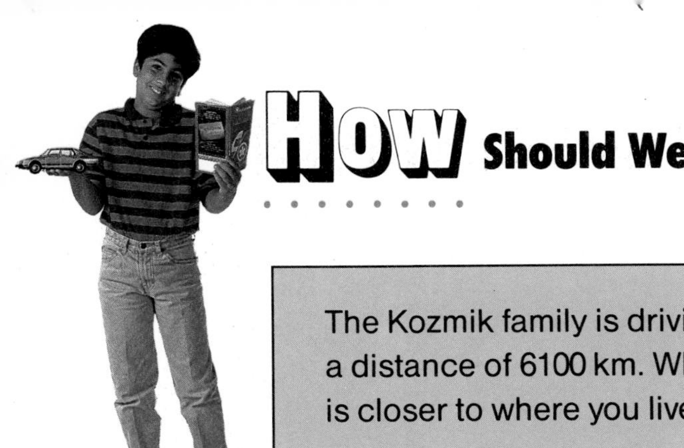

HOW Should We Go?

The Kozmik family is driving from Halifax to Vancouver, a distance of 6100 km. Which of these cities is closer to where you live?

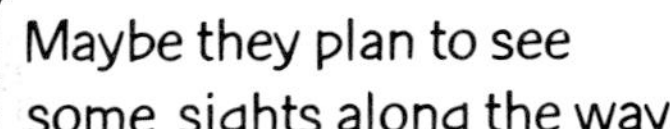

Maybe they plan to see some sights along the way.

1. Their car uses gasoline at a rate of about 10 L for every 100 km travelled. At an average price of 60¢ for every litre used, about how much will they spend on gasoline to get to Vancouver?

2. They hope to average about 80 km every hour on the drive. How far might they get in a day? How many days could it take them to reach Vancouver?

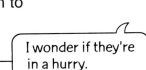

I wonder if they're in a hurry.

3. They budget $70 a night for motel rooms along the way. About how much will they spend on motels getting to Vancouver?

4. They budget $80 a day for food. About how much will they spend on food getting to Vancouver?

5. What is the approximate total cost of their drive to Vancouver?

6. How much would it cost the four members of the Kozmik family to fly to Vancouver and back?

INVOICE
HALIFAX TO VANCOUVER
RETURN AIRFARE $840.00
TAXES $101.60
FLIGHT BOARDING PASS
CARTE D'EMBARQUEMENT

Which way— driving or flying— is cheaper? By about how much?

7. A flight leaves Halifax at 8:12 a.m., and arrives in Vancouver at 12:57 p.m. What is the actual time for the flight?

8. List some advantages of each way of travelling to Vancouver from Halifax.
Which way would you go? Why?

9. Make a table like this to help you find how much time is saved by driving faster.

Travelling 500 km

Speed	80 km per hour	90 km per hour	100 km per hour	110 km per hour
Time	?	?	?	?

By how much time might the trip be shortened if they averaged 90 km per hour? 100 km per hour? Is an average speed of 100 km per hour realistic for driving across Canada? Explain.

10. When they reach Regina, the Kozmiks decide to go to Edmonton. Which route is shorter? By how much? Why might they decide not to take the shorter route? Use a ruler to measure each distance to the nearest tenth of a centimetre. Then multiply by 75.

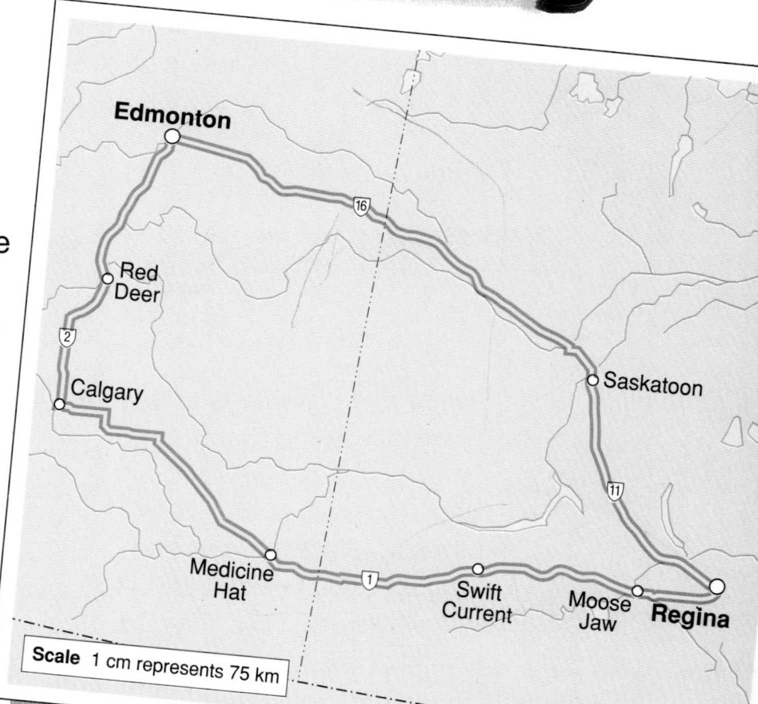

11. Plan a trip to a place at least 1000 km away. Investigate the costs and time required for different ways to get there.

Did You Know...?

On an average day, 44 210 Canadians are on a holiday within Canada.

▶ Is that more or less than 1% of 27 million Canadians?

? I Wonder... ?

FARES

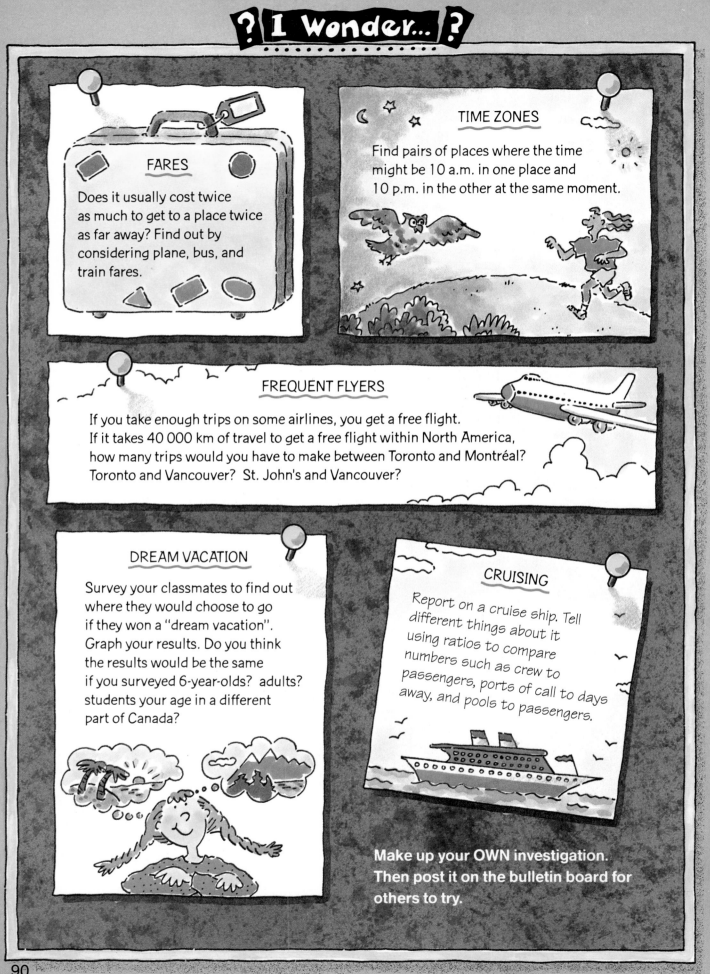

Does it usually cost twice as much to get to a place twice as far away? Find out by considering plane, bus, and train fares.

TIME ZONES

Find pairs of places where the time might be 10 a.m. in one place and 10 p.m. in the other at the same moment.

FREQUENT FLYERS

If you take enough trips on some airlines, you get a free flight. If it takes 40 000 km of travel to get a free flight within North America, how many trips would you have to make between Toronto and Montréal? Toronto and Vancouver? St. John's and Vancouver?

DREAM VACATION

Survey your classmates to find out where they would choose to go if they won a "dream vacation". Graph your results. Do you think the results would be the same if you surveyed 6-year-olds? adults? students your age in a different part of Canada?

CRUISING

Report on a cruise ship. Tell different things about it using ratios to compare numbers such as crew to passengers, ports of call to days away, and pools to passengers.

Make up your OWN investigation. Then post it on the bulletin board for others to try.

Thinking Back . . .

Tell six things the graph shows about where Canadians travel. Why do you think this graph excluded the United States?

Foreign Destinations of Canadian Travellers (excluding the United States)

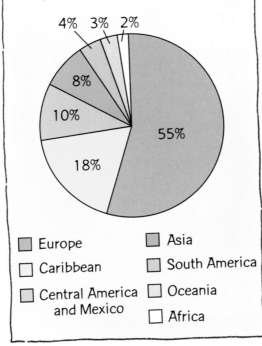

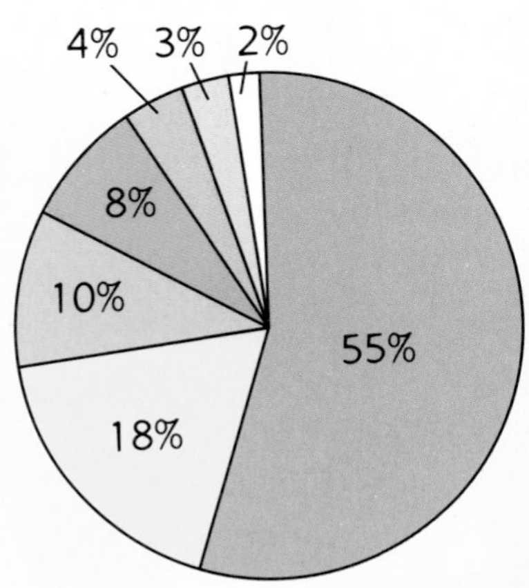

- Europe
- Caribbean
- Central America and Mexico
- Asia
- South America
- Oceania
- Africa

Tell how you might use measurements, calculations, and schedules if you were the manager of a vacation resort.

To find the cost of a trip, when might you need to multiply? to divide?

Some schedules follow the 24 hour clock and others follow the 12 hour clock. What are some advantages of each?

What else would you like to know about transportation? Tell what you would do to find out.

6 Extending Multiplication

What multiplication sentence is suggested?
What division sentence?

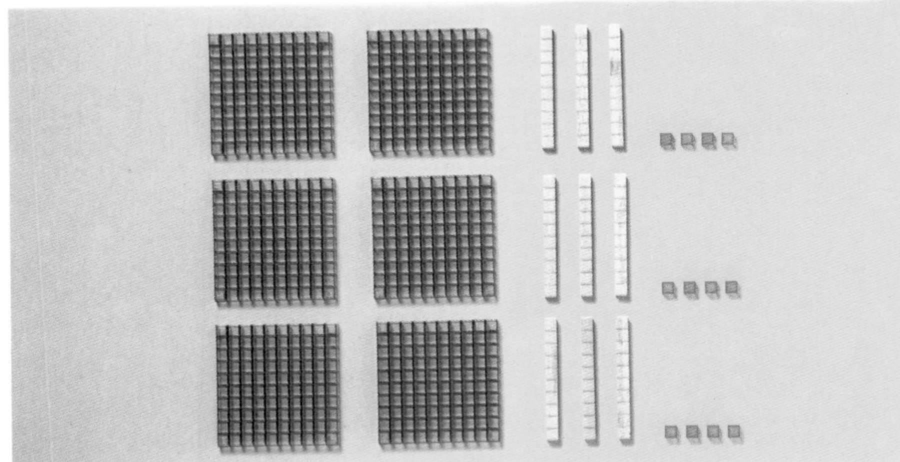

How many tiles are in this array?
How did you decide?
Describe two other arrays with the same number of tiles.

Try this trick.
Think of a number.
Multiply the number by 35.
Divide the product by 7.
Add the original number to the quotient.
Divide the sum by 6.
What happens?

and Division

- Complete this table.

Number of Complete Turns in the Same Amount of Time

Large gear	1	12	?	78	?
Small gear	6	72	120	?	720

- Write the scale as 1 cm represents ? km.
About how far apart are Dawson and Whitehorse?
What two places are about 900 km apart?
Tell how you decided.

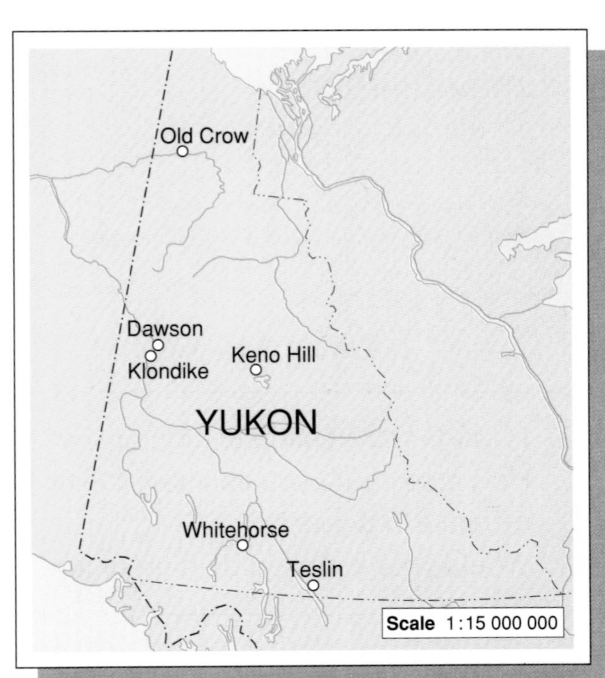

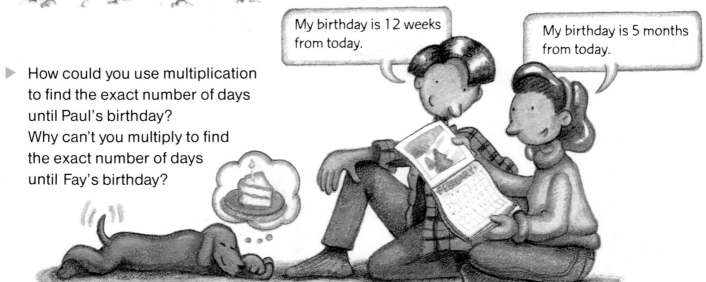

My birthday is 12 weeks from today.

My birthday is 5 months from today.

- How could you use multiplication to find the exact number of days until Paul's birthday?
Why can't you multiply to find the exact number of days until Fay's birthday?

How can you cut a pancake into 8 pieces with only 3 straight cuts?

Estimating Winks and Blinks

Using approximate numbers

Wink

I took 40 winks
yesterday afternoon
and another 40 today.
In fact I get through
about 280 winks a week.
Which is about 14 560
winks a year.
(The way I'm going on
I'll end up looking like a wink).

by Roger McGough
from *The Kingfisher Book of Comic Verse*

How did the author likely decide he had about 14 560 winks in a year?

Marianne thought he likely multiplied 280 and 52.
She estimates to check.

280 → 300 → 3 hundreds
x 52   x 50   x 50
150 hundreds
or 15 000

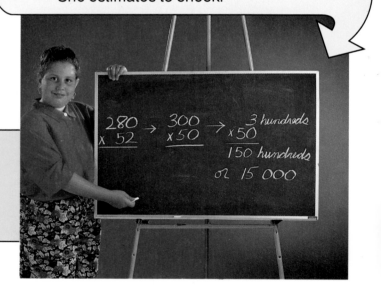

Is Marianne's estimate high or low? Why?
How else could you estimate the number of winks in a year?
Would your estimate be high or low? Why?

1. Most people blink about 20 000 times per day.
Gord is estimating how many times he blinks in an hour.

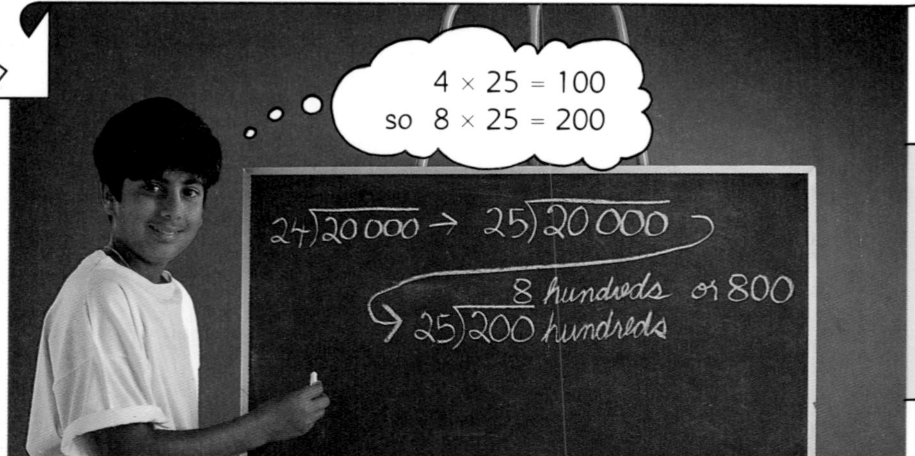

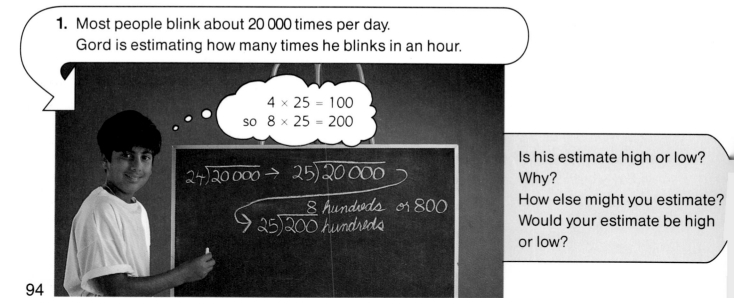

Is his estimate high or low?
Why?
How else might you estimate?
Would your estimate be high or low?

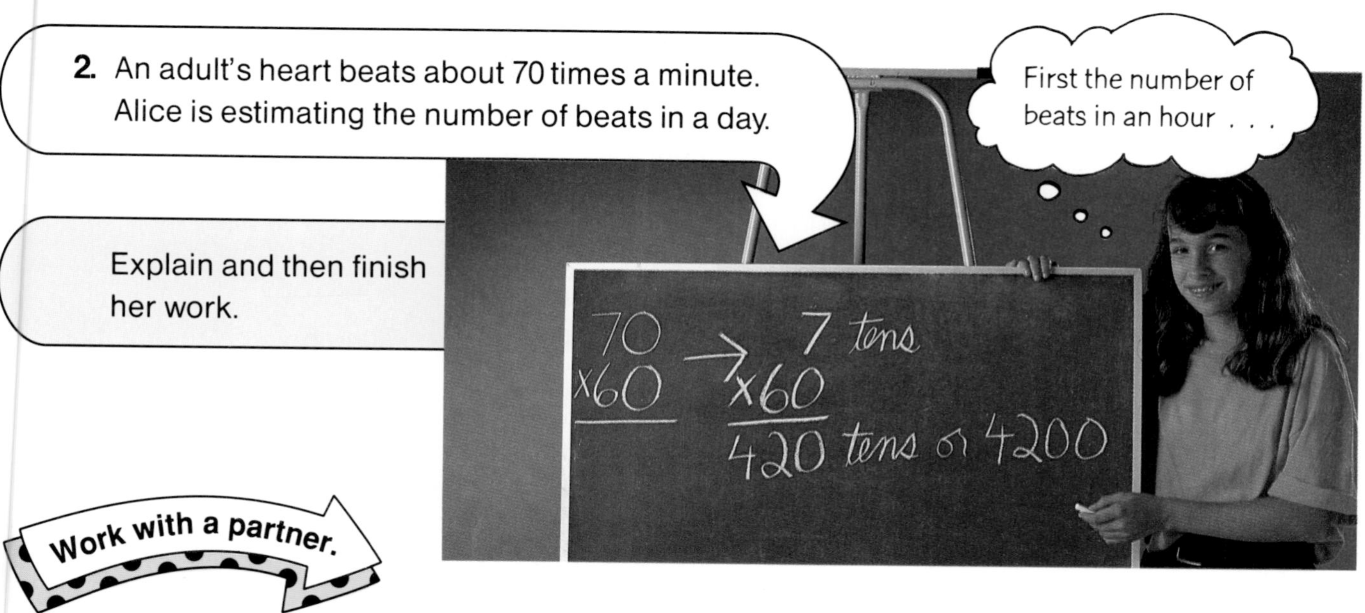

First the number of beats in an hour . . .
70 → 7 tens
×60 ×60
420 tens or 4200
Work with a partner.

2. An adult's heart beats about 70 times a minute. Alice is estimating the number of beats in a day.

Explain and then finish her work.

3. A child's heart beats about 85 times a minute. About how many times has your heart beat in the last week?

4. A person's heart pumps about 8400 L of blood each day. Use numbers you can work with in your head to estimate the number of litres pumped each hour.

5. There are about 96 500 km of blood vessels in the human body. The distance across Canada is about 6000 km. Which calculation would you perform to estimate the number of times your blood vessels would cross Canada? Why?

96 thousands ÷ 6 thousands
90 thousands ÷ 6 thousands
100 thousands ÷ 5 thousands

Would your estimate be high or low? Explain.

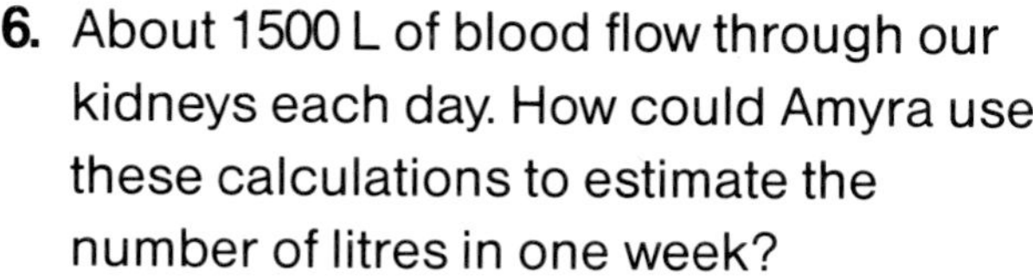

6. About 1500 L of blood flow through our kidneys each day. How could Amyra use these calculations to estimate the number of litres in one week?

- 7 × 1000
- 7 × 2000

How do you think Amyra might estimate the number of litres in a month?

7. Most people shed about 18 kg of skin in a lifetime. How many grams is that? What age is reasonable for an average lifetime? About how many grams of skin would you shed each year? each month?

8. Most people lose about 80 scalp hairs each day. About how many scalp hairs would you lose in a year? Have you lost more than 1 million so far? Will you in your lifetime?

9. Use information about the body. Make up two estimation problems involving multiplication or division for another pair to solve.

Copy this path.
How can you travel it completely without going over a side more than once?

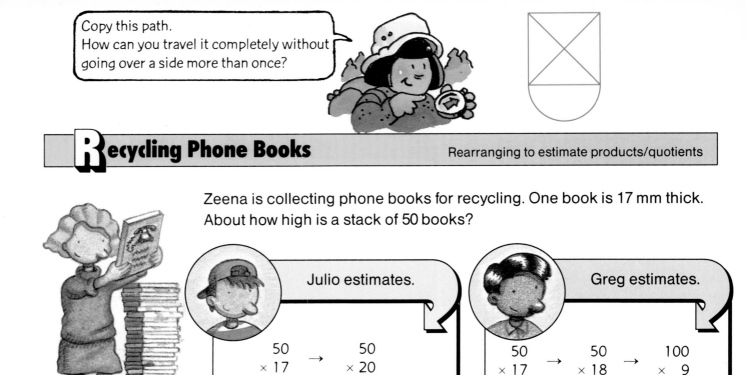

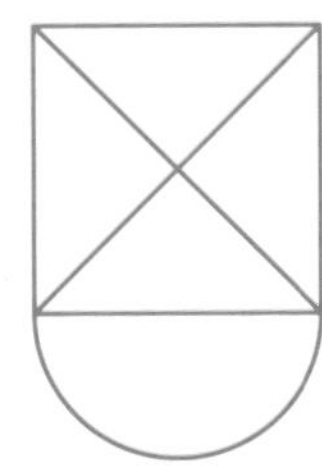

Recycling Phone Books

Rearranging to estimate products/quotients

Zeena is collecting phone books for recycling. One book is 17 mm thick. About how high is a stack of 50 books?

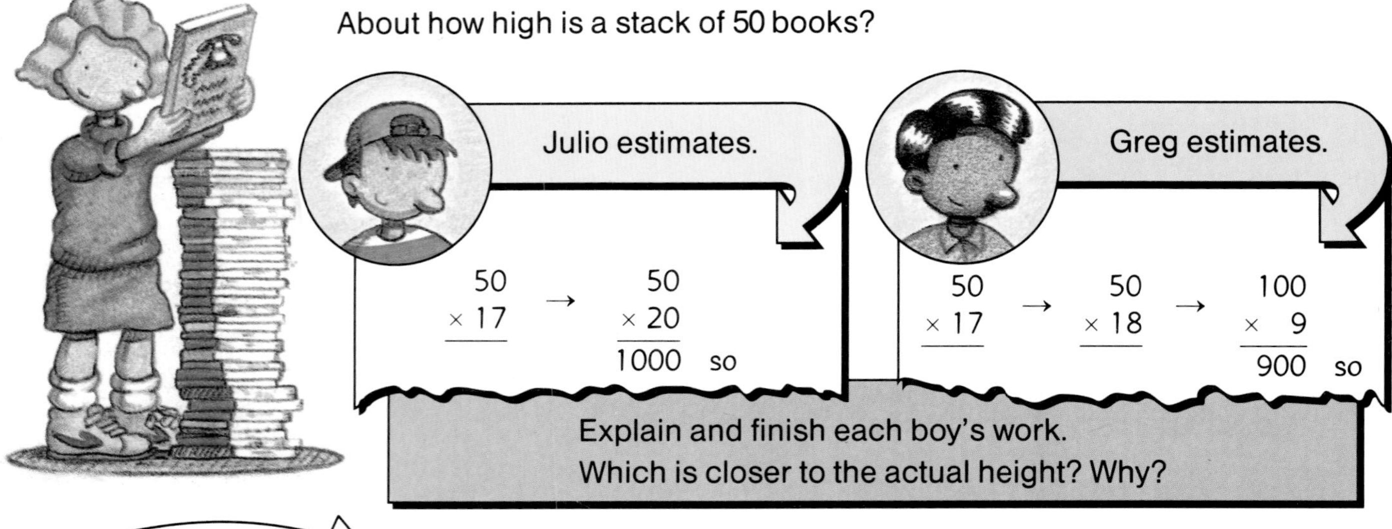

Julio estimates.
50 × 17 → 50 × 20 = 1000 so
Greg estimates.
50 × 17 → 50 × 18 → 100 × 9 = 900 so
Explain and finish each boy's work.
Which is closer to the actual height? Why?

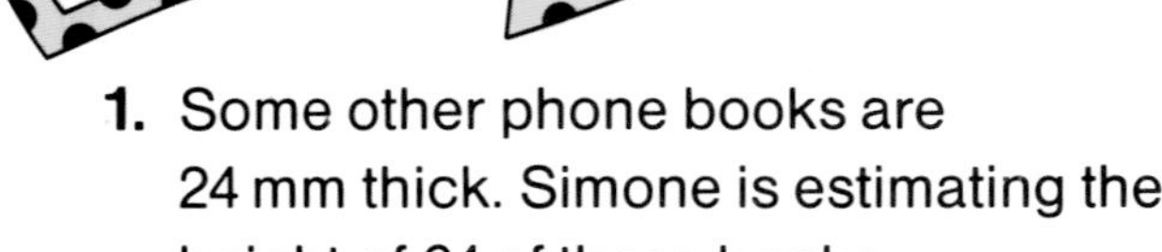

1. Some other phone books are 24 mm thick. Simone is estimating the height of 64 of these books.

   $24 \times 64 \rightarrow 25 \times 64 \rightarrow 50 \times 32$

   Explain and finish Simone's work.

2. Estimate the height of each stack.
   - 84 phone books each 26 mm thick
   - 124 phone books each 24 mm thick
   - 78 phone books each 48 mm thick

3. Alex is estimating how high a stack of 32 phone books, each 27 mm thick, would be.

   $32 \times 27 \rightarrow 33 \times 27 \rightarrow 99 \times 9$

   Explain and finish his work.

4. 1235 phone books are collected. One carton holds 48 of them. Amy is estimating how many cartons are needed.

   $48\overline{)1235} \rightarrow 50\overline{)1200} \rightarrow 50\overline{)1000}$

   Explain and finish her work.

5. Estimate how many cartons are needed.
   - 1798 phone books, 52 to a carton
   - 1130 phone books, 24 to a carton
   - 1989 phone books, 34 to a carton

6. Estimate and then check the thickness of a phone book. About how high would a stack of 25 be? 48? 34?

Take Your Pick

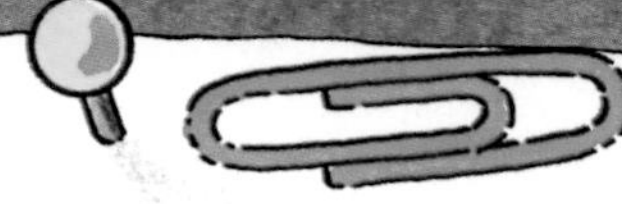

PAPER CLIPS

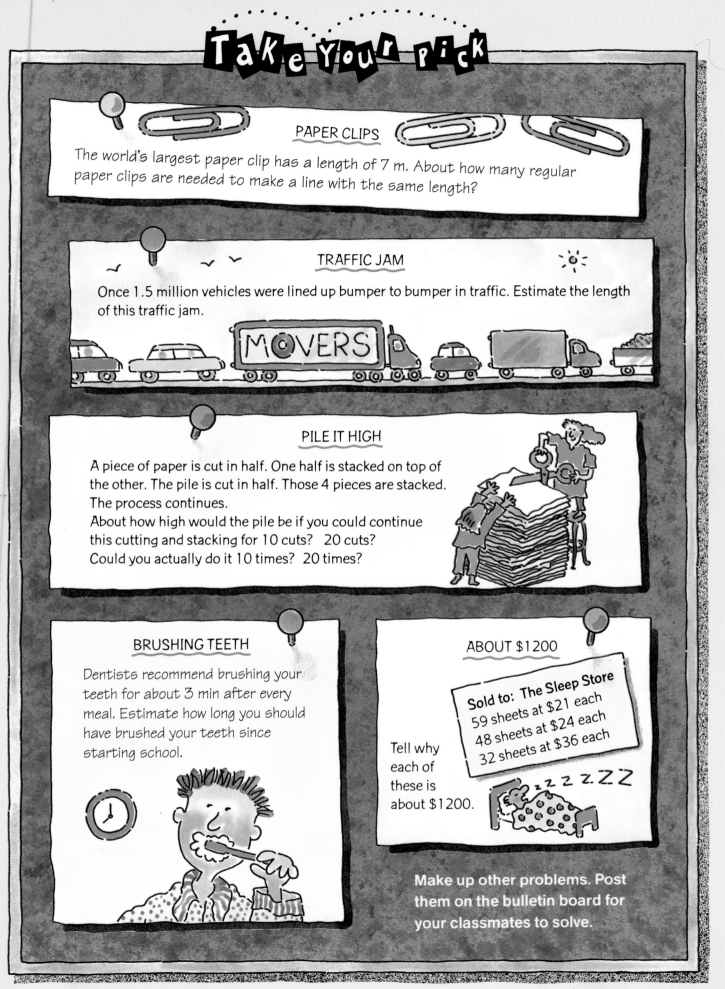

The world's largest paper clip has a length of 7 m. About how many regular paper clips are needed to make a line with the same length?

TRAFFIC JAM

Once 1.5 million vehicles were lined up bumper to bumper in traffic. Estimate the length of this traffic jam.

PILE IT HIGH

A piece of paper is cut in half. One half is stacked on top of the other. The pile is cut in half. Those 4 pieces are stacked. The process continues.

About how high would the pile be if you could continue this cutting and stacking for 10 cuts? 20 cuts?

Could you actually do it 10 times? 20 times?

BRUSHING TEETH

Dentists recommend brushing your teeth for about 3 min after every meal. Estimate how long you should have brushed your teeth since starting school.

ABOUT $1200

Sold to: The Sleep Store
59 sheets at $21 each
48 sheets at $24 each
32 sheets at $36 each

Tell why each of these is about $1200.

Make up other problems. Post them on the bulletin board for your classmates to solve.

1 000 000 is 1000 thousand.
1 000 000 cm is 10 km.
Tell five other things that are true about 1 000 000.
21
17

Keeping in Shape

Using informal methods to multiply

Lia jogs 15 km a week — 10 km on weekdays and 5 km on weekends.

Copy and complete this table.

Distance Jogged (km)

Number of weeks	1	4	8	12	16	20	24
Distance jogged (km) • on weekdays	10	?	?	?	?	?	?
• on weekends	5	?	?	?	?	?	
• all week	15	?	?				

Work with a partner.

How do the numbers in the weekend row relate to the numbers in the weekday row?
What method for multiplying by 15 does the table suggest to you?

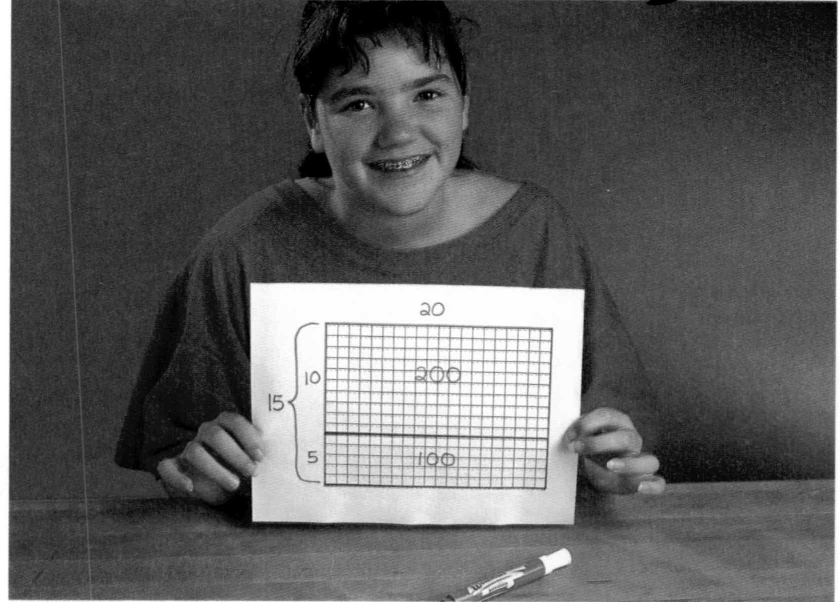
20
15
10
200
5
100

1. How far does Lia jog in 36 weeks? 52 weeks? 78 weeks? 43 weeks? 27 weeks?

2. Katia jogs 14 km a week and Jill jogs 16 km a week. How could you use the product of 15 and 36 from Problem 1 to find the distance each girl jogs in 36 weeks? How far does each girl jog in a year?

3. Kirk runs 11 km each week.
Copy and complete the table.

Number of weeks	3	6	9	12	15	18	21	24
Distance run (km)	33	66	99	?	?	?	?	?

double 33

66 + 33

4. 11 is a special factor. $15 \times 11 = 1\ 6\ 5$
Does this method work for other numbers in the table above? Which ones?

5. How far does Kirk run in 34 weeks?
26 weeks? 63 weeks?
52 weeks? 44 weeks?

6. This method works because, for example,

$$11 \times 24 = 10 \times 24 + 1 \times 24$$
$$= 240 + 24$$

and

$$\begin{array}{r} 2\,4\,0 \\ +\ \ 2\,4 \\ \hline 2\,6\,4 \end{array}$$

How does this help you adapt this method to find the distance Kirk runs in 64 weeks?
29 weeks?

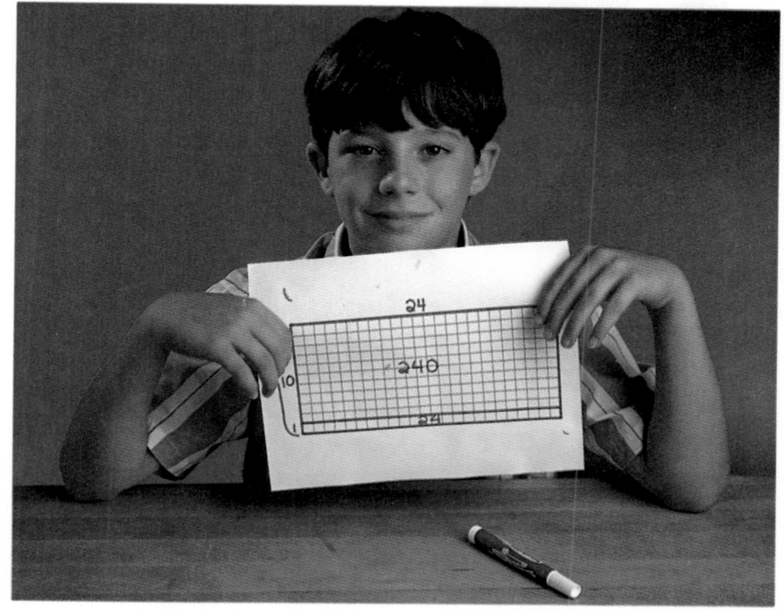

7. Eli cycles 199 km on his exercise bike each month.
How can you calculate in your head how far he cycles in 8 months?

8. Describe an "easy" way to find the distance each student covers in 26 weeks.
- Brad runs 9 kilometres per week
- Lena walks 25 kilometres per week
- Joy cycles 20 kilometres per week
- Franz jogs 19 kilometres per week

Describe the car trip shown by the graph.

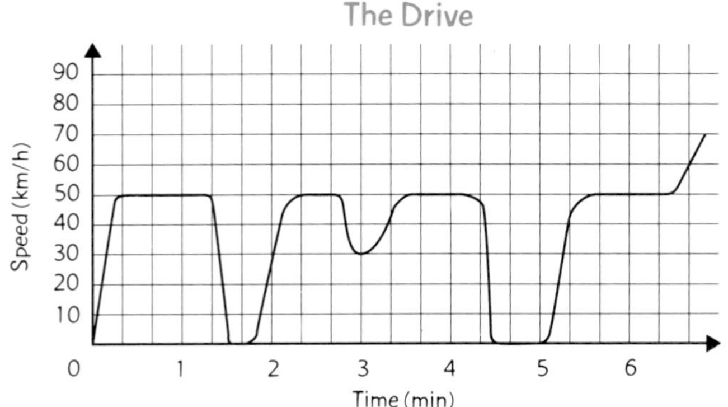

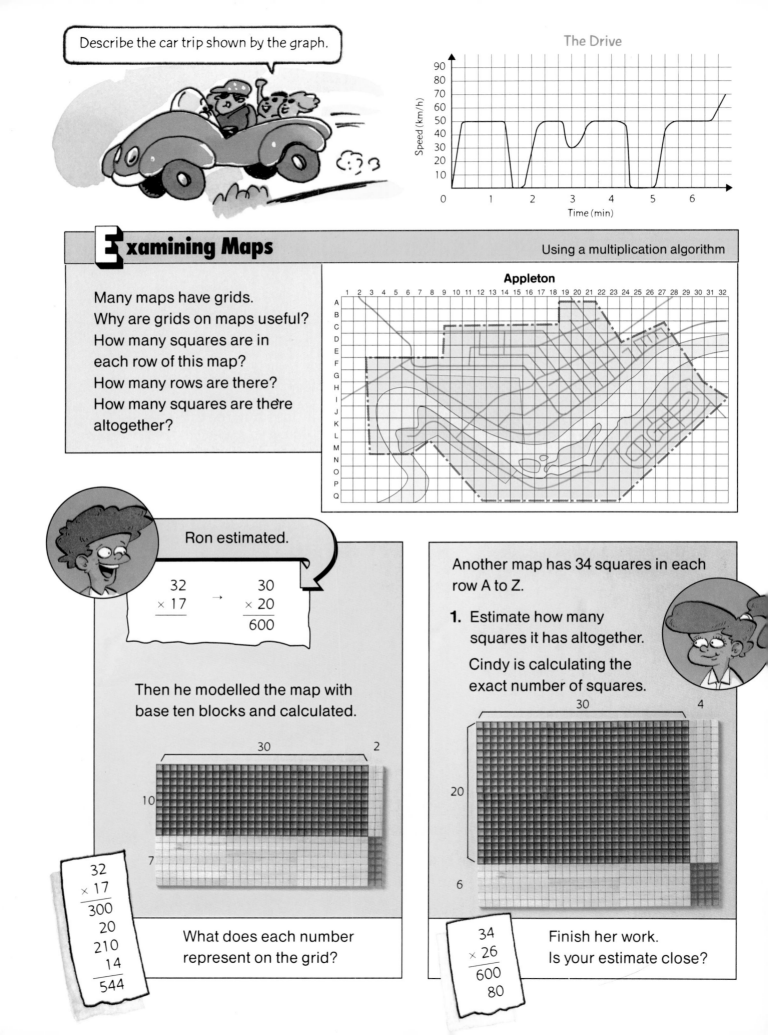

Examining Maps

Using a multiplication algorithm

Many maps have grids.
Why are grids on maps useful?
How many squares are in each row of this map?
How many rows are there?
How many squares are there altogether?

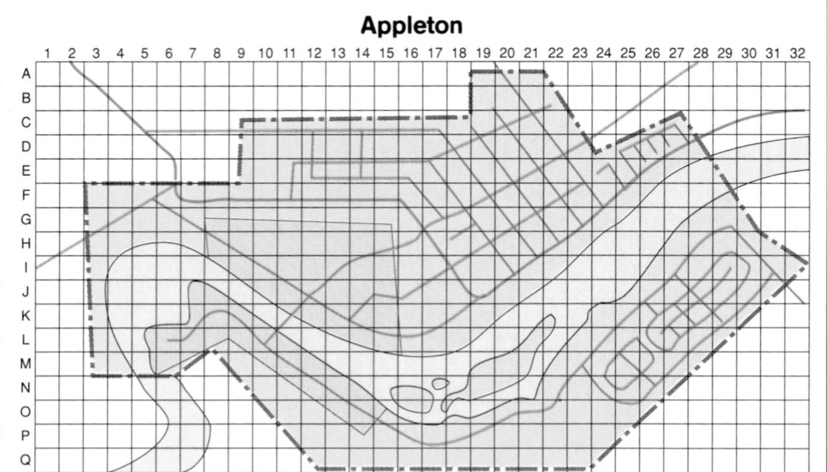

Ron estimated.

$$\begin{array}{r} 32 \\ \times\ 17 \\ \hline \end{array} \rightarrow \begin{array}{r} 30 \\ \times\ 20 \\ \hline 600 \end{array}$$

Then he modelled the map with base ten blocks and calculated.

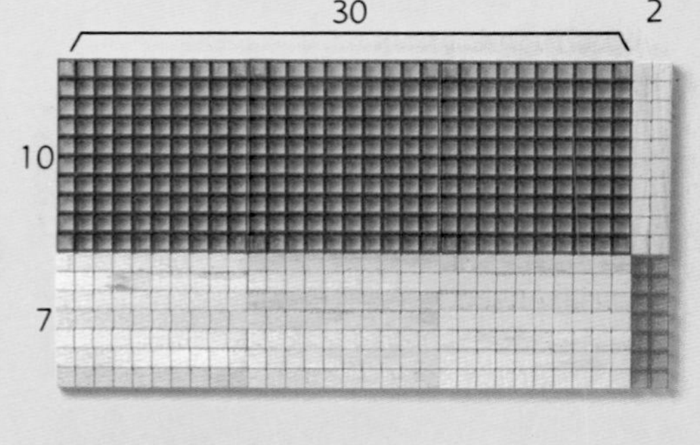

$$\begin{array}{r} 32 \\ \times\ 17 \\ \hline 300 \\ 20 \\ 210 \\ 14 \\ \hline 544 \end{array}$$

What does each number represent on the grid?

Another map has 34 squares in each row A to Z.

1. Estimate how many squares it has altogether.

Cindy is calculating the exact number of squares.

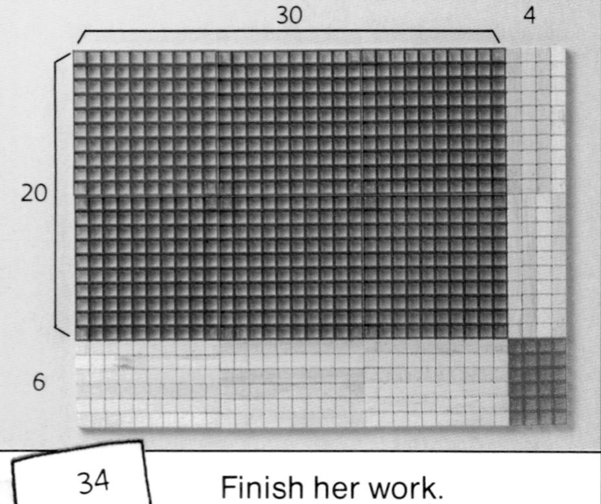

$$\begin{array}{r} 34 \\ \times\ 26 \\ \hline 600 \\ 80 \end{array}$$

Finish her work.
Is your estimate close?

Use base ten blocks or grids to model.

2. To find the total number of squares on a map with 47 squares in each row A to W, Roberto made this model and multiplied.

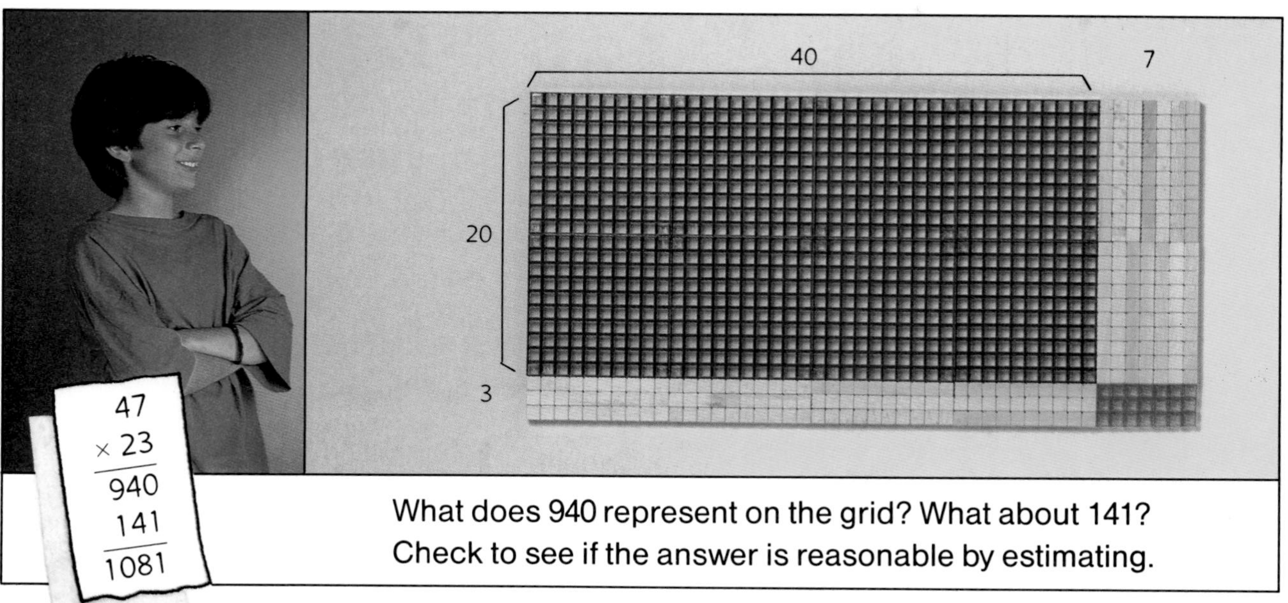

What does 940 represent on the grid? What about 141?
Check to see if the answer is reasonable by estimating.

3. Could Roberto also have multiplied this way? Explain.

$$\begin{array}{r} 47 \\ \times 23 \\ \hline 141 \\ 94 \\ \hline 1081 \end{array}$$

4. Find the total number of squares on each map.
   - Boomtown — 38 squares in each row A to X
   - Carsville — 45 squares in each row A to S
   - Drumborough — 39 squares in each row A to L

5. Tell how finding the total number of squares on the first map can help you find the total number of squares on the others.
   - Endville — 24 squares in each row A to Q — 24×17
   - Fairtown — 24 squares in each row A to R
   - Grantford — 34 squares in each row A to Q
   - Hiborough — 23 squares in each row A to Q

6. A map has 22 squares in each row A to O.
   Why might you multiply 11 by 30 to find the total number of squares?
   What other multiplication might you do?

7. How are these maps related?
   - Innisvale — 15 squares in each row A to X
   - Jamtown — 24 squares in each row A to O

Explain the pattern.

$9 = 3 \times 3 + 0 \times 4$ $12 = 4 \times 3 + 0 \times 4$

$10 = 2 \times 3 + 1 \times 4$ $13 = 3 \times 3 + 1 \times 4$

$11 = 1 \times 3 + 2 \times 4$ $14 = 2 \times 3 + 2 \times 4$

Write 81, 82, and 83 as groups of 3s and 4s.

Making Lunches

Multiplying decimals and whole numbers

"I have a great idea! I'll give you my lunch money if you'll make my lunch every day."

Jenny did some arithmetic in her head. The school lunch cost \$1.50. \$1.50 times 5 days a week = \$7.50 a week.

from *What's Cooking Jenny Archer?* by Ellen Conford

How would you find \$1.50 × 5?

Finish each student's work.

1. How much would Jenny earn in a month that has 20 school days?
2. Estimate how much she would earn in a school year if there are 194 school days. Then predict whether the estimate is greater or less than the exact amount. Check your prediction by using a calculator.
3. Of the 194 school days, 8 are Professional Development days. How can you find the maximum Jenny can earn if she makes her friend's lunch every day they are at school?

Write the number sentences.

4. If Jenny uses an average of 3 loaves a month, about how many will she use in a school year?
Estimate the total cost of the bread. Predict whether the estimate is greater or less than the actual cost. Then check.

Jenny made clam dip and mushroom sandwiches.

5. Estimate and then calculate the cost of 5 containers of clam dip.

How does estimating help you check your calculation?

6. Explain how to find the cost of 1.5 kg of mushrooms.

7. Suppose Jenny also made peanut butter, banana, and bacon sandwiches and cream cheese, walnut, and olive sandwiches.
Estimate the cost of each ingredient, and the total.

3 kg peanut butter at $4.29/kg
2 kg bananas at $1.08/kg
2 pkg bacon at $3.69/pkg
800 g cream cheese at $1.69/100g
700 g walnut pieces at $1.355/ 100 g
600 g olives at $0.885/ 100 g

Will $50.00 be enough to pay for all the ingredients? Explain.

8. How much more money would Jenny earn in a week if she sold lunches to 4 friends at $1.75 each instead of at $1.50? How did you find the difference?

9. About how much would Jenny need to charge for each of 4 lunches if she wanted to earn as much as selling 5 lunches at $1.50?

10. How much would it cost Jenny to make a cream cheese and bacon sandwich for every member of your class? How much profit would she make?

11. Why does finding the cost of items usually involve multiplying decimals and whole numbers? How is multiplying decimals like multiplying whole numbers?

Multiplying Decimals

There are lots of ways to calculate 2.56×8.
Here are some. Can you think of any more?

1. You could show 2.56 eight times using decimal grids.

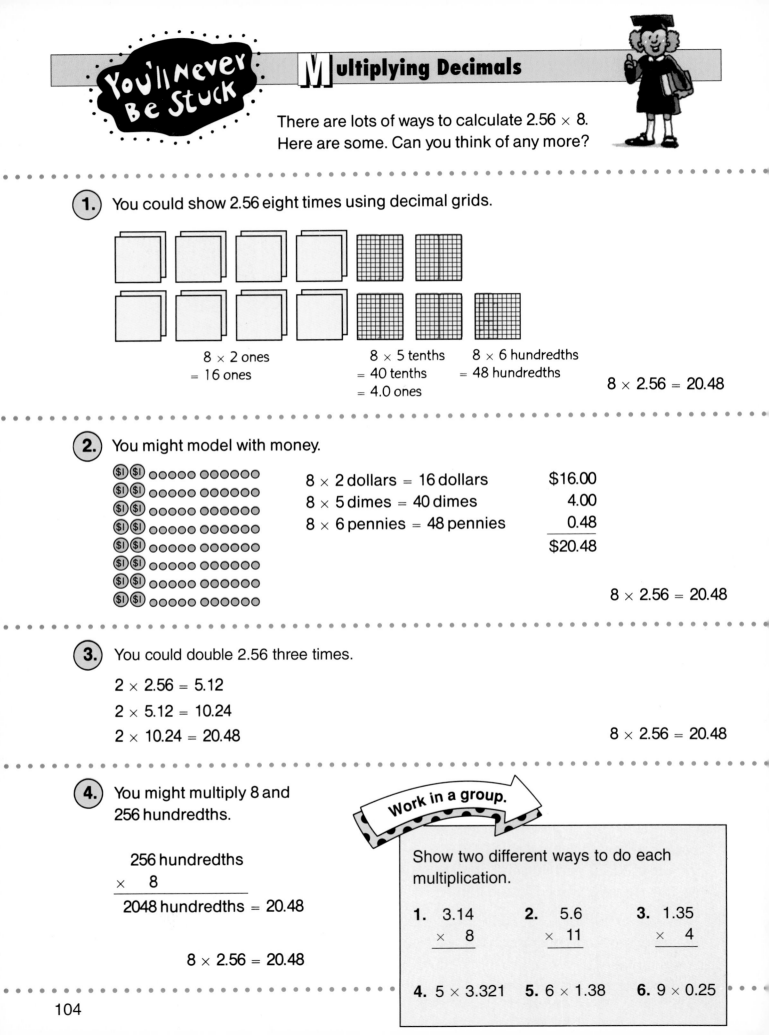

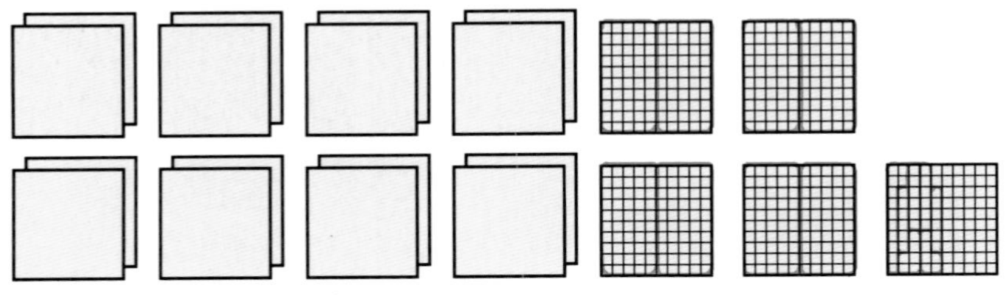

8 × 2 ones
= 16 ones

8 × 5 tenths
= 40 tenths
= 4.0 ones

8 × 6 hundredths
= 48 hundredths

$8 \times 2.56 = 20.48$

2. You might model with money.

8 × 2 dollars = 16 dollars	\$16.00
8 × 5 dimes = 40 dimes	4.00
8 × 6 pennies = 48 pennies	0.48
	\$20.48

$8 \times 2.56 = 20.48$

3. You could double 2.56 three times.

$2 \times 2.56 = 5.12$

$2 \times 5.12 = 10.24$

$2 \times 10.24 = 20.48$

$8 \times 2.56 = 20.48$

4. You might multiply 8 and 256 hundredths.

```
  256 hundredths
×   8
 2048 hundredths = 20.48
```

$8 \times 2.56 = 20.48$

Show two different ways to do each multiplication.

1. 3.14×8

2. 5.6×11

3. 1.35×4

4. 5×3.321

5. 6×1.38

6. 9×0.25

Take Your Pick

ONES DIGIT

What is the ones digit of the product of the numbers from 1 to 99? Tell why.

TWELVE PIECES

If a flat represents 1. what product is suggested by these blocks?

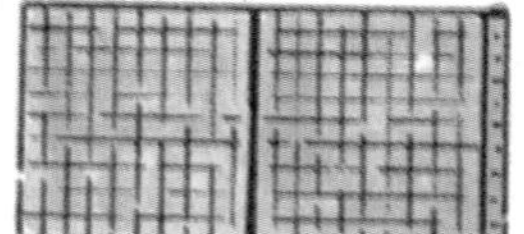 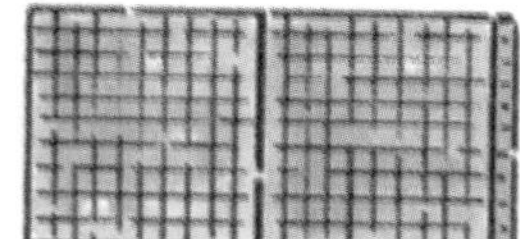 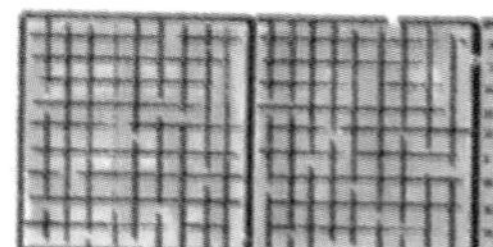 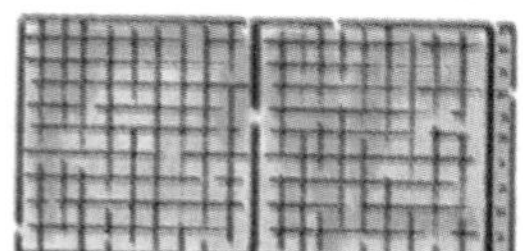

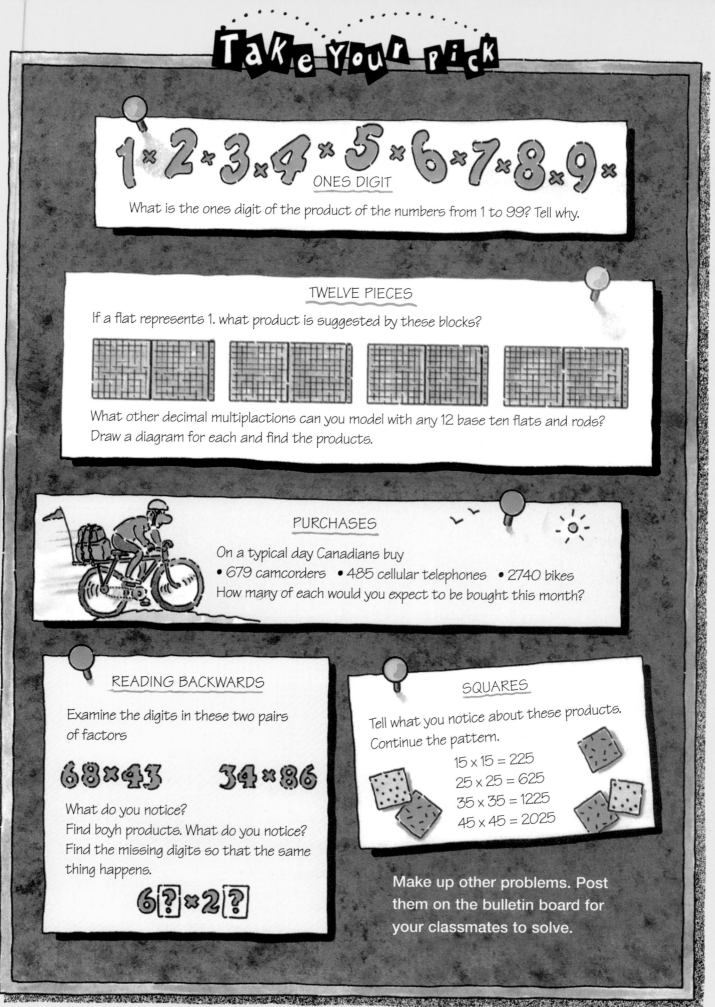

What other decimal multiplactions can you model with any 12 base ten flats and rods? Draw a diagram for each and find the products.

PURCHASES

On a typical day Canadians buy

- 679 camcorders
- 485 cellular telephones
- 2740 bikes

How many of each would you expect to be bought this month?

READING BACKWARDS

Examine the digits in these two pairs of factors

68×43 34×86

What do you notice?
Find boyh products. What do you notice?
Find the missing digits so that the same thing happens.

SQUARES

Tell what you notice about these products. Continue the pattern.

$15 \times 15 = 225$
$25 \times 25 = 625$
$35 \times 35 = 1225$
$45 \times 45 = 2025$

Make up other problems. Post them on the bulletin board for your classmates to solve.

If all the checkers sold in 1 year
by one manufacturer could be stacked,
they would make a tower 90 km high.
About how many checkers were sold by one manufacturer?

Comparing Animals

Dividing by 2-digit divisors

To find how many porpoises are needed to have the same mass as the cow, Clark made this table.

There must be a shorter way.

Number of porpoises	1	2	3	4	5	6	7	8	9	10	11	1		4	15	16	17	18
Mass (kg)	47	94	141	188	235	282	329	376	423	470	51			05	752	799	846

How do you think he found 799 and 846?
How many porpoises would be needed?

Anya suggested dividing.

First she estimated.

816 ÷ 47 is about 800 ÷ 50
= 80 tens ÷ 5 tens
= 16

Is her estimate high or low? Why?

Then she calculated using long division.

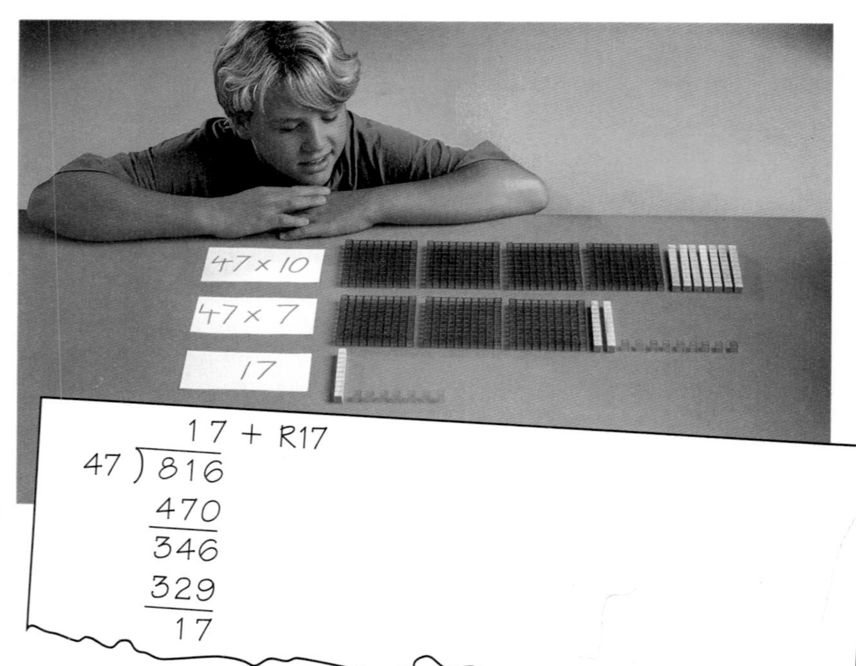

1. How do you know that more than 100 porcupines are needed to have the same mass as the walrus?
Is the answer closer to 100 or 200?

How many porcupines are needed?

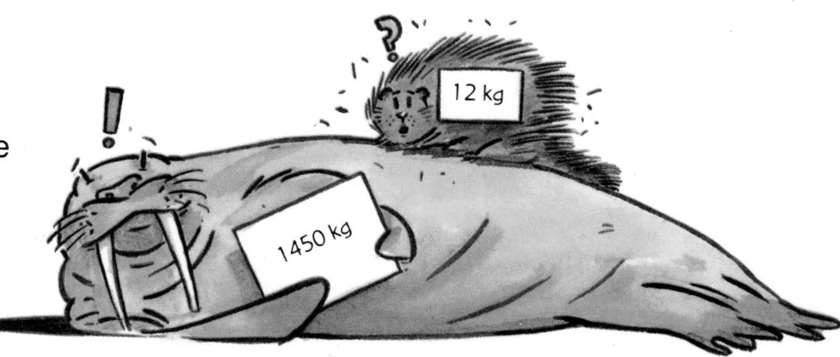

Estimate and then calculate. Use base ten blocks if you wish.

2. How many of each type of animal are needed to have the same mass as the 816 kg cow?

How did you find the number of coyotes?
About how many times as many raccoons as sheep are needed? Why?

3. How many of you would be needed to have the same mass as the cow?

4. How many mice are needed to have the same mass as each of these animals?

5. How many mice are needed to have the same mass as this monkey?

6. How many times as tall as the cat is each animal?

7. The height of a horse is 160 cm.
Without calculating, how many times as tall as the cat is it? How do you know?

8. How many times as tall as the cat are you?

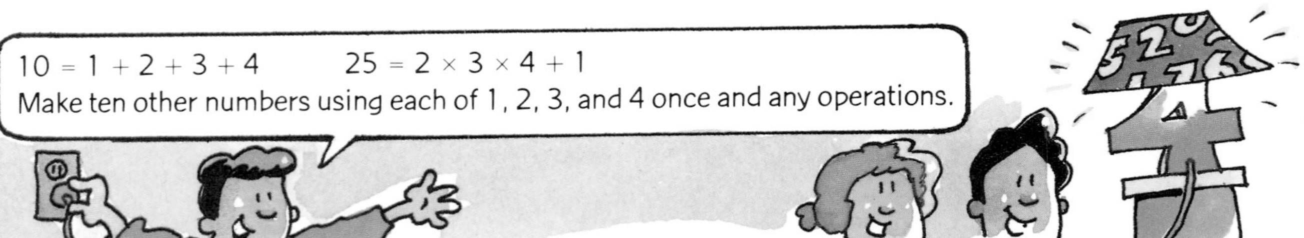

10 = 1 + 2 + 3 + 4 25 = 2 × 3 × 4 + 1
Make ten other numbers using each of 1, 2, 3, and 4 once and any operations.

Earning Money

Interpreting decimal remainders

Zoki, Brad, and 4 friends broke a window when they were playing ball. It cost $236 to replace.

Zoki and Brad divide to find each friend's share.

First they estimate.

$236 \div 6$ is about $240 \div 6 = 40$

Zoki uses short division.

3 9 + R2
6)23⁵6
Each share is $39
and 1/3 of a dollar.

Brad uses a calculator.

Each share is $39.33.

39.333333

Why did he say $\frac{1}{3}$ of a dollar?

Compare the two answers. What do you notice?

What keys did he press?
Why did he round to 2 decimal places?

1. Suppose only 4 friends were playing ball when the window was broken. Would each share be greater or less than with 6 friends? Use a calculator to find each share.

Divide using a calculator.
Predict what the whole number remainder will be.
Then divide without a calculator to check your prediction.

2. Three of the friends mowed lawns and earned $40 altogether. Find each friend's share.

3. The other three friends delivered flyers and earned $47 altogether. Find each friend's share.

4. Five students earned $296 during the summer doing yard work. What is each share in dollars and cents? Why do you think the calculator only showed one digit after the decimal point?

5. A group of students cleaned up debris and earned $158. Find the share for each number of students from 2 to 8.

Number of students	Each share (in dollars) as a decimal	with a remainder
2	79.0	79 + R0
3		
4		
5		
6		
7		
8		

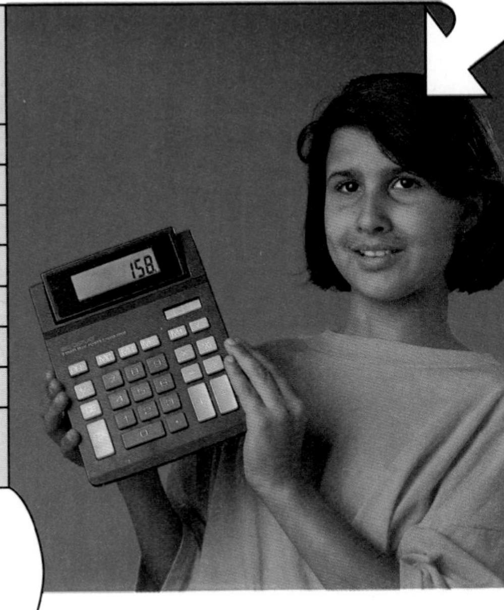

For which numbers were there no digits after the decimal point? one digit? two? more than two? Which could you have predicted? Why?

6. Use each share of $158 earned by 3 students and by 4 students from the previous problem. Compare the digits after each decimal point and compare the remainders. What do you notice?

7. A group of students earned $[?].00. Each share is $29.75. What can you tell about how many students might have been in the group? Explain.

8. Explain why you can get decimal remainders even when you divide whole numbers.

How could you find the thickness of one sheet of paper?

Comparing Prices

Dividing decimals by whole numbers

To find which is the better buy, Mario found the **unit price**.

First he estimated.

\$1.98 ÷ 3 is less than 210¢ ÷ 3 = 70¢

Why less than?

\$2.50 ÷ 4 is greater than 240¢ ÷ 4 = 60¢

Why greater than?

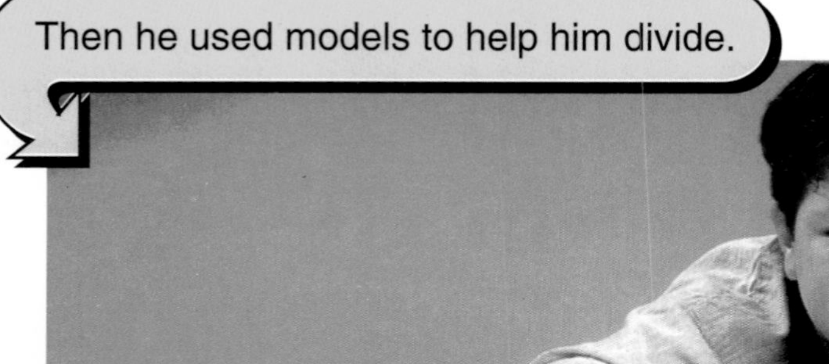

Then he used models to help him divide.

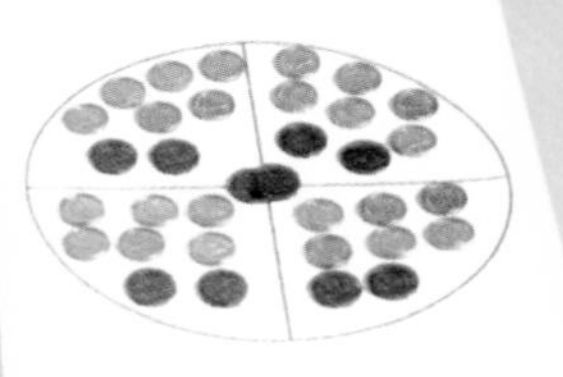

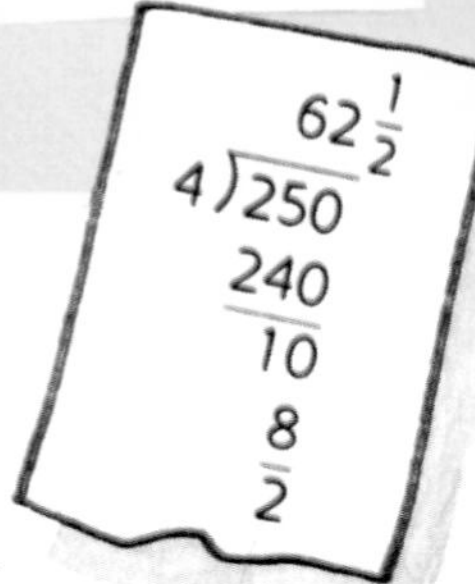

Which is less expensive?
What might make the more expensive one the better buy?

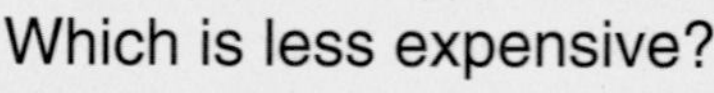

1. Peggy calculated $3\overline{)1.98}$. Use her method to find $4\overline{)2.500}$.

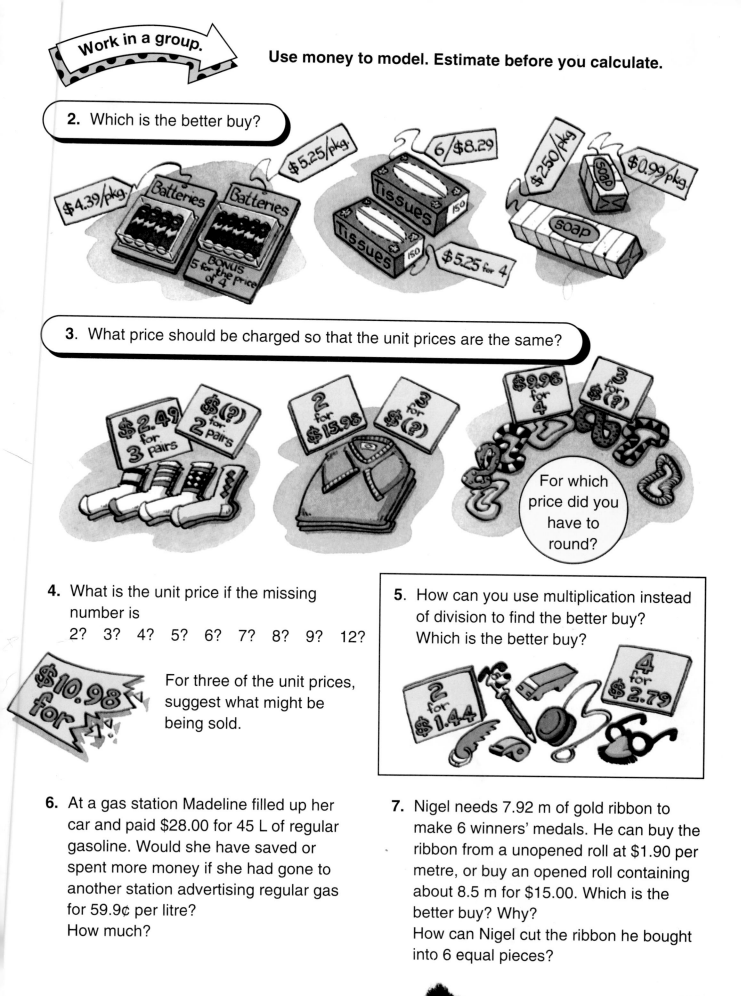

Use money to model. Estimate before you calculate.

2. Which is the better buy?

3. What price should be charged so that the unit prices are the same?

4. What is the unit price if the missing number is
2? 3? 4? 5? 6? 7? 8? 9? 12?

For three of the unit prices, suggest what might be being sold.

5. How can you use multiplication instead of division to find the better buy?
Which is the better buy?

6. At a gas station Madeline filled up her car and paid $28.00 for 45 L of regular gasoline. Would she have saved or spent more money if she had gone to another station advertising regular gas for 59.9¢ per litre?
How much?

7. Nigel needs 7.92 m of gold ribbon to make 6 winners' medals. He can buy the ribbon from a unopened roll at $1.90 per metre, or buy an opened roll containing about 8.5 m for $15.00. Which is the better buy? Why?
How can Nigel cut the ribbon he bought into 6 equal pieces?

Dividing Decimals

There are lots of ways to calculate 7.92 ÷ 6. Here are some. Can you think of any more?

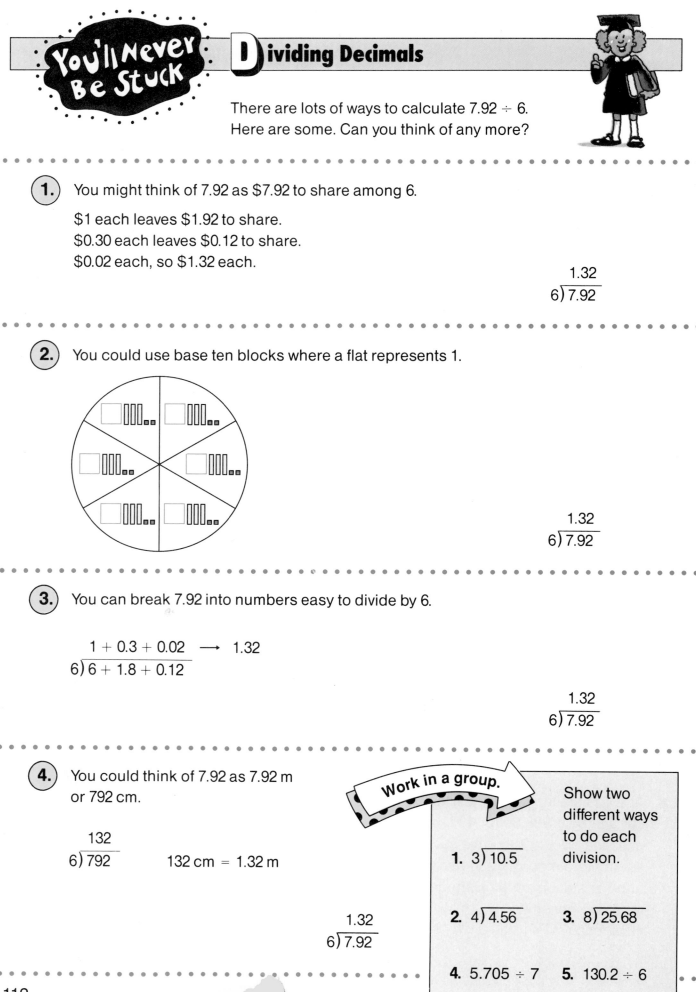

1. You might think of 7.92 as $7.92 to share among 6.

$1 each leaves $1.92 to share.
$0.30 each leaves $0.12 to share.
$0.02 each, so $1.32 each.

$$6\overline{)7.92}\quad 1.32$$

2. You could use base ten blocks where a flat represents 1.

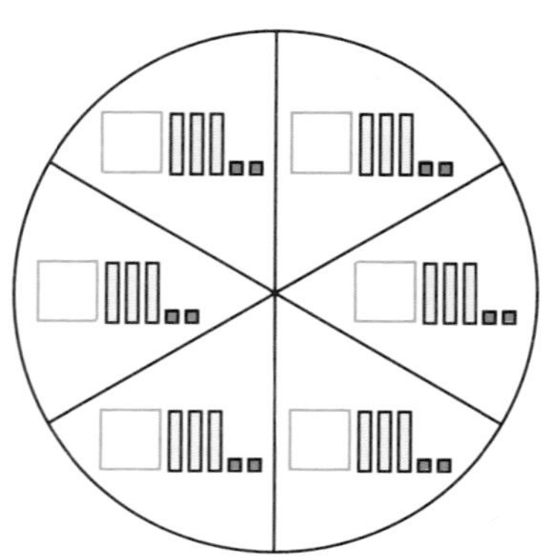

$$6\overline{)7.92}\quad 1.32$$

3. You can break 7.92 into numbers easy to divide by 6.

$$\begin{array}{r} 1 + 0.3 + 0.02 \\ 6\overline{)6 + 1.8 + 0.12} \end{array} \longrightarrow 1.32$$

$$6\overline{)7.92}\quad 1.32$$

4. You could think of 7.92 as 7.92 m or 792 cm.

$$\begin{array}{r} 132 \\ 6\overline{)792} \end{array} \qquad 132 \text{ cm} = 1.32 \text{ m}$$

$$6\overline{)7.92}\quad 1.32$$

Show two different ways to do each division.

1. $3\overline{)10.5}$
2. $4\overline{)4.56}$
3. $8\overline{)25.68}$
4. 5.705 ÷ 7
5. 130.2 ÷ 6

Take Your Pick

JUST DROP IT

To estimate the quotient of a 3-digit number and a 2-digit number, you can drop the ones digit in both numbers.
For example, to estimate 978 ÷ 32, divide 97 by 3.
Try a few times. Check using a calculator.
Is it a good method?

CALCULATING DIVISION

A whole number less than 30 was divided by a 1-digit whole number.

This was the result. **3.2857142**

Are there any 1-digit whole numbers you are certain could not be the divisor?
If so, what are they? Explain. What were the numbers?

GROCERIES

In 1991 the typical Canadian family of four spent $135.45 a week on groceries.
What was the typical daily cost for the family?
What would you expect the typical daily cost was for a family of three?

7, 11, AND 17

Write a 3-digit number.
Repeat the digits to make a 6-digit number.
Divide the 6-digit number by 7.
Then divide that quotient by 11.
Divide the last quotient by 13.
What do you notice?
Try this with some other 3-digit numbers.

WHAT'S MISSING?

The same digit replaces all the squares.
Another digit replaces all the circles.
What are the missing digits?

Make up other problems. Post them on the bulletin board for your classmates to solve.

Solving a Problem by Guessing and Testing

Try this problem before going on.

CATCH UP

A bike is travelling at 35 km per hour. A car travelling at 80 km per hour is 180 km behind the bike. How long will it be before the car catches up to the bike?

Sylvie's group solved this problem by guessing and testing.

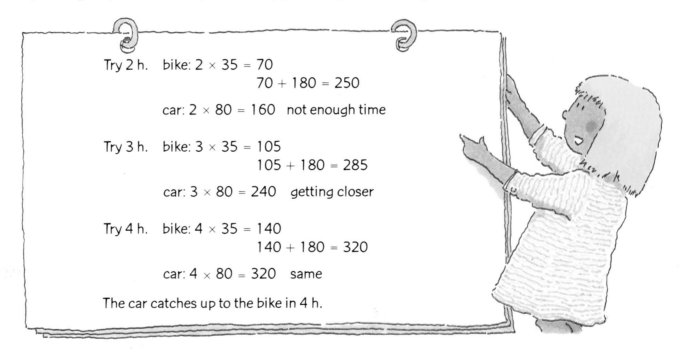

Try 2 h. bike: $2 \times 35 = 70$
$70 + 180 = 250$
car: $2 \times 80 = 160$ not enough time

Try 3 h. bike: $3 \times 35 = 105$
$105 + 180 = 285$
car: $3 \times 80 = 240$ getting closer

Try 4 h. bike: $4 \times 35 = 140$
$140 + 180 = 320$
car: $4 \times 80 = 320$ same

The car catches up to the bike in 4 h.

Solve these problems by guessing and testing.

TWO DIGITS

Find digits to replace A, B, and C.

$$\begin{array}{r} AA \\ \times\ AA \\ \hline BCB \end{array}$$

MEASURE IT

Suppose you have only a 3 L container, a 5 L container, and a large container of unknown capacity, all without any markings. How could you measure 7 L? 4 L?

NINES

Find a pair of 2-digit factors where the product has
- one 9
- two 9s

Practising What You've Learned

1. There are 448 tiles in a rectangular array. How many tiles are in each row if there are 8 rows? 14 rows? 16 rows?

2. Estimate each product or quotient. Tell what you did.
   - 9 × 15.135
   - 458.1 × 23
   - 789.4 ÷ 36

3. Describe a situation which might lead to each computation.
   - 15 × 365
   - 285 ÷ 60

4. Find the unknown digits.
   - ? 536 ÷ 15 is about 300
   - ? 4 × ? 36 is about 3300

5. Complete the table.

Number of steps	1	2	4	8	16
Height (cm)	18	?	?	?	?

Describe the pattern in each row.
About how many steps are as tall as you are?

6. Eddie divided 439 by 7 to find the number of weeks in 439 d. Is there an exact number of weeks?
If not, about how many days are left over?

7. How many doughnuts are in 98 boxes of 6?

8. 435 children enrolled for baseball. How many teams of 12 players can be formed? How many more children are needed to form 1 more team?

9. When Lou's mom leaves for work, the odometer on her car reads 34 527.0 km. She drives 45.3 km each way. What will the odometer read when she arrives at work? returns home?

10. In the last two months, Angie ran 275 km. Based on a 30-day month, how many kilometres did she run each day? Round your answer to the nearest tenth of a kilometre.

11. Travis is 1.5 times as tall as his sister who is 102 cm tall. How tall is Travis?

Playing Games for Practice

Play this game with another player.

Three in a Row

- Spin both spinners and divide.
- Place a counter in the square for the quotient on the gameboard if it's there and not already occupied.
- Take turns. Use a different color of counters.
- The winner is the first player to get 3 in a row, column, or diagonal.

Example

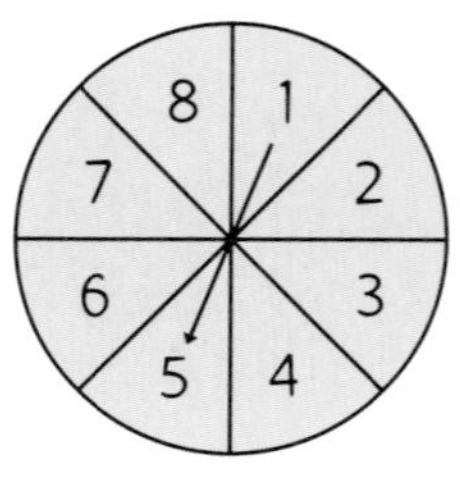

Dividend

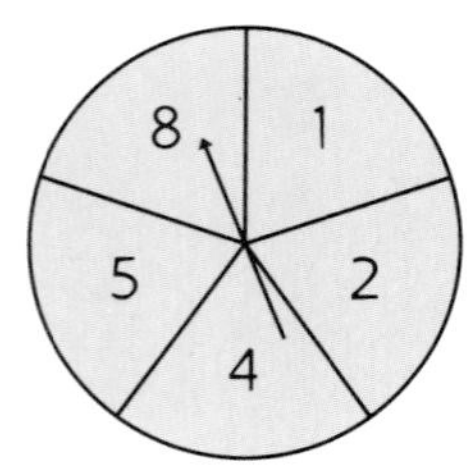

Divisor

$$8\overline{)5.000}\quad = 0.625$$

0.75	0.125	0.6	1.0	1.5
0.25	4.0	3.0	3.5	0.625
0.5	0.4	7.0	5.0	2.0
1.2	0.8	0.875	1.25	6.0
2.5	1.4	0.2	0.375	1.75

Play this game in a group of 2, 3, or 4.

Pick Three for Four

- Make these multiplying and dividing frames.

  ? × ? . ? ?) ? . ?

- Use aces as 1s and remove the face cards and 10s from a deck of cards.
- Shuffle the other cards, 1s to 9s, and deal each player three cards.
- Arrange your cards in either frame, trying to get an answer that is as close to 4 as possible.
- Score 1 point if your answer is between 3 and 5.
- Take turns shuffling and dealing.
- The first player with 5 points wins.

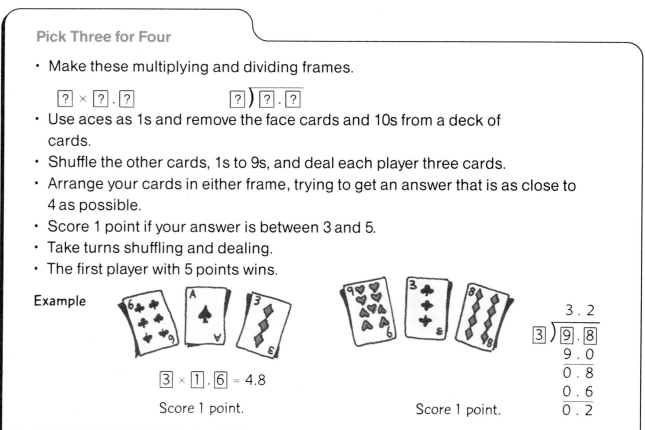

Example

3 × 1 . 6 = 4.8

Score 1 point.

Score 1 point.

```
     3 . 2
3 ) 9 . 8
    9 . 0
    0 . 8
    0 . 6
    0 . 2
```

Take Your Pick

LEGO BLOCKS

About 6 million Lego blocks are made each year. How far out in space would a stack of that many blocks go?

FINAL DIGIT

What is the final digit of the product when 89 sevens are multiplied together? Hint: Use a pattern.

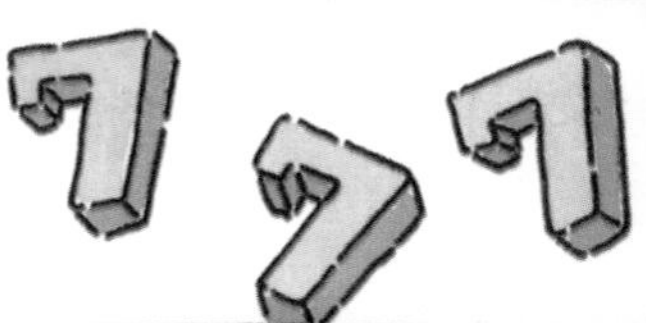

GROWING

The adult heigth of a male is about 1.23 times his height at age 11, or about 1.19 times his height at age 12.

The adult height of a female is about 1.14 times her height at age 11, or about 1.07 times her height at age 12.

How do you think these numbers were found? What is your height? Predict your adult height.

PATTERNS

Examine the whole number parts of the products. What do you notice?

1.2 x 3 2.3 x 4 3.4 x 5 4.5 x 6

Continue the pattern. What happens?

BIRTH RATES

There are about 106 boys born for every 100 girls. How many boys would you expect for 3500 girls?

Make up other problems. Post them on the bulletin board for your classmates to solve.

Showing What You Know

1. Explain how you could do each calculation in your head.
   - 2440 × 0.5
   - 34 567 ÷ 1000
   - 4422.22 ÷ 22
   - 4.005 × 12

2. How would you arrange 2, 4, and 5 in ? × ? . ? to get the greatest product? the least? How much greater is the greatest than the least?

3. How many CDs were likely sold if almost $200 was received? How many at the regular price of $21.99 would need to be sold to receive about the same amount?

4. To estimate 36 × 26, Dominique multiplied 9 × 100. Explain her thinking.

5. Estimate the savings. Explain what you did and why.

6. To estimate 2457 × 36, Chris multiplied 2000 and 40. Tell how he knows that his estimate ends with 4 zeroes.

7. The ratio of the sides of two squares is 5 to 1. What is the ratio of the area of the larger square to that of the smaller one?

8. How is each dividend related to the first one? Use the first division to find the other quotients.

   436 ÷ 8 = 54 + R4

   444 = 8 + 436 so $8\overline{)444}$ is the same as $8\overline{)436 + 8}$ (54 + 1 + R4)

   - 444 ÷ 8
   - 1236 ÷ 8
   - 516 ÷ 8
   - 872 ÷ 8

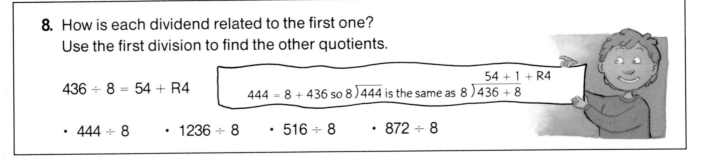

9. Use a calculator to find the greatest number of $5 bills you could receive from a $378 cheque. How do you know that is $3 short?

10. What's the greatest product possible when you multiply two 2-digit numbers?

11. What's the least quotient possible when you divide a 4-digit number by a 2-digit number?

Thinking Back . . .

Which would you use to estimate
3546 ÷ 34? Why?
3600 ÷ 30
3400 ÷ 34
3500 ÷ 35
Would your estimate be high or low? Why?

How can you use money to show how to divide 1 by 5?

How are dividing decimals and dividing whole numbers alike? different?

Do you find it easier to multiply in your head by 15 or by 14? Tell why.

Would you estimate or calculate an exact answer to find

- how many hours it would take to travel 552 km?
- each person's share of expenses for a trip?
- the cost of 5 hamburgers and 5 drinks?

Tell why.

What questions do you still have about multiplication and division?

7

Examining Motion

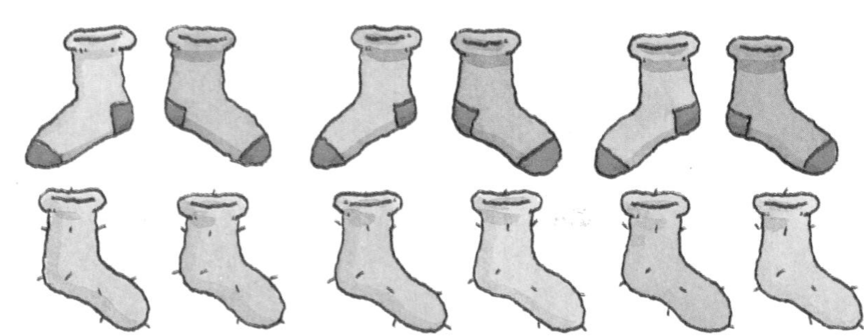

▶

Which row of socks shows slides? flips?

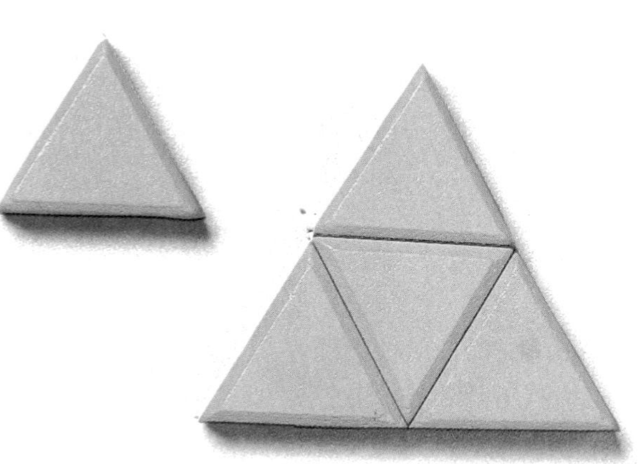

▶

Would you describe the small and large triangles as congruent? Why?

Continue the pattern and make another triangle. Build other shapes using a different type of pattern block.

◀ Trace a shape from this basket-weaving pattern. Move the tracing to decide where a sliding or a flipping motion is suggested by this pattern.

Geometry

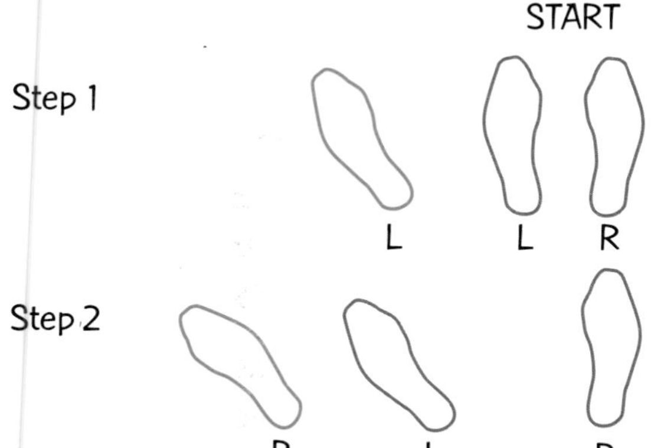

Try these steps of the ancient dance, Branle.
Describe the motions you used.

Make up two other dance steps.
Sketch footprints for them.
Have a classmate try them and describe the motions.

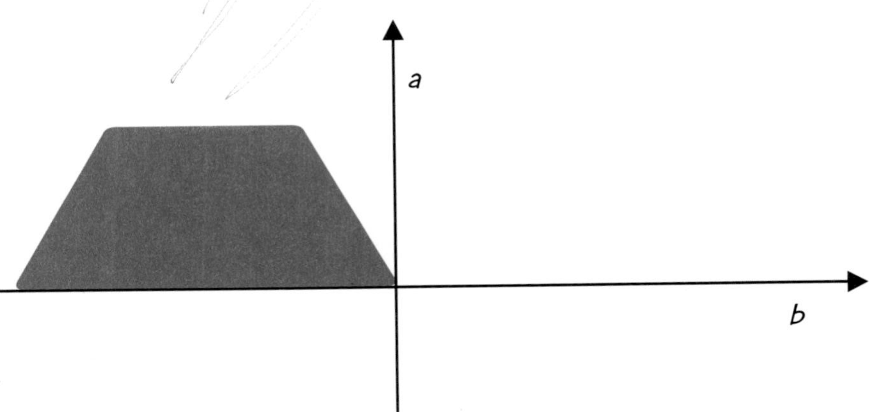

Place a trapezoid pattern block as shown.
Flip it in line *a*.
Show and describe a single motion that results in the same final image.

Investigate how different shapes look when they are reflected in shiny curved surfaces.
Make sketches to show others.

Arrange these fractions and decimals from least to greatest.

$\frac{99}{100}$ 1.05 $\frac{3}{4}$ 1.001 $\frac{1}{2}$ 0.9 1.1

Which is closest to 1?

Plotting Diagrams

Sliding shapes

A plotter arm **slides** along paper by following rules sent to it by a computer.

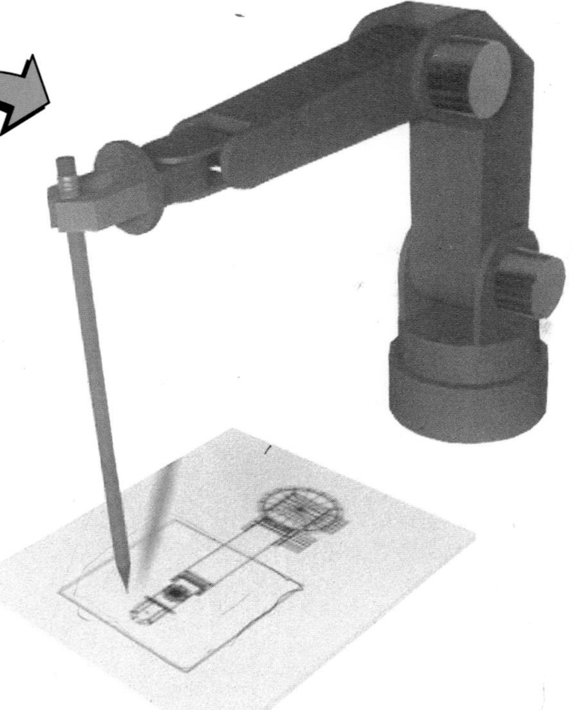

It appears as if a plotter arm copied the blue triangle by sliding it according to the **rule right 4, up 2** or **(R4, U2).** The red triangle is the **slide image.**

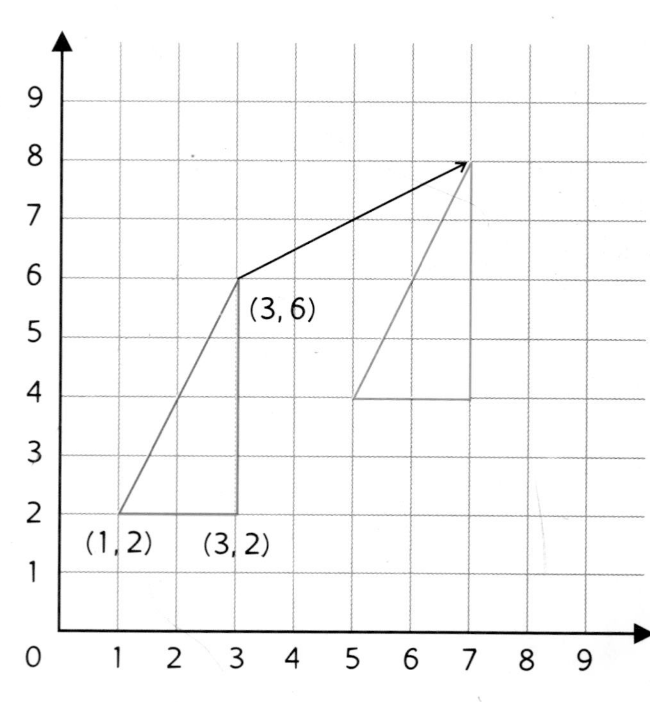

What do you notice about

- the coordinates of the corresponding or matching vertices of the blue and red triangles?
- the size and the shape of the blue and red triangles?

What rule would slide the arm back from the red triangle to the blue one?

Use grid paper.

1. Copy the blue triangle from the bottom of page 122.
   Locate its slide image using each rule. Tell what you notice.
   (R1, U1) (R2, U2) (R3, U3)

2. Draw a different triangle. Slide it (R1, U3). Slide that image (R2, U1).
   Then slide that image (L3, D4).
   How could you have predicted the location of the final image?
   Would it matter if the rules were followed in a different order? Explain.

3. Draw any quadrilateral. Use any slide arrow or rule to locate a slide image.
   Draw a line from each vertex of your original quadrilateral to the corresponding vertex of its slide image. Tell what you notice.

4. A triangle has vertices at (1, 1), (3, 1), and (3, 4).
   Another has vertices at (5, 4), (5, 2), and (8, 2).
   Draw both triangles. Could they be slide images of one another?
   Explain why or why not.

5. A triangle has vertices at (1, 2), (3, 3), and (2, 6).
   One vertex of a slide image is at (7, 5).
   What slide arrows or rules are possible?
   What slide images are possible?

6. The rule (R3, D3) locates the same slide image as (R1, D5) followed by (R2, U2). Find four other pairs of rules that locate the same slide image as (R3, D3).

7. Draw a triangle. Then double each number in the coordinates of each vertex. For example, (2, 3) becomes (4, 6). Draw a triangle with the new vertices. Are the triangles slide images of each other?

8. How are slides (R2, U2) and (R8, U8) alike? different?

Consider these fractions in pairs. Tell how they are like each other, but different from the other one.

$\frac{4}{5}$ $\frac{7}{8}$ $\frac{12}{15}$

Drawing Solids and Skeletons

Using slides to sketch 3-D shapes

Stack a pile of identical pattern blocks.

What shape is the top face? the bottom face? each side face?

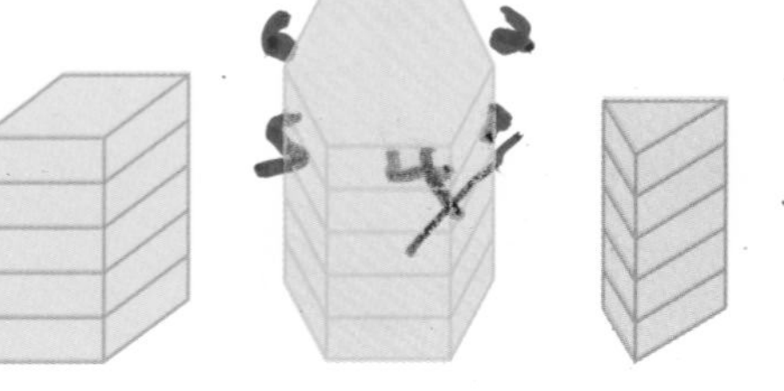

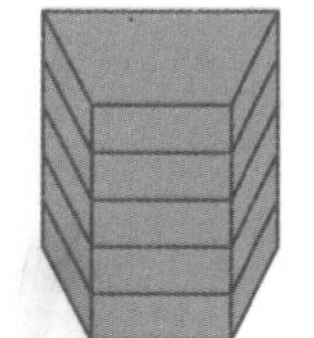

These solid shapes are all prisms because they have identical top and bottom faces, joined by rectangular side faces.

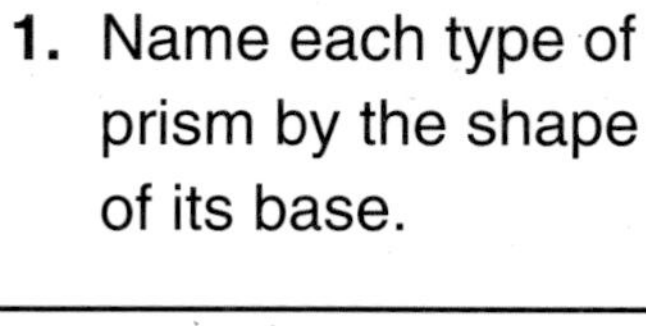

1. Name each type of prism by the shape of its base.

You can sketch a diagram of a prism by

- tracing around the pattern block on blank paper
- sliding the pattern block and tracing around it again
- joining the matching corners (vertices) with a ruler to form the edges

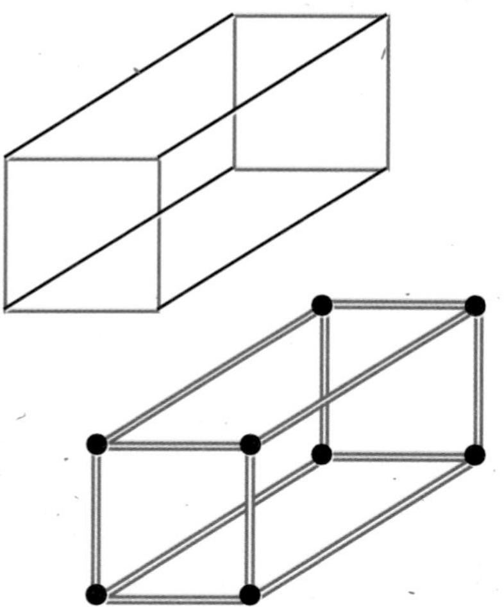

2. Draw a square prism. Draw a dot at each corner.
   How many dots (vertices) are there?
   How many lines (edges) did you draw?
   How is your drawing like that of a **skeleton** made with pipe cleaners and balls of plasticine?

3. On blank paper draw a diagram of a
   - triangular prism
   - hexagonal prism
   - trapezoidal prism
   - rhomboidal prism

4. For each prism, record the number of faces, edges, and vertices in the chart.

Type of prism	Type and number of faces	Edges	Vertices
square prism	4 rectangular side faces + 2 square end faces	12	8
triangular prism			

5. How is this drawing like that of a **solid** made out of plasticine?

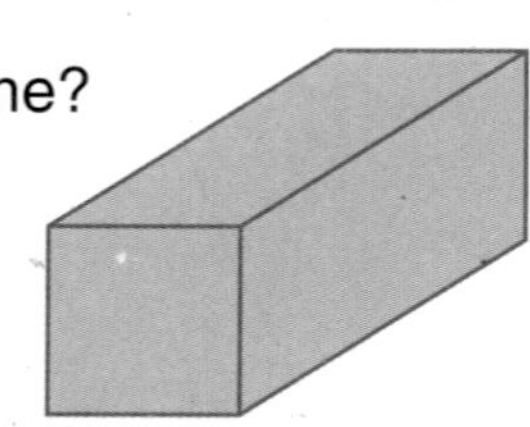

You can sketch a diagram of a prism by using different types of dot paper.

6. Explain how each shape is drawn. Describe the sliding motion in each diagram.

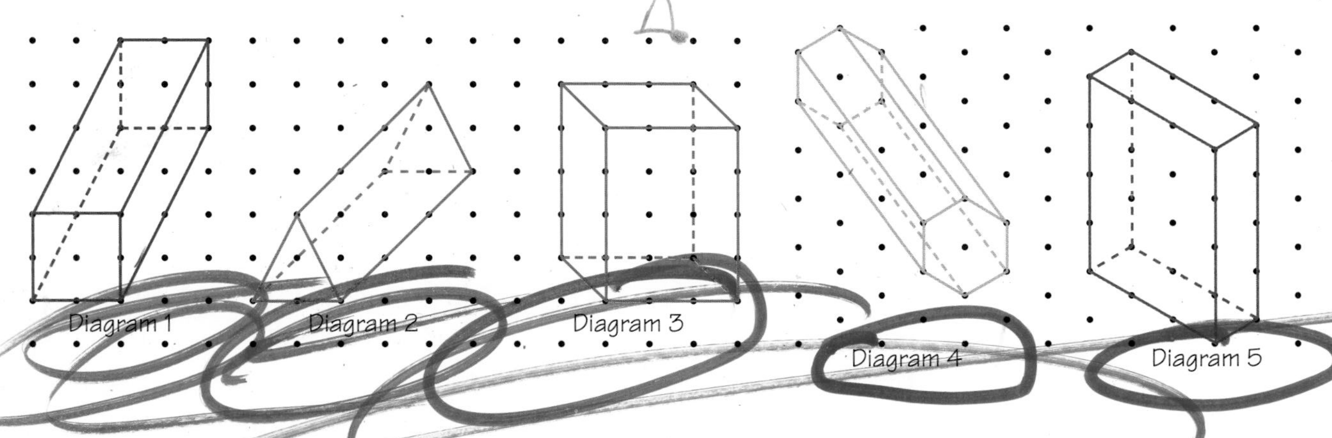

7. How does changing the angle and/or the distance of the slide for the opposite face affect the appearance of the prism?

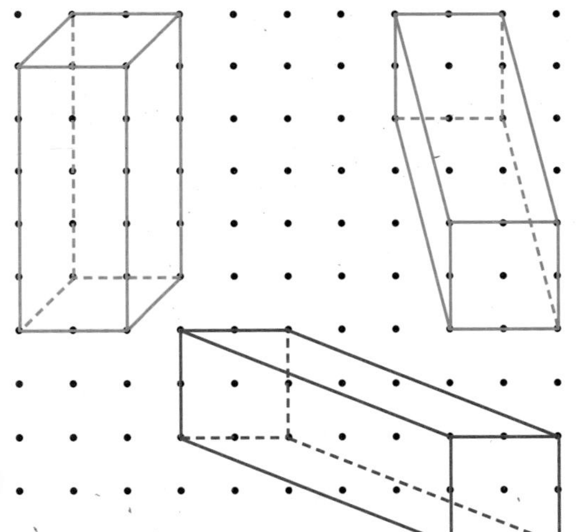

8. Which diagram, 3 or 5, do you think is better for accurately drawing the dimensions of a single-serving cereal box that is 9 cm wide, 3 cm deep, and 12 cm high? Justify your choice.

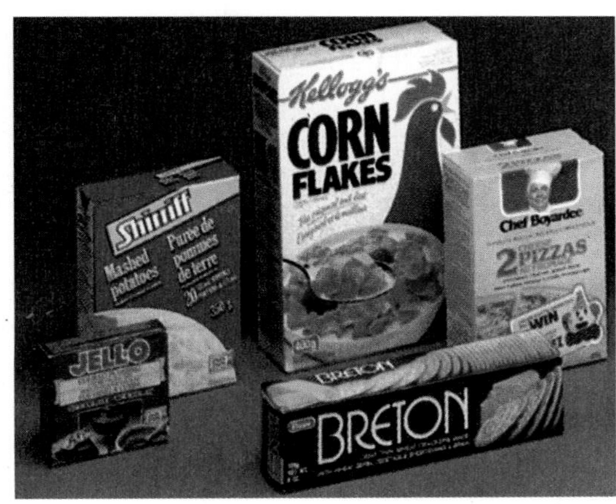

9. A larger box of the same cereal is 3 times as wide, deep, and high. Draw the actual size of both boxes on a large plain sheet of paper.

10. Measure a box, then draw a diagram of it on dot paper.
Measure a cube, then draw a diagram of it on dot paper. Why is it a special type of rectangular prism?

11. How is drawing a cylinder the same as drawing a prism? How is it different? Is using dot paper helpful?

12. Try drawing solids that end in a point - such as cones, or square pyramids (or triangular or hexagonal pyramids). Explain your method.

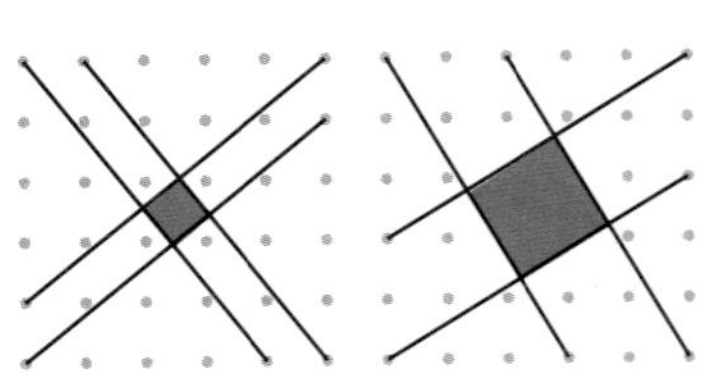

Continue this pattern.
Are the purple shapes squares?
Why or why not?

Comparing Opposite Places

Flipping shapes

Going back upstairs, Toby saw himself in a mirror. Something looked very strange. What was wrong? He put out his hand to touch the mirror – and walked right through it! He was out in the street. It seemed like the same old street, but was it?

from *Through the Magic Mirror*
by Anthony Browne

The path that Toby walks is the **flip image** of the same path in the real world. Suppose Toby walks this path. How could you locate the flip image of it?

mirror

Pierre traced the path and the flip line onto paper. Then he folded the paper along the flip line. What could he do next to locate the flip image?

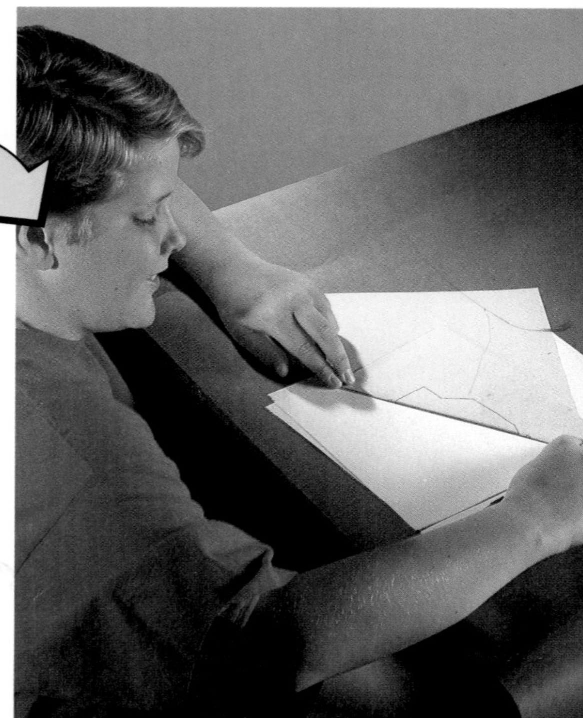

Trace the path and locate the flip image. Draw a line from each vertex of the path to the corresponding vertex of its flip image. Measure the angles formed by these lines and the flip line. What do you notice?

Measure the distance along the lines just drawn from each vertex to the flip line. What do you notice?

How can you use this information to find the flip image of this path?

Trace each diagram. Use a ruler and protractor. Then check by folding.

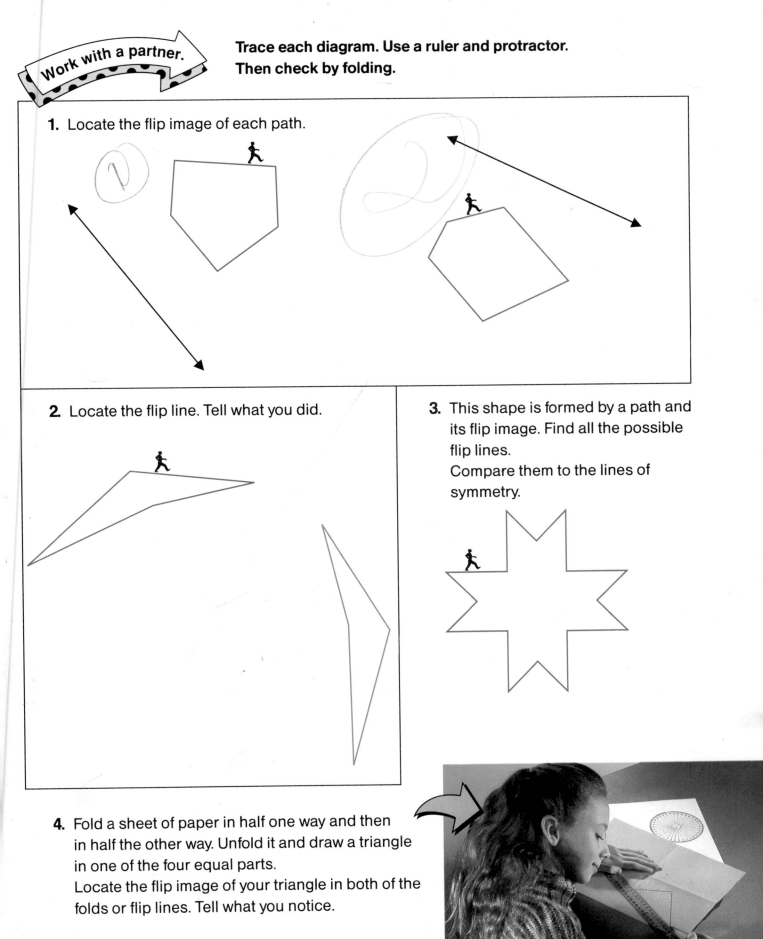

1. Locate the flip image of each path.

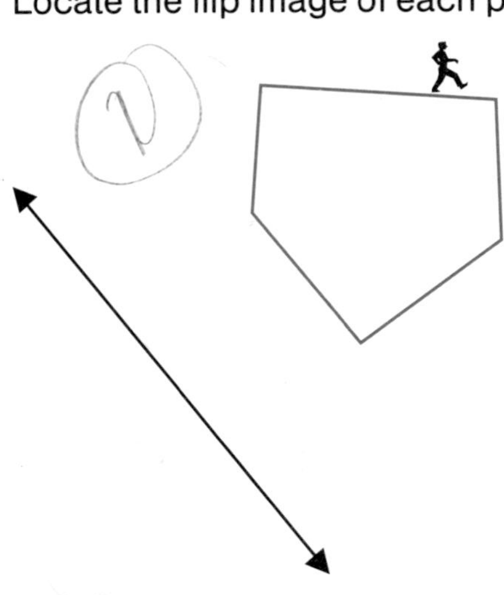

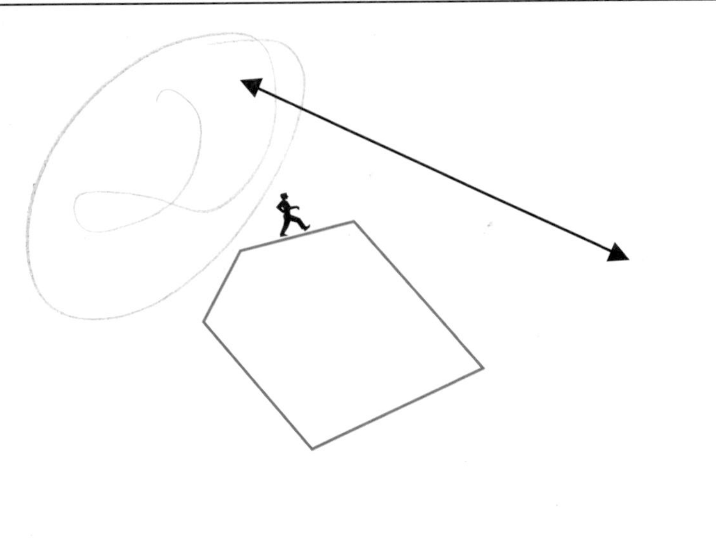

2. Locate the flip line. Tell what you did.

3. This shape is formed by a path and its flip image. Find all the possible flip lines.
   Compare them to the lines of symmetry.

4. Fold a sheet of paper in half one way and then in half the other way. Unfold it and draw a triangle in one of the four equal parts.
   Locate the flip image of your triangle in both of the folds or flip lines. Tell what you notice.

5. Draw a quadrilateral path and a flip line for another pair of students to locate the flip image.

Examining Line Symmetry

Applying flips to line symmetry in polygons

Trace each diagram on a separate piece of tracing paper, and fold on the dotted line. Then turn over the paper and trace the shape again. Unfold the paper.

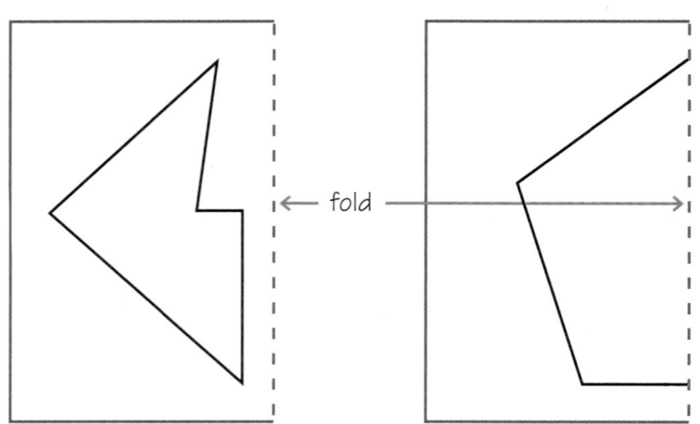

1. Describe the flipping motion of the shape about the flip line. When is a flip line also a line of symmetry?

The shape in the first diagram is a pentagon because it has 5 sides. The unfolded shape from the second diagram is a **regular** pentagon.

2. What do you think **regular** means? (Hint: Measure the sides and the angles. What do you notice?)

3. How can you fold a rectangular piece of paper so that one half matches the other half? How many lines of symmetry does the rectangle have? Do you think a diagonal of a rectangle is a line of symmetry? Fold to check.

diagonals

4. Repeat the procedure in question 3 using a square piece of paper. Are the diagonals of a square lines of symmetry? How many lines of symmetry does a square have? Why can a square be called a regular quadrilateral?

5. Fold your tracing paper model of a regular pentagon to determine where all the lines of symmetry are.

6. Use all the pattern block pieces. Which of the pieces are regular polygons? Explain.
Determine how many lines of symmetry each shape has and record this data with the others in the chart below.

Shape	Number of lines of symmetry
trapezoid	
blue rhombus	
tan rhombus	
rectangle	2
equilateral triangle	
square	4
regular pentagon	5
regular hexagon	

7. Find the number of lines of symmetry in this regular heptagon. Then extend the chart in question 6 and record your result.

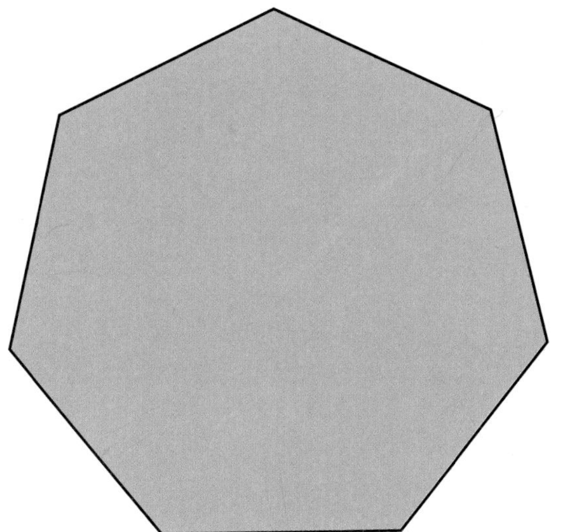

8. Predict how many lines of symmetry there are in a regular octagon.

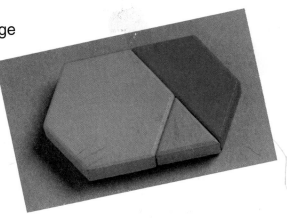

9. Form a shape by combining two identical pattern blocks so that they share a common side. Is a sliding or flipping motion involved? Trace around the shape.
How many lines of symmetry does your shape have?
Does combining pairs of identical shapes usually change the number of lines of symmetry?

10. Make a design that has line symmetry by combining any number of pattern blocks.
How many lines of symmetry does your design have?
Can you create a design with more than 6 lines of symmetry?

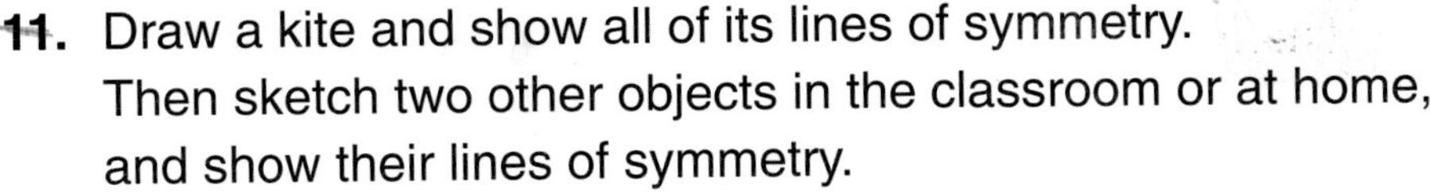

11. Draw a kite and show all of its lines of symmetry.
Then sketch two other objects in the classroom or at home, and show their lines of symmetry.

About 280 million cans of one brand of cola are sold each day. About how many days does it take to sell enough cans to make a stack that would reach the moon, which is about 385 000 km away?

Looking at Illusions

Examining congruent shapes

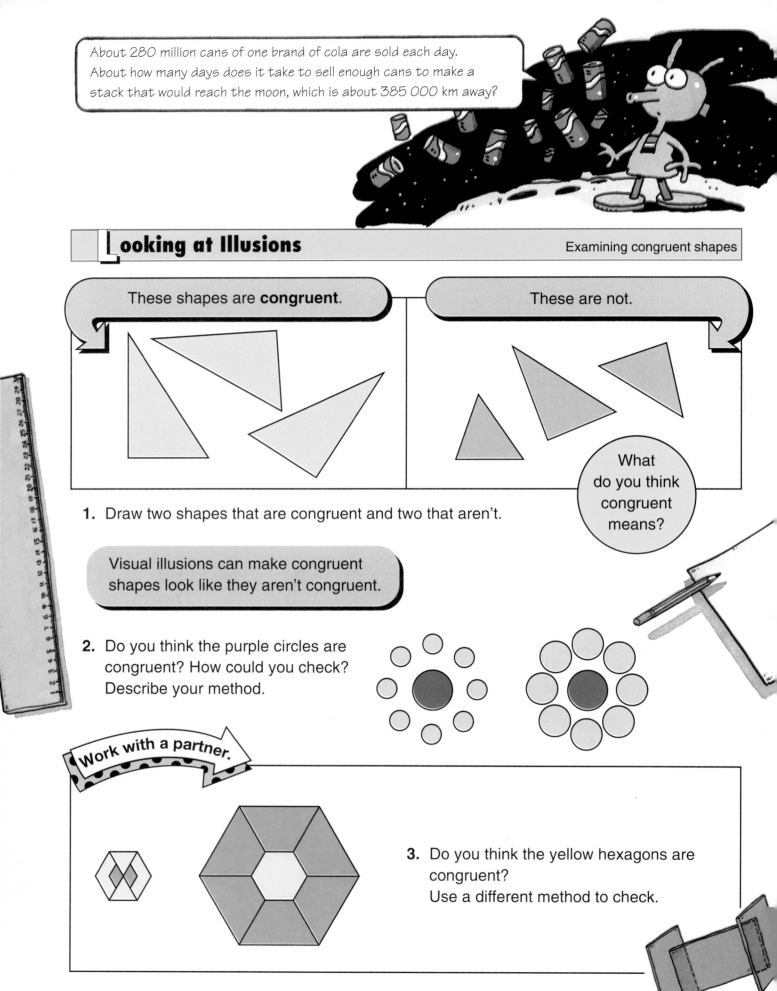

These shapes are **congruent**.

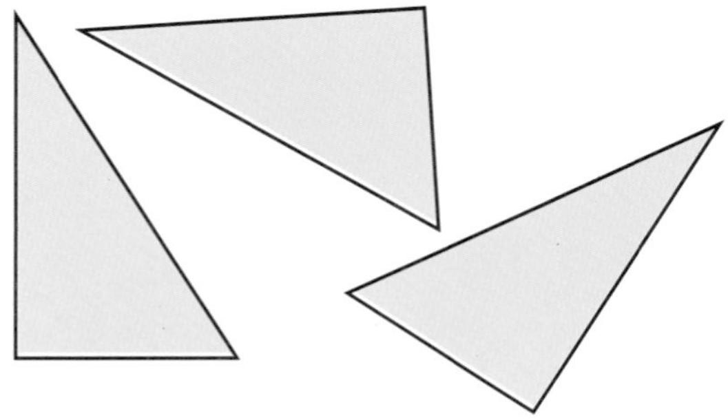

These are not.

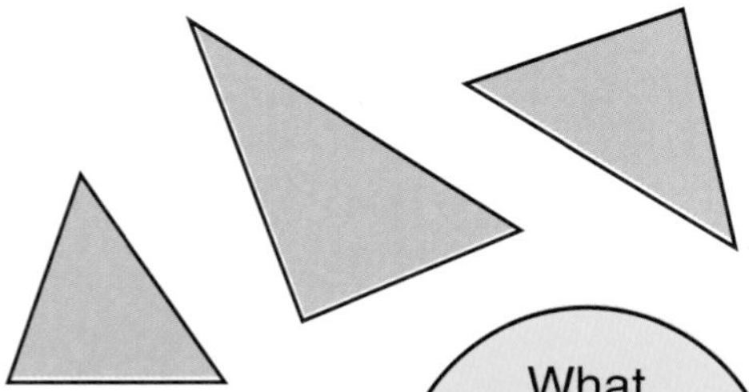

What do you think congruent means?

1. Draw two shapes that are congruent and two that aren't.

Visual illusions can make congruent shapes look like they aren't congruent.

2. Do you think the purple circles are congruent? How could you check? Describe your method.

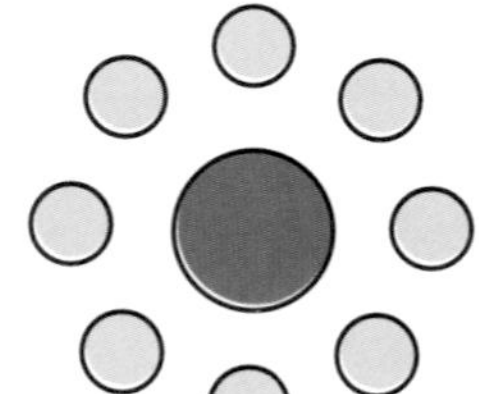

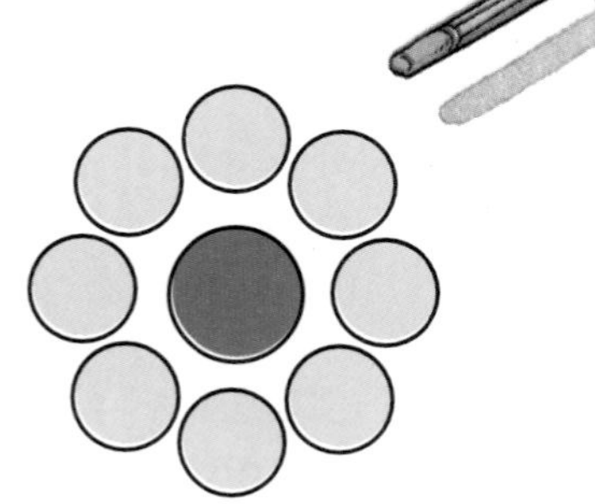

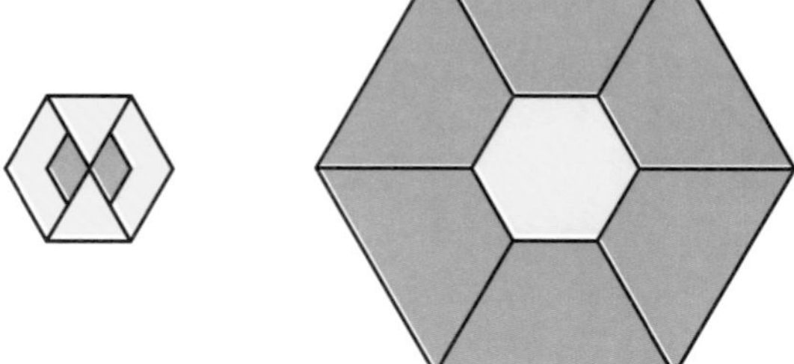

3. Do you think the yellow hexagons are congruent? Use a different method to check.

4. Do you think the blue triangles are congruent? Use a different method to check.

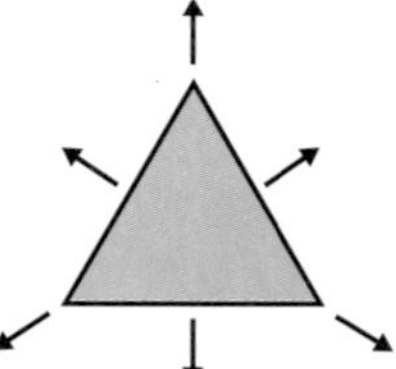

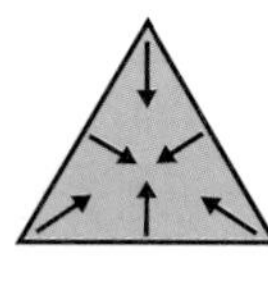

5. Use your favorite method to determine which pairs of squares are congruent. Which pairs cannot be checked easily with a Mira?

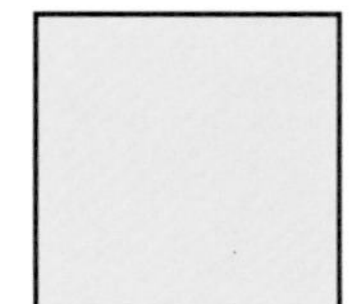

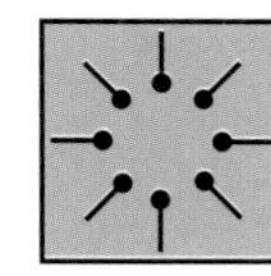

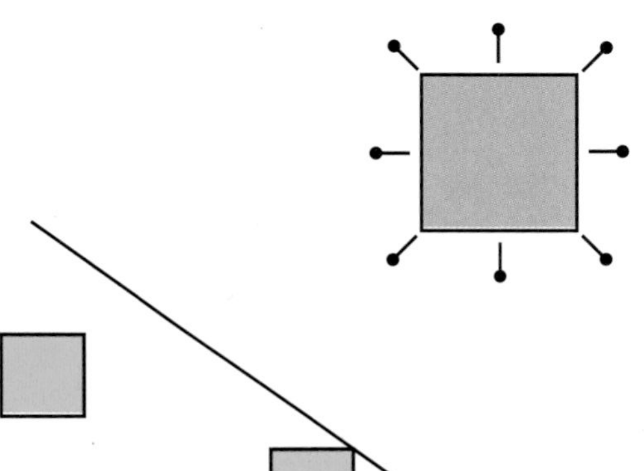

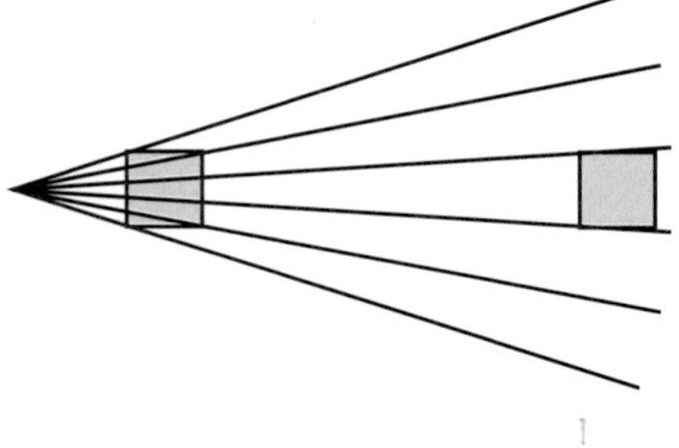

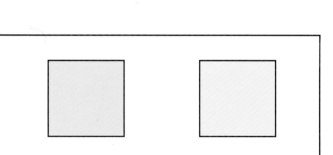

6. What is it about the diagrams that helps to create the illusions?

7. Are these characters congruent? Check. yes

8. Make your own visual illusion.

A B C
× C
C D E
Replace each letter with a different number to make this true. Can you do it more than one way?

Plotting Designs

Combining motions on a coordinate grid

Dana plotted and joined these sets of points on a coordinate grid:
A (1, 9), B (5, 9), C (5, 13) and D (9, 9), E (9, 5), F (13, 5).

Show and describe how to move the blue triangle to the red triangle using

- a slide and a flip
- a flip and a slide
- 2 or more flips

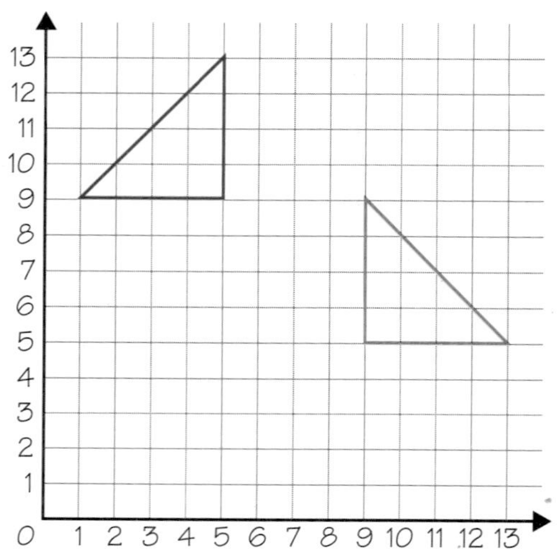

First I slid it (R4, D4). Now I will flip it in the vertical line for 9.
How many different ways can you find?

Use coordinate grid paper.

1. Use the same combinations of motions as listed above. Show and describe how to move the blue triangle to the red triangle. Are any of these combinations not possible?

2. Draw a polygon on a grid. Use any combination of motions listed above to move it. Give your diagram to another pair of students to decide which combination you used.

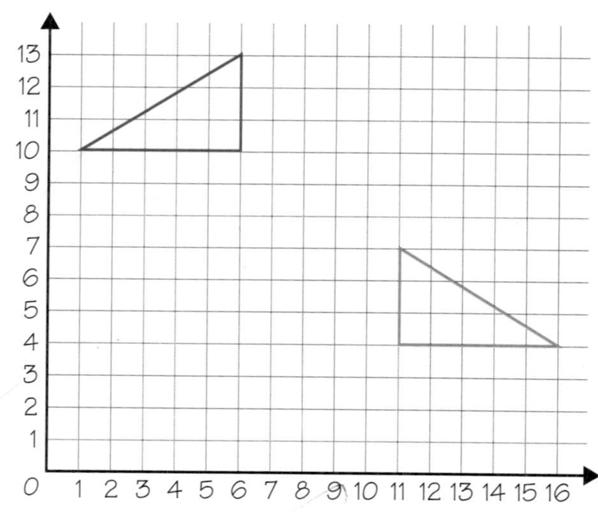

3. Plot and join these points: A (0, 3), B (6, 3), and C (6, 6). Use this triangle to show how 2 flips gives the same final image as a slide.
Then make up a similar problem using a quadrilateral instead of a triangle.

4. Recreate this design by

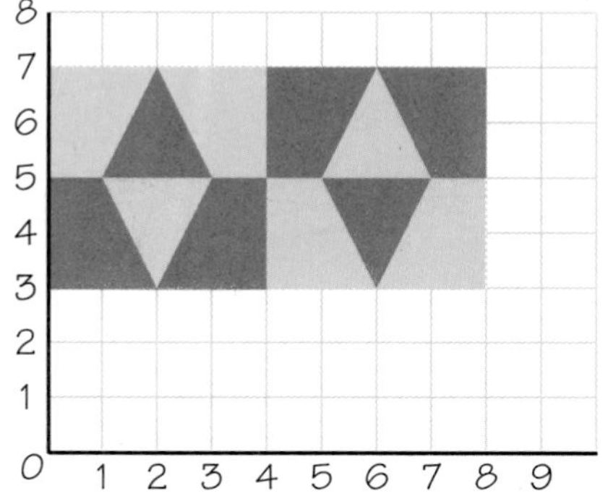

- plotting points A (1, 5), B (3, 5), and C (2,7) to form triangle ABC
- flipping the triangle about the line joining (0, 5) and (8, 5)
- flipping both triangles about the line joining (4, 3) and (4, 7)
- drawing a rectangle so that the two flip lines are its lines of symmetry.

How else could you move from one triangle to another?
Describe this design by plotting and moving the trapezoid instead of the triangle.

5. What combinations of motions do you see in this design?

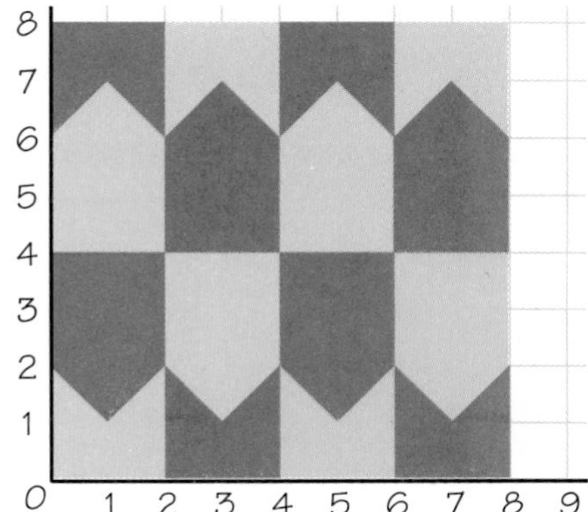

Write instructions for plotting the vertices of one of the pentagons. Then tell how to slide and/or flip the shape to make this design.

Try giving your instructions to an older student or family member to see if they can recreate the design.

6. Plot these points A (2, 3), B (4, 5), and C (2, 7) to form triangle ABC.
Flip the triangle about the vertical line through point B, and label the corresponding points A' and C'. (Read as A prime and C prime.)
Join C to C'. Join A to A'.
What type of polygon does the entire design form? How many lines of symmetry does it have?

7. Plot and join these points: A (1, 3), B (4, 3), C (6, 5), and D (3, 5).
What shape did you form?
Flip the shape about side BC. What type of polygon do both shapes form?

There is a special name for this type of shape - a chevron.
How many lines of symmetry does it have?

Make a design by flipping the chevron about side DC, then flipping both chevrons about the vertical line through point C.
How many lines of symmetry do you think the entire design has?
Cut and fold the design to check.

Take Your Pick

SLIDING ARROWS

Copy the diagram onto dot paper. Trace it and slide the tracing (R5, U0). How would you describe the position of the arrows in relation to each other?

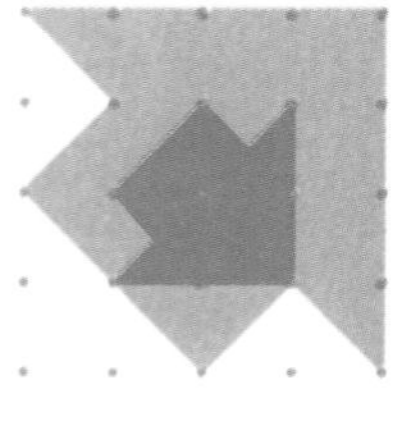

SWITCHING ORDER

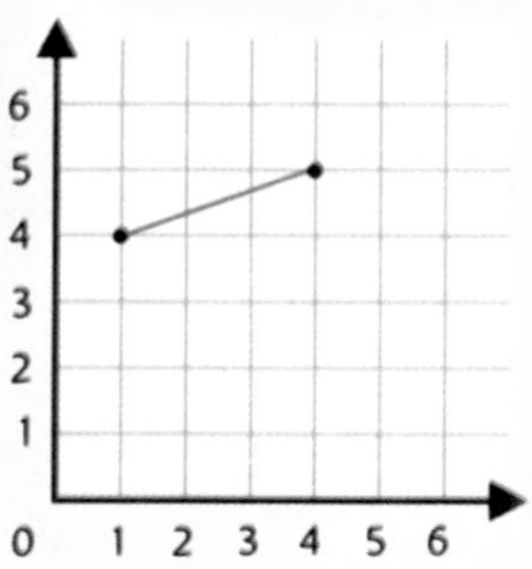

Draw this line on a grid. Switch the order of the numbers in the coordinates of each end point.

Plot the new end points and draw the new line. Is the second line a slide or fllip image of the first one? Try it with other lines. Tell what you notice.

FLIP AND SLIDE

Copy the diagram onto grid paper. Locate the filp image of *P* in line *a*. Slide the image point (R5, U0). Draw a line to join *P* and the final image. Measure the length of that line from each end point to the flip line. What do you notice? Try flipping and sliding other points. Do you always get similar results?

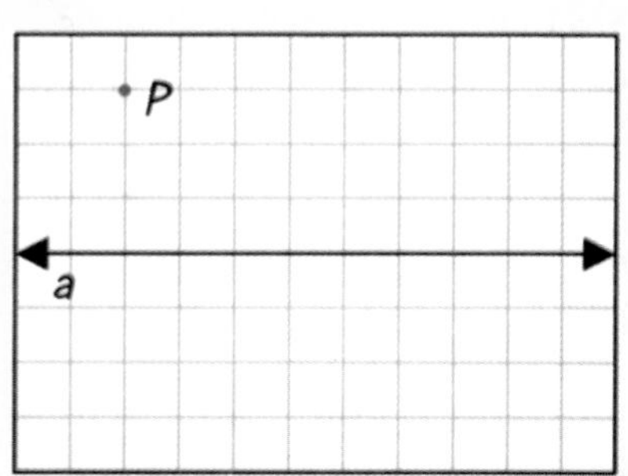

MIRROR, MIRROR, . . .

Investigate automobile side mirrors, makeup or shaving mirrors, and store security mirrors. Report on how they change the apperance of objects.

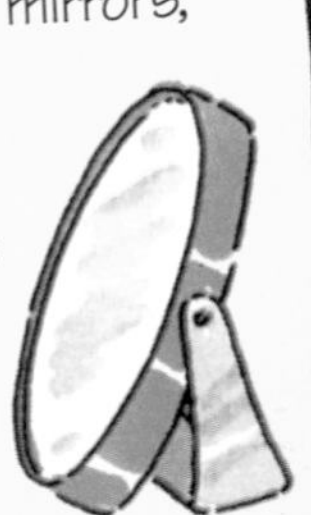

MOVING QUARTERS

The upper quarter is slid so that it is directly under the lower one. What slides might have been made?

Make up other problems. Post them on the bulletin board for your classmates to solve.

Solving a Problem by Working Backward

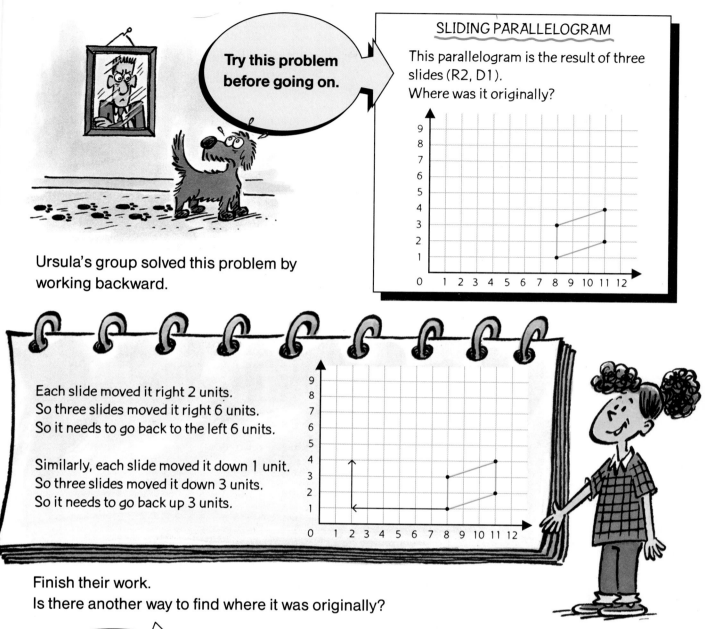

SLIDING PARALLELOGRAM

This parallelogram is the result of three slides (R2, D1).
Where was it originally?

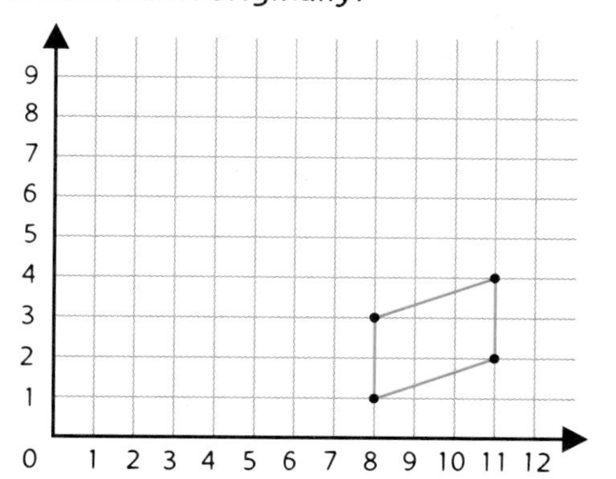

Ursula's group solved this problem by working backward.

Each slide moved it right 2 units.
So three slides moved it right 6 units.
So it needs to go back to the left 6 units.

Similarly, each slide moved it down 1 unit.
So three slides moved it down 3 units.
So it needs to go back up 3 units.

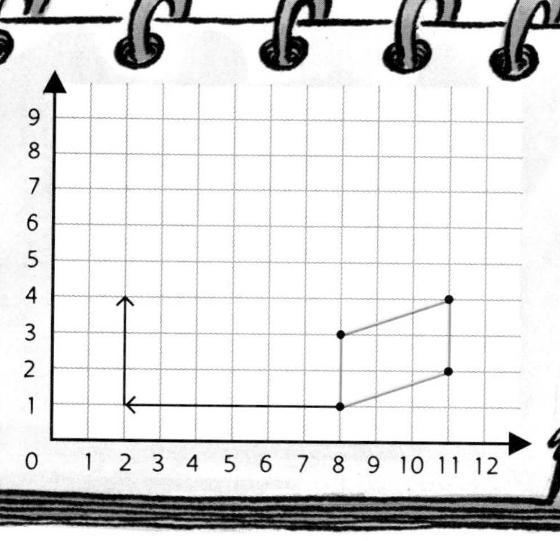

Finish their work.
Is there another way to find where it was originally?

Solve each problem by working backward.

TWO FLIPS

The point (2, 2) is the result of the point (6, 8) being flipped and then its image being flipped.
Locate the two flip lines.
Tell what you did.

SLIDING

A line with end points (5, 2) and (7, 4) is the result of a line being slid (R3, U1).
What are the end points of the original line?

HOTCAKES

Each day twice as many hotcakes were sold as the day before. If 256 hotcakes were sold on March 18, on what day was only one hotcake sold?

Practising What You've Learned

1. Which pairs of points are images of each other when flipped in line *a*? Why?

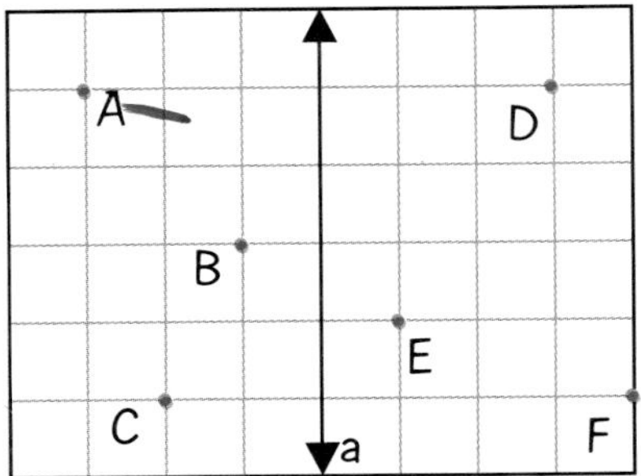

2. To enter a 7 after entering 3, your finger slides (L2, D2) from 3 to 7. What slides are used to enter the digits of a phone number you call often?

3. Locate the image of this pentagon when slid (R3, D2).

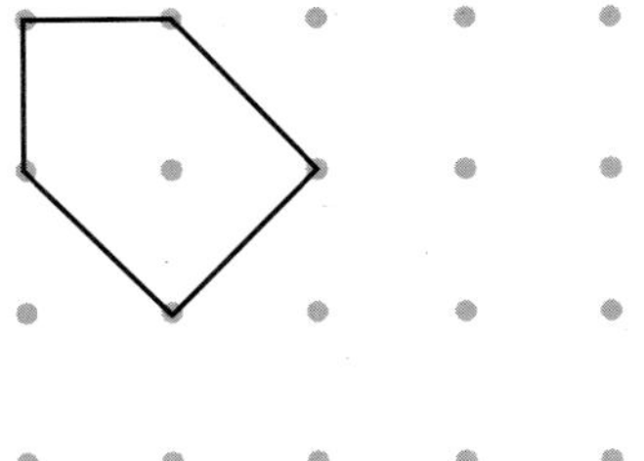

4. This quadrilateral is flipped in line *a*. What are the coordinates of the vertices of the image?

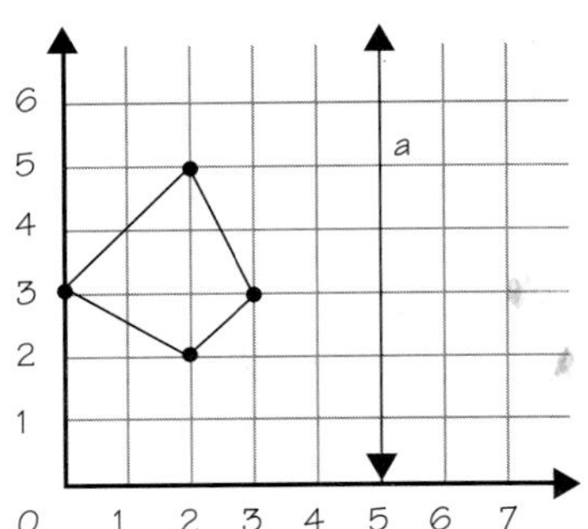

5. Tell how to flip pattern blocks so that the images look like slide images.

6. Show how to move point (2, 4) to (8, 8) using two slides.

7. Locate a flip line so that the peak of the roof does not move when the house is flipped in that line. Draw the flip image.

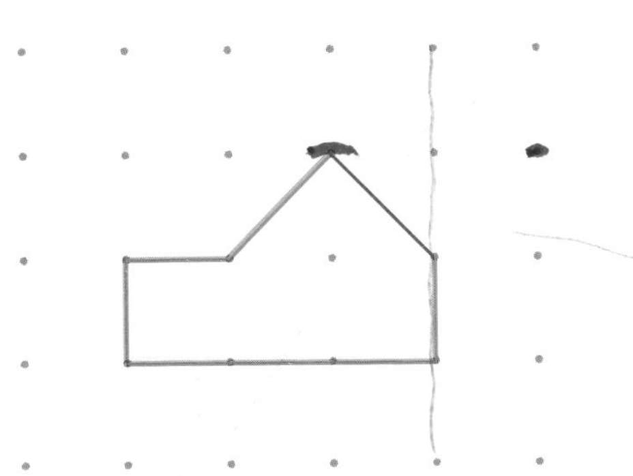

8. Locate the flip line that will flip one half of the diagram onto the other half. What is this type of flip line called?

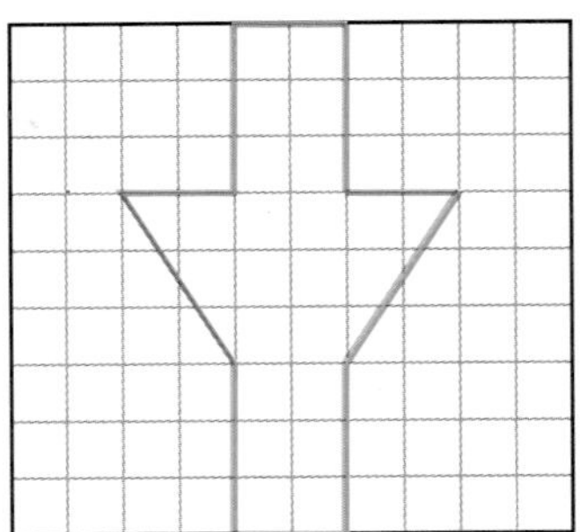

9. Explain why a parallelogram has no lines of symmetry.

Playing Games for Practice

Play each game in a group of 2, 3, or 4.

Capturing Squares

- Place your L shape anywhere on a 10 by 10 grid.
- Spin the spinner.
- Move your shape to any unoccupied squares using the motion spun.
- Color the captured squares.
- Take turns.
- Continue until all squares are captured or no player can move.
- The winner is the player with the most captured squares.

Example

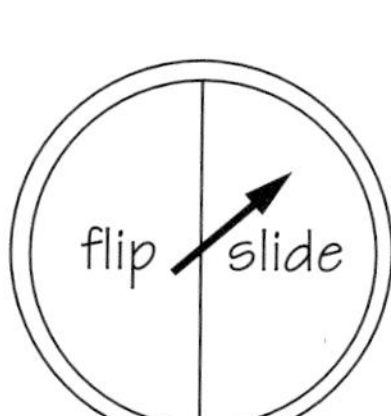

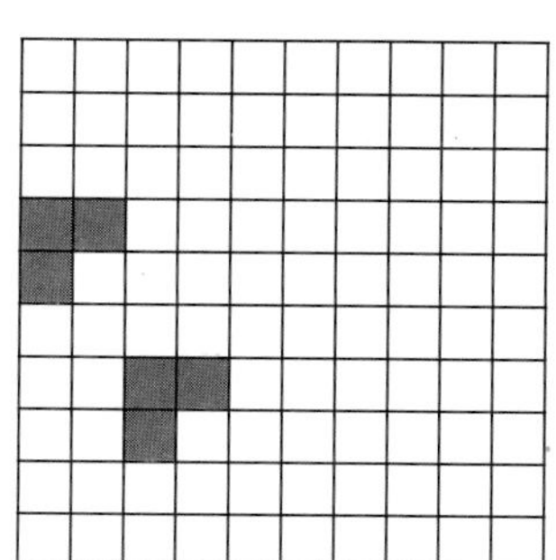

Enlarging Rectangles

- Roll two dice.
- Use the numbers rolled as the length and width of a rectangle.
- Draw the rectangle on your sheet of grid paper.
- Double the size of your rectangle by flipping it.
- Find its area.
- Score as many points as the number of square units in the area of your doubled rectangle.
- Take turns.
- The winner is the first player to get a total score greater than 500 points.

Example

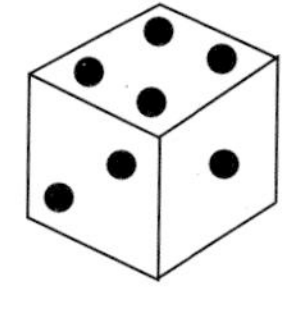

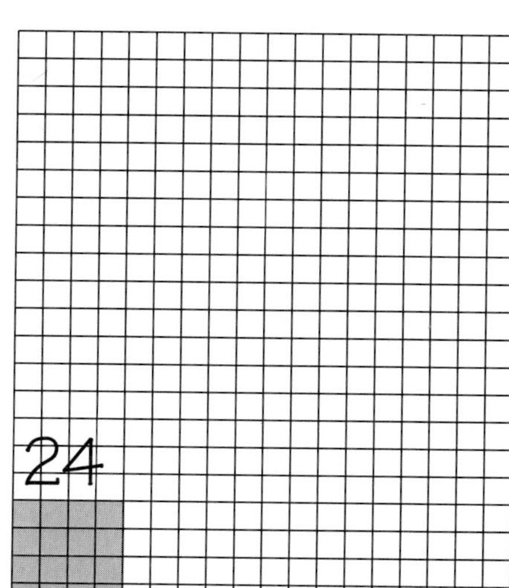

Showing What You Know

1. Tell if the size and shape usually change when a shape is
   - reflected in a bathroom mirror
   - taken up an escalator
   - reflected in a spoon
   - photographed

   Use a chart to organize your answers.

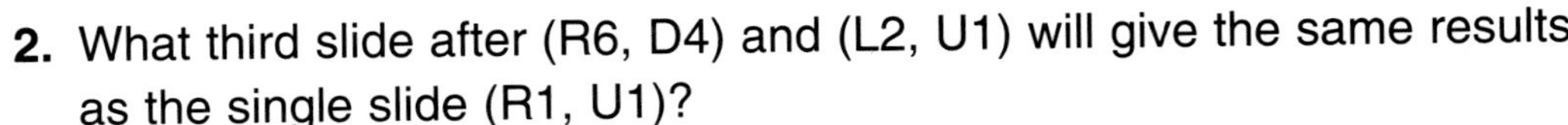

2. What third slide after (R6, D4) and (L2, U1) will give the same results as the single slide (R1, U1)?

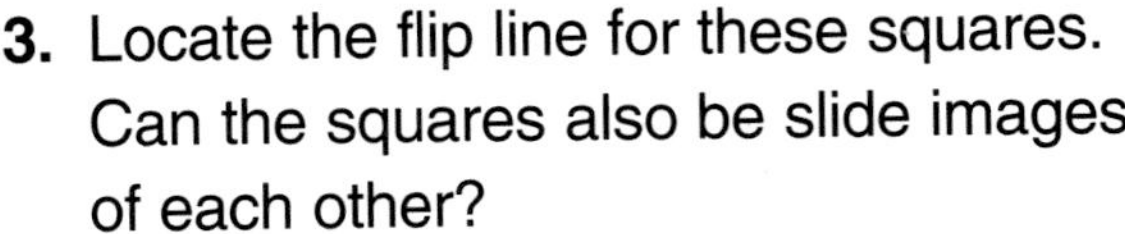

3. Locate the flip line for these squares. Can the squares also be slide images of each other?

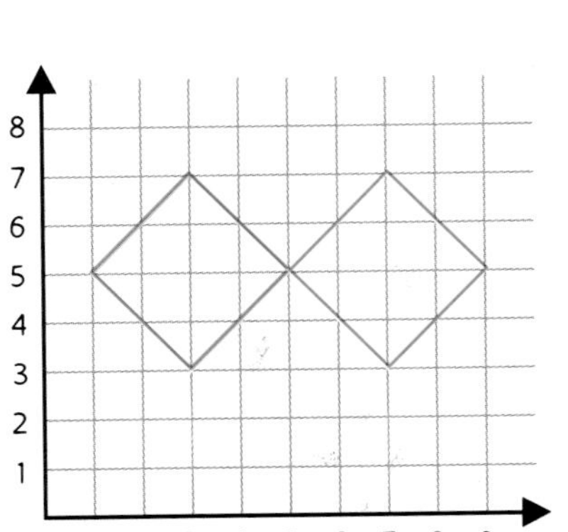

4. Use a ruler to locate the midpoint of each line joining two vertices. Draw a straight line through these points. What is this line called? At what angle does this line intersect each of the other lines?

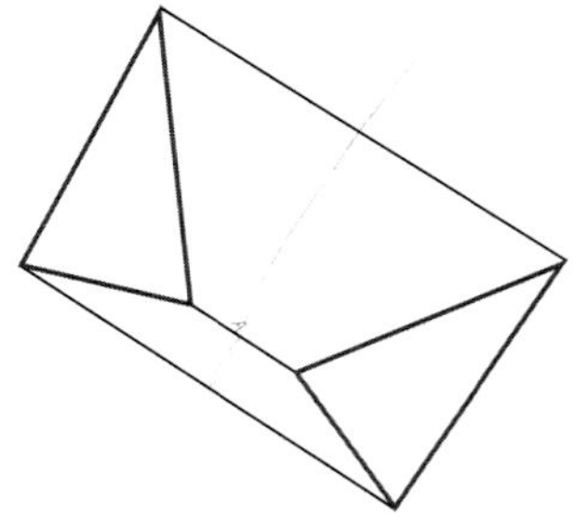

5. Which of the Ts are slide and flip images of each other?

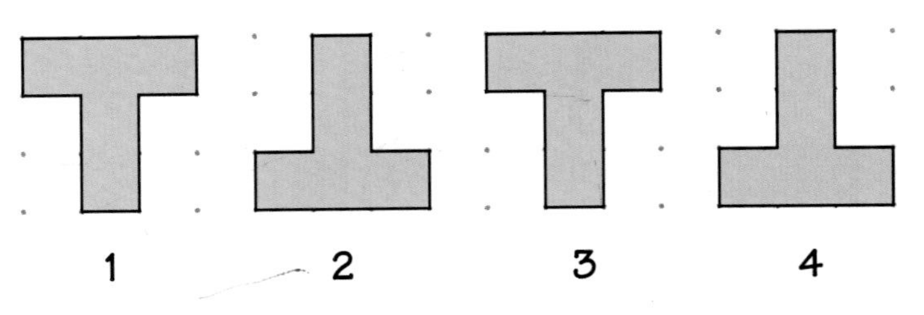

6. Draw the triangle that results from a flip across line AB.

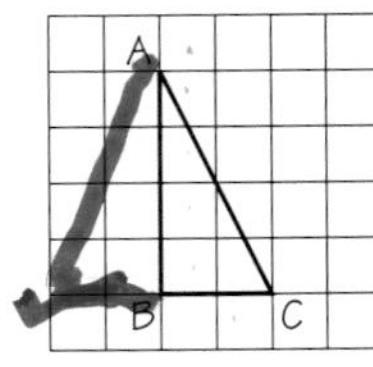

7. Draw the quadrilateral that results from a flip across line AD.

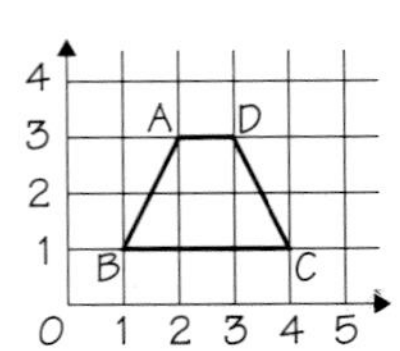

8. How many lines of symmetry does a circle have?

9. Draw a rectangular prism on dot paper. Describe the sliding motion used.

Thinking Back . . .

What parts of this can are translation images of each other? Explain.

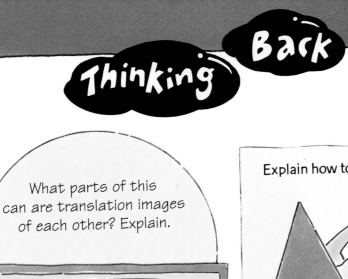

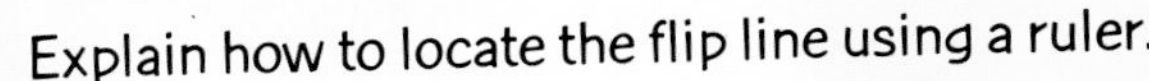

Explain how to locate the flip line using a ruler.

Draw the flip lines you would use to flip the blue part of the pattern to make the rest of the pattern.

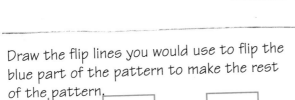

Who is correct? Explain.

These squares are not congruent.
These squares are congruent.

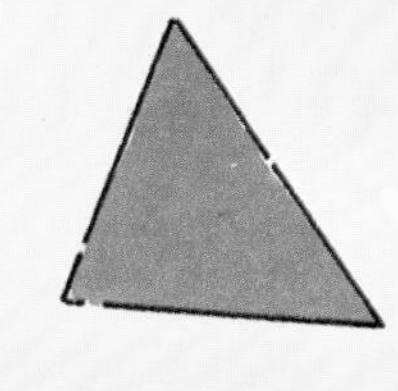

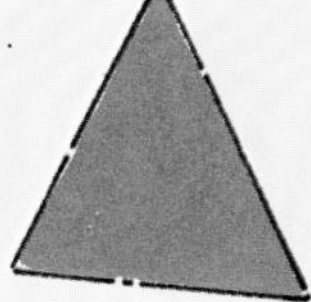

One shape looks like it's a slide image of another.
Describe one way you could determine if it really is.

What questions do you still have about motion geometry?

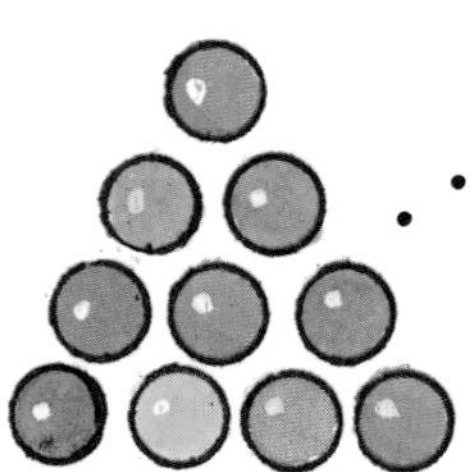

Examining

◀ Josh says the nickels are worth $34.18.
Do you think he's right? Explain.

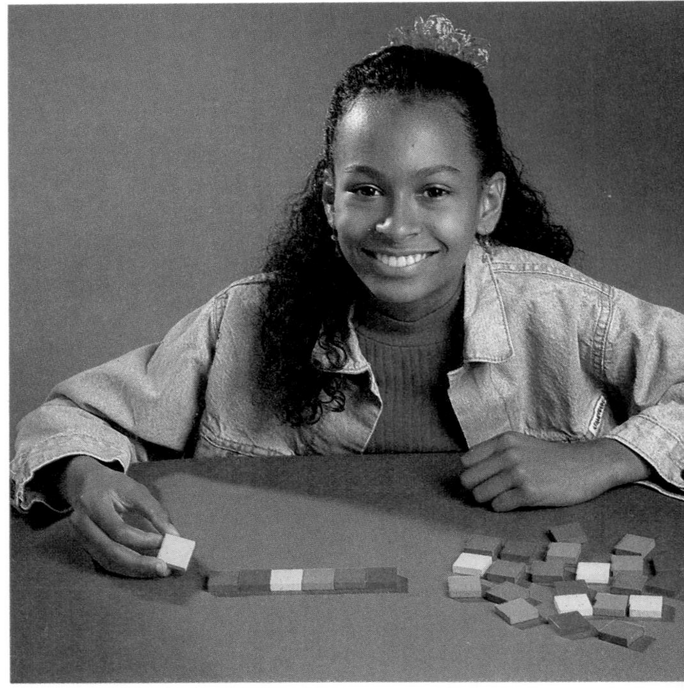

▲ How many different rectangular arrays can you make if each array has 29 squares? 39 squares? 49 squares?
Tell something about each number — 29, 39, and 49 — that makes it different from the other two.

▼ Sonja bought 240 stars.
How many of these packages did she buy?

What other ways could 240 stars be packaged with an equal number in each package?

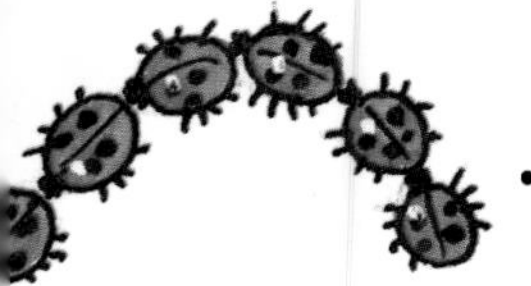

Number Theory

▼ Complete this table.

a

a	b
b	b

a	b	c
b	b	c
c	c	c

a	b	c	d
b	b	c	d
c	c	c	d
d	d	d	d

Number of letters						
on each side	1	2	3	4	5	6
altogether	1	4	?	?	?	?
that are a	1	1	?	?	?	?
that are b	0	3	?	?	?	?
that are c	0	0	?	?	?	?
that are d	0	0	?	?	?	?
that are e	0	0	?	?	?	?
that are f	0	0	?	?	?	?

How did you complete the last two columns?
Describe the pattern in the table.

▶ Erin is buying the same number of picnic plates as picnic glasses.
How many of each might she be buying?
How many packages of each would that be?

Is it easier to write an even number or an odd number as the product of two other numbers? Explain.

Choose two numbers from 1 to 9. Multiply one of them by 5. Add 7 and double the sum.
Add the other number and subtract 14. Try this with a different pair of numbers. Tell what happens.

Creating Equal Groups

Finding factors

There are 24 students to be placed in equal groups for science projects. Could each group have 5 students? 4 students? Why?

Tara, Rebecca, and Aaron are finding all the possible ways to create equal groups from 24.

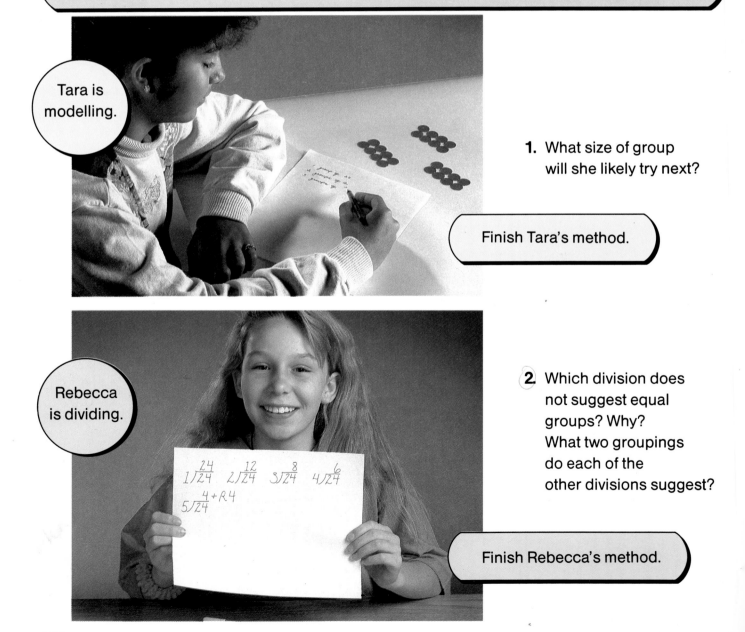

Tara is modelling.

1. What size of group will she likely try next?

Finish Tara's method.

Rebecca is dividing.

2. Which division does not suggest equal groups? Why? What two groupings do each of the other divisions suggest?

Finish Rebecca's method.

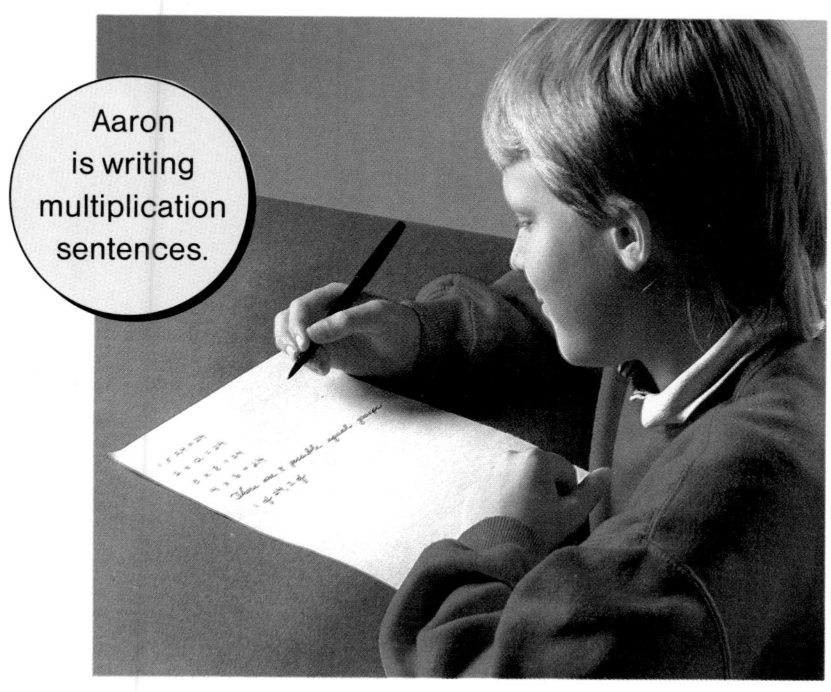
Aaron
is writing
multiplication
sentences.

3. Why did he decide to write only four multiplication sentences?

Will his method find the same groupings as the others?

4. Which groupings do you think are practical for science project groups? Why?

5. Why are the group sizes of 1, 2, 3, 4, 6, 8, 12, and 24 **factors** of 24?

Work with a partner.

Use any of the methods you wish.

6. What are the different ways to create equal groups of 27 students? 18 students? 20 students? 29 students? 40 students? What are all the factors of each number?

7. If equal groups of 6 are possible, what other equal groups must also be possible? Why?

8. If 2, 3, and 5 are factors of the number of students in a class, why are 6, 10, and 15 also factors? How many students would likely be in the class?

9. What are the factors of these numbers of students?
   - 85
   - 42
   - 56

10. If the number of students becomes greater, does this mean there will be a greater number of factors? Explain.

11. There are six factors of 28. What are they? Find two other numbers greater than 20 with exactly six factors.

I had $1 000 000 and I gave away one-fourth of it.
Then I give away one-fourth of what was left.
Once more I gave away one-fourth of what was left.
How much money do I still have?

Lining Up Insects

Finding multiples and least common multiple

How many chinch bugs placed end to end are as long as one of the longest insect?

Honeybee
12 mm

Giant Water Bug
48 mm

Termite
7 mm

Cornfield Ant
3 mm

Silverfish
20 mm

Chinch Bug
4 mm

Ladybug
6 mm

Lawrence is modelling to find 10 different lengths that a line of chinch bugs could have with no spaces between them. He is using counting rods on a metre stick.

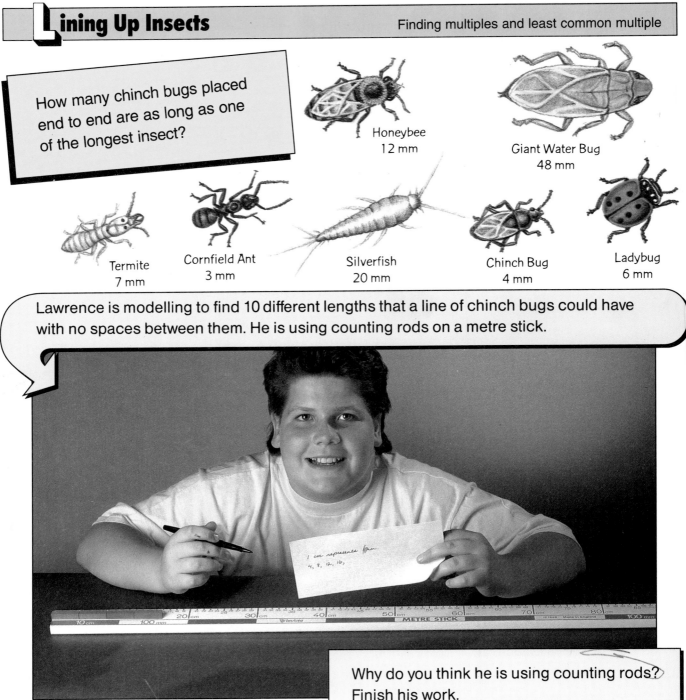

Why do you think he is using counting rods?
Finish his work.
These lengths are **multiples** of 4. Why?

1. Find 10 different lengths that a line of ladybugs could have with no spaces between them. What number are these lengths multiples of?

2. Model a line of ladybugs as long as a line of chinch bugs.

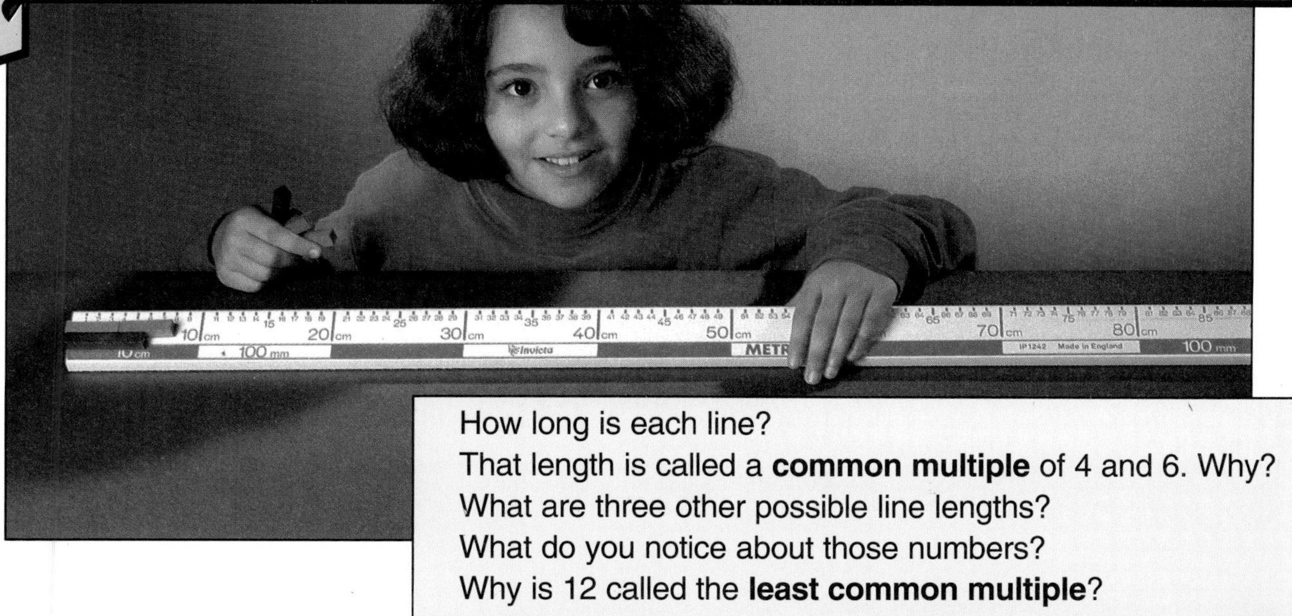

How long is each line?
That length is called a **common multiple** of 4 and 6. Why?
What are three other possible line lengths?
What do you notice about those numbers?
Why is 12 called the **least common multiple**?

Use counting rods or centimetre strips and a metre stick if you wish. Remember, there are no spaces between the insects.

3. What are three common multiples of the lengths of these insects? What is the least common multiple for each?
   - ladybugs and honeybees
   - chinch bugs and termites
   - termites and cornfield ants
   - honeybees, cornfield ants, and chinch bugs

4. What are five multiples of the length of a silverfish? Is 4 a factor of each length? Why? What else do you notice about these numbers?

5. Which types of insect could form a line 1 m long?

6. A line of honeybees is 96 mm long. Which types of insect could form a line the same length? How many of each would be in the line?

7. Which types of insect could form a line the same length as just one of another type of insect?

8. Which statements are true?
   - Multiples of even numbers are always even.
   - Multiples of odd numbers are always odd.
   - Common multiples of two even numbers are always even.
   - Common multiples of two odd numbers are always odd.

Identify 4 different types of solids with exactly 6 faces.

Cutting Squares

Determining common factors and the greatest common factor

Derek and Celine have a 90 cm by 60 cm piece of cloth to cut congruent squares from without any cloth left over.

To find the sizes of squares possible, Derek is using a measuring tape.

Celine is listing the factors of 90 and 60.

Side lengths
1 cm ✓ ✓
2 cm ✓ ✓
3 cm ✓ ✓
4 cm ✓ ✗
5 cm ✓ ✓
6 cm ✓ ✓
7 cm ✗ ✗
8 cm ✗ ✗
9 cm ✗ ✓
10 cm ✓

1 cm, 2 cm, and 3 cm are possible for both 60 cm and 90 cm.
Which side is 4 cm not possible for?
Finish his work.

Why is she listing the factors?
Why has she circled some factors?
Finish her work.

The possible sizes of the squares — 1, 2, 3, 5, 6, 10, 15, and 30 — are called **common factors** of 90 and 60. Why?
Why is 30 called the **greatest common factor**?

Remember, no cloth is to be left over.

1. What sizes of congruent squares are possible from cloth that measures
   - 90 cm by 10 cm?
   - 90 cm by 30 cm?
   - 90 cm by 40 cm?
   - 90 cm by 16 cm?
   - 35 cm by 45 cm?
   - 42 cm by 63 cm?

   What is the greatest common factor for each?

2. Which number is always a common factor of any pair of numbers? Why?

3. All the common factors of 110 and 45 except 1 are multiples of the same number. What's the number?

4. If 3 is not a common factor of a pair of numbers, what other numbers can't be common factors? Explain.

Take Your Pick

NINETY NINES

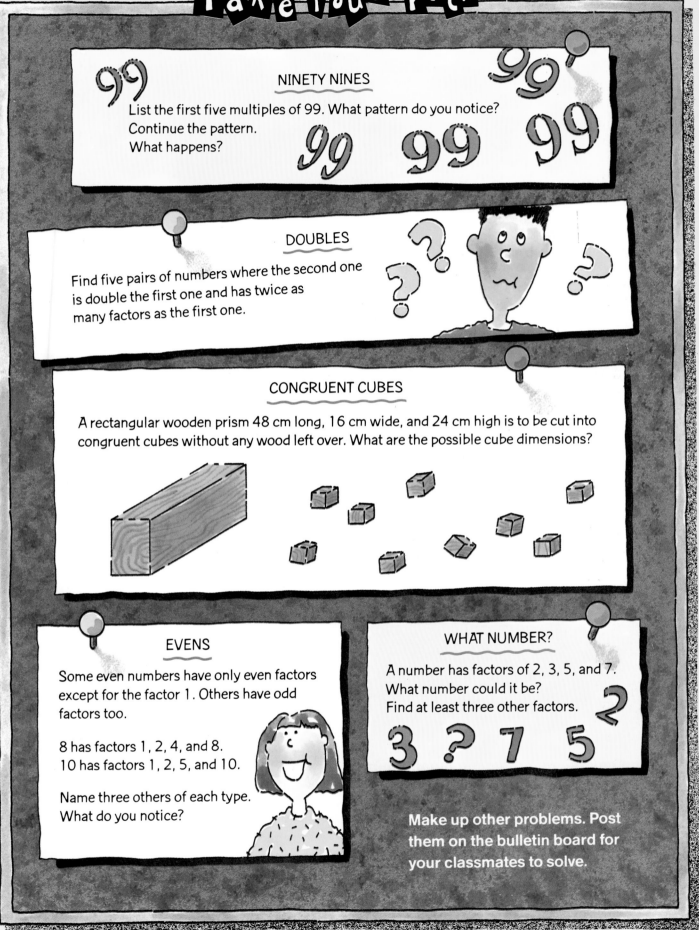

List the first five multiples of 99. What pattern do you notice?
Continue the pattern.
What happens?

DOUBLES

Find five pairs of numbers where the second one is double the first one and has twice as many factors as the first one.

CONGRUENT CUBES

A rectangular wooden prism 48 cm long, 16 cm wide, and 24 cm high is to be cut into congruent cubes without any wood left over. What are the possible cube dimensions?

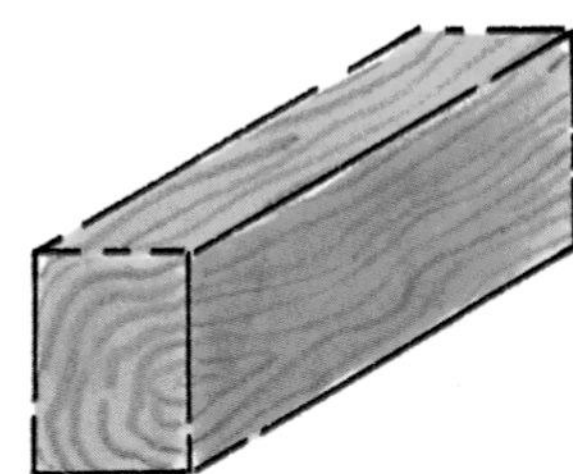

EVENS

Some even numbers have only even factors except for the factor 1. Others have odd factors too.

8 has factors 1, 2, 4, and 8.
10 has factors 1, 2, 5, and 10.

Name three others of each type.
What do you notice?

WHAT NUMBER?

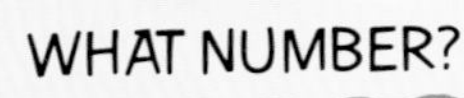

A number has factors of 2, 3, 5, and 7.
What number could it be?
Find at least three other factors.

Make up other problems. Post them on the bulletin board for your classmates to solve.

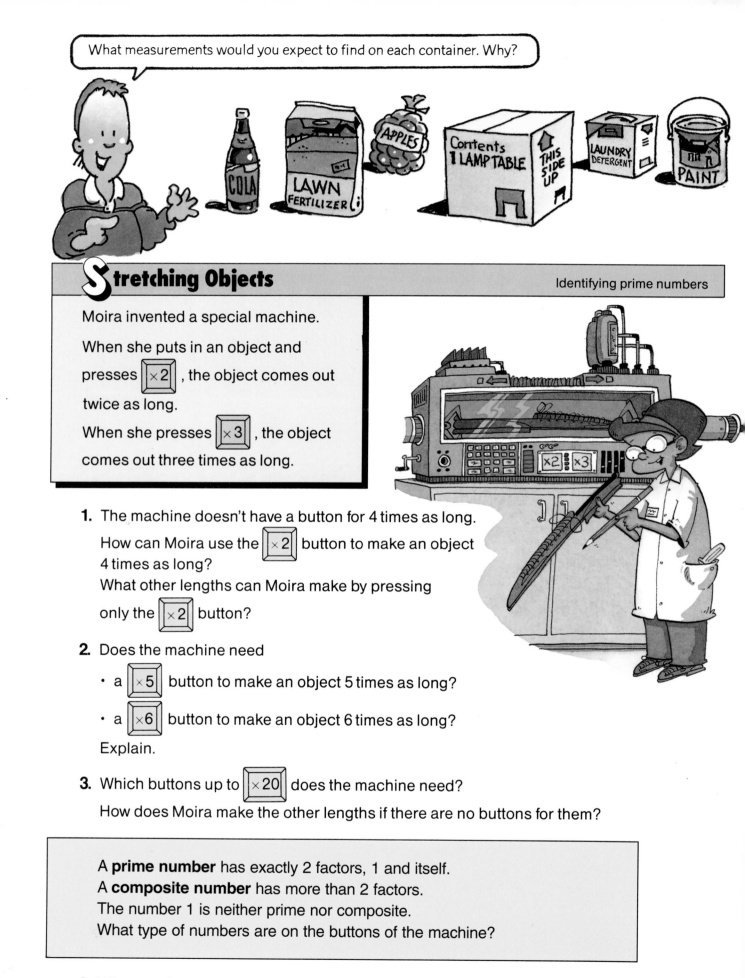

Stretching Objects

Identifying prime numbers

Moira invented a special machine.

When she puts in an object and presses [×2], the object comes out twice as long.

When she presses [×3], the object comes out three times as long.

1. The machine doesn't have a button for 4 times as long.
   How can Moira use the [×2] button to make an object 4 times as long?
   What other lengths can Moira make by pressing only the [×2] button?

2. Does the machine need
   - a [×5] button to make an object 5 times as long?
   - a [×6] button to make an object 6 times as long?

   Explain.

3. Which buttons up to [×20] does the machine need?
   How does Moira make the other lengths if there are no buttons for them?

A **prime number** has exactly 2 factors, 1 and itself.
A **composite number** has more than 2 factors.
The number 1 is neither prime nor composite.
What type of numbers are on the buttons of the machine?

4. What are the prime numbers to 20?

5. Which of these numbers are composite? Explain.
   12 5 13 16 22 23 39 41

6. Does the machine need buttons for any multiples of 3? of 5?
   Does it need buttons for numbers that are multiples of any other numbers? Explain.
   How can the machine make an object 24 times as long? 45 times as long? 70 times as long?

7. Use a hundreds chart. Put a diamond around 1. Circle each prime number to 20. Cross out each composite number to 20.

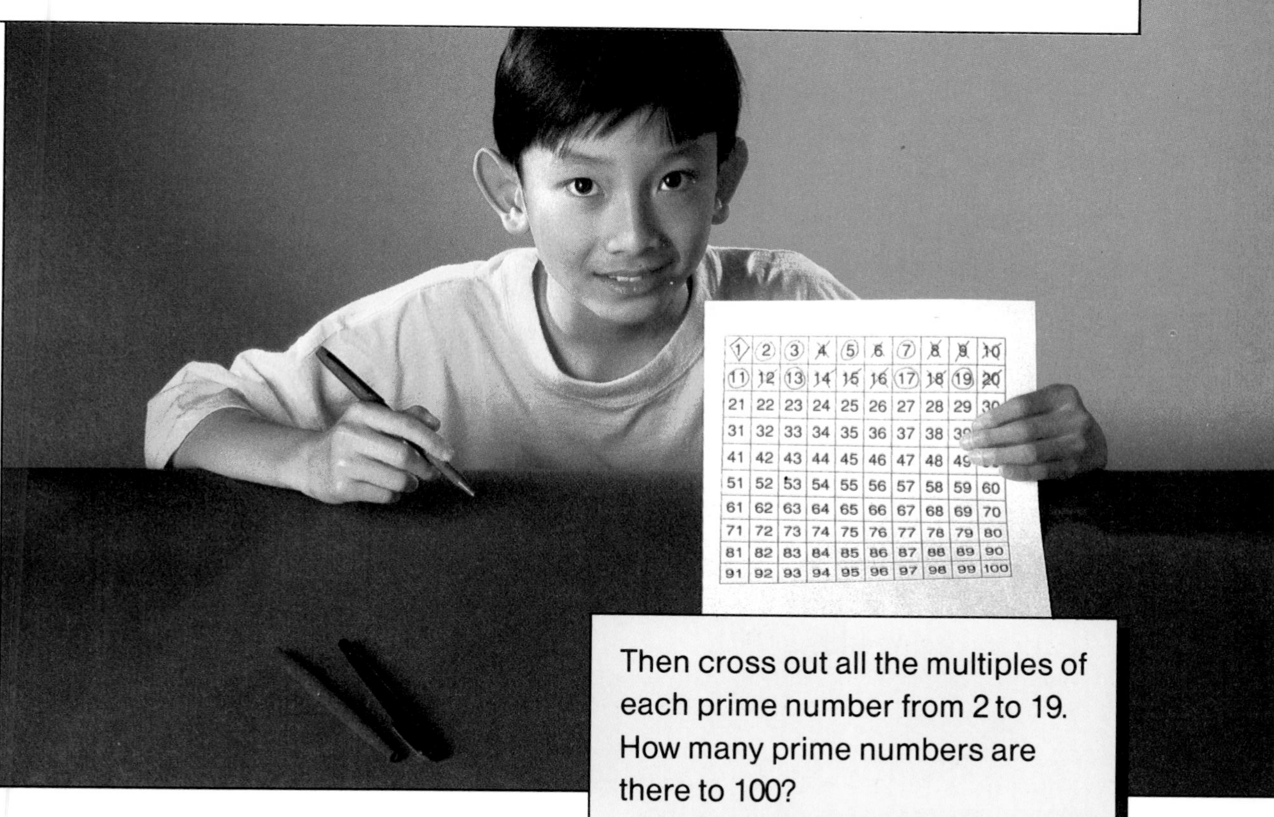

Then cross out all the multiples of each prime number from 2 to 19. How many prime numbers are there to 100?

8. Which ones digits appear in prime numbers? Which one appears least often? most often?

9. How can you tell if a number is prime by listing its factors?

10. Why are there fewer prime numbers than composite numbers?

11. How would you explain what prime and composite numbers are to a friend who has not yet learned about them?

One pencil can write about 45 000 words.
About how many words can be written for each centimetre of pencil?
for each millimetre of pencil?

Sorting Numbers

Using prime factorization to sort groups of numbers

Katy-Anne drew this Venn diagram to sort all the whole numbers from 2 to 20.

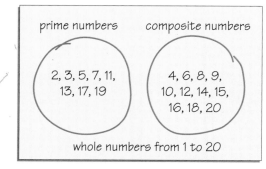

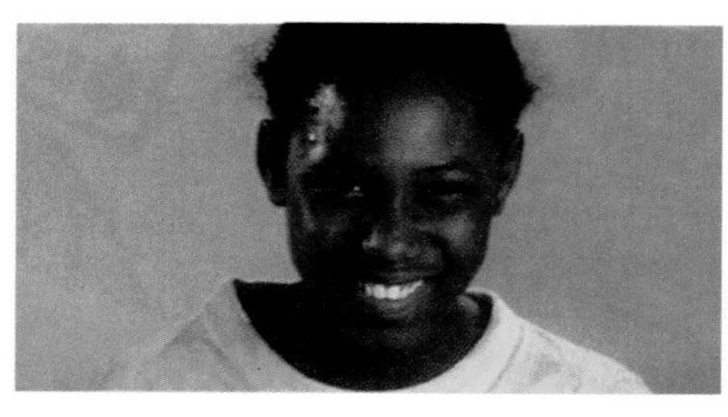

prime numbers: 2, 3, 5, 7, 11, 13, 17, 19

composite numbers: 4, 6, 8, 9, 10, 12, 14, 15, 16, 18, 20

whole numbers from 1 to 20

1. Where would you place the number 1? Explain.

2. Make a Venn diagram for the numbers to 50.
   Then write each of the prime numbers as a product of its factors.
   How are the prime numbers alike?

   $2 = 2 \times 1$

Numbers can be sorted in other ways by first writing the **prime factorization**.

This means write a number as the product of its prime factors.

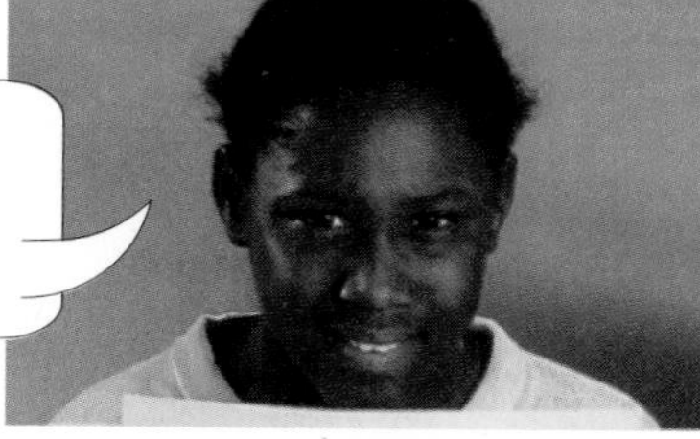

3. Explain what Katy-Anne did.

$$\begin{aligned} 24 &= 2 \times 12 \\ &= 2 \times 3 \times 4 \\ &= 2 \times 3 \times 2 \times 2 \end{aligned}$$

4. List the prime factorizations for the composite numbers from 1 to 50.

5. Use the list of prime factorizations for the numbers from 1 to 50 to write
   - the multiples of 7
   - the numbers that have only three prime factors
   - the numbers that have only four prime factors

6. Which number(s) less than 50 has the most prime factors?
   Do you think it also has the most pairs of factors?
   Test your prediction.

7. List the numbers from 1 to 50 where all of the prime factors are different.

8. Which numbers from 1 to 50 have only identical prime factors?

9. Gord used this approach to predict which numbers from 51 to 100 have only identical prime factors.
$8 \times 8 = 64$
$9 \times 9 = 81$
$10 \times 10 = 100$
Do you agree? Explain.

10. Peggy used this approach to find numbers with identical prime factors.

2 x 2 x 2 x 2 x 2 x 2
=4 =8 =16 =32 =64

3 x 3 x 3 x 3
=9 =27 =81

5 x 5 =25

7 x 7 =49

11 x 11 =121

13 x 13 =169

Use a calculator to find the next number in each of Peggy's patterns.

11. Use this Venn diagram to help you find the prime factorization of the composite numbers from 51 to 100.

12. Which number(s) from 1 to 100 has the greatest number of prime factors?

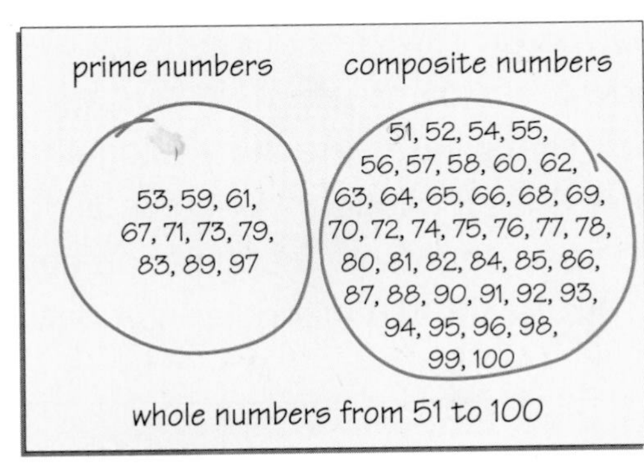

Make this true without using the digits 1 or 2.
Try it three different ways.
[?][?][?][?] ÷ [?][?] = 93

Arranging Cards

Relating number and geometry patterns

What polygon is suggested by these cards arranged for playing solitaire?

1 tells the number of cards in the first column.
$1 + 2 = 3$ tells the total number of cards in the first two columns.
$1 + 2 + 3 = 6$ tells the total number of cards in the first three columns.

Continue the addition pattern for the remaining columns.
Why do you think 1, 3, 6, 10, . . . are called **triangular numbers?**
Model the 5th triangular number.

1. Continue the pattern to find the first 20 triangular numbers.

2. What pattern of odd and even numbers do you notice?

3. Are there more triangular numbers between 1 and 25 or between 25 and 50? between 1 and 100 or between 100 and 200? Why?

4. Which digits have not appeared as ones digits?

5. A triangular arrangement can be viewed as part of a rectangle.

   For the 4th triangular number,
   - how many rows are in the rectangle?
   - how many cards are in each row?
   - how many cards are there altogether?
   - how does the number of cards altogether compare to the 4th triangular number?

   Try this for the 5th triangular number.

6. Use the idea suggested by Problem 5 to find the number of cards in the 19th triangular number. Did it work?
   What is the 50th triangular number? the 99th?

Take Your Pick

SQUARE NUMBERS

Here are the first four **square numbers**.

1

4

9

16

Show the next five. How many dots did you add to one to get the next?

SPECIAL SUMS

Find the sums of the first five pairs of consecutive triangular numbers.

1 + 3 3 + 6 6 + 10 10 + 15 15 + 21

What do you notice about these sums?

They are called **square numbers**. Predict the next five sums.

OPENING DOORS

There are 100 closed doors in a row. You open every 2nd door. Then you open every 3rd door unless it is already open. Next you open every 5th, and finally every 7th door. What doors will still be open?

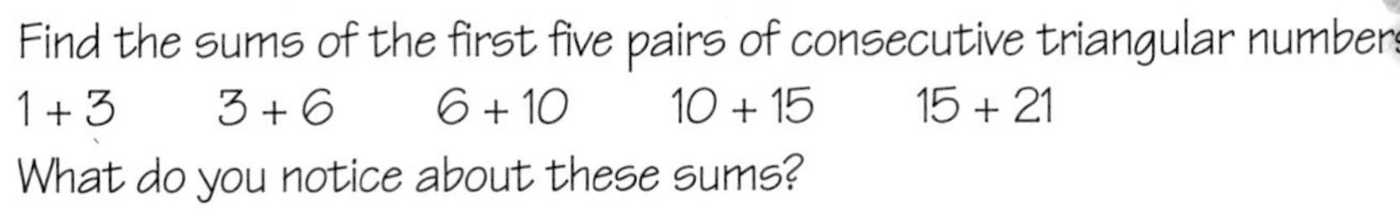

WORD POWER

Write at least 10 words of 4 letters or more using the word COMPOSITE.

BACKWARD

Is 13 a prime number?
Reverse the digits.
Is that number prime?
Find another pair of numbers like this pair.

Make up other problems. Post them on the bulletin board for your classmates to solve.

Using the centres of squares on a hundreds chart as vertices, draw a parallelogram so that the numbers at the vertices have a sum of 182.

Generalizing Patterns

Describing relationships and creating expressions

Lewis made this table to show the relationship between the number of ducks in a pen and the number of their legs.

Number of Ducks (D)	0	1	2	3	4	5
Number of Legs (L)	0	2	4	6		

How many legs are there when there are no ducks in the pen?
Why does the number of legs increase by 2 each time a duck is added to the pen?

1. Copy and complete the table for up to 7 ducks.

2. What do you think the equation $D \times 2 = L$ means?
   Do you think this equation $L = 2 \times D$ means the same thing? Explain.

3. Copy and complete the list of the eight ordered pairs for (D , L). (0, 0), (1, 2), (2, 4), (3, ?), (4, ?), (? ,?), (?, ?), (? ,?)
   Then plot the points for the ordered pairs on a coordinate grid.
   What pattern do the points show in the graph?

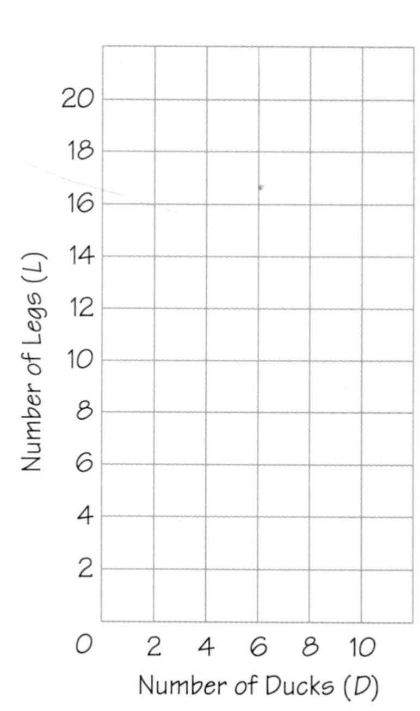

4. Use your graph or one of the equations to help you answer these questions. Explain what you did.
   - How many legs would there be for 8 ducks? 20 ducks?
   - How many ducks would there be if there were 18 legs? 56 legs?
   - If 1000 ducks were counted, how many legs would there be?

5. These 3 models, built with connecting cubes, show a pattern. Describe how to build the fourth model in the series.

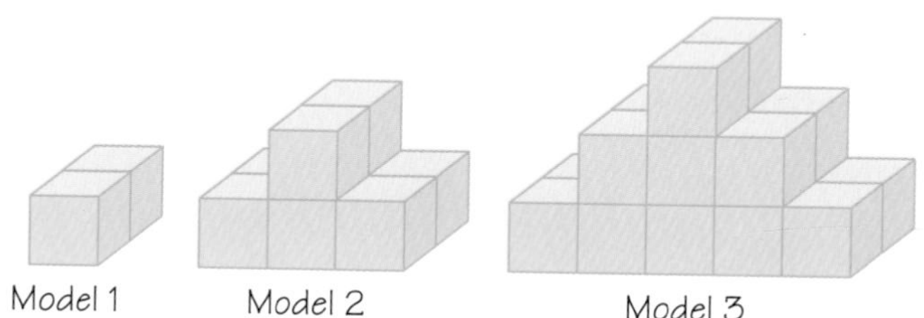

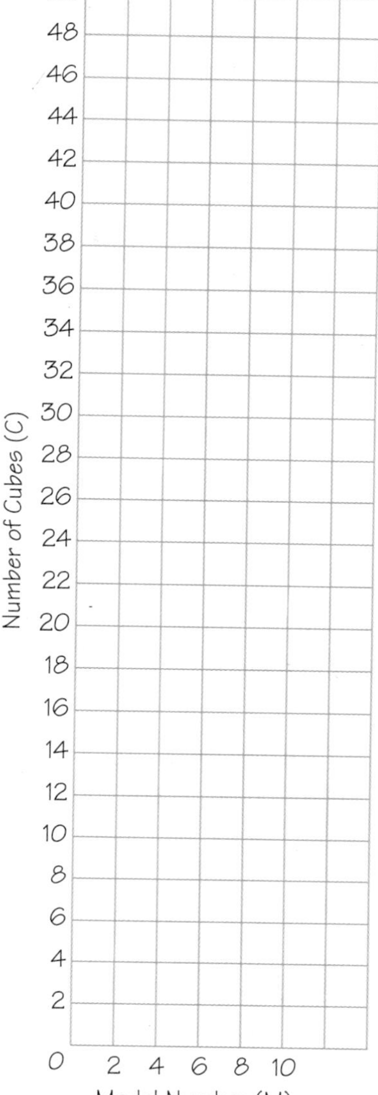

6. Make a table showing the number of cubes needed to build the first 5 models.

Model Number (M)	1	2	3	4	5
Number of Cubes (C)	2				

List the ordered pairs (M , C) for the model number, and the number of cubes.
Then plot the points on a coordinate grid.
Is there a pattern in the graph? If so, describe it.

7. Use your pattern to predict the number of cubes needed to build the sixth and seventh models.

8. Shauna used cubes to build rectangles that expand in two directions. Then she made this table to show the relationship.

Model Number (M)	1	2	3	4
Number of Cubes (C)	2	6	12	20

Draw or use cubes to construct the first 4 models in Shauna's series.
How are the numbers in each column in the table related?
Will 60 be a number that appears in the table if it is extended? Explain.

9. Use Shauna's table to list the ordered pairs (M , C). Then plot them on a coordinate grid.
Describe any pattern you see in the graph.

Use a globe, a string, and these facts. The distance across Canada is about 6000 km. The Canadian coastline is about 250 000 km. If the coastline could be straightened out and stretched around the equator, about how many times would it go around?

Balancing Objects

Understanding equality by balancing objects

Each of the cubes on the right side of the balance scales has a mass of 1 g. What is the mass of the small stone on the left side? How do you know?

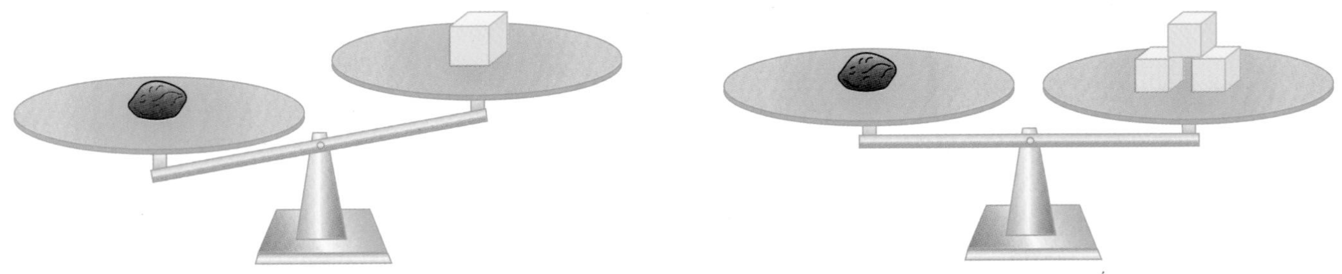

Meagan wrote this equation to describe when the scales balance. $s = 3$
What do you think the s stands for?

What happens to the balance if you add

- 2 cubes on the right side?
- then 2 cubes on the left side?

Explain how the equation $s + 2 = 5$ describes what you did.

Does the mass of the rock change?

What happens if you now take 1 cube from each side? Write the new equation.

1. The equation $t + 2 = 9$ describes the situation shown on the balance scales. What is the mass, in grams, of the trapezoid pattern block, t? Explain how you know.

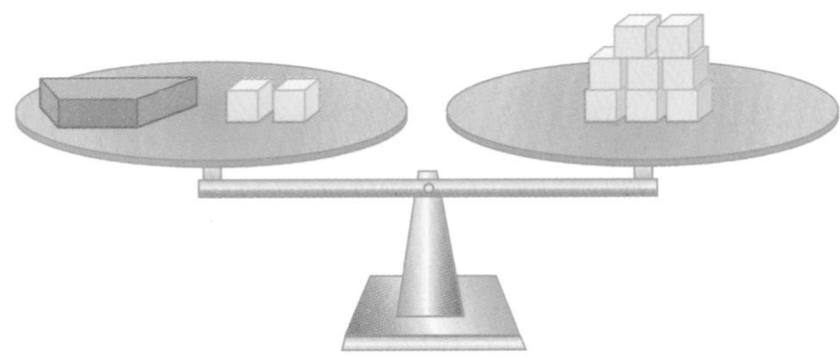

2. How many cubes must you add to make the scales balance?

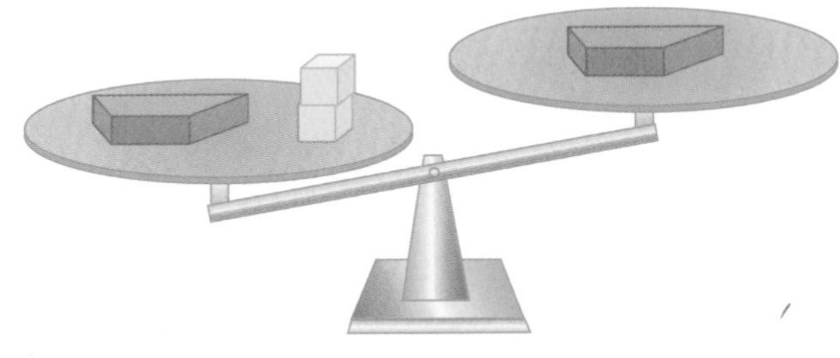

3. The equation $n + 1 = 6$ describes the situation shown on the balance scales. How many cubes must you take off to find the mass, in grams, of the nickel, n?

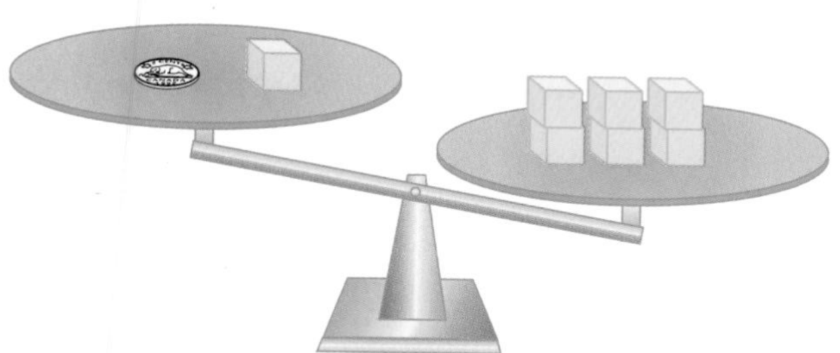

4. How many cubes must you add to make the scales balance 2 nickels?

5. About how many cubes would you need to balance a roll of 50 nickels? Explain.

6. The equation $4r + 1 = 5$ describes the situation shown on the balance scales. How can you find the mass, in grams, of one raisin, r?

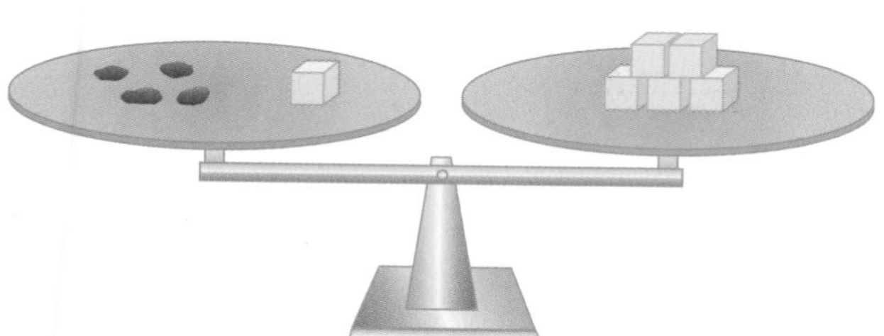

7. How many cubes must you add to make the scales balance 5 raisins?

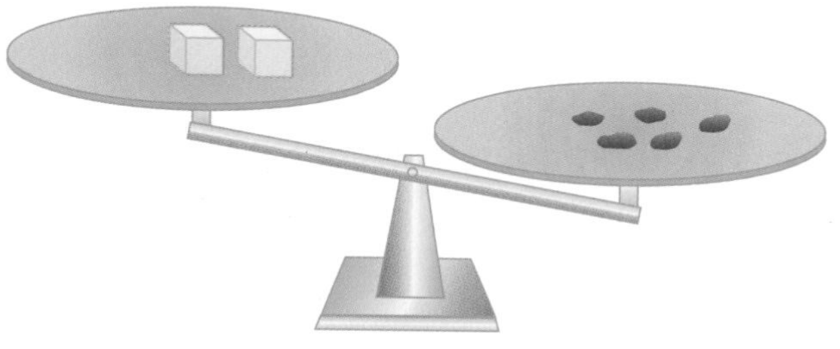

8. About how many cubes would you need to balance a small box of raisins? Explain.

9. What fraction of the hexagon pattern block is the trapezoid? the blue rhombus? How many of each must you place on the scales to make it balance?

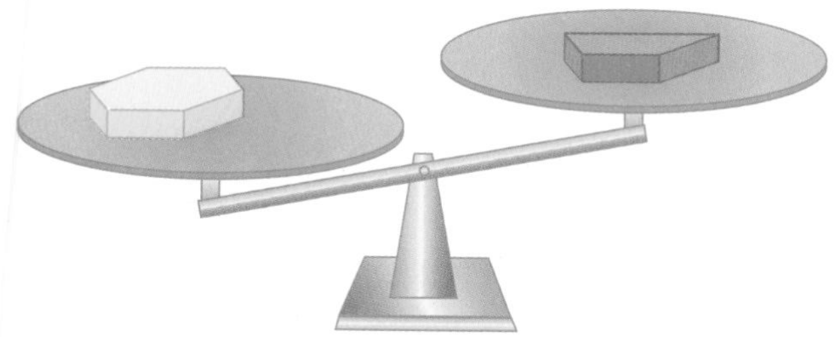

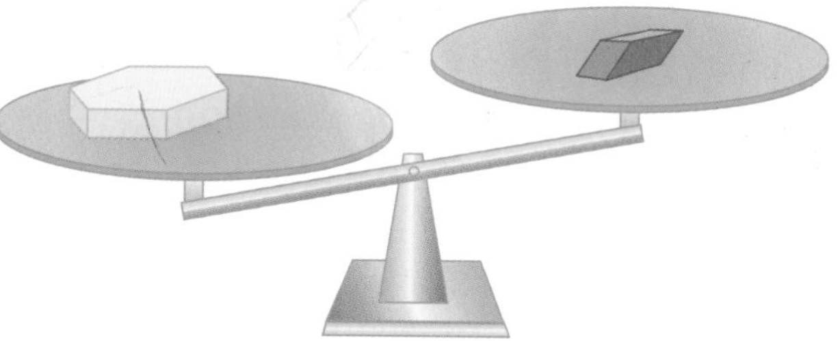

10. How can you find the mass, in grams, of 1 hexagon? 1 blue rhombus?

Find the mass, in grams, of each parcel. Explain what you did.

11.

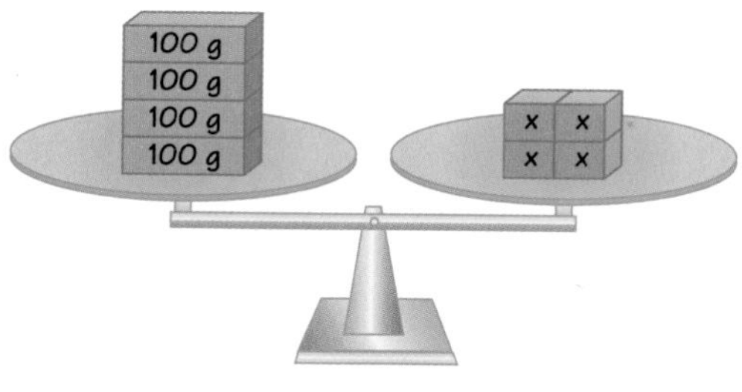

12.

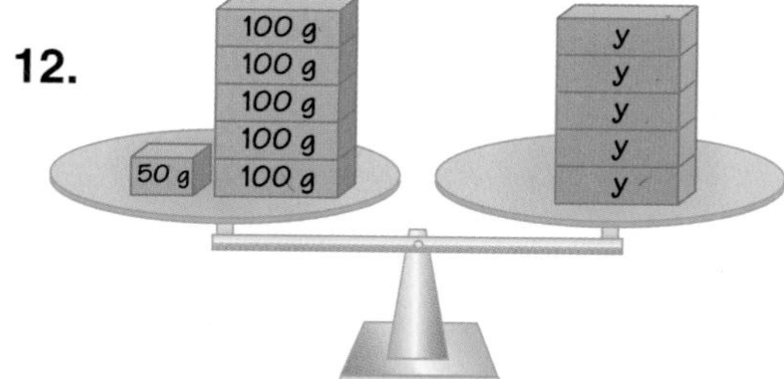

Modelling Equality

Explaining equality using models and diagrams

Monique is using centicubes to model this equation. 24 – ▢ = 16

How many cubes should she put on the right side? the left side?

How many cubes must she take away on the left side to produce an equality statement?

Monique drew this diagram to record what she did.

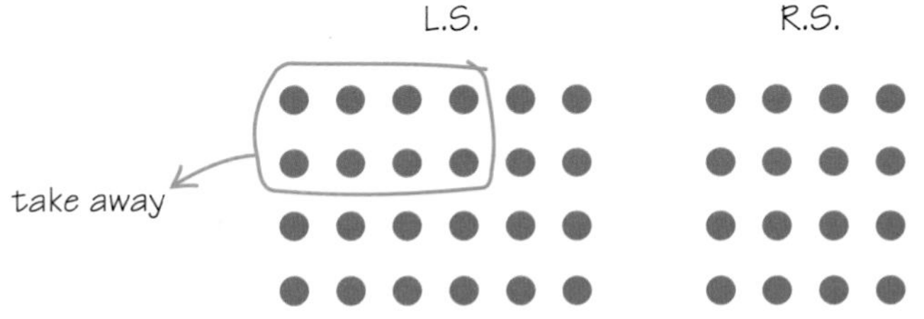

Does the left side equal the right side? Copy and complete the equation.

1. Monique modelled the equation 21 = 14 + ▢. How many cubes did she add on the right side to produce an equality statement?

   Do you agree with her diagram? Explain.

   Copy and complete the equation.

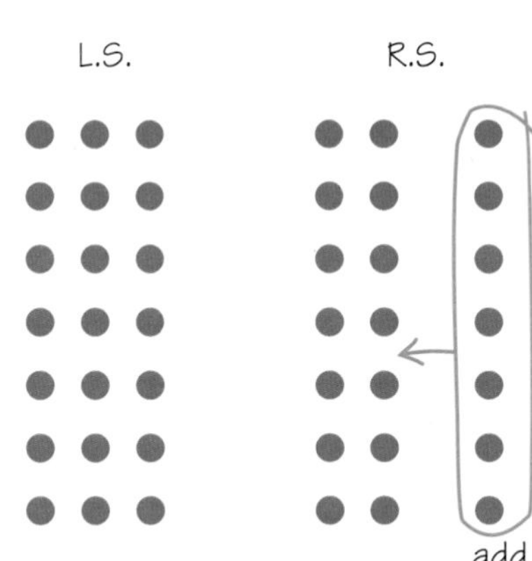

2. Model using cubes. How many cubes are needed to produce an equality statement in each case?

$\square + 12 = 13$ $10 + \square = 15$ $\square - 4 = 8$ $24 = \square + 8$ $15 = \square - 8$

Then copy and complete each equation.

3. Write six ways that the right side of each equation can be changed so that it is still true.

$4 = 2 + 2$ $6 = 1 + 5$ $7 = 0 + 7$ $10 = 5 + 5$

4. Use cubes to model. Draw a diagram to record what you did.

$7 + \square = 9 + 4$ $16 - 7 = 3 + \square$ $\square + 3 = 12 - 7$ $11 - \square = 18 - 7$

Then copy and complete each equation.

Use cubes and/or diagrams to help you answer questions 5 to 8.

5. For each equation, find the value of the left side. Then find the missing number in the right side.

$16 \div 2 = \square + 1$ $60 \div 2 = \square \times 6$ $2 \times (3 + 5) = \square - 4$

Then copy and complete the equation.

6. For each equation, find the value of the right side. Then find the missing number in the left side.

$12 \div \square = 24 \div 4$ $37 - \square = 33 - 12$ $\square + 4 = (3 \times 2) + 4$

Then copy and complete the equation.

7. Create your own equation like the ones in question 5 or 6 for your partner to solve.

8. Each box represents the same number. How can you solve this by guessing and testing?

$\square + (3 \times 6) = \square + \square + 15$

Each of these numbers is $\frac{3}{4}$ of the way from 0 to another number.

300 9 33 1.5

What are the other numbers?

Finding Unknowns

Using pre-algebra strategies to solve single-variable equations

Calvin used a **variable** to write this equation. $22 = a + 3$

What number plus 3 equals 22?
3 + 19 = 22

He found the missing number by working backward.

Check that the left side equals the right side.

L.S. = 22 R.S. $= a + 3$
$= 19 + 3$
$= 22$

L.S. = R.S.

So, the missing number is 19.

How else can you solve the equation?

Try subtracting 3 from each side. Why does the equation stay balanced?

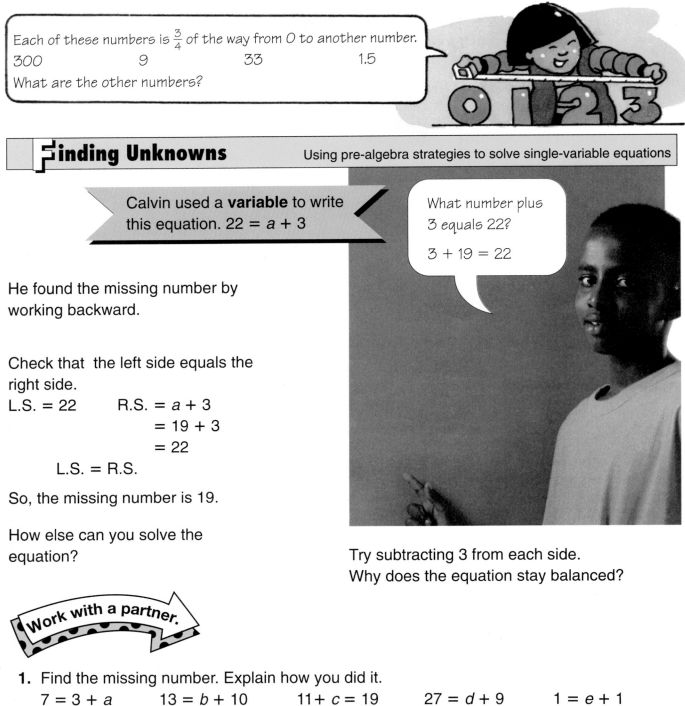

Work with a partner.

1. Find the missing number. Explain how you did it.

$7 = 3 + a$	$13 = b + 10$	$11 + c = 19$	$27 = d + 9$	$1 = e + 1$
$5 = 7 - f$	$15 = g - 5$	$28 - h = 13$	$i - 7 = 18$	$j - 3 = 13$
$6 = 2 \times k$	$36 = m \times 3$	$n \times n = 49$	$p \div 8 = 5$	$60 \div q = 5$

2. Write an equation that has the solution 10, where a number must be subtracted from both sides to find its solution.

3. Solve each equation. Explain what you did.

$16 \div 2 = r + 1$	$60 \div 2 = s \times 6$	$2 \times (3 + 5) = t - 4$
$12 \div u = 24 \div 4$	$37 - v = 33 - 12$	$w + 4 = (3 \times 2) + 4$

Take Your Pick

MISSING NUMBERS

In this table, the product of the first two numbers in any row or column is the third number.

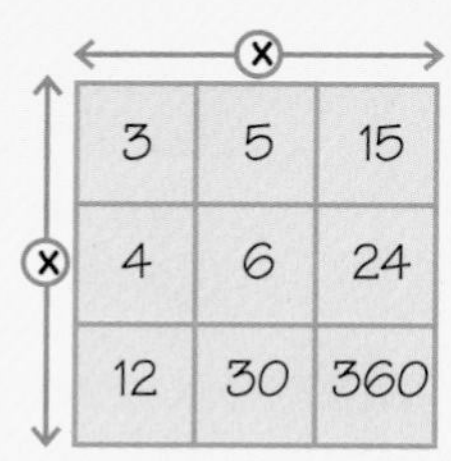

3	5	15
4	6	24
12	30	360

Solve.

(×)

6	A	18
B	9	45
30	27	C

(+)

5	X	12
Y	13	21
13	20	Z

GUESS MY NUMBER

- Choose a number.
- Increase it by 6.
- Multiply the result by 8.
- Divide this number by 4.
- Decrease the result by 12.
- Divide this number by 2.

What's the answer?

Try another number.

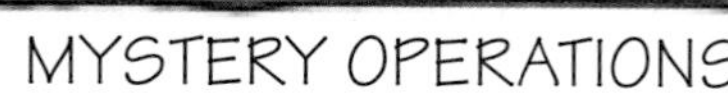

MYSTERY OPERATIONS

512 * 68 = A

A * 4 = B

B * 3 = 114

Replace each * with +, −, or ÷.
Show how I got the answer.

A RACE CAR'S TIME

What is the expression for the number of laps travelled in t minutes?

Time (min)	Laps
1	2
2	4
3	6
4	8

AGE PUZZLES

Solve.

- Six times Freida's age is 42. How old is she?
- When twice Robert's age is increased by 1, the result is 19. How old is he?

Make up similar problems. Post them on the bulletin board for your classmates to solve.

Solving a Problem by Finding and Extending a Pattern

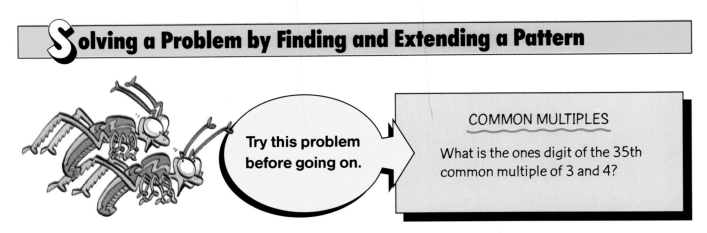

Try this problem before going on.

COMMON MULTIPLES

What is the ones digit of the 35th common multiple of 3 and 4?

Leo's group solved the problem by finding and extending a pattern.

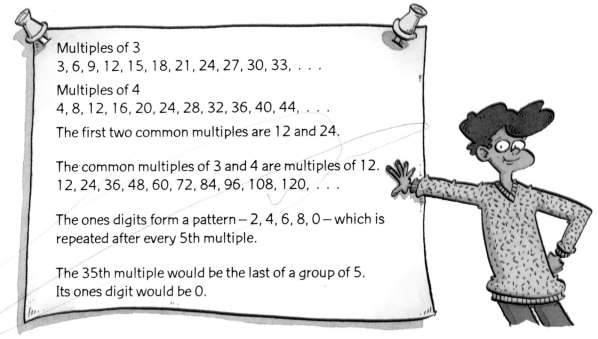

Multiples of 3
3, 6, 9, 12, 15, 18, 21, 24, 27, 30, 33, . . .

Multiples of 4
4, 8, 12, 16, 20, 24, 28, 32, 36, 40, 44, . . .

The first two common multiples are 12 and 24.

The common multiples of 3 and 4 are multiples of 12.
12, 24, 36, 48, 60, 72, 84, 96, 108, 120, . . .

The ones digits form a pattern – 2, 4, 6, 8, 0 – which is repeated after every 5th multiple.

The 35th multiple would be the last of a group of 5.
Its ones digit would be 0.

What is the ones digit of the 47th common multiple of 3 and 4?

Solve these problems by finding and extending a pattern.

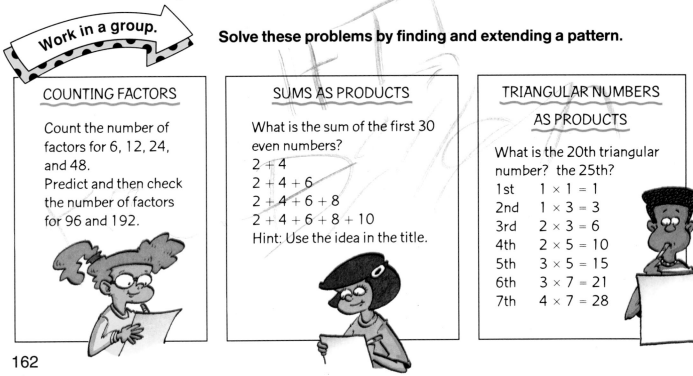

COUNTING FACTORS

Count the number of factors for 6, 12, 24, and 48.
Predict and then check the number of factors for 96 and 192.

SUMS AS PRODUCTS

What is the sum of the first 30 even numbers?

2 + 4
2 + 4 + 6
2 + 4 + 6 + 8
2 + 4 + 6 + 8 + 10

Hint: Use the idea in the title.

TRIANGULAR NUMBERS AS PRODUCTS

What is the 20th triangular number? the 25th?

1st	1 × 1 = 1
2nd	1 × 3 = 3
3rd	2 × 3 = 6
4th	2 × 5 = 10
5th	3 × 5 = 15
6th	3 × 7 = 21
7th	4 × 7 = 28

Practising What You've Learned

1. How many different rectangular arrays can you create with 19 counters? 20 counters?
   What does that tell you about 19? about 20?

2. Draw a picture to show that
   - 7 is not a factor of 48
   - 6 is a common factor of 18 and 24
   - 30 is a common multiple of 6 and 5
   - 15 is not prime
   - 64 is a square number
   - 55 is a triangular number

3. Write these numbers as a product of their prime factors.
   - 14 • 44 • 76 • 80

4. Find all the factors of each number.
   - 12 • 45 • 28

5. Find the greatest common factor for each pair of numbers.
   - 6 and 18 • 24 and 36 • 45 and 60

6. Find the least common multiple of each pair of numbers.
   - 2 and 4 • 4 and 6 • 12 and 20

7. Which of these numbers do you know for sure are not prime? Explain.
   - 50 • 25 • 19
   - 34 • 20 • 75

8. Which two triangular numbers are 12 apart?

9. Write an equation that has the solution 2, where a number must be added to both sides to find its solution.

What does one triangle equal in each diagram?

10.

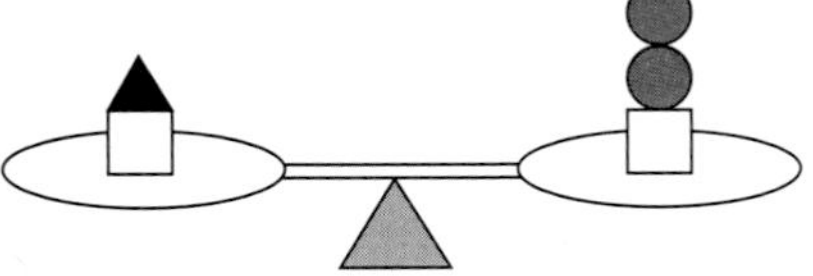

11.

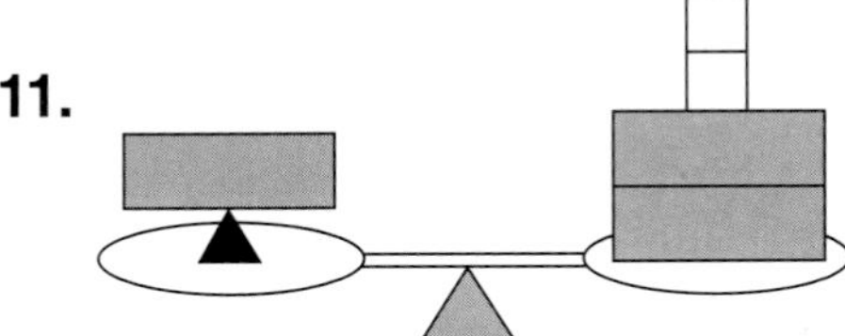

Playing Games for Practice

Play this game with another player.

Factor Sums

- Record the composite numbers to 40.
- Cross out a number. Score that number of points.
- Find the sum of that number's factors except the number itself. The other player scores that number of points.
- Switch roles.
- Continue playing until no numbers are left.
- The winner is the player with the most points.

Example A player crosses out 15 and scores 15 points.
The other player scores $1 + 3 + 5$ or 9 points.

A player crosses out 12 and scores 12 points.
The other player scores $1 + 2 + 3 + 4 + 6$ or 16 points.

Play this game in a group of 2, 3, or 4.

Going Down to Prime

- Roll a pair of dice to get a 2-digit number.
- Subtract any factor except the number itself. Use that difference as the number to factor on your next turn.
- Take turns.
- The first player to get a difference that is a prime number scores a point.
- Roll again and repeat the process.
- The winner is the first player to score 5 points.

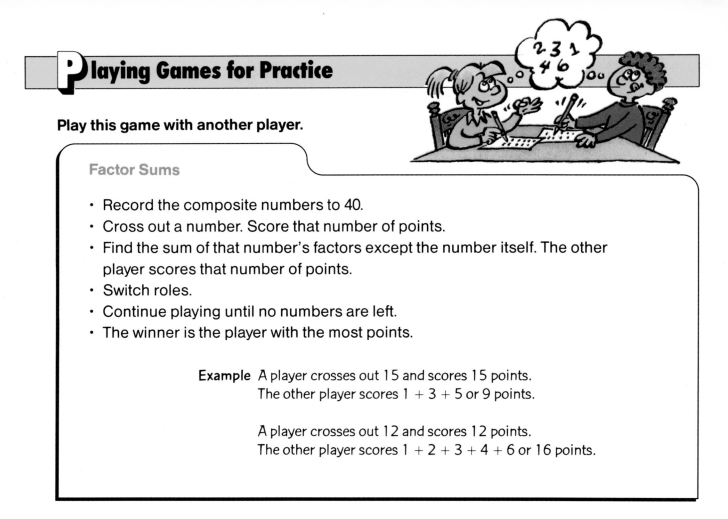

Example	Player 1	Player 2
First turn	Use 36 or 63.	Use 56 or 65.
	36	65
	− 18	− 13
	18	52
Second turn	− 9	− 26
	9	26
Third turn	− 3	− 13
	6	13 is prime. Score 1 point.

Take Your Pick

THREE FACTORS

Which numbers from 1 to 50 have exactly three factors? What do you notice? Predict four other numbers that have exactly three factors. Check your predictions.

HEXAGONAL NUMBERS

Here are the first three hexagonal numbers.

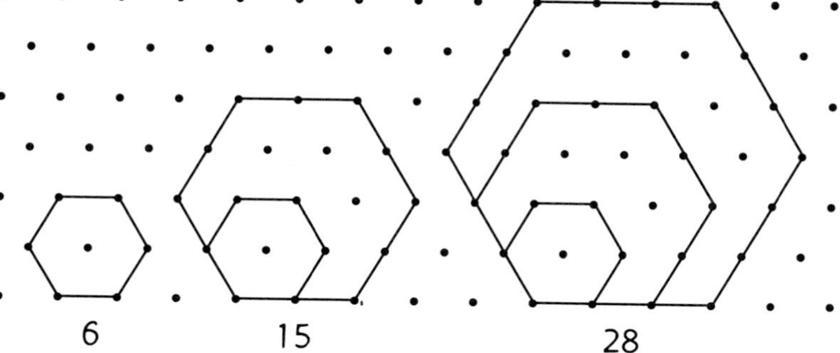

Find the next three hexagonal numbers. Then plot the ordered pairs (diagram number, number of dots) on a coordinate grid. Describe the pattern.

BY FOUR

x4

Multiply each number by 4.

- 28
- 79
- 130
- 56
- 107

What do you notice about the last digits in each product?

TWIN PRIMES

Primes like 11 and 13, which are two apart, are called twin primes. What other pairs of twin primes are there between 1 and 100?

9 10 11 12 13 14 15 16

DIFFERENCE OF 0

A factor of 20 is subtracted from a factor of 36. How many pairs of these factors differ by 0? What were you really finding?

Make up other problems. Post them on the bulletin board for your classmates to solve.

Showing What You Know

1. Write all the factors of these numbers.

   16 18 24 30

   32 42 72 99

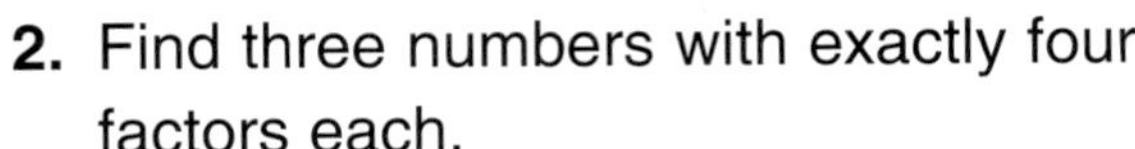

2. Find three numbers with exactly four factors each.

3. Find two square numbers whose sum is also a square number.

4. How can you tell that 63 isn't prime?

5. Can the product of two different prime numbers be prime? Why or why not?

6. Find the least common multiple for these circles divided into different numbers of parts. What does this least common multiple mean?

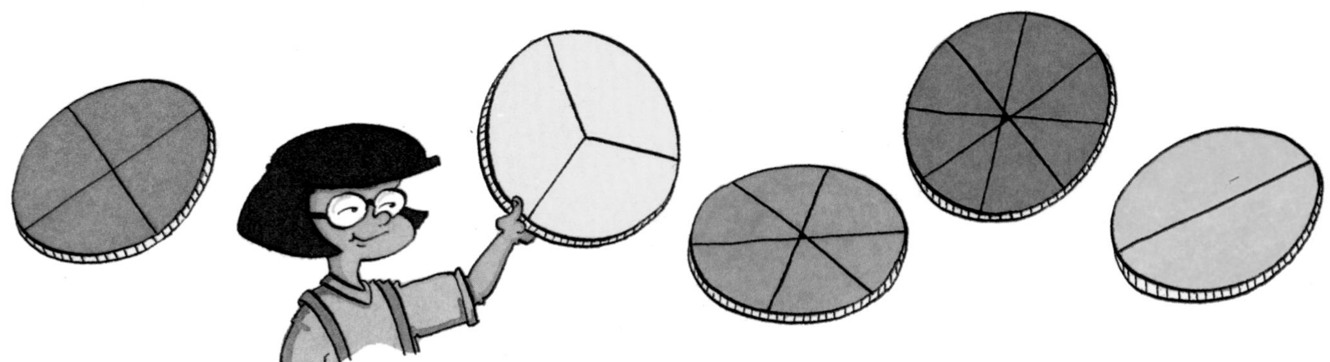

7. Two factors of a number are 6 and 15. What other numbers must also be factors of that number?

8. How many factors does the product of two different primes have? Is this true no matter which two primes are multiplied?

9. A common factor of two numbers is 10. What do you know about the other common factors? about the numbers themselves?

10. Find 2 multiples of 8 between 50 and 100 that are also multiples of 6.

11. List all the factors of 15. Write all the ratios of a lesser factor to a greater factor. Which ratios are equivalent?

12. Why are 2 and 3 the only prime numbers that differ by 1?

13. A number, x, has 10 added to it. The result is 11. What was the original number, x?

14. A number, y, has 7 subtracted from it. The result is 2. What was the original number, y?

Thinking Back . . .

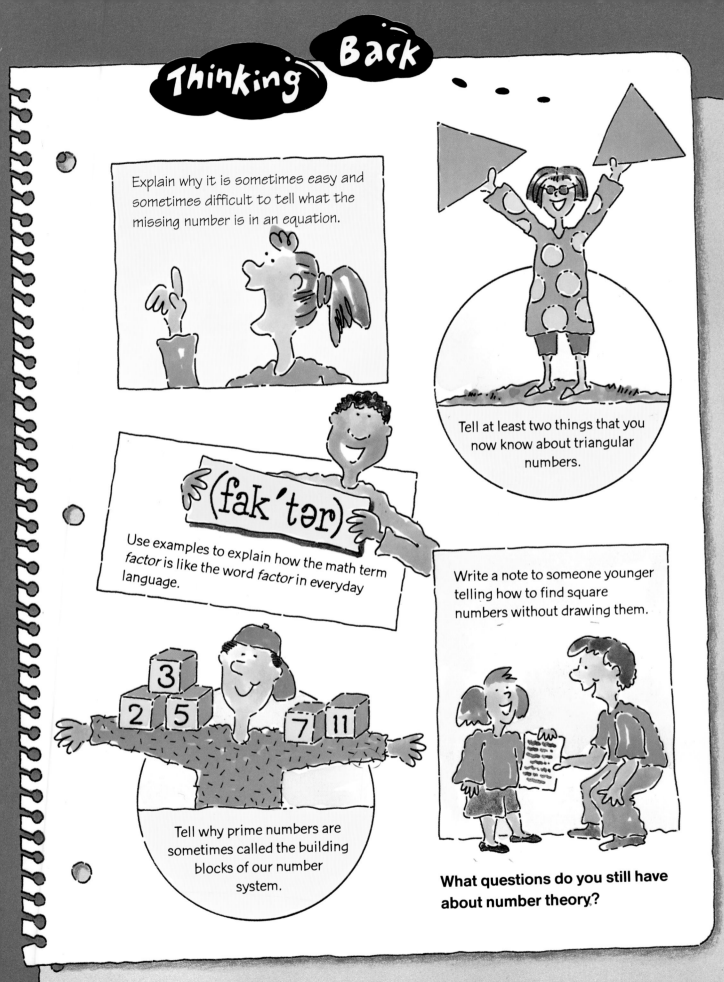

Explain why it is sometimes easy and sometimes difficult to tell what the missing number is in an equation.

Tell at least two things that you now know about triangular numbers.

Use examples to explain how the math term *factor* is like the word *factor* in everyday language.

Tell why prime numbers are sometimes called the building blocks of our number system.

Write a note to someone younger telling how to find square numbers without drawing them.

What questions do you still have about number theory?

UNIT

9

Exploring

► In each sample, which type of fish is
- the most common?
- the least common?
- about $\frac{1}{5}$ of the total?

Is it likely that the samples were taken from the same lake? Explain.

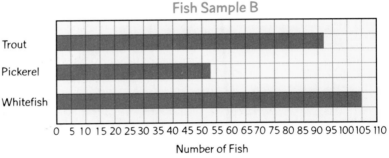

Fish Sample A

Trout	
Pickerel	
Whitefish	
One [fish] represents 1 fish.	

Fish Sample B

Trout

Pickerel

Whitefish

0 5 10 15 20 25 30 35 40 45 50 55 60 65 70 75 80 85 90 95 100 105 110

Number of Fish

◄ These 10 picture cards of pattern blocks are put in a bag.
A card is removed and examined.
Then it is returned to the bag.
If 100 cards are examined, what fraction of them will likely have a shape that
- is red?
- has right angles?
- has more than 5 sides?
- has all sides the same length?

▼ In 3 computer games, some routes eventually reach a treasure.

Game A: 5 out of 6 routes do
Game B: half of its routes do
Game C: 1 in 3 routes do

Which of the coin, the spinner, or the die could you use to simulate the number of times you might reach a treasure when playing each game? Explain.

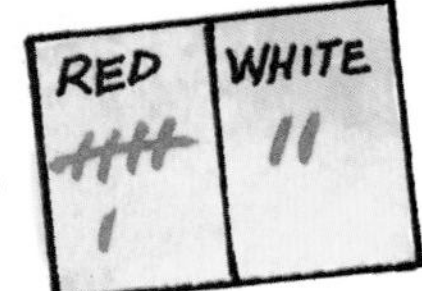

Probability and Statistics

▶ How could you find which of 5 pencils has the middle length?

▼ About how many people lived on farms in 1931? in 1971?
About how many times as many people lived on farms in 1931 as in 1971?
How many would you expect lived on farms in 1936? this year?
What overall impression do you get from this graph?

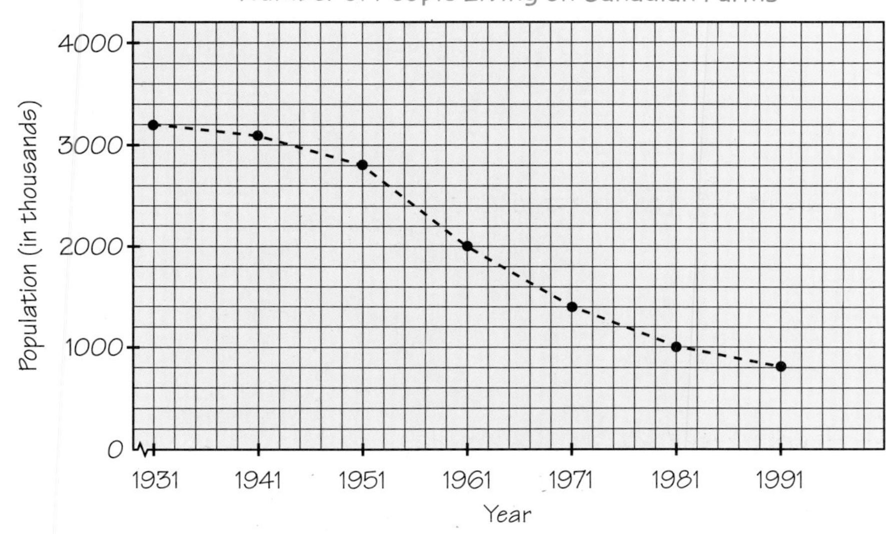

Tell about some situations you might want to know the probability or chance of them happening.

About how long a line would the toothpicks in this full box make if they were laid end to end?

Sampling Socks

Predicting by sampling

The Sock Monster

There's a thing stealing socks in our dryer, we know,
It's stealing them one by one;
It never grabs panties or stuff that won't show,
It just grabbles up socks by the tonne.

I get so depressed when I start to get dressed
With that hopeless, disastrous feeling;
I'm all the time late when I can't find a mate,
Our sock pile goes up to the ceiling.

On a pretty good day there's a black and a grey
And my pants meet my shoes real nice;
When everything's right there's a cream and a white
And people don't even look twice.

If I ever find that sock-grabbing thing
It better prepare to be dead;
I'll stomp it to death with my stocking feet . . .
A yellow one. And a red.

from *An Armadillo Is Not a Pillow* by Lois Simmie

How could you find the exact number of each color of sock in a pile like this?

How could you predict the fraction of each color of sock in a pile like this?

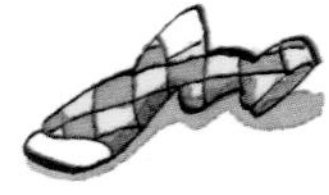

Use a container of 100 colored cubes to represent a pile of socks.

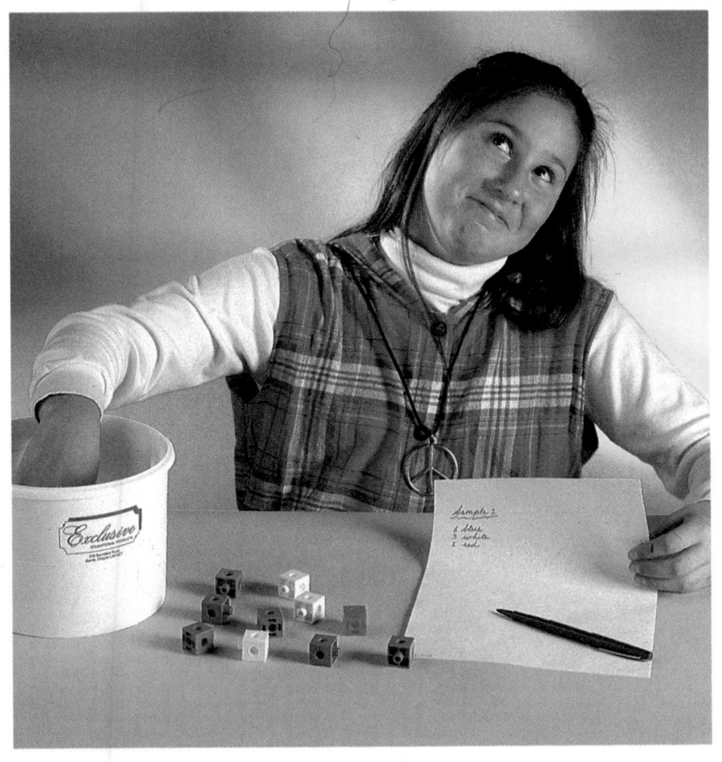

1. Mix up the cubes.
   Choose a sample of 10 without looking.
   Record the number of each color.
   Replace the cubes.

   What fraction of your sample is each color?
   What percent?

2. How could you use your results to predict the fraction and percent of each color in the container?

3. Repeat Problem 1 for three more samples of 10.

4. Calculate the middle number of each color found in your samples. Now what fraction and percent of each color do you predict is in the container?

5. Repeat the sampling process and find fractions and percents of each color for four samples of 20 and for the middle number of the four samples of 20.

6. Examine your results. Which do you think provides the best prediction of the fraction of each color of the container?
   - a sample of 10
   - the middle number of 4 samples of 10
   - a sample of 20
   - the middle number of 4 samples of 20

   Explain. Check by counting the colored cubes. What fractions and percents did you find?

7. Which of these predictions can usually be made by sampling socks?
   - the most common color
   - the least common color
   - the ratio of the colors
   - the fraction having holes
   - the percent that are knee highs

   Explain.

8. Why do sock manufacturers test the strength of a sample of socks rather than every sock they make?

What fraction of a turn does each turn of the lock represent?

How many degrees will be turned through to open this lock?

Right to 30.
Left to 15.
Right to 45.
Pull to open.

Describing Families

Simulating outcomes

Some events have equally likely outcomes.
Birth is one.
A baby boy is as equally likely as a baby girl.
What other events have equally likely outcomes?
What are their equally likely outcomes?

The children in this family are all girls.

What other combinations are possible for families of 3 children?

Martin simulated the outcomes for a family of 3 children.
He used 3 coins. Why? What else could be used?
He tossed the 3 coins 25 times, tallied the results, and drew a bar graph.

Describe Martin's graph.
Which combinations are most common? least common?

Use 25 tosses for each simulation.

1. Try Martin's simulation and graph your results. Compare your graph to Martin's and to other pairs of students'. Tell what you notice.

2. What are the boy-girl combinations for families of 4 children? Try a simulation for this size of family. Which combinations are most common? least common?

3. What are the boy-girl combinations for families of 5 children? Explain how the results of your simulations for families of 3 and 4 children could be used to predict which combinations are most common and least common for 5 children.

4. For every 1000 families of 10 children, about one family will be all boys. About how many families will be all girls? Explain.

5. The Harrison family had 12 children— all girls! They had one more child. Was this child
   - more likely to be a girl than a boy?
   - more likely to be a boy than a girl?
   - equally likely to be a boy or a girl?

6. The probability that children born in a certain family will be able to roll their tongues into a U-shape is $\frac{1}{2}$. Tell how coin tossing can be used to find out how many children might be born before there are 5 tongue-rollers.

On an average day, 14 521 *Archie, Veronica,* and *Jughead* comic books are sold in Canada. At this rate, how many days does it take to sell one million?

Playing Games

Comparing theoretical and experimental probabilities

Pugasaing was a game played by the Cree.
It used three sticks, each with one red side and one white side.
The sticks made from bone, wood, or horn were usually shaken in a basket and tossed onto the ground.

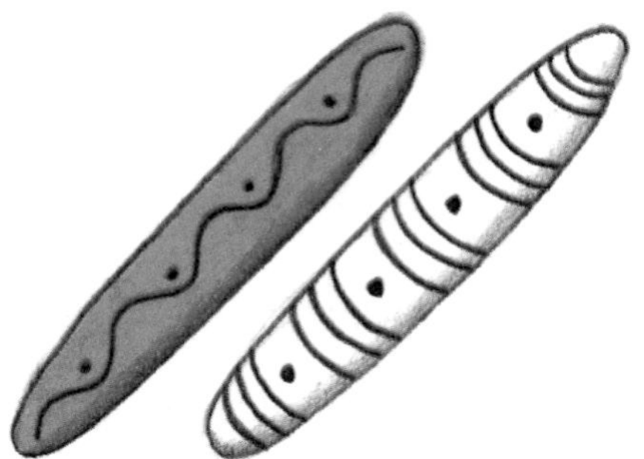

Red side White side

How many outcomes are there for one Pugasaing stick?
What are they?

Why can you use a coin to simulate these outcomes?

The outcomes are equally likely.
What fraction represents the **theoretical probability** for each outcome?

What decimal represents the theoretical probability for each outcome?

1. Use a coin to simulate the outcomes for a Pugasaing stick. Perform an experiment by tossing your coin 20 times and recording the results. How does your experimental probability compare to the theoretical probability?

2. You have a cube with the faces numbered 1 to 6. How many equally likely outcomes are possible? Name them.

3. For a cube numbered 1 to 6, what is the theoretical probability for these outcomes:
   a 1? a 4? a 7?
   Perform an experiment with a die and compare results.

4. What is the probability of tossing a prime number with a die? a composite number? a number that is neither prime nor composite?

5. For Problem 4, what is the probability of not tossing each outcome? Explain.

6. Why must the probability of all outcomes in an event total 1?

7. Complete this tree diagram to find the total number of outcomes possible when 3 two-color tiles are tossed at the same time.
   What is the probability of tossing 3 reds?
   3 whites?
   2 whites and a red?
   2 reds and a white?

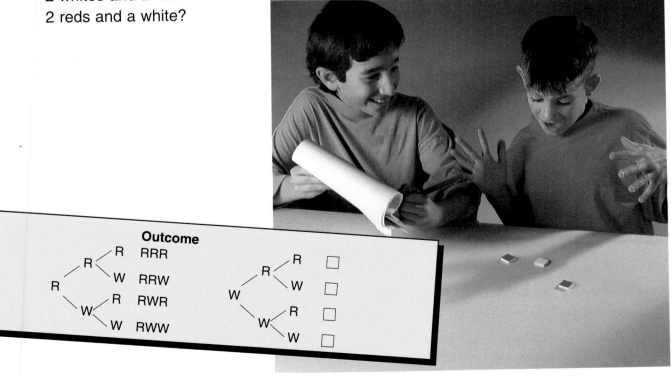

			Outcome
R	R	R	RRR
		W	RRW
	W	R	RWR
		W	RWW
W	R	R	☐
		W	☐
	W	R	☐
		W	☐

Emma earned $8 per hour at one job and $12 per hour at another. She earned $192 altogether. How many hours might she have worked at each job?

Using Different Dice

Relating the number of faces on a die to probability

What is the probability of rolling a prime number using a regular die?

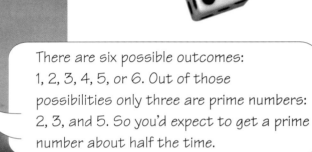

There are six possible outcomes:
1, 2, 3, 4, 5, or 6. Out of those
possibilities only three are prime numbers:

number about half the time.

Do you agree with June's statement? Why or why not?

Suppose you used a different shape of die.

This die is made from the net of an equilateral triangular pyramid.

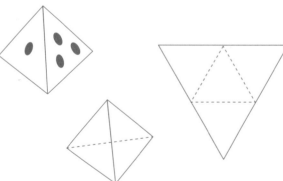

1. How many faces are identical?
   Do you think that each face has an equal chance of landing up when the die is thrown? Explain.

2. If you label the faces from 1 to 4, what is the probability of rolling a prime number?

3. Predict how many times you'd expect to get a 2 or a 3 in 50 tosses.
   Then make the 4-sided die and record your results for 50 tosses.
   Find the experimental probability.
   Is your experimental probability close to the theoretical probability?

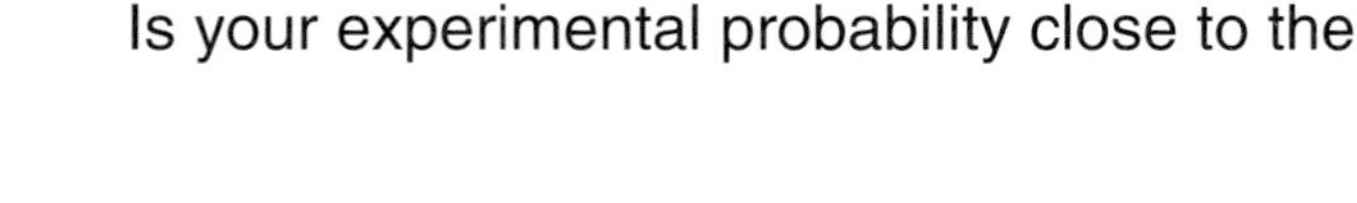

4. This die is made from the net of a square pyramid.
Do you think that each face has an equal chance of landing up when the die is thrown? Explain.
Would you say that this die is fair or unfair? Why?

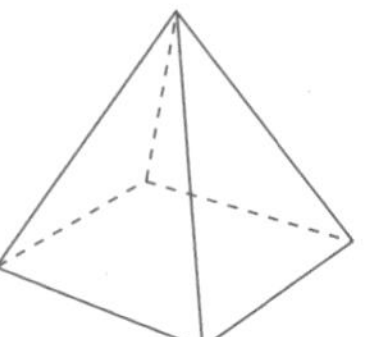

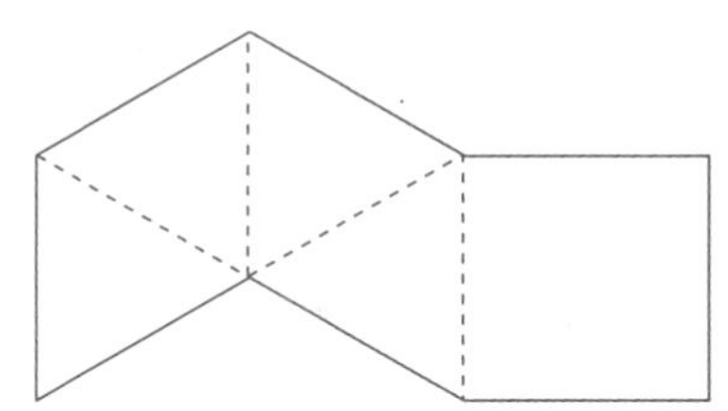

5. Draw a net for a die with 6 congruent faces. Will this die be fair or unfair? Why?
If you label each face from 1 to 6, what is the probability of rolling an odd number?
How could you label the die so that the probability of rolling an odd number is $\frac{5}{6}$?

6. How many times would you expect to get a 1, 3, or 5 in 30 tosses? 60 tosses?
Try the experiment and record your results for 30 tosses, then 60 tosses.
Find the experimental probability for each number of tosses.
Which experimental probability comes closest to the theoretical probability?

7. How can you make a die with 8 congruent faces using the 2 square pyramids?
Draw a net for a die with only 8 congruent faces.

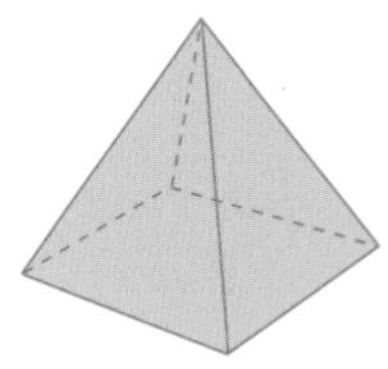

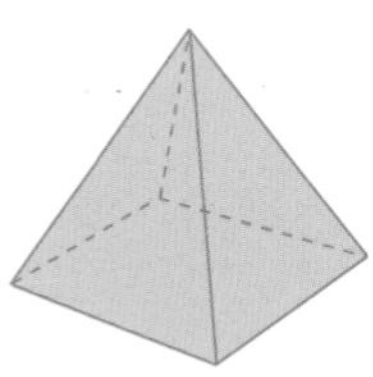

8. Use the die in question 7. If you label each face of the die from 1 to 8, what's the probability of rolling a multiple of 2?
How can you label the die so that the probability of rolling a multiple of 2 is $\frac{5}{8}$?

9. Suppose you made a die from the net below and labelled each face with the counting numbers starting at 1.
What is the probability of rolling an even number?

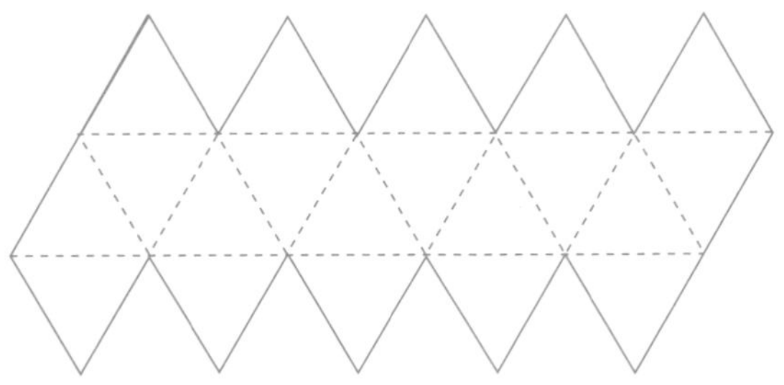

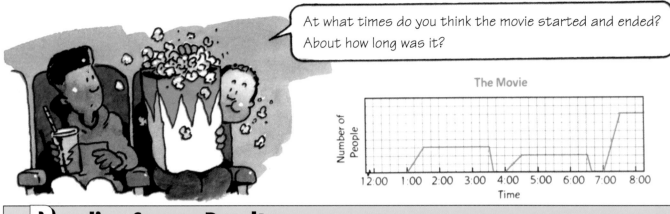

At what times do you think the movie started and ended? About how long was it?

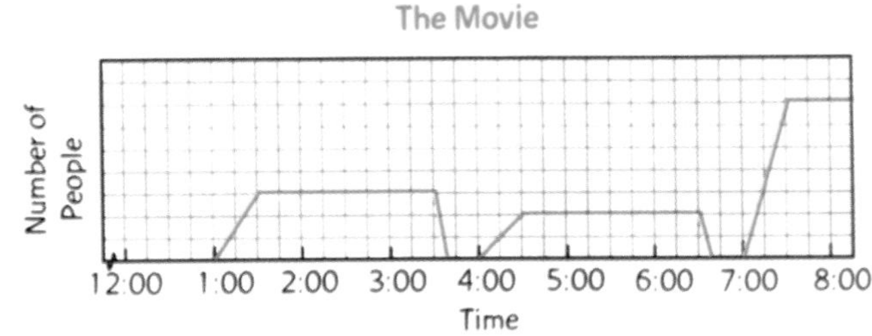

Reading Survey Results

Displaying data in various ways

Why is a histogram used here instead of a bar graph?

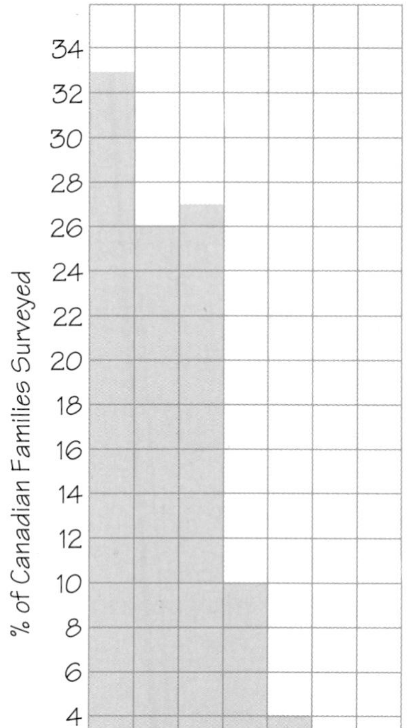

1. Copy and complete the table if the number of families surveyed was
   • 100 • 200 • 150 • 75

Number of Children at Home	0	1	2
Number of Families Out of 100			
Out of 200			
Out of 150			
Out of 75			

   Describe the mental math you used, if any, to do the calculations.

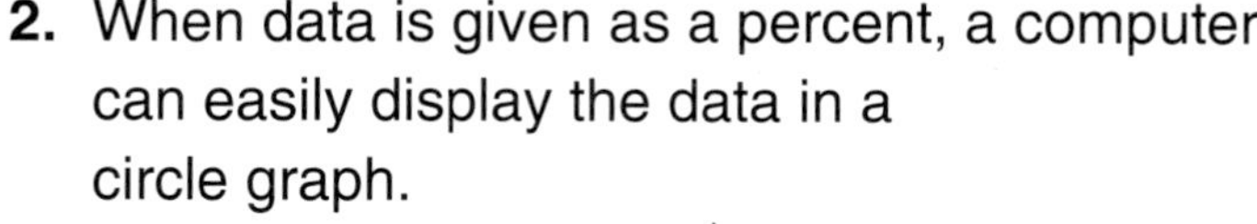

2. When data is given as a percent, a computer can easily display the data in a circle graph.
   Which section is about $\frac{1}{3}$ of the circle?
   Which 2 sections together make up slightly more than half the circle?

Number of Children at Home

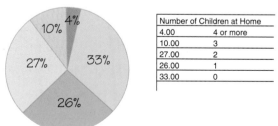

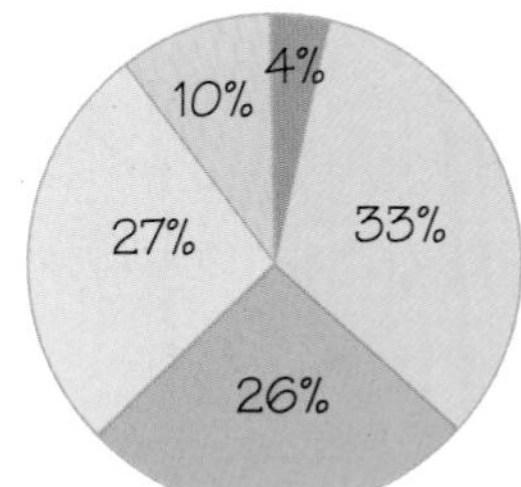

Number of Children at Home	
4.00	4 or more
10.00	3
27.00	2
26.00	1
33.00	0

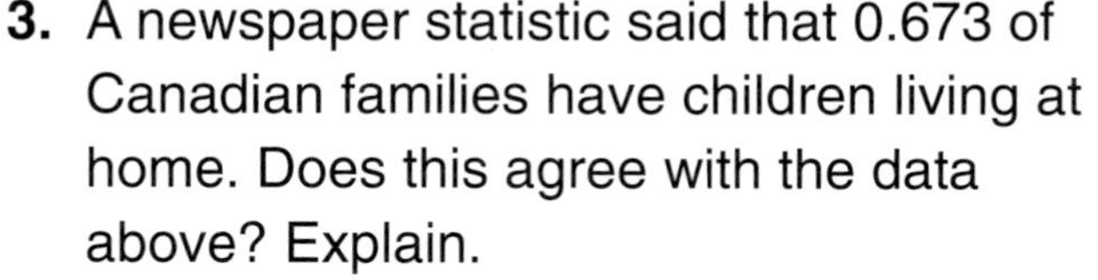

3. A newspaper statistic said that 0.673 of Canadian families have children living at home. Does this agree with the data above? Explain.

4. If you surveyed your classmates and recorded the number of children at home, would your data be similar to that shown above? Why or why not?

5. Morag surveyed her classmates.

Number of children at home	Our Class	Percent
0	0	0
1	9	36
2	10	?
3	4	?
4 or more	2	?

Which category would have the same number for your class as it has for Morag's? How do you know?
How many students were surveyed?
Is 36% correct for 1 child at home? How many can you tell?

6. Would it be easier or harder to find percents if 22 students had been surveyed? Explain.

7. What conclusions can you make from this double bar graph?
Explain your reasoning for each.
What important information is not provided in this graph?
Could this graph be true for the students in your class? your school? Why?

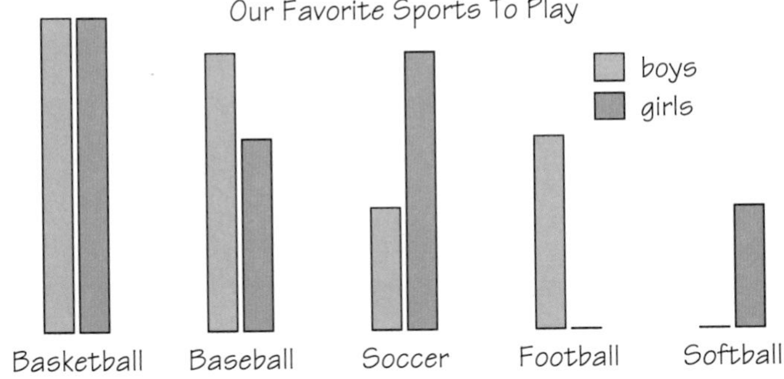

8. Another survey showed that in Canadian households,
- 8% owned a CD player in 1991, and 33% in 1993
- 71% owned a clothes dryer in 1991, and 75% in 1993
- 13% owned a computer in 1991, and 23% in 1993
- 68% owned a microwave in 1991, and 79% in 1993
- 98% owned a telephone in 1991, and 99% in 1993
- 99% owned a TV in 1991, and 99% in 1993

Display the data in a graph. Justify why you chose the graph you did.
Why do you think it's unreasonable to display the data in a circle graph?

9. Other statistics show that in Canadian households
- 60% own their own homes
- 21% are one-person households

In each case, describe what the data might look like.
How would you graph each set of data? Justify your choice.

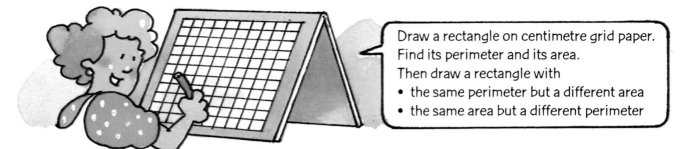

Draw a rectangle on centimetre grid paper.
Find its perimeter and its area.
Then draw a rectangle with

- the same perimeter but a different area
- the same area but a different perimeter

Comparing Lengths of Movies

Using stem-and-leaf plots

The **range** of this data is from 90 min to 145 min, the smallest and largest value.
What do you think range means?

Length (in minutes) of the Top 20 Movies in 1989									
126	127	113	93	90	102	124	107	128	95
97	100	106	97	102	112	115	145	106	107

How could you display this data so it's easier to use?

Helena made a **stem-and-leaf-plot**.
The ones digit in each number is the leaf.
The tens or hundreds and tens digits are the stems.
Then she reorganized the ones digits in each row from least to greatest.

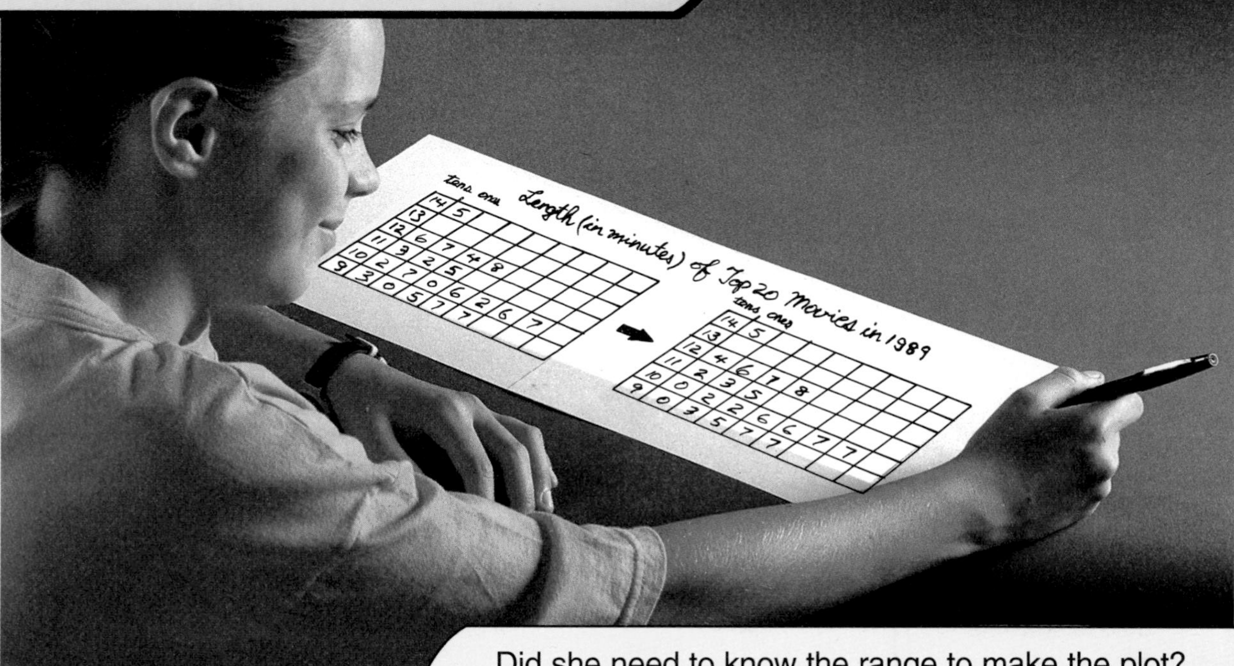

Did she need to know the range to make the plot? Explain.
Why do you think this is called a stem-and-leaf plot?
What is the stem and the leaf for each number?

1. Find the number of movies, the **frequency**, of each movie length.
2. What fraction of the movies are longer than 2 h? less than 110 min?
3. Tell how you could use the plot to find the middle length. Find it.
4. What are the most common lengths?
5. What is the range of this data?

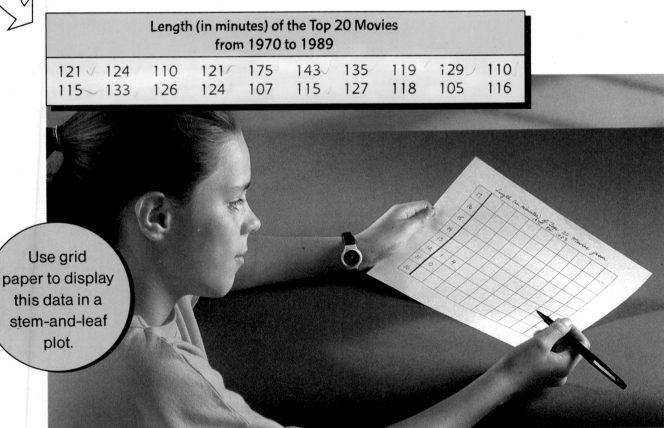

Length (in minutes) of the Top 20 Movies from 1970 to 1989									
121	124	110	121	175	143	135	119	129	110
115	133	126	124	107	115	127	118	105	116

Use grid paper to display this data in a stem-and-leaf plot.

6. Compare your plot with the *Movies in 1989* plot. What do you notice?
7. What fraction of these movies are less than 110 min? longer than 2 h?
8. What is the middle length? the most common length? Compare these lengths to those in the *Movies in 1989* plot.
9. Find the lengths of at least 20 movies enjoyed by your class. Display them in a stem-and-leaf plot.
   Make up two questions about your plot for another group to answer.

Take Your Pick

MOST COMMON NUMBER OF FACTORS

How many factors does each number from 1 to 10 have?
Find the most common number of factors.
Predict whether the most common number of factors for the numbers from 11 to 20 will be greater or less.
Check your prediction.

DICEY DICE

Draw and label the net of a die so that the chance of rolling a prime number is $\frac{0}{4}$.
What other types of dice could you make where the chance of rolling a prime number is 0?

BACK AND FORTH

Draw a number line from -15 to 15. Start at 0. Toss a coin.
Move one place to the right for heads and 1 place to the left for tails. Toss the coin 24 more times, numbering your moves. Compare your results with others. What do you notice?
Is it possiable to reach 15 or -15?
Is it likely? Explaine.

FREE-THROW SHOOTER

A basketball player sinks 5 out of every 6 free-throw shots she tries.
Use a die to simulate her shooting.
Find the number of free-throw shots she might have to try before she sinks 8 in a row.

GUESS THE NUMBER

Fill a clear container with dried beans.
Have at least 25 students estimate the number of beans.
Record their estimates on a stem and leaf plot.
Repeat with much younger students.
What do you notice?

Make up other problems. Post them on the bulletin board for your classmates to solve.

Solving a Problem by Finding Relevant Information

Discuss this problem before going on.

BIKE HELMETS

What percent of students wear bike helmets?
Why don't all students?

Theo's group solved the problem by finding relevant information.

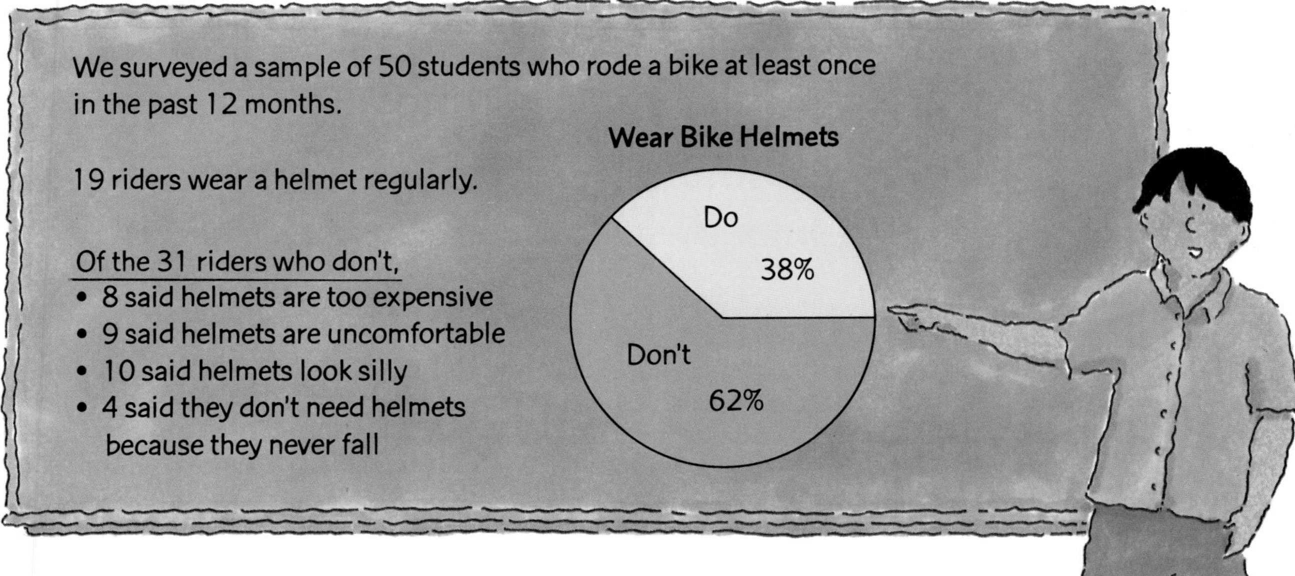

We surveyed a sample of 50 students who rode a bike at least once in the past 12 months.

19 riders wear a helmet regularly.

Of the 31 riders who don't,

- 8 said helmets are too expensive
- 9 said helmets are uncomfortable
- 10 said helmets look silly
- 4 said they don't need helmets because they never fall

Would you expect similar results at your school?

Discuss how to find the relevant information to solve these problems.

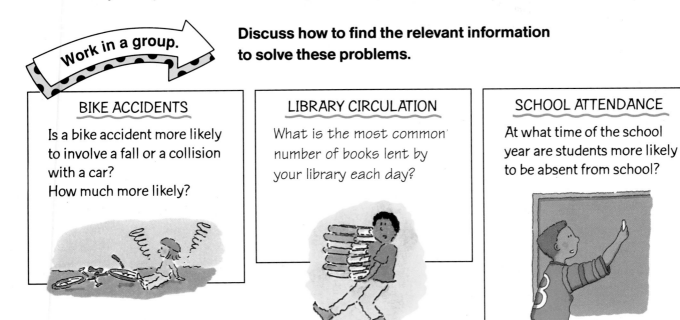

BIKE ACCIDENTS

Is a bike accident more likely to involve a fall or a collision with a car?
How much more likely?

LIBRARY CIRCULATION

What is the most common number of books lent by your library each day?

SCHOOL ATTENDANCE

At what time of the school year are students more likely to be absent from school?

Practising What You've Learned

1. A sample of 25 jellybeans from a large jar included 4 red, 8 yellow, 12 green, and 1 purple. What can you predict about the jellybeans in the jar? What can't you predict?

2. Tommy makes his bed about $\frac{1}{3}$ of the time. Explain how to use a spinner to simulate Tommy's bed-making. By simulating, how could you find the number of days that might pass before he makes his bed four days in a row?

3. How many possible outcomes are there when you toss a die? What is the theoretical probability for each outcome?

4. What are the theoretical probabilities for a cube numbered 1 to 6?
   - getting a prime number
   - getting a composite number
   - getting a number that is neither prime nor composite

5. Find the middle and the most common lengths of the cube trains. Tell what you did.

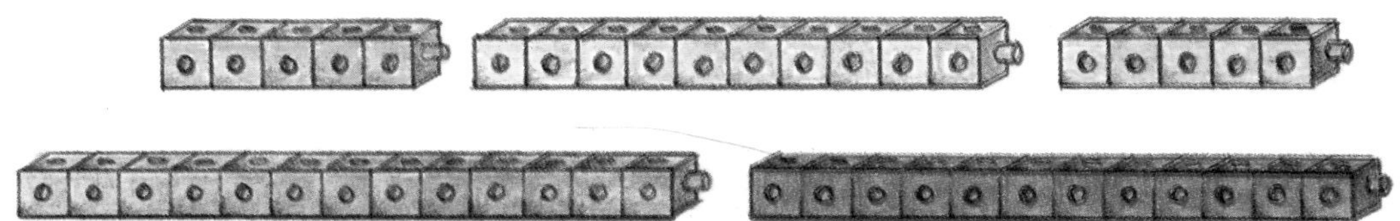

6. What is the most common price? What is the range of prices?

7. The price tags from Problem 6 are placed in a bag. What is the probability of drawing a price tag that is more than $5? Express your answer as a decimal.

8. Calculate the range for this data. Then display the data in a stem-and-leaf plot. What is the most common number of goals scored?

Goals Scored by NHL Scoring Champions from 1970–71 to 1991–92										
76	66	55	68	46	56	56	60	47	53	55
92	71	87	73	52	62	70	85	40	41	44

9. How could you label a 6-sided die so that the probability of rolling an even number is $\frac{2}{3}$?

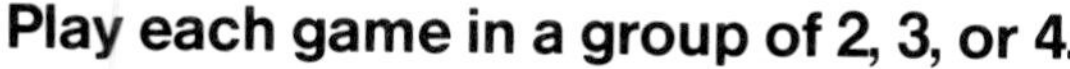

Playing Games for Practice

Play each game in a group of 2, 3, or 4.

Predict a Sum

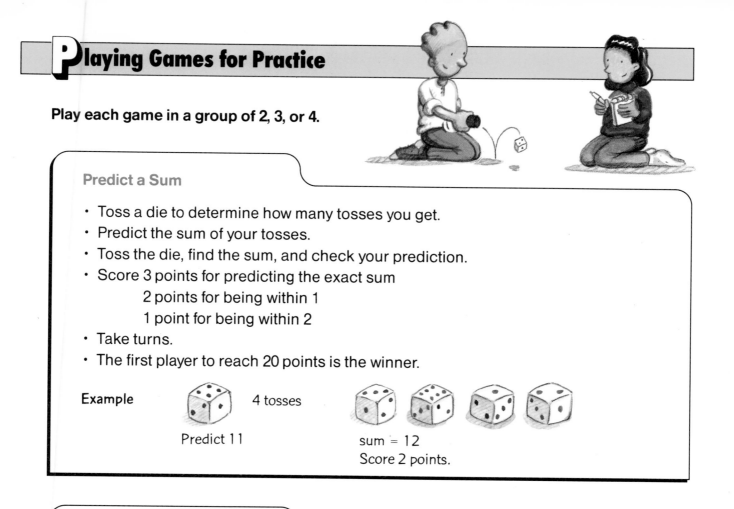

- Toss a die to determine how many tosses you get.
- Predict the sum of your tosses.
- Toss the die, find the sum, and check your prediction.
- Score 3 points for predicting the exact sum
  2 points for being within 1
  1 point for being within 2
- Take turns.
- The first player to reach 20 points is the winner.

Example

Predict 11

4 tosses

sum = 12
Score 2 points.

Greater, Less, or Equal

- Remove the face cards from a deck of playing cards.
- Shuffle the remaining cards.
- Deal 5 cards in a row face down.
- Turn over the first, the third, and the fifth cards.
- Before the second card is turned over, each player records a prediction of whether it will be within the range of turned up numbers. Check the predictions.
- Score 1 point for each correct prediction.
- Score 2 points if the card shows the middle number between the 2 turned up numbers.
- Repeat with the fourth card.
- Then, play again with a different set of 5 cards.
- The winner is the first player to reach 20 points.

Example

Take Your pick

GUESSING COMBINATIONS

Some bicycle combination locks have 4 dials, each with the digits from 1 to 6.
How many combinations are possiable?
What is the theoretical probability that someone could guess the combination on the first guess?

GO TO JAIL

In Monopoly, rolling a double gets you an extra turn, but rolling 3 doubles in a row gets you to jail.
Simulate playing Monopoly by rolling a pair of dice.
Find the number of turns that might be taken before 3 consecutive doubles are rolled.
Compare your results with others.

CALENDAR SQUARES

Add all the numbers in the 3 x 3 array surrounding the middle number. How many times greater than the middle number is the sum?
Repeat using other 3 by 3 arrays.
Tell what you notice.

MARCH

S	M	T	W	T	F	S
		1	2	3	4	5
6	7	8	9	10	11	12
13	14	15	16	17	18	19
20	21	22	23	24	25	26
27	28	29	30	31		

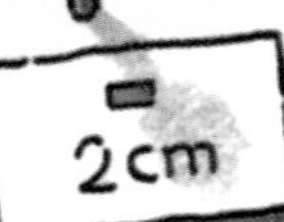

PICKING RODS

These 5 picture cards of rods are placed in a bag, shaken, and 1 is removed.
What is the theoretical probability of getting a length that is

- an even number of centimetres?
- an odd number of centimetres?
- less than or equal to 8 cm?
- less than or equal to 12 cm?

SAMPLING PHONE NUMBERS

Use sampling to determine if some digits are used more often than others in phone numbers.

Make up other problems. Post them on the bulletin board for your classmates to solve.

Showing What You Know

1. A spinner with 8 different colored sections is spun. What is the probability of spinning any one color? What is the probability of spinning no color? What's the probability of spinning a color?

2. A spinner with 9 sections numbered 1 to 9 is spun. What is the probability of spinning a prime number? a composite number? a number that is neither prime nor composite?

3. About $\frac{2}{3}$ of the time it will be a wet day in St. John's, NF. Show how to simulate the weather in St. John's. By simulating, find how many days might have to pass to get three consecutive days that are not wet.

4. A survey of 50 households showed that
   - 12 own one or more dogs
   - 11 own one or more cats
   - 6 own one or more other pets

   What is the percent of each category? What is the ratio of dog owners to cat owners?

5. What is the range of the masses of tomatoes? What is the middle mass? About how many times larger is the world's largest tomato? Round your answer to the nearest hundredth.

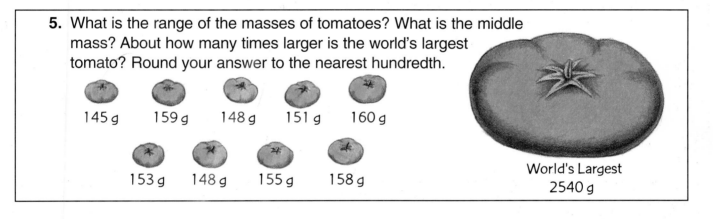

145 g 159 g 148 g 151 g 160 g

153 g 148 g 155 g 158 g

World's Largest
2540 g

6. Tell what you notice about this graph. Predict the cost in 1969 and for this year.

7. What is the difference between theoretical and experimental probability?

8. Create a stem-and-leaf plot. Present it to a classmate. Have them tell you the range of the data, the middle number, and the most common number.

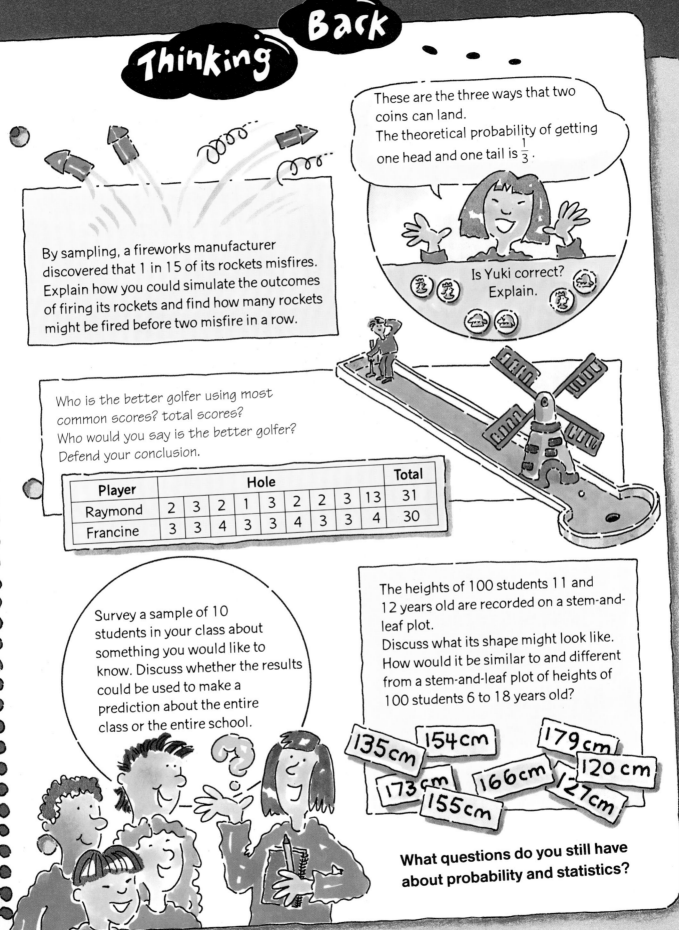

Thinking Back . . .

By sampling, a fireworks manufacturer discovered that 1 in 15 of its rockets misfires. Explain how you could simulate the outcomes of firing its rockets and find how many rockets might be fired before two misfire in a row.

These are the three ways that two coins can land. The theoretical probability of getting one head and one tail is $\frac{1}{3}$.

Is Yuki correct? Explain.

Who is the better golfer using most common scores? total scores? Who would you say is the better golfer? Defend your conclusion.

Player	Hole									Total
Raymond	2	3	2	1	3	2	2	3	13	31
Francine	3	3	4	3	3	4	3	3	4	30

Survey a sample of 10 students in your class about something you would like to know. Discuss whether the results could be used to make a prediction about the entire class or the entire school.

The heights of 100 students 11 and 12 years old are recorded on a stem-and-leaf plot. Discuss what its shape might look like. How would it be similar to and different from a stem-and-leaf plot of heights of 100 students 6 to 18 years old?

What questions do you still have about probability and statistics?

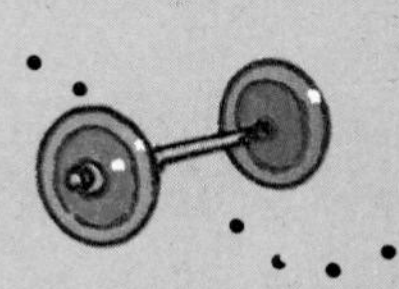

UNIT 10

Investigating Sports

What sports do the students in your class participate in?

Tell what you notice about the bar graph. About what percents of males and females in each age group do not participate in a competitive sport?

Do you think the graph describes your classmates? Tell what you could do to find out.

What do you think the graph would look like if other age groups were included?

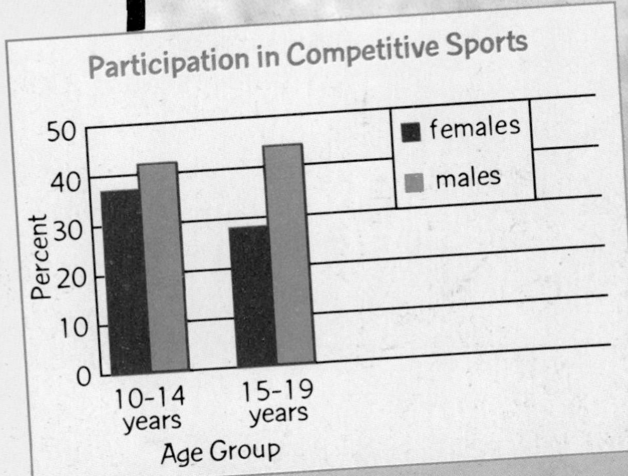

WHAT Are Some Highlights in Sports?

Torch Relay Sets Records!
The 1988 Olympic Torch Relay set a record for the longest distance covered at 18 000 km. It also took the longest time to complete at 88 days. 6953 athletes and volunteers participated in the relay and about 2.9 million people watched along the route.

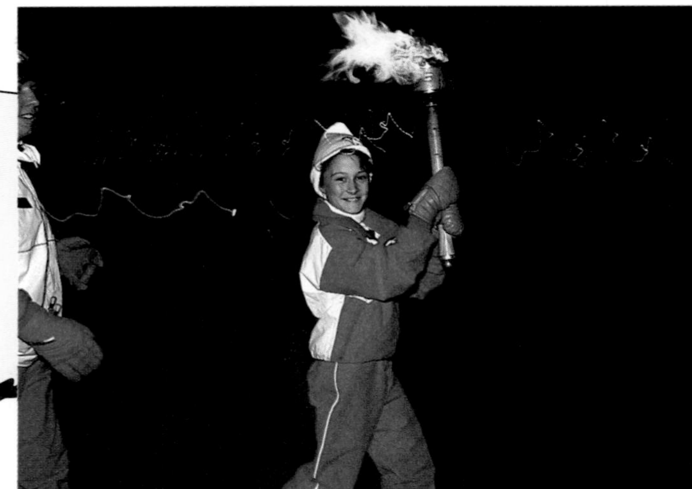

What was the approximate distance travelled by
- the torch each day?
- each torchbearer?

Ten million applications for volunteer torchbearers were sent to Canadian households. 6500 volunteers were selected from the 6.6 million applications returned.
- How many applications for volunteers were not returned?
- About what percent were returned?
- What was the theoretical probability of being selected as a torchbearer for those who returned one application?

Work with a partner.

Canada Captures Gold!
Alwyn Morris and Hugh Fisher became gold-medal winners in a two-man kayak event at the 1984 Summer Olympics. The winning team completed the 1000 m event in a record time of 3:24.22.

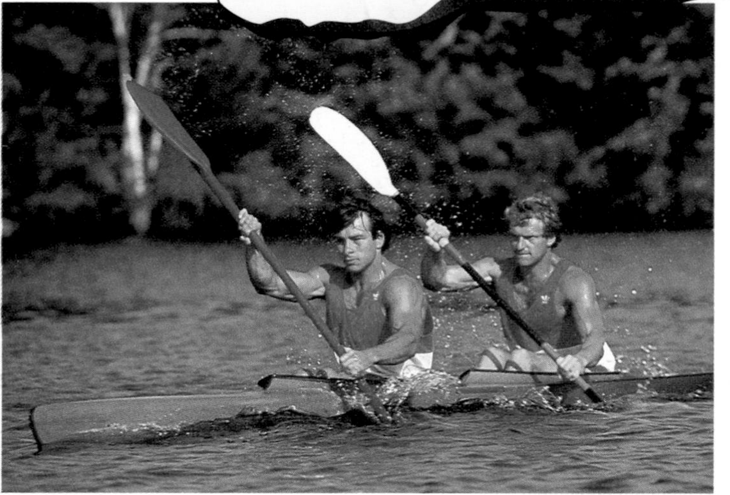

1. Express the winning time as a decimal to the nearest tenth of a minute.
2. The kayakers averaged about 130 strokes each minute. About how many strokes did each man make in the winning race?
3. What was the approximate distance the kayak travelled for each stroke?
4. What was the approximate speed of the kayak in kilometres per hour?

Swimming the Distance
Vicki Keith has made the greatest number of crossings of Lake Ontario by a swimmer. Her record for the Butterfly stroke for the 51.2 km distance across the lake is 31 h.

5. What was Vicki's approximate speed? About how long would you expect her to take to do the Butterfly across Lake Winnipeg, a distance of 29 km?

6. About how many lengths of a 50 m swimming pool equal her swim across Lake Ontario?

Powerlifting Highlights
Joy Burt of Canada, who weighed in the 56 kg category, lifted a mass of 200.5 kg to set a world record. Lars Noren of Sweden, weighing in the 125 kg category, lifted a mass of 387.5 kg.

7. Explain why Joy might be considered stronger than Lars. If you had the same strength as one of these athletes, what mass would you be able to lift?

8. About how many attended each of the 81 home games?

Attendance Soars
The Toronto Blue Jays set the major league baseball attendance record in 1992 of 4 028 318.

9. The Colorado Rockies averaged over 55 000 spectators for each home game in 1993. Did they break the Blue Jays' record? About what percent of the 76 000 seats were filled each game?

10. Investigate and report on a highlight of a sport you enjoy. Make up a math problem for someone else to solve.

Did You Know...?

In 1990, Andre Viger established the best performance for a Canadian athlete in the wheelchair marathon by travelling 42 km in 1:32.20.

- What was his approximate speed in kilometres per hour?
  How much faster was he than the Olympic marathon runner who finished the same distance in 2:12.23?

HOW Can We Measure Sports Balls?

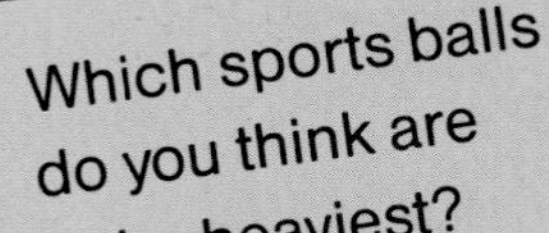

Which sports balls do you think are
- the heaviest?
- the smallest?
- the most bouncy?

Work in a group.

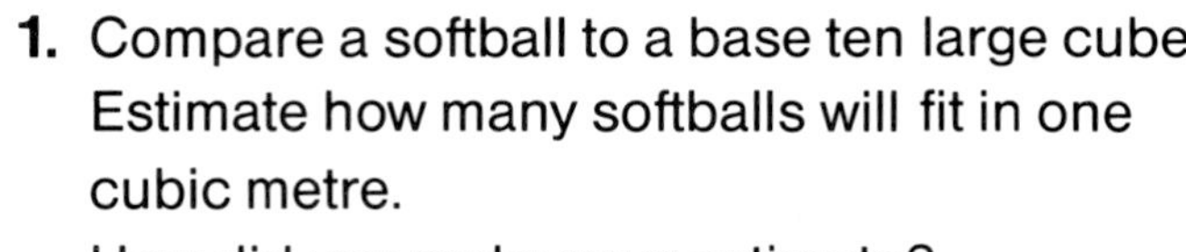

1. Compare a softball to a base ten large cube.
   Estimate how many softballs will fit in one cubic metre.
   How did you make your estimate?

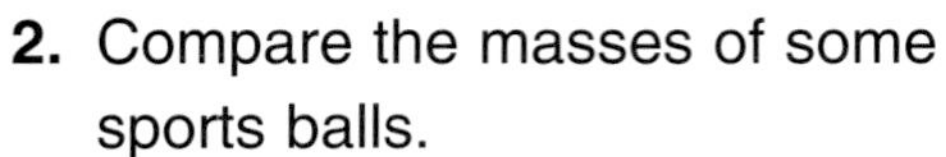

2. Compare the masses of some sports balls.
   How many times as heavy as your lightest ball is your heaviest ball?

3. What regular polygons can you see on a regulation soccer ball?
   What is the measure of the angles at each vertex?
   Would these shapes form a tiling pattern on a flat surface? Explain.

4. Diane dropped a golf ball from various heights and measured how high it bounced each time. She plotted the results in a graph as ordered pairs (drop height, bounce height). What do you notice about the graph? Estimate how high the ball will bounce if dropped from a height of 2.0 m.

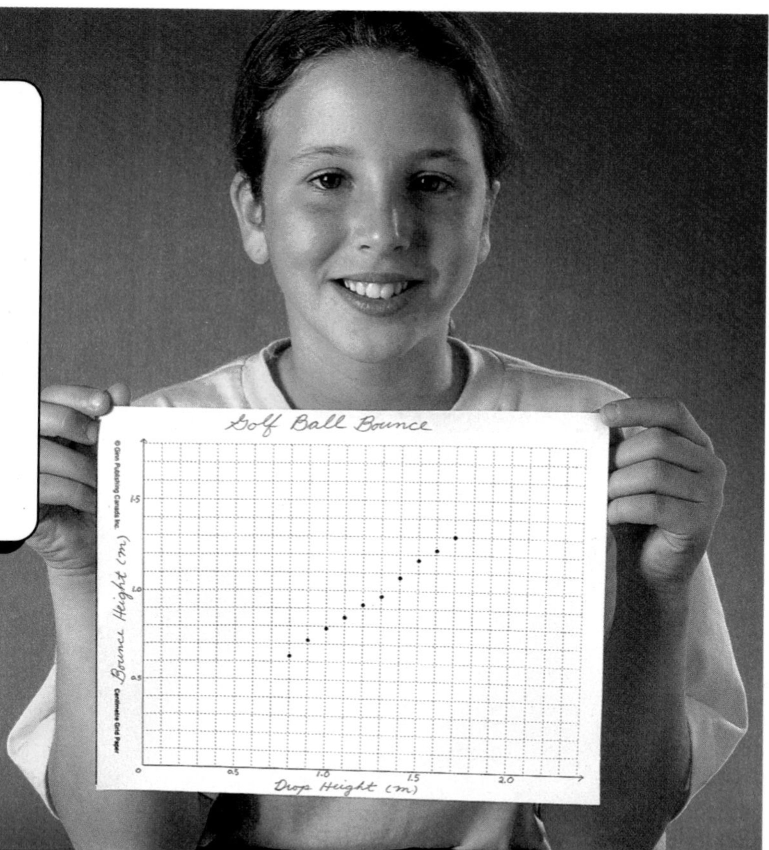

5. Measure the bounce of another ball from various heights. Graph the results. How is your graph different from Diane's graph? How is it alike?

6. Ljiljana Ljubific won a medal for Canada in the 1992 Paralympics shotput event with a 9.96 m throw. The distance around a shot is about 30 cm. About how many turns would the shot make if it was rolled this distance?

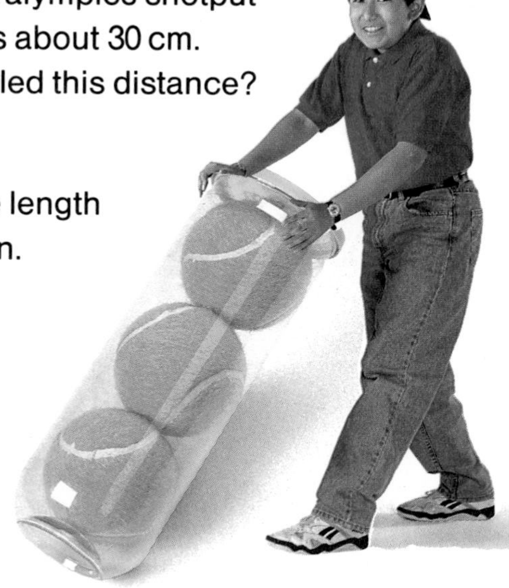

7. Measure the distance around another ball. Predict the number of turns it will make when rolled the length of your classroom. Roll the ball to check your prediction.

8. Compare the height of three tennis balls in a container with the distance around a tennis ball. Explain what you notice. Use this result to predict the height of a package of three golf balls each with a distance around of 13.5 cm.

Did you Know...?

Every ball used in professional sports must meet a standard of bounciness. For example, a lacrosse ball must bounce between 1.1 m to 1.2 m when dropped from a height of 1.8 m onto a wooden floor. Tennis balls must bounce between 135 cm to 147 cm when dropped from a height of 254 cm onto a concrete base.

▶ About what percent of the height of the drop is the bounce in each situation? Explain why different sports have different bounciness standards.

WHAT Can We Learn About Hockey Statistics?

About what fraction of shots by the top National Hockey League players score a goal?

About what fraction of shots are stopped by the top goalies?

Success of Top NHL Players' Shots on Goal (1992-93)

Craig Simpson	Edmonton Oilers	26.4 %
Petr Nedved	Vancouver Canucks	25.5 %
Dimitri Khristich	Washington Capitols	24.4 %
Mario Lemieux	Pittsburg Penguins	24.1 %
Luc Robitaille	Los Angeles Kings	23.8 %

Shots Saved by Top NHL Goalies (1992-93)

Curtis Joseph	St. Louis Blues	91.1 %
Felix Potvin	Toronto Maple Leafs	91.0 %
Ed Belfour	Chicago Black Hawks	90.6 %
Tom Barrasso	Pittsburgh Penguins	90.1 %
John Vanbiesbrouck	New York Rangers	90.0 %

1. Which spinners could you use to simulate
   - goal scoring?
   - goal saving?

   Explain.

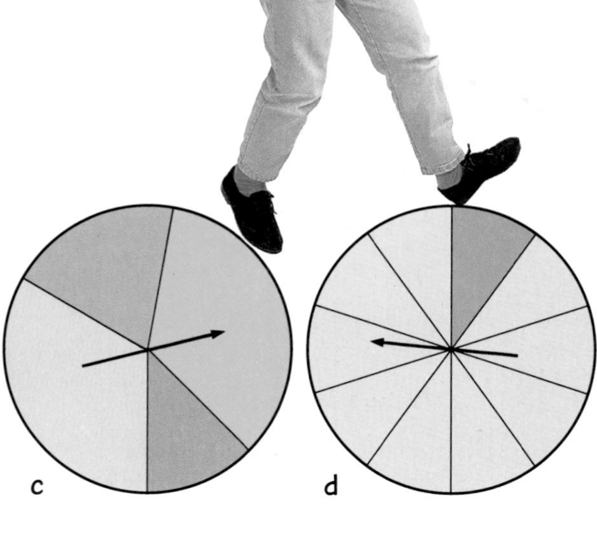

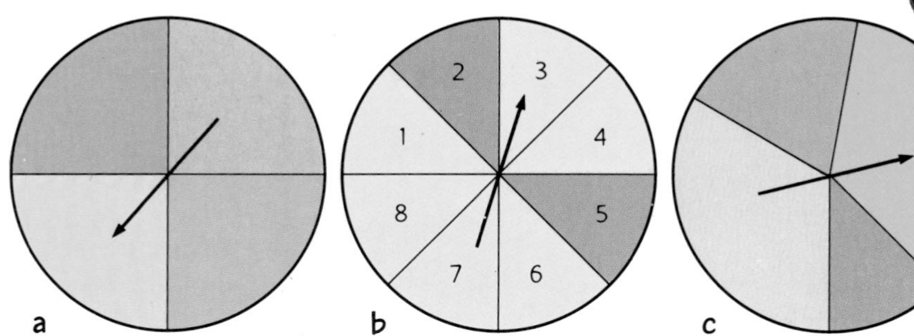

2. Simulate 25 shots on goal by a top player. Record the number of scores and misses.
What percent of shots scored? missed?
Make a grid graph to show your results.

3. Simulate 25 shots handled by a top goaltender. Record the number of saves and goals.

What percent of shots were saved?
What is the ratio of saves to goals?

Top Five All-Time NHL Point Leaders (to end of 1992–93 season)

Player	Seasons	Games	Goals	Assists	Points
1. Wayne Gretzky	14	1044	765	1563	2328
2. Gordie Howe	26	1767	801	1049	1850
3. Marcel Dionne	18	1348	731	1040	1771
4. Phil Esposito	18	1282	717	873	1590
5. Stan Mikita	22	1394	541	926	1467

4. How does the order of the top five players change when the approximate number of points per game is found?

5. What other numbers can you use to compare these players? How does the order change?

6. Do you think statistics can be used to compare present players and teams with past players and teams? Explain.

Did You Know...?

Several players have scored a goal within 5 s of the start of a game.

▶ If they kept scoring at this rate, how many goals would they score in a regulation game of three 20 min periods?

? I Wonder... ?

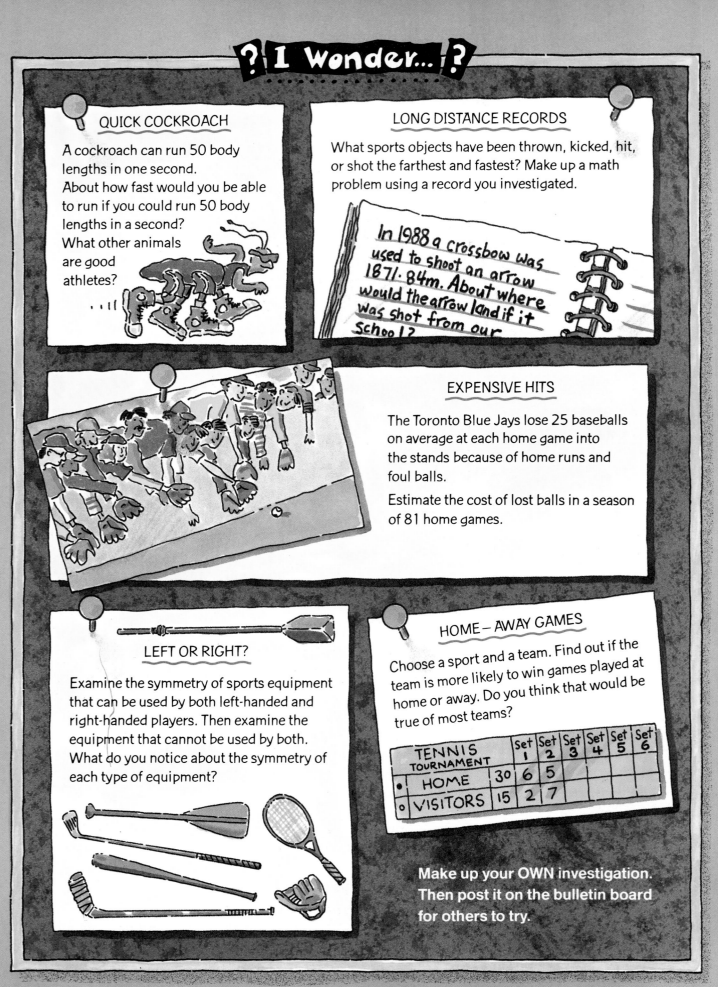

QUICK COCKROACH

A cockroach can run 50 body lengths in one second.
About how fast would you be able to run if you could run 50 body lengths in a second?
What other animals are good athletes?

LONG DISTANCE RECORDS

What sports objects have been thrown, kicked, hit, or shot the farthest and fastest? Make up a math problem using a record you investigated.

In 1988 a crossbow was used to shoot an arrow 1871.84m. About where would the arrow land if it was shot from our school?

EXPENSIVE HITS

The Toronto Blue Jays lose 25 baseballs on average at each home game into the stands because of home runs and foul balls.

Estimate the cost of lost balls in a season of 81 home games.

LEFT OR RIGHT?

Examine the symmetry of sports equipment that can be used by both left-handed and right-handed players. Then examine the equipment that cannot be used by both. What do you notice about the symmetry of each type of equipment?

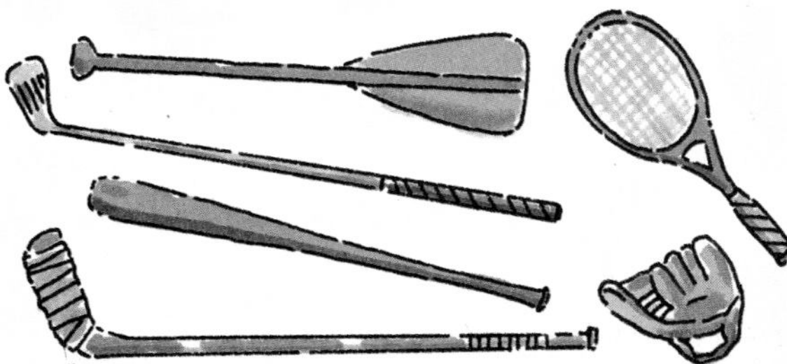

HOME – AWAY GAMES

Choose a sport and a team. Find out if the team is more likely to win games played at home or away. Do you think that would be true of most teams?

TENNIS TOURNAMENT		Set 1	Set 2	Set 3	Set 4	Set 5	Set 6
• HOME	30	6	5				
○ VISITORS	15	2	7				

Make up your OWN investigation. Then post it on the bulletin board for others to try.

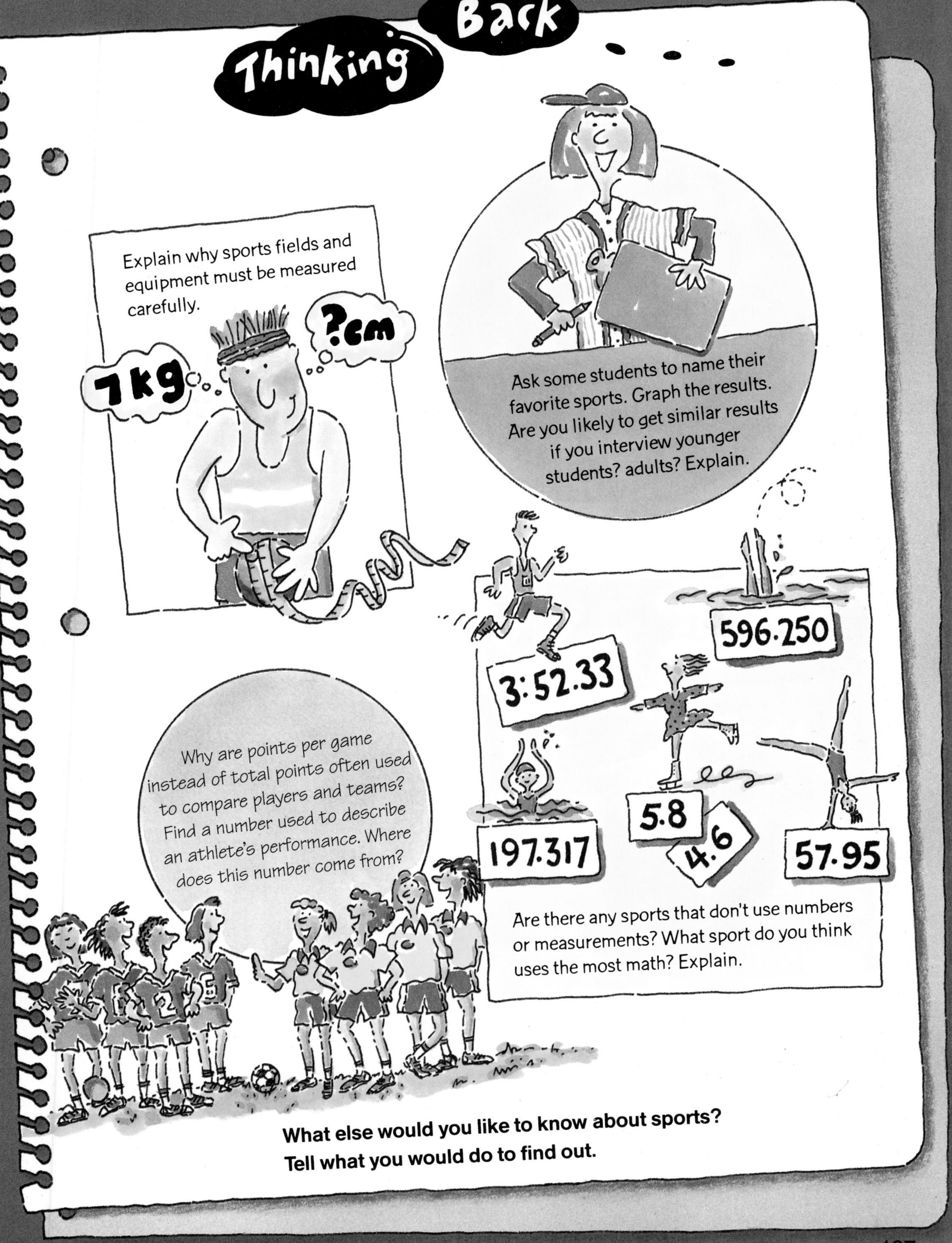
Thinking Back
Explain why sports fields and equipment must be measured carefully.
7kg
?cm
Ask some students to name their favorite sports. Graph the results. Are you likely to get similar results if you interview younger students? adults? Explain.
596.250
3:52.33
Why are points per game instead of total points often used to compare players and teams? Find a number used to describe an athlete's performance. Where does this number come from?
5.8
4.6
197.317
57.95
Are there any sports that don't use numbers or measurements? What sport do you think uses the most math? Explain.
What else would you like to know about sports? Tell what you would do to find out.

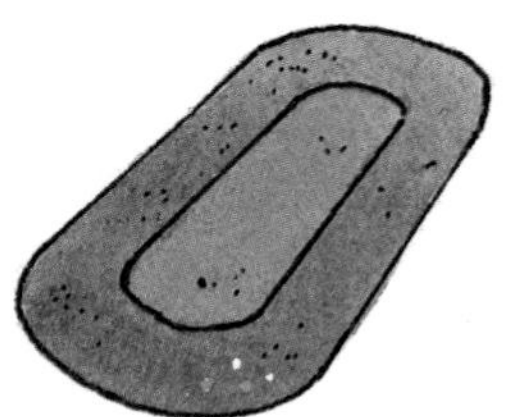

Exploring

▶ Draw a symmetrical shape on triangular dot paper with a perimeter of 11 units.

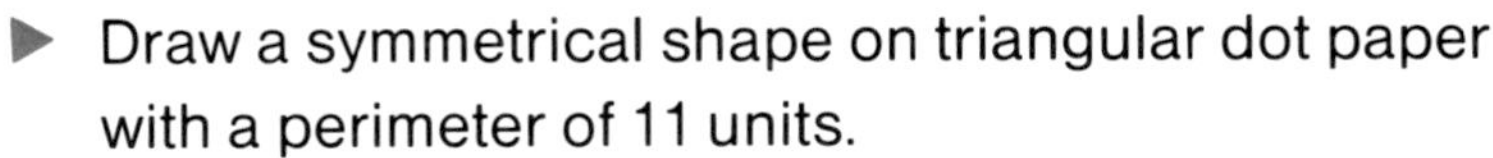

◀ Make a circle with 6 students with outstretched arms.

Predict how many students with outstretched arms would fit across the circle through its centre. Check your prediction.

Use your results to predict how many would fit across a circle made by

- 9 students
- 21 students
- all the students in your class

▶ Use square dot paper. Copy the shapes and cut them out. Cut the triangle and parallelogram so that each will cover the square. Draw a rectangle that has the same area.

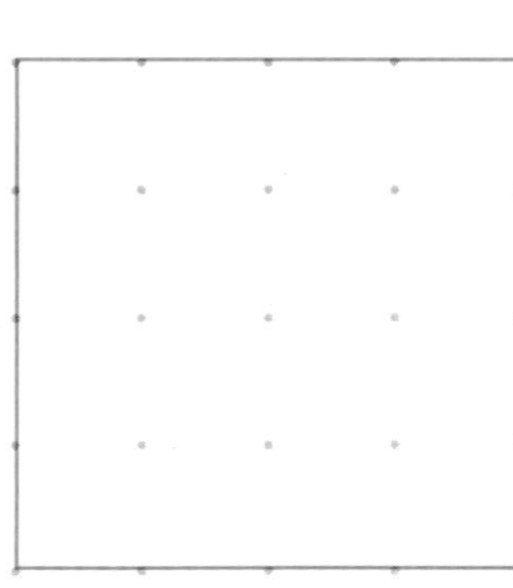

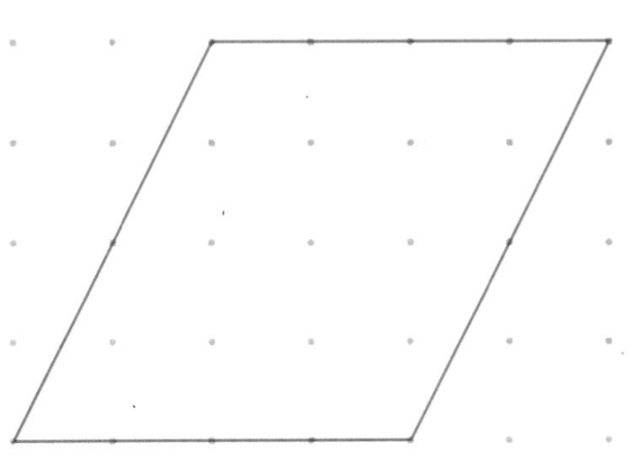

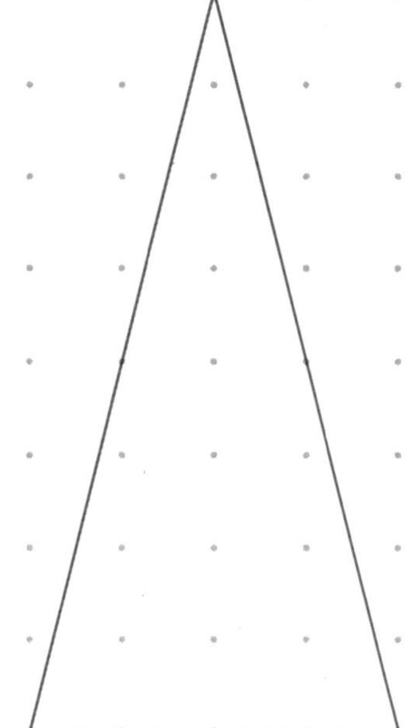

Measurement Shortcuts

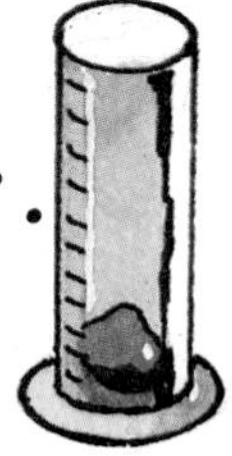

▶ In each square centimetre of your skin, there are about

- 2 cold sensors
- 10 heat sensors
- 165 pain sensors
- 2480 nerve endings

Estimate the number of each on the palm of your hand.

◀ Make this prism.
Find its volume in cubic units.

Make a different prism with the same volume.

Is it possible to build a cube with the same volume? Explain.

▶ Explain why it is easier to find the area of the square than the hexagon.

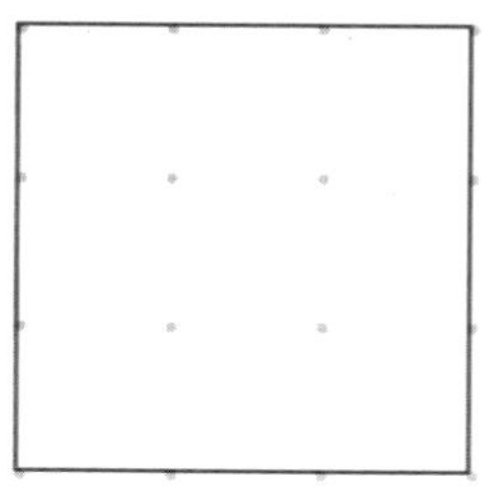

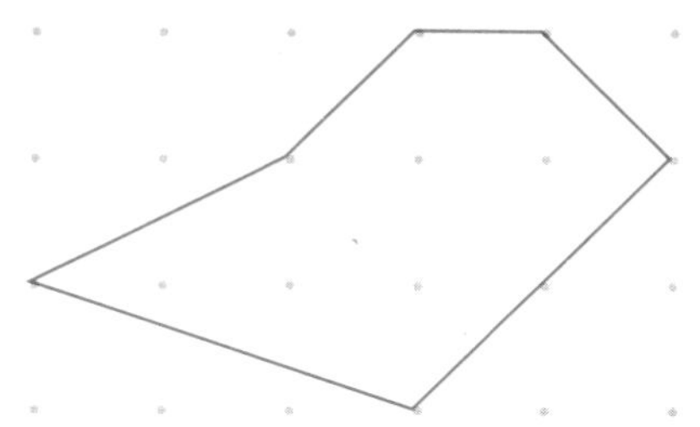

Cara and Kevin are dealt 26 cards each from a deck of 52 playing cards.
Cara's score is the number of red cards she receives.
Kevin's score is the number of black cards he receives.
Who will have the greater score? Explain.

Racing Around

Relating side lengths and perimeters of polygons

Average Speeds

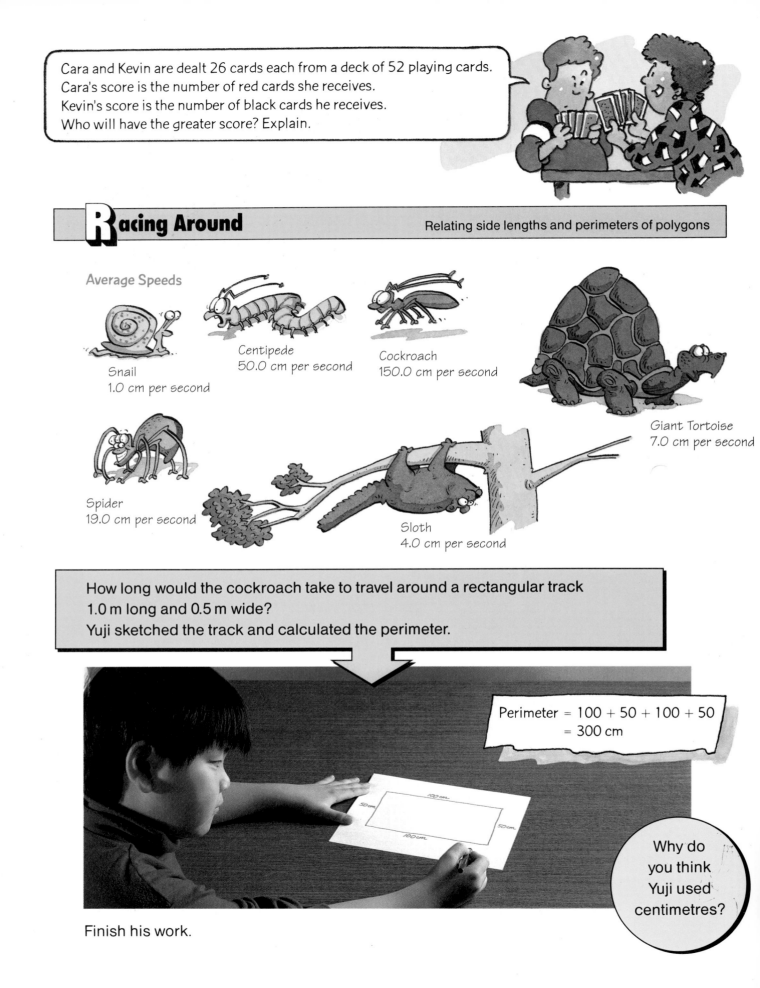

Snail
1.0 cm per second

Centipede
50.0 cm per second

Cockroach
150.0 cm per second

Giant Tortoise
7.0 cm per second

Spider
19.0 cm per second

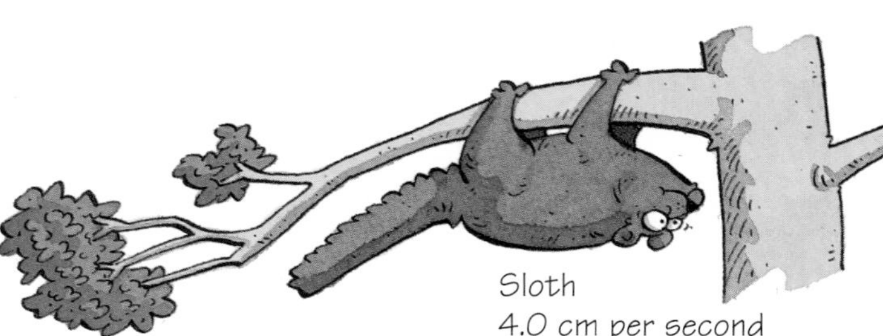

Sloth
4.0 cm per second

How long would the cockroach take to travel around a rectangular track 1.0 m long and 0.5 m wide?
Yuji sketched the track and calculated the perimeter.

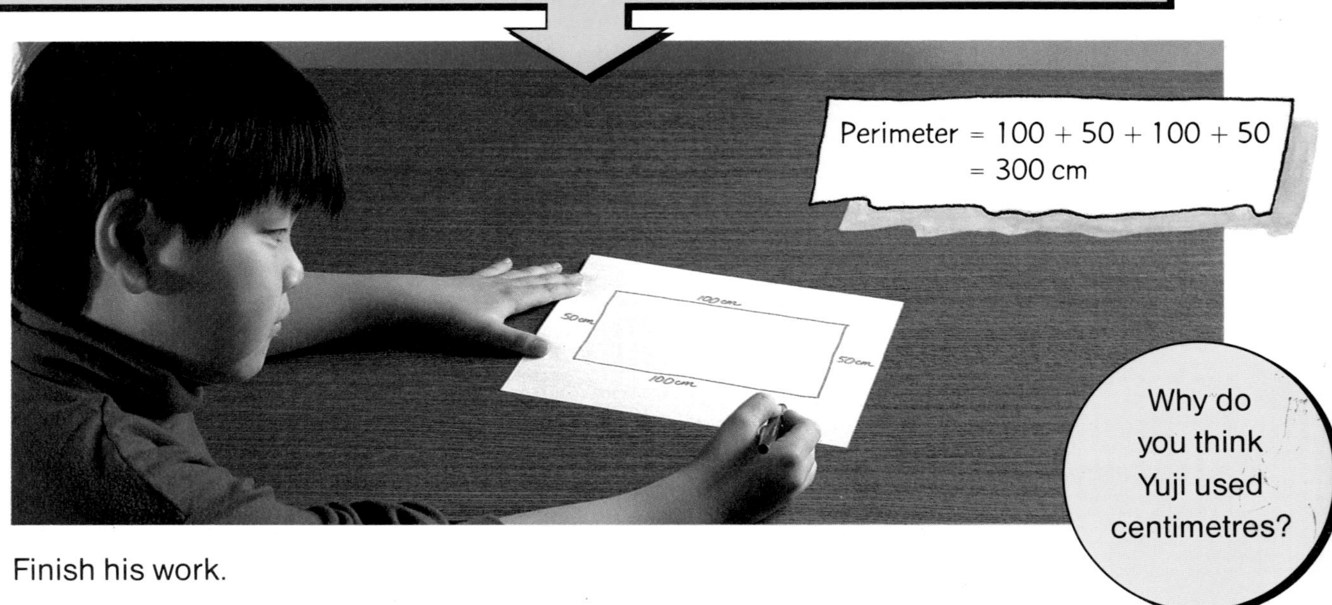

Finish his work.

Sketch and label diagrams to help you.

1. Explain Shelley's method of finding the perimeter of the rectangular track.

100 + 50 = 150
2 × 150 = 300
Perimeter = 300 cm

2. Estimate and then calculate the number of seconds the tortoise would take to travel around a rectangular track 1.0 m long and 0.25 m wide.
Explain what you did.

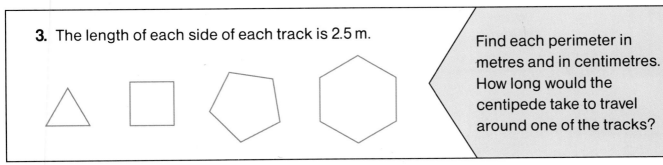

3. The length of each side of each track is 2.5 m.

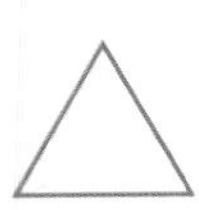 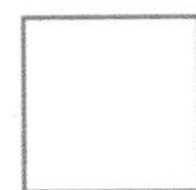 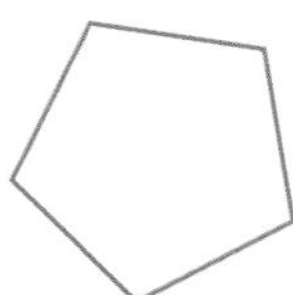 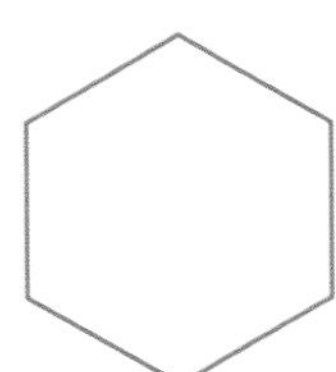

Find each perimeter in metres and in centimetres.
How long would the centipede take to travel around one of the tracks?

4. How can the perimeters of the tracks in Problem 3 be found without adding every side length? Explain.

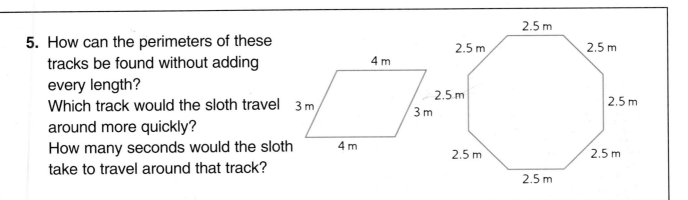

5. How can the perimeters of these tracks be found without adding every length?
Which track would the sloth travel around more quickly?
How many seconds would the sloth take to travel around that track?

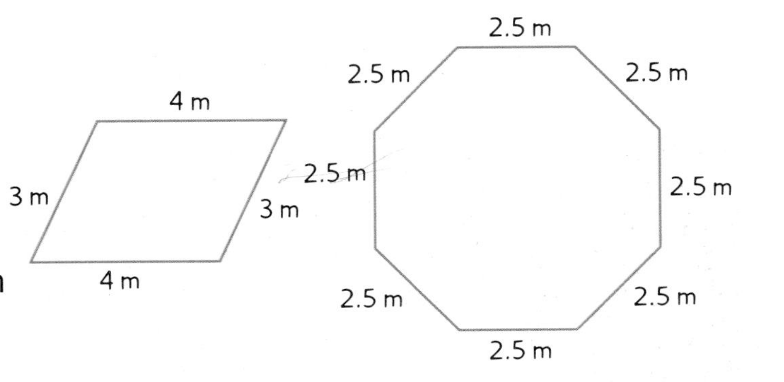

6. A rectangular track has a perimeter of 36 m.
Its length is twice as long as its width.
What are its dimensions?

7. A cockroach travels around a 12 m track in the same time a centipede travels around a square track. What is the length of each side of that square track?

8. Use whole numbers. How many different rectangles are there with a perimeter of 12 cm?
What are the dimensions? Use grid paper to draw your rectangles.

9. Use whole numbers. How many different rectangles are there with a perimeter of 24 cm?
What are the dimensions? Use grid paper to draw your rectangles.

A sock drawer contains 3 green socks and 4 red socks. The room is dark and the socks are not in pairs. How many socks do you have to pick from the drawer to be sure to have a matching pair?

Considering Polygons

Using expressions to find the perimeter of polygons

Three students wrote different equations for the perimeter of a rectangle to solve this problem.

What is the missing dimension in this garden?

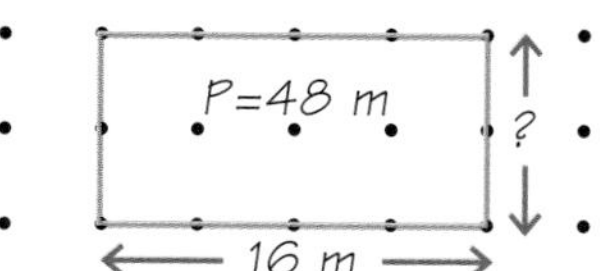

Greta wrote:
$P = L + W + L + W$
$48 = 16 + W + 16 + W$

1. Describe Greta's rule in words. What do the variables in Greta's rule represent? What did she do in the second line of her work?

Darin wrote:
$P = (2 \times L) + (2 \times W)$
$48 = (2 \times 16) + (2 \times W)$

2. Describe Darin's rule in words. Compare Darin's rule with Greta's. How are they related? What did he do in the second line of his work?

Why do you think that parentheses are used in the right side of the equation?

Estelle wrote:
$P = 2 \times (L + W)$
$48 = 2 \times (16 + W)$

3. Describe Estelle's rule in words. Compare Estelle's rule with Greta's. How are they related?

Can the equation $P = 2 \times L + W$ be used to find the perimeter of the rectangle? Explain.

Choose one student's method and finish solving the problem. What is the missing dimension? Explain why you chose the method you did.

Does the equation still work if the garden is a parallelogram?

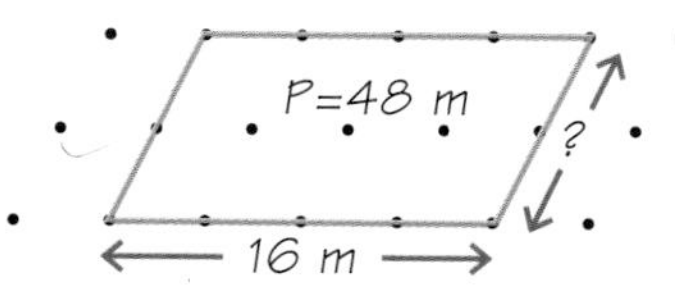

4. Darin wrote these equations for the gardens below. Do you agree with his work? Tell when it's possible to write the shorter rule.

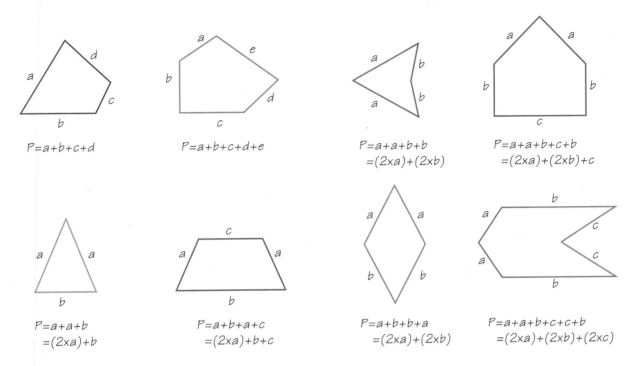

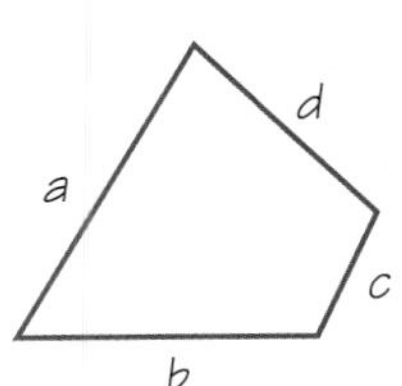

$P=a+b+c+d$

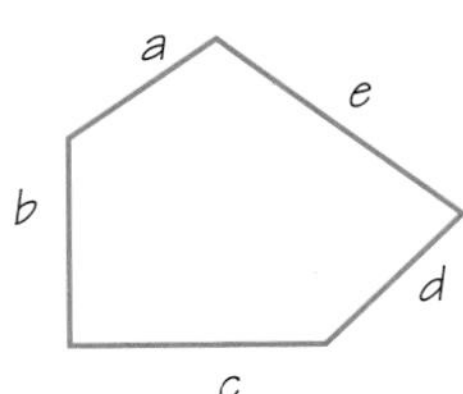

$P=a+b+c+d+e$

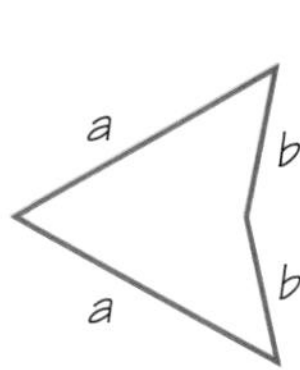

$P=a+a+b+b$
$=(2\times a)+(2\times b)$

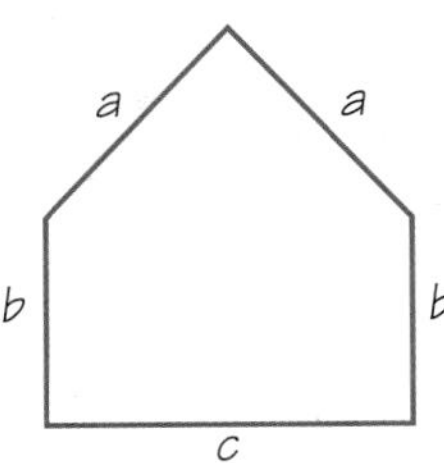

$P=a+a+b+c+b$
$=(2\times a)+(2\times b)+c$

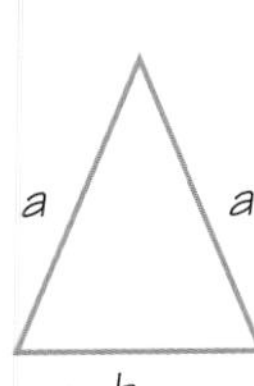

$P=a+a+b$
$=(2\times a)+b$

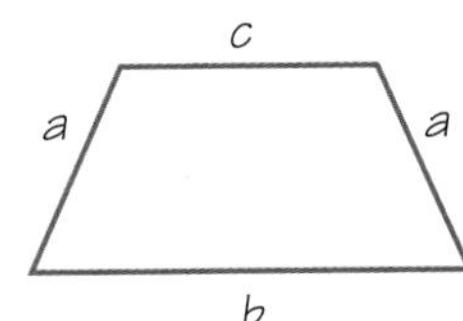

$P=a+b+a+c$
$=(2\times a)+b+c$

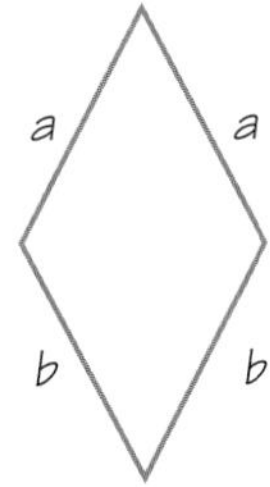

$P=a+b+b+a$
$=(2\times a)+(2\times b)$

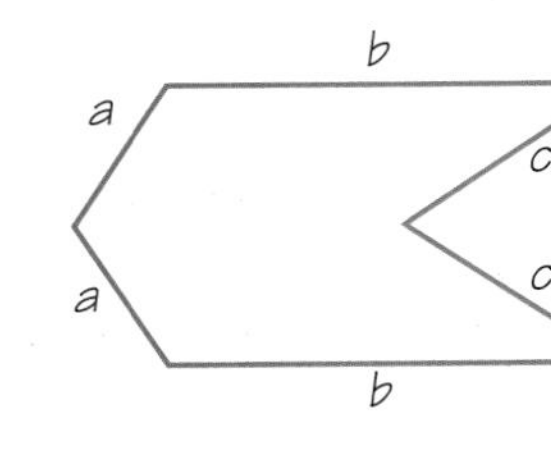

$P=a+a+b+c+c+b$
$=(2\times a)+(2\times b)+(2\times c)$

5. Write an equation to find the perimeter of each regular polygon. What does your variable represent?

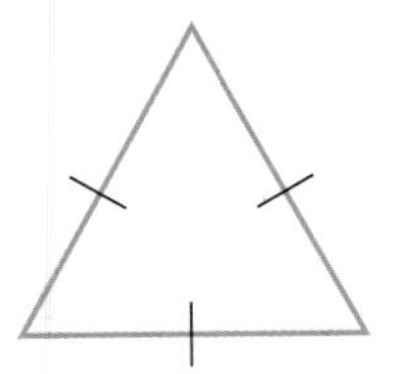

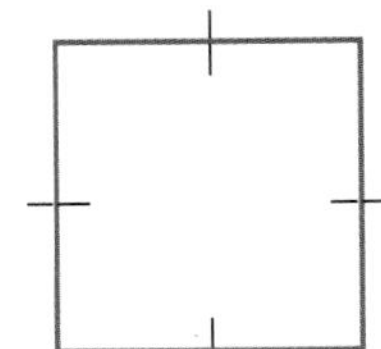

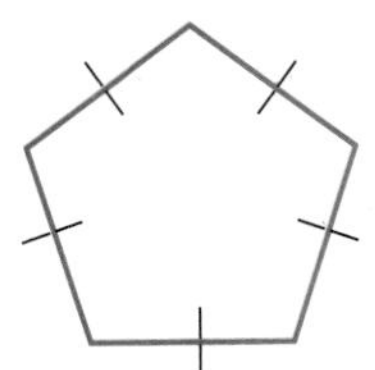

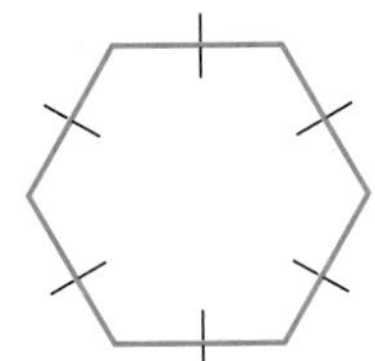

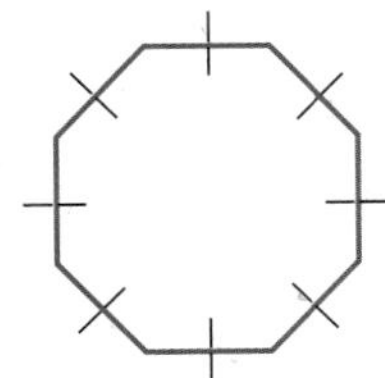

6. Use your equations for the polygons in question 5. What is the perimeter of each polygon if the length of a side is 5 cm? 230 mm? 1.7 cm?

For each problem below, copy the diagram and label the length of each side. Write an equation. Solve the problem, then check your solution.

7. In a rectangular garden, side two is 7 m longer than side one. If the perimeter of the garden is 34 m, what is the length of each side?

8. A triangular garden has a different length on each side. Side two is 8 m longer than side one. Side three is 3 m shorter than side one. The perimeter of the garden is 65 m. What is the length of each side?

Estimate the percent of each section of the graph. What might each section represent for your class?

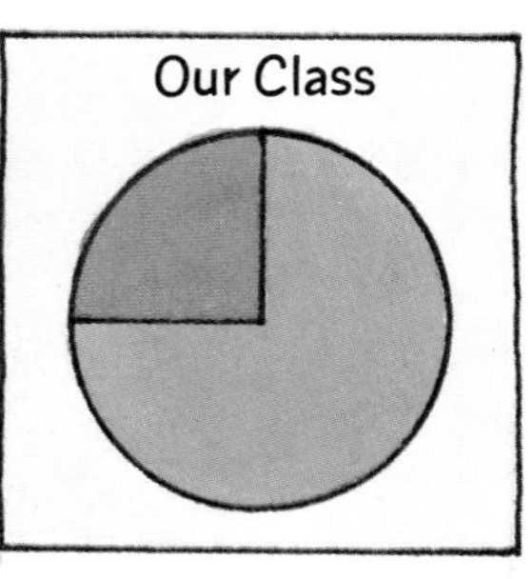

Measuring Labels

Relating dimensions and areas of rectangles

How could Lara find the area of this label?

She placed a transparent centimetre grid over the label. Then she traced the label.

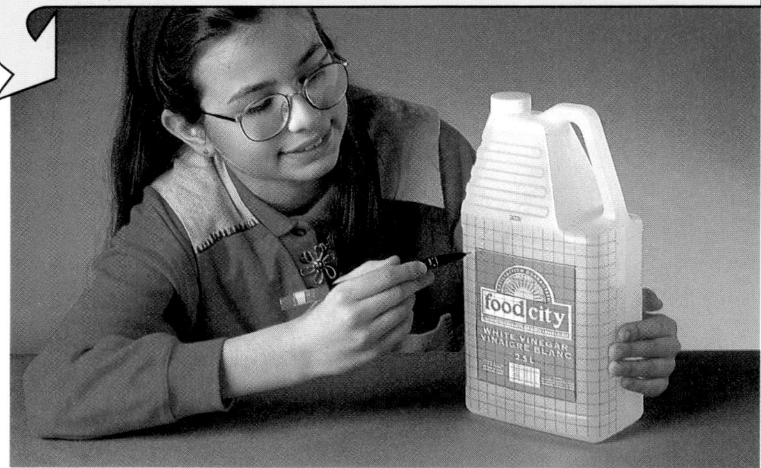

What is the area of the label?
Tell what you did.
What are the length and height of the label?
How does knowing the length and height help you find the area?

Use centimetre grid paper when needed.

1. Draw each label and find its area.
   - one 8 cm long and 6 cm high
   - one 9.5 cm long and 5 cm high
   - one 12 cm long and 4.5 cm high

2. Find the area of two rectangular labels. Tell what you did.

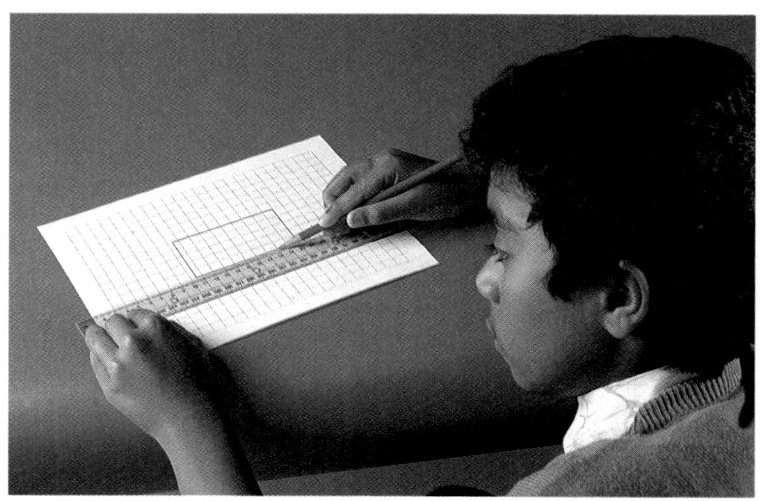

3. How can you find the area of a rectangular label if you have a ruler but no centimetre grid paper?

4. Predict which labels have the least and greatest areas.
Find each area. Tell what you did.

Container	Length (cm)	Height (cm)
Ginger Ale	36	13
Tonic Water	9	12
Olive Oil	5	17
Tomatoes	33	11
Vinegar	9.5	7
Tuna	3.5	28

5. A square label has an area of 144 cm^2.
What is the length of each side?

6. Do these labels have the same area? Explain.

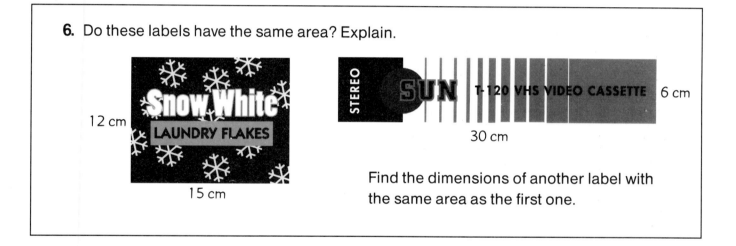

12 cm

15 cm

6 cm

30 cm

Find the dimensions of another label with the same area as the first one.

7. How many rectangles with an area of 20 m^2 are possible? List the dimensions. Calculate each perimeter. Use grid paper to draw the rectangles.

8. How many rectangles are possible with an area of 36 mm^2? List each set of dimensions. Calculate each perimeter. Use grid paper to draw your rectangles.

9. Tell why manufacturers would want to know the area of their labels.

10. The area of a large garden is 1 hectare (ha). A hectare is a square that measures 100 m on each side. What is the area of the garden in square metres?

Which of these numbers is likely prime?

197 2 456 045 12 321

Considering Rectangles

Using expressions to find the area of rectangles

Reed wrote this equation to find the area of the rectangle.

$A = r \times n$

where r represents the number of rows, and n represents the number of squares in each row.

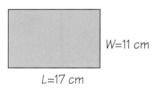

The area of a figure is the number of square units that covers its surface.

1. Substitute the values for r and n into the equation to find A. How is Reed's equation related to the equation $A = L \times W$?

2. Use an equation to find the area of this rectangle, and its perimeter.

W=11 cm
L=17 cm

Work with a partner.

3. What is the area and perimeter of each rectangle?
   - $L = 5$ cm, $W = 4$ cm
   - $L = 9.2$ cm, $W = 4.4$ cm
   - $L = 10$ m, $W = 3$ m
   - $L = 18$ mm, $W = 12$ mm
   - $L = 1.4$ m, $W = 1.1$ m
   - $L = 2.5$ km, $W = 500$ m

4. Find the length of the rectangle and its perimeter when $A = 1200$ cm^2 and $W = 25$ cm.

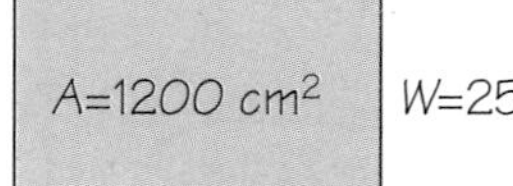
A=1200 cm²
W=25 cm

5. A rectangle has an area of 12 km^2. Draw and label the whole number dimensions on a diagram of the rectangle that has the greatest perimeter. the least perimeter.

6. If you double the length and width of a rectangle, does its area double as well? Explain.

7. Reed wrote this equation to find the area of a square. $A = s \times s$
What does the variable s represent?
What is the area of a square when $s = 70$ mm?
What is the length of each side when $A = 121$ m^2?

8. The centres of these loonies are the vertices of a square. If the radius of a loonie is 13 mm, what is the area of the square?

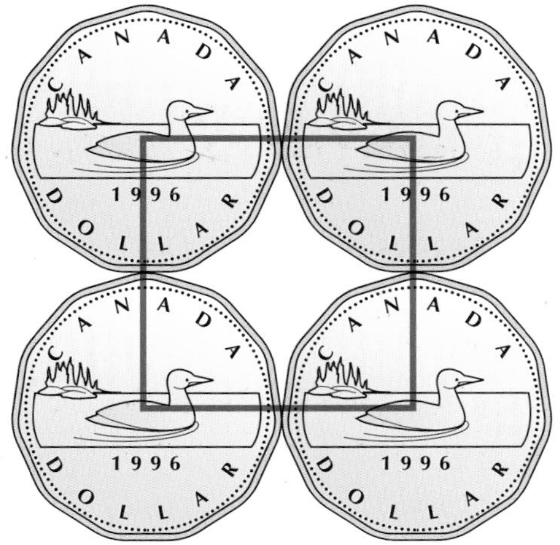

9. Cut the right-angled triangle off one end of the parallelogram below. How can you move the triangle so that the two shapes form a rectangle?

For the rectangle,
$P = 2 \times (a + b)$ and $A = a \times b$.
Do these equations apply to the parallelogram as well? Explain.

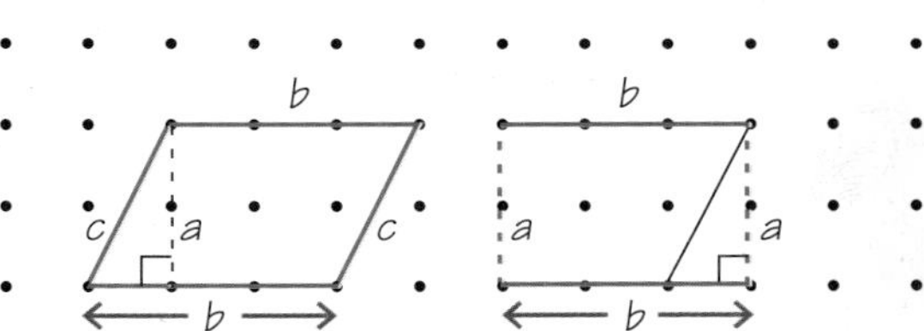

10. Is the perimeter of the rhombus and the square the same?
Is the area the same? Explain.

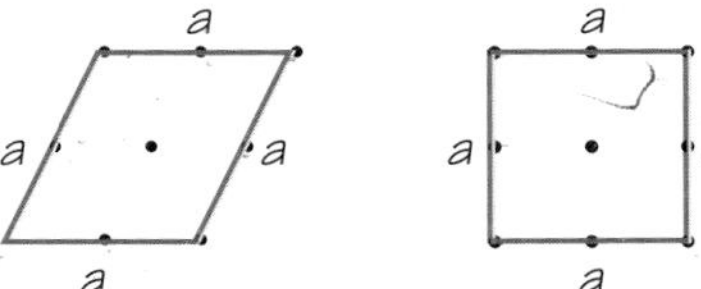

11. Cut the isosceles triangle below in half. Flip one half about the horizontal base. Then slide it so that the two shapes form a rectangle.

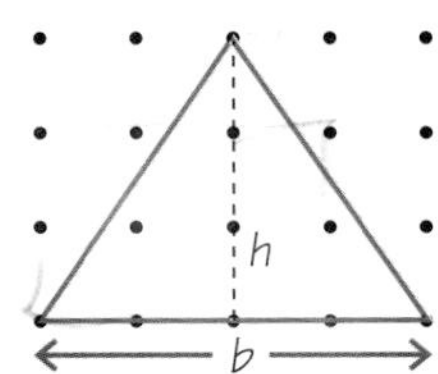

What is the area of the rectangle? the original triangle?
How is the height, h, of the original triangle related to the width, W, of the rectangle?
How is the base, b, of the original triangle related to the length, L, of the rectangle?

Which costs more per kilogram? How much more?

Examining Boxes

Determining surface area of right rectangular prisms

What is the shape of each face of this box?
How can you use length and width to find the area of each face?
Which faces have the same area?

Measure, then find the area of each different face.

1. How can you find the total area of all the faces of the box?
   Why do you think **surface area** is a good name for this area?

2. What is the surface area of
   - this box?
   - a different box?
   - this textbook?
   - a metre stick?

   Calculate to the nearest square centimetre.

3. Describe the shapes of the faces on any rectangular prism.
   Draw the nets of some different rectangular prisms.
   Explain how to find the surface area of any rectangular prism.
   What shortcut can you use to find the surface area of a cube?

4. The world's largest box of popcorn measures 12.18 m tall, 6.31 m wide, and 2.44 m deep. It was filled with popcorn by elementary students in Florida in 1994.
   Estimate, then calculate its surface area to the nearest square metre.

5. Find the surface area of a 10 cm × 3 cm × 5 cm rectangular prism. Then double each dimension of the prism. Predict and then calculate the new prism's surface area.
   Compare the surface areas of the larger and smaller prisms. What do you notice?

Take Your Pick

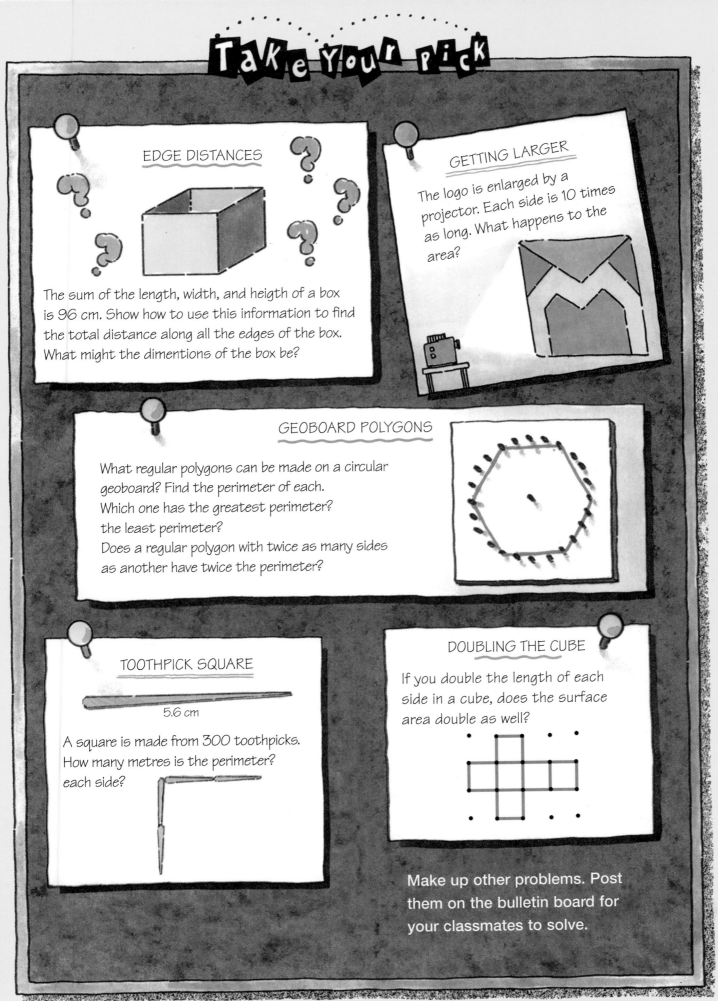

EDGE DISTANCES

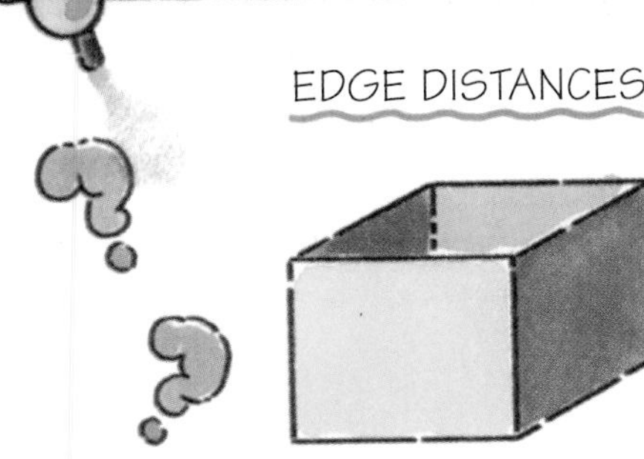

The sum of the length, width, and heigth of a box is 96 cm. Show how to use this information to find the total distance along all the edges of the box. What might the dimentions of the box be?

GETTING LARGER

The logo is enlarged by a projector. Each side is 10 times as long. What happens to the area?

GEOBOARD POLYGONS

What regular polygons can be made on a circular geoboard? Find the perimeter of each.
Which one has the greatest perimeter?
the least perimeter?
Does a regular polygon with twice as many sides as another have twice the perimeter?

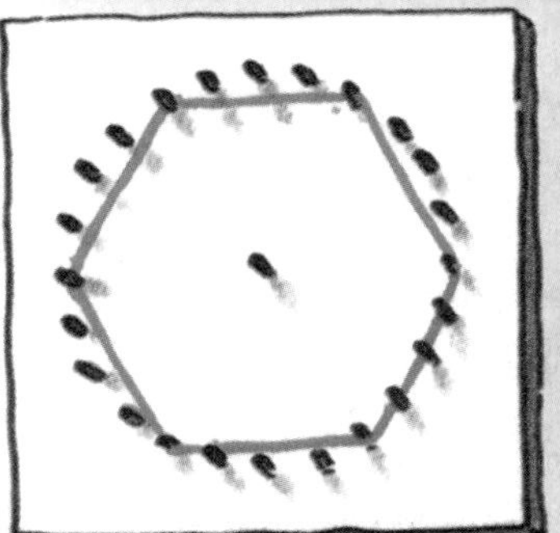

TOOTHPICK SQUARE

5.6 cm

A square is made from 300 toothpicks. How many metres is the perimeter? each side?

DOUBLING THE CUBE

If you double the length of each side in a cube, does the surface area double as well?

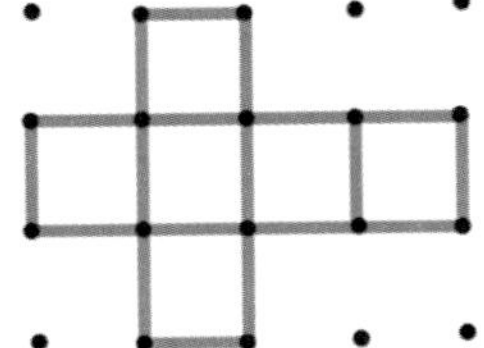

Make up other problems. Post them on the bulletin board for your classmates to solve.

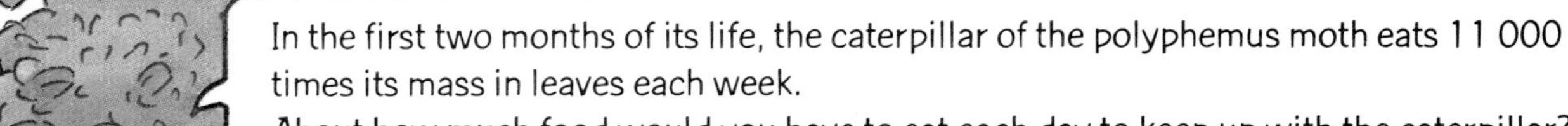

In the first two months of its life, the caterpillar of the polyphemus moth eats 11 000 times its mass in leaves each week.
About how much food would you have to eat each day to keep up with the caterpillar?

Digging Up Artifacts

Relating dimensions and volumes of rectangular prisms

At Wanuskewin Heritage Park in Saskatoon, archaeologists have dug up Plains Indian artifacts twice as old as the Egyptian pyramids.

To help record the location of artifacts, they make square grids of string.
Each square is 1 m by 1 m.

In order to protect artifacts, the earth is dug up slowly and carefully.

To find the volume of earth removed from a hole 10 cm long, 10 cm wide, and 5 cm deep, Orysia built a model.

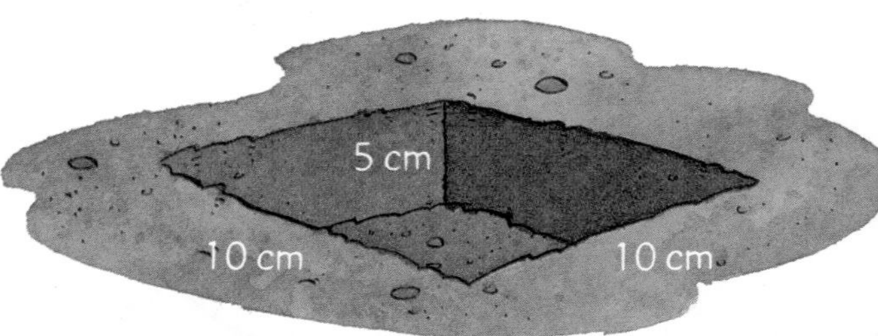

How many cubic centimetres are in one layer?
How many layers are there?
How many cubic centimetres are there altogether?
What is the volume of earth removed?
How does knowing the dimensions help you find the volume?

Use base ten blocks to model the earth removed.

1. Each hole is 10 cm long, 10 cm wide, and
   - 10 cm deep
   - 12 cm deep
   - 15 cm deep

   How many layers of 100 cm^3 are removed from each hole?
   What is the volume of each hole?

2. For these holes, what would you use as the depth of one layer?
   How many layers does each hole have?
   What is the volume of one layer of each hole? all its layers?
   - 5 m long, 2 m wide, 2 m deep
   - 4 m long, 3 m wide, 4 m deep
   - 10 m long, 4 m wide, 3 m deep
   - 10 m long, 5 m wide, 2 m deep

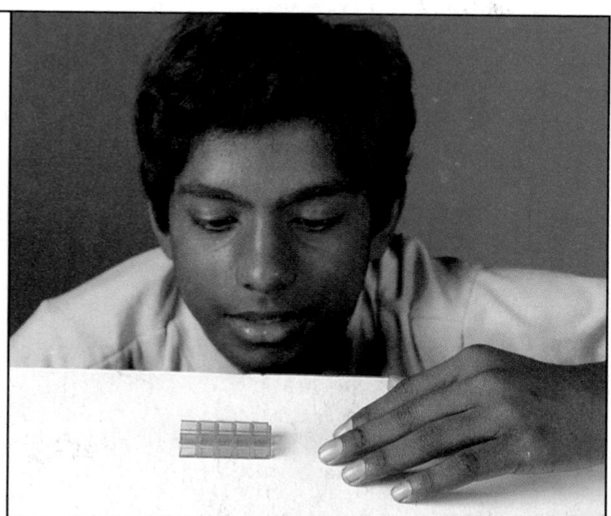

3. A hole is 5 m long and 2 m wide and has a volume of 40 m^3. How deep is it?

4. What is the volume of a 10 m by 4 m by 2 m hole?
   How does knowing the volume of that hole help you find the volume of these holes?
   - 10 m by 4 m by 1 m
   - 5 m by 8 m by 2 m
   - 2.5 m by 16 m by 2 m

5. Double all the dimensions of each hole in Problem 4.
   Tell what happens to each volume.

6. Find the dimensions of three different holes, each with a volume of 64 m^3.

7. Find the dimensions of a cube-shaped hole with a volume greater than 200 m^3.

8. Why might archaeologists want to know how much earth is removed in a dig?

I added the ages of my relatives and then divided by the number of people. The result is 43. Can the sum of their ages be 268? Explain.

Considering Prisms

Using rules to find volume of right rectangular prisms

What is the volume of this box?

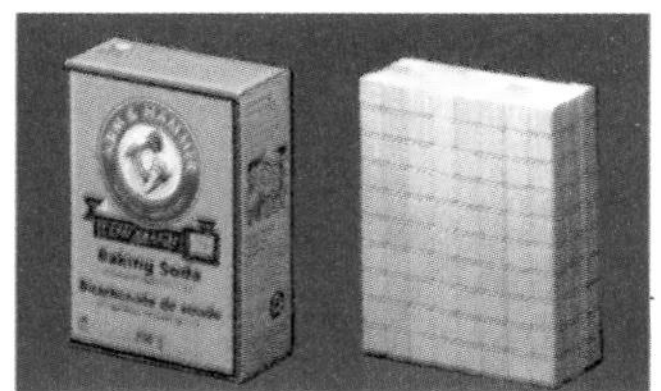

Alexis wrote this equation to find the volume of the box.
$V = A \times H$,
where A represents the area of the base, and H represents the height.
How is this equation related to $V = L \times W \times H$?

1. What shape is the base in any rectangular prism?

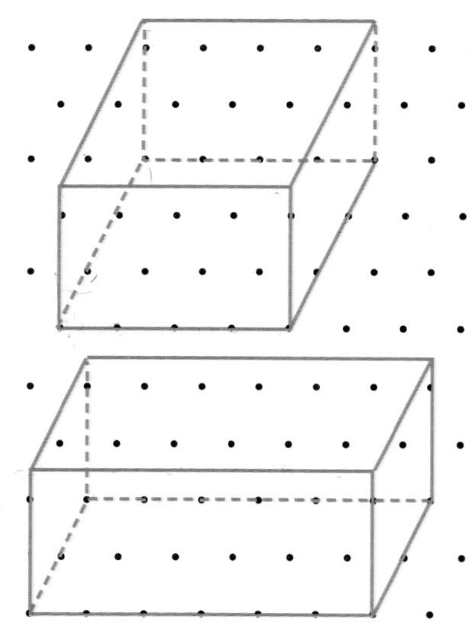

2. In both diagrams at the right, 1 grid interval represents 1 cm. What is the length and width of each box? Do they have the same area of the base?

   Both boxes have a height of 2 cm. Do they have the same volume? Explain.

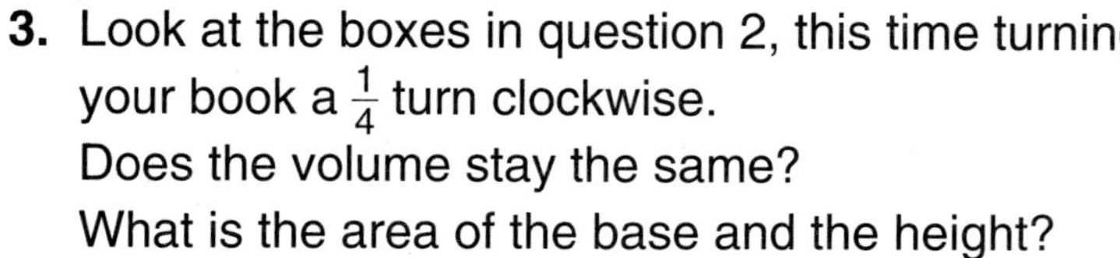

3. Look at the boxes in question 2, this time turning your book a $\frac{1}{4}$ turn clockwise.
   Does the volume stay the same?
   What is the area of the base and the height?

4. Find the volume of a rectangular prism with $A = 16$ cm^2 and $H = 2$ cm.
   What whole number dimensions are possible for the length and width?
   Sketch the possible boxes on triangle dot paper using the method on page 124.

5. Use the equation $V = A \times H$ or $V = L \times W \times H$ to find the volume of each.

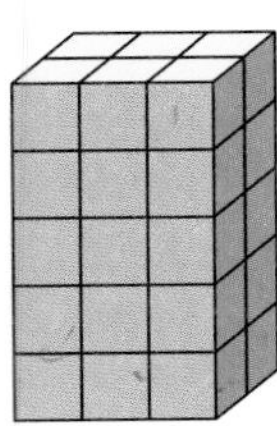

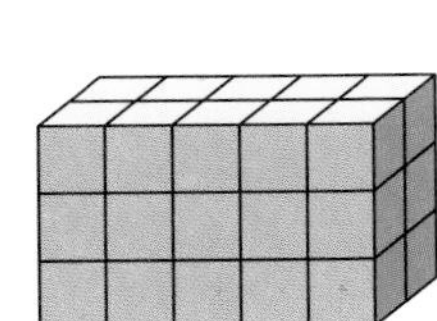

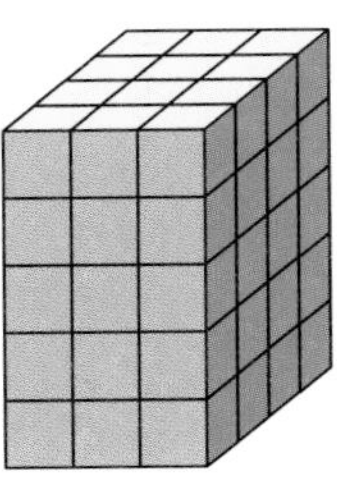

6. Find the volume of each rectangular prism.

- $L = 10$ m, $W = 8$ m, $H = 3$ m
- $L = 11$ cm, $W = 11$ cm, $H = 2$ cm
- $L = 30$ mm, $W = 1$ mm, $H = 6$ mm
- $L = 16$ mm, $W = 2$ mm, $H = 7$ mm
- $L = 20$ m, $W = 10$ m, $H = 5$ m
- $L = 17$ m, $W = 2$ m, $H = 13$ m

7. The Almeida family is renting a truck to move their 33 m^3 of belongings.
Estimate the volume of each truck in the chart.
Which of the trucks are large enough for their belongings?

Truck		Dimensions			Rental Charge	
		length	width	height	each day	each kilometre
Rent a Truck	A	2.9 m	1.7 m	1.4 m	$32.95	18¢
	B	4.6 m	2.3 m	2.0 m	$39.95	18¢
	C	7.3 m	2.4 m	2.2 m	$59.95	22¢
You Move It	D	3.5 m	2.3 m	2.1 m	$29.95	35¢
	E	4.3 m	2.3 m	2.2 m	$34.95	35¢
	F	6.8 m	2.3 m	2.6 m	$44.95	39¢

2.9 is about 3
1.7 is about 2
1.4 is about 1
6 cubes so 6 m^3

Does the longest truck always have the greatest volume? Explain.

8. Which truck that will hold their belongings has the lower cost if they

- are moving locally?
- are moving about 400 km away?

What are the factors of 4? 8? 16?
For each number, add the factors except the number itself.
What do you notice about the sums?
Find three other numbers with similar sums.

Making Stone Soup

Finding the volumes of irregular solids

"Good folk," she said as the peasants drew near. "I am but a poor, hungry lass, out to seek my fortune. Until I find it, I must ask for help. Since you have no food, we'll have to use my magic stone to make stone soup."
The peasants leaned forward. Stone soup? Surely that was impossible.
"First we'll need a large iron pot," Grethel said.

from *Stone Soup* retold by John Warren Stewig

How might you estimate the volume of a stone like Grethel's stone?

Carlos estimated the volume of a stone by measuring the length, width, and height needed for a box that could hold his stone.

length 9 cm
width 4 cm
height

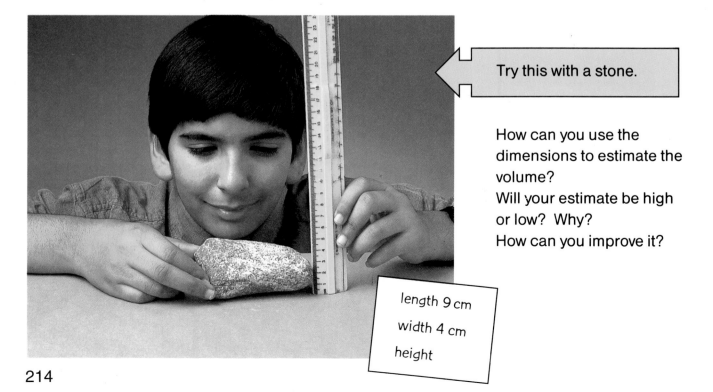

Try this with a stone.

How can you use the dimensions to estimate the volume?
Will your estimate be high or low? Why?
How can you improve it?

Use a measuring cylinder and water.

1. Pour 200 mL of water into a measuring cylinder.
   Drop in ten centimetre cubes.
   How many cubic centimetres are the ten cubes?
   How many millilitres did the water level change?

2. Predict the change in the water level in millilitres after a different number of cubes are dropped in. Drop in the cubes.
   How close is your prediction?

3. Explain how your results from Problems 1 and 2 can help you find the volume of this stone in cubic centimetres.

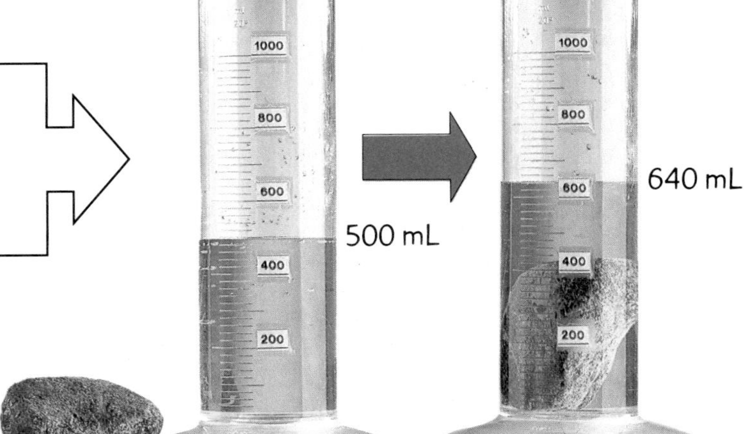

4. Estimate the volumes of three different stones by finding the dimensions for a box that would hold each one. Then check your estimates by dropping each stone into a measuring cylinder of water.

5. The peasants brought vegetables and other food to add to Grethel's stone soup.
   Estimate the volume of some vegetables you might use to make soup.
   Find the volume by dropping each into a measuring cylinder of water.

6. How can you use this method to find the volume of objects that float?

HOLEY WOOD

A 3 cm by 3 cm by 3 cm hole is cut out of a solid block of wood 5 cm by 5 cm by 3 cm.
Find the volume of the wood that is left.

MODEL BUILDINGS

These model buildings are made from base ten rods.
What is the volume of each building?
What building would likely be built next to continue the pattern?
What is its volume?

BALL AND BOX

Find the approximate volume of a golf ball that fits exactly in a box where each side is 4.3 cm.
If a golf ball was placed in the box, about what percent of the space in the box would the ball take?

COIN VOLUME

What is the volume of $100 in pennies? in dollar coins?
Tell what you did to find out.

LEAF VOLUME

Show how to estimate the volume of one leaf in a large book.

Make up other problems. Post them on the bulletin board for your classmates to solve.

Solving a Problem by Making a Model

Try this problem before going on.
KITE FLYING
What is the area of a kite with a cross piece that measures 8 dm and is 6 dm from the top and 10 dm from the bottom?

Margo's group solved the problem by making a model.

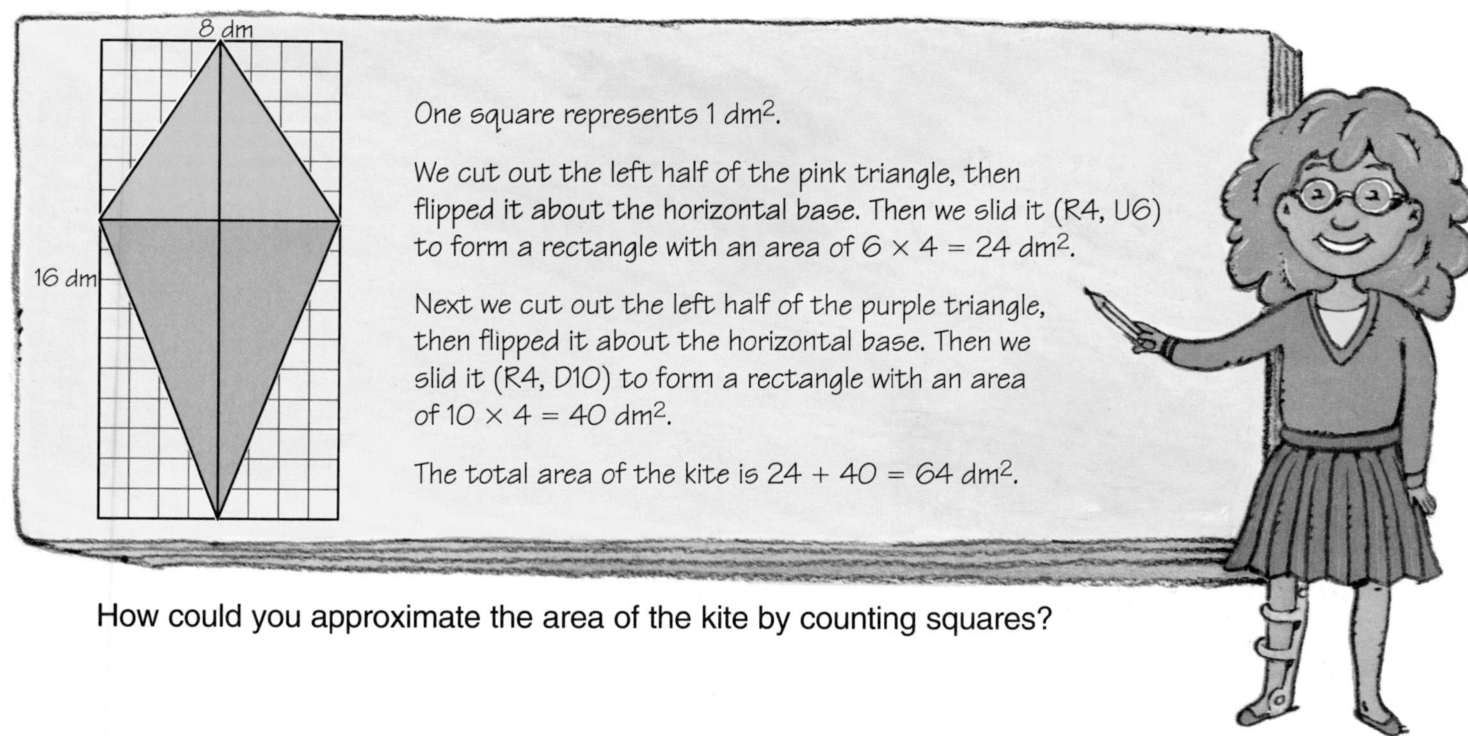

We cut out the left half of the pink triangle, then flipped it about the horizontal base. Then we slid it (R4, U6) to form a rectangle with an area of 6 × 4 = 24 dm².
Next we cut out the left half of the purple triangle, then flipped it about the horizontal base. Then we slid it (R4, D10) to form a rectangle with an area of 10 × 4 = 40 dm².

How could you approximate the area of the kite by counting squares?

Work in a group. **Solve each problem by making a model.**

DIAGONAL LENGTH

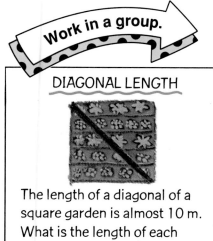

The length of a diagonal of a square garden is almost 10 m. What is the length of each side? What is the area?

CYLINDRICAL TANK

A cylindrical tank fits on a square base with an area of 25 dm². What is the greatest distance across the bottom that the tank could have?

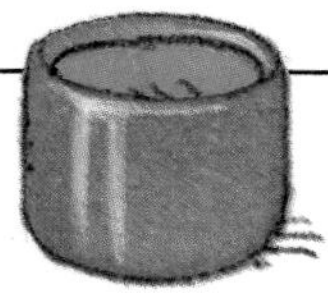

CUBE RATIOS

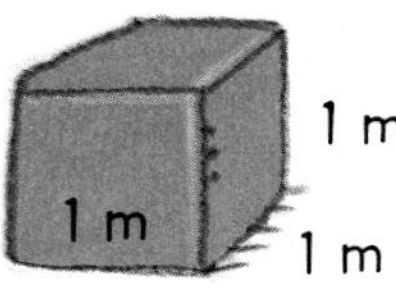

What is the volume of the cube? the area of all its faces? the ratio of these numbers (volume to area of faces)? Do all cubes have this ratio?

Practising What You've Learned

1. Find the perimeter of each.

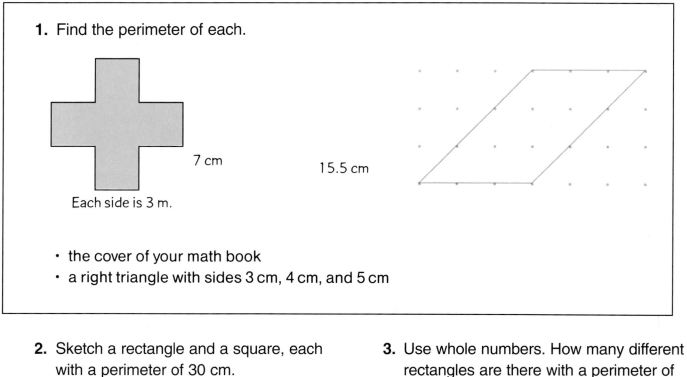

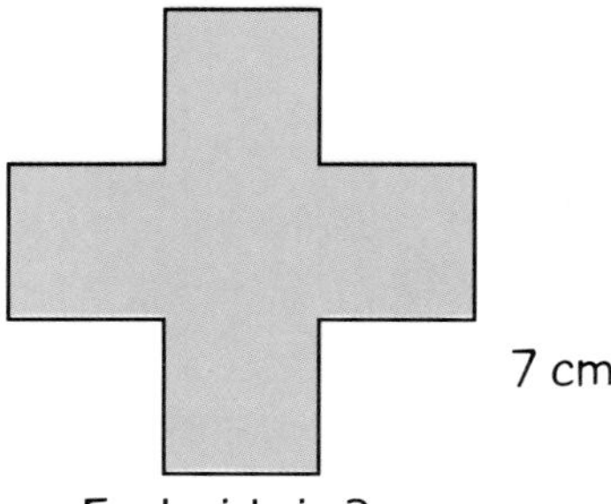

7 cm

15.5 cm

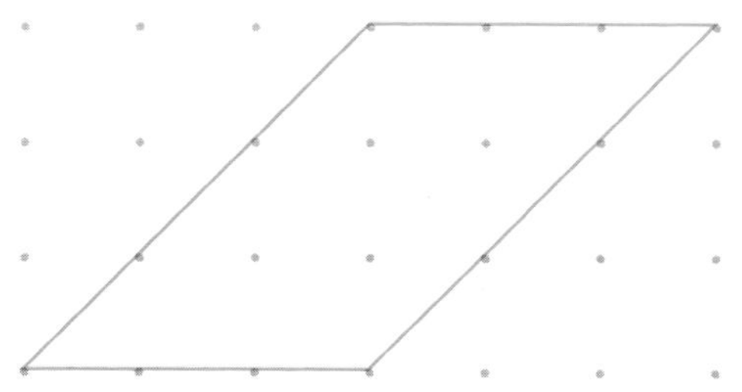

Each side is 3 m.

- the cover of your math book
- a right triangle with sides 3 cm, 4 cm, and 5 cm

2. Sketch a rectangle and a square, each with a perimeter of 30 cm.

3. Use whole numbers. How many different rectangles are there with a perimeter of 18 cm? What are the dimensions? Use grid paper to draw the rectangles.

4. Find the dimensions of a rectangle that has a perimeter of 22 cm and an area of 30 cm^2.

5. How many different rectangles are possible with an area of 49 mm^2? List each set of dimensions. Calculate each perimeter.

6. Each block measures 5 cm by 4 cm by 4 cm.

Find the volume and surface area of this shape.

7. About how many millilitres of salt can this box hold?

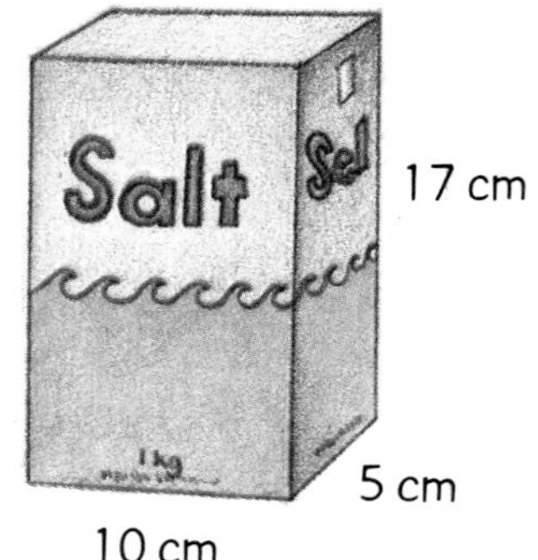

8. There is 30 mL of water. What is the volume of the grape?

Playing Games for Practice

Play each game in a group of 2, 3, or 4.

Rolling Rectangles

- Roll a pair of dice.
- Use one number to represent the length and the other to represent the width of a rectangle.
- Form a rectangle with these dimensions on a geoboard.
- Find the area in square units.
- Score 1 point for each square unit.
- Take turns.
- The winner is the first player with more than 50 points.

Example

Area = 12 square units
Score 12 points.

Building Towers

- Spin to get the base of a tower.
- Roll a die to find the height.
- Calculate the volume in cubic centimetres.
- Build the tower to check your answer.
- Score 1 point for each cubic centimetre if your answer is correct.
- Take turns.
- The winner is the first player with more than 75 points.

Example

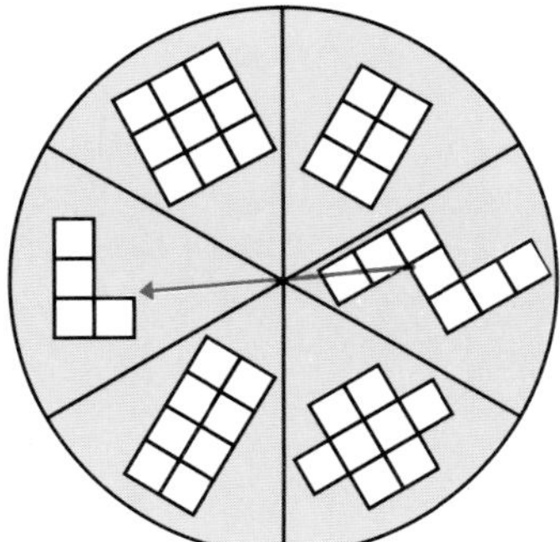

Volume = 12 cm^3

Volume is correct.
Score 12 points.

Take Your Pick

WRAPPING STRING

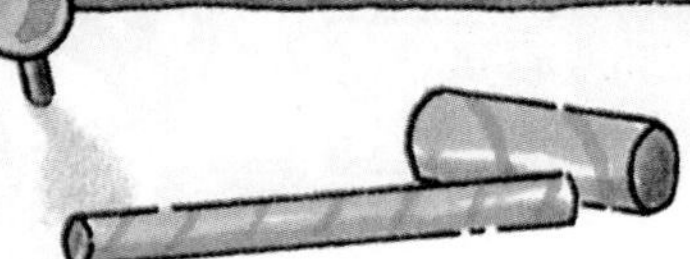

Predict the length of string that can be wrapped in a single layer around a tube. Check your prediction.

LARGE LASAGNA

One of the largest lasagnas ever made was 15.2 m long by 1.5 m wide and had a mass of about 1637 kg. Find the area of the top surface. Would the lasagna fit on the floor of your classroom? Explain.

WRAP IT UP

Investigate the length and width of plastic wrap, aluminum foil, or wax paper.
What area does one roll cover?
About how many rolls would you need to cover your classroom floor?

PACKAGE LIMITS

A shipping company charges extra if the sum of the length, width, and heigth of a package is greater than 30 cm.
What is the greatest volume of a package that can be sent without being charged extra?

PIE PERIMETER

Estimate the perimeter of the pie that this slice was cut from.
Explain what you did.

Make up other problems. Post them on the bulletin board for your classmates to solve.

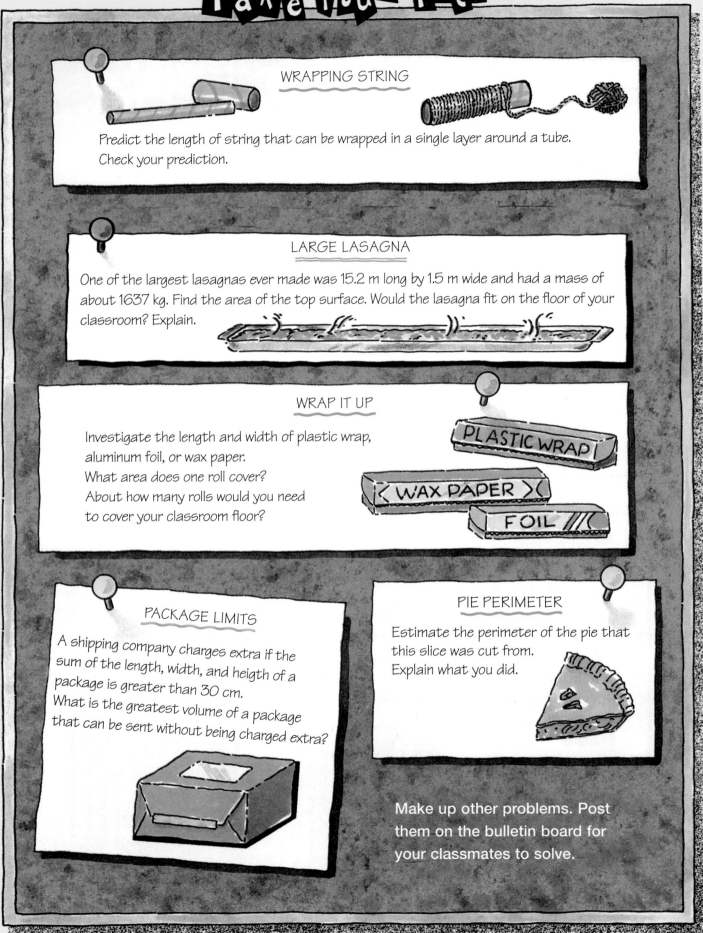

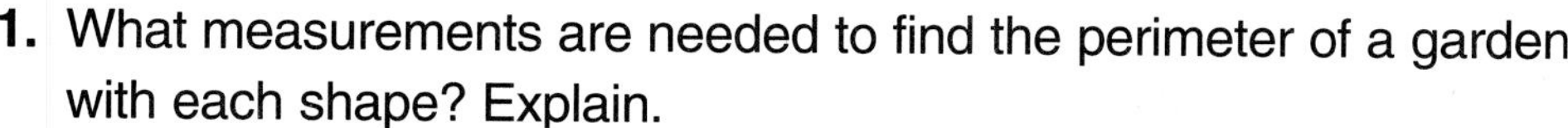

Showing What You Know

1. What measurements are needed to find the perimeter of a garden with each shape? Explain.
   - a square
   - a rectangle
   - a regular hexagon
   - a triangle

2. How can the perimeter of a square and a rectangle be found without adding every side length?

3. Draw a rectangle with a perimeter of 14 cm and an area of 10 cm^2. What are the dimensions?

4. If a dart lands somewhere on this rectangle, what is the theoretical probability it is on the blue part?

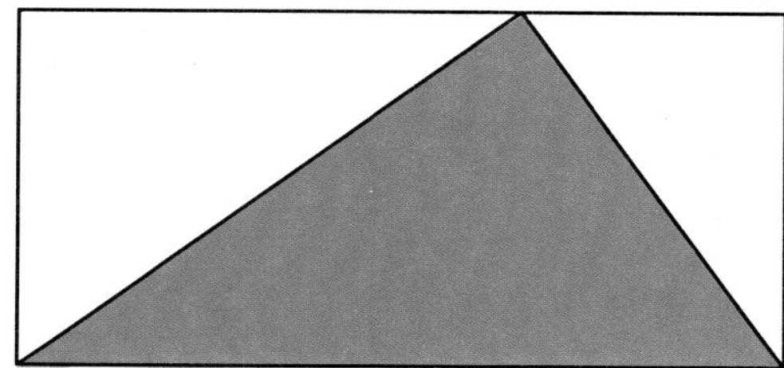

5. How many rectangular fields are possible with an area of 28 km^2? List each dimension. Calculate each perimeter.

6. Draw a 6 cm by 4 cm rectangle on dot paper. Connect the midpoints of the sides. What percent of the area of the rectangle is the area of the inner shape? Would you get the same result with different rectangles? Explain.

7. In which units — metres, square metres, or cubic metres — would you expect to buy carpeting? garden soil? chain-link fencing? Why?

8. What is the perimeter around each face?
   - the area of each face?
   - the volume of butter?

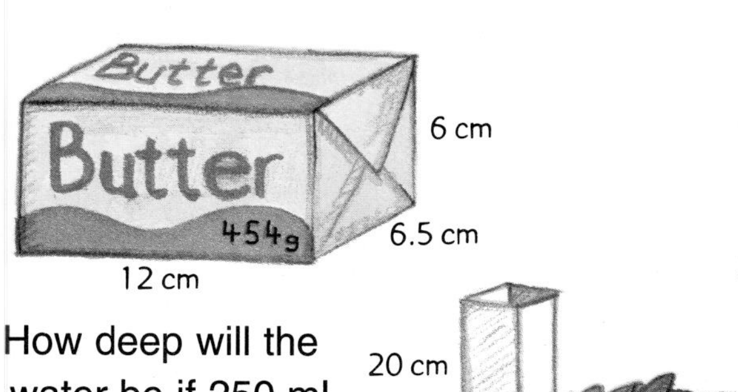

9. What would you expect to pay for the other cake? Explain.

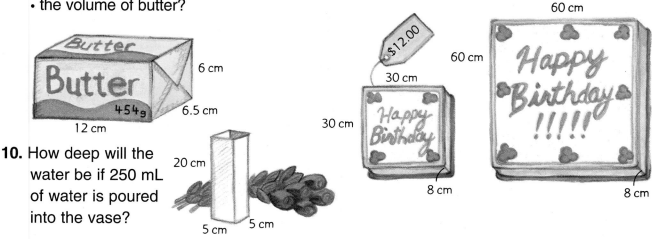

10. How deep will the water be if 250 mL of water is poured into the vase?

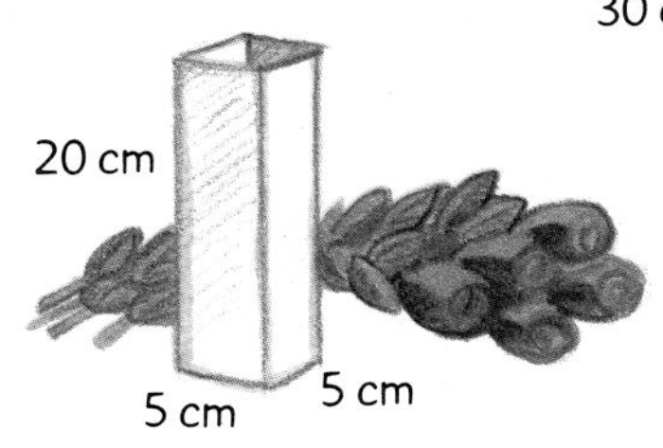
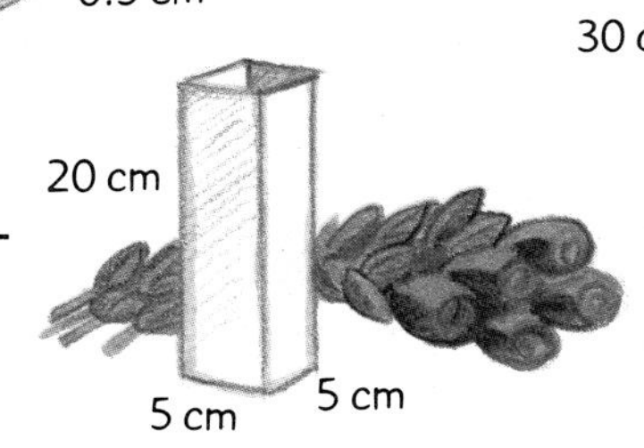

11. Explain how you know that a 10 cm by 10 cm by 10 cm plastic container can hold 1 L of water.

12. Write an equation for finding the perimeter of a 9-sided regular polygon.

Thinking Back . . .

You can find the area of the parallelogram by moving the geostrips to make a rectangle.

Is Vesna correct? Explain why or why not.

This book shows the equation for the perimeter of a rectangle as P = (2 × L) + (2 × W). A shortcut way I'd write it is P = 2 × L + W.

Do you agree with Tim? Explain.

Draw an octagon so that you need to measure the lengths of only two sides to find the perimeter. Draw another one so that you need to measure every side.

Write a note to a younger student explaining how the amount of room in a lunch box can be calculated.

Which piece of this square cake would you prefer? Why?

What questions do you still have about measurement shortcuts?

Investigating the Environment

The average Canadian creates 1.8 kg of household waste each day.
About how many kilograms are created by your family in a day? a week? a year?
About how many kilograms are created by your community in a day? a week? a year?
Norwegians create only about 0.4 as much household waste as Canadians.
About how much waste does an average Norwegian create in a day?
About how much waste would a Norwegian community the size of yours create in a year?
Why might Norwegians have so much less household waste?
What can we do to reduce household waste in Canada?

HOW Do We Use Water?

Each day an average Canadian uses about 350 L of water.
About how much is used in litres and in kilolitres (1 kL = 1000 L) by an average Canadian in a week? a month? a year?

1. The human body needs only about 1.5 L of water each day for drinking. Is this more or less than 1% of an average Canadian's use? About how many times as much water is used for non-drinking as for drinking?

2. How long would a shower last if it used $\frac{1}{2}$ of the daily water use? The flow of water is about 20 L every minute.

3. How long a shower would use the same amount of water as a bath in a tub filled to a depth of 25 cm? Explain.

It's 113 cm long and 55 cm wide.
1 mL = 1 cm^3 so 1 L = 1000 cm^3

4. Some "low-flow" shower heads use only about $\frac{1}{3}$ of the water that a regular shower head uses every minute. About how much water would a low-flow shower head use in 1 min? About how much water could be saved in an 8 min shower by changing shower heads?

5. How could you find how much water comes out of a tap in 1 min without wasting any water?

6. Dentists recommend brushing your teeth 4 times a day for 3 min each time.
If you leave the tap running while brushing your teeth the recommended time, about how much water runs down the drain in a day?
About how much water is saved by turning the water on only to wet your brush and then to rinse at the end?

7. Over $\frac{1}{3}$ of the water that Canadians use each day goes down the toilet.
One flush uses about 12 L of water. Environment Canada suggests that placing two small bricks in the toilet tank can reduce the amount of water used by 20%. Estimate the volume of a small brick.

8. The capacity of a washing machine is about 80 L.
One load of laundry uses about 240 L of water. Explain.

9. A dishwasher uses about 40 L of water to wash and rinse a load of dishes. Tell how you could find out how much more or less water is used by washing and rinsing dishes in the sink.

10. 97% of the world's water is too salty to use. 2% is frozen.
What percent is left to use?
Show the percents on a grid graph.
Suppose all the world's water could fit in a 100 L tank.
How much water would be usable?
Only 2 mL of the 100 L of water would be drinkable.
What fraction of usable water is drinkable?
What fraction of all the water is drinkable?

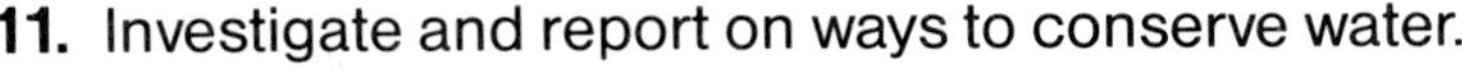

11. Investigate and report on ways to conserve water.

Did You Know...?

Canadians pay about 47¢ for 1000 L of water.

- What is the ratio of the cost of water to the cost of other things you drink?

HOW Many Mosquitoes Surround Us?

In Saskatoon, mosquitoes are counted once or twice a week at 15 light traps around the city.

How do you think a light trap works?
About how many counts might be taken in one month?
How might large numbers of mosquitoes in a trap be estimated?

1. What is the range of this data?
   Show the male and female data in a double stem-and-leaf plot.

Number of Mosquitoes Trapped

Week of	Greenhouse Trap		Golf Course Trap	
	Female	Male	Female	Male
May 14	24	6	92	15
May 21	6	0	8	2
May 28	4	2	53	7
June 4	2	0	2	2
June 11	129	46	117	79
June 18	8	1	31	6
June 25	15	1	81	26
July 2	0	0	6	0
July 9	9	0	36	3
July 16	11	0	37	6
July 23	84	17	293	87

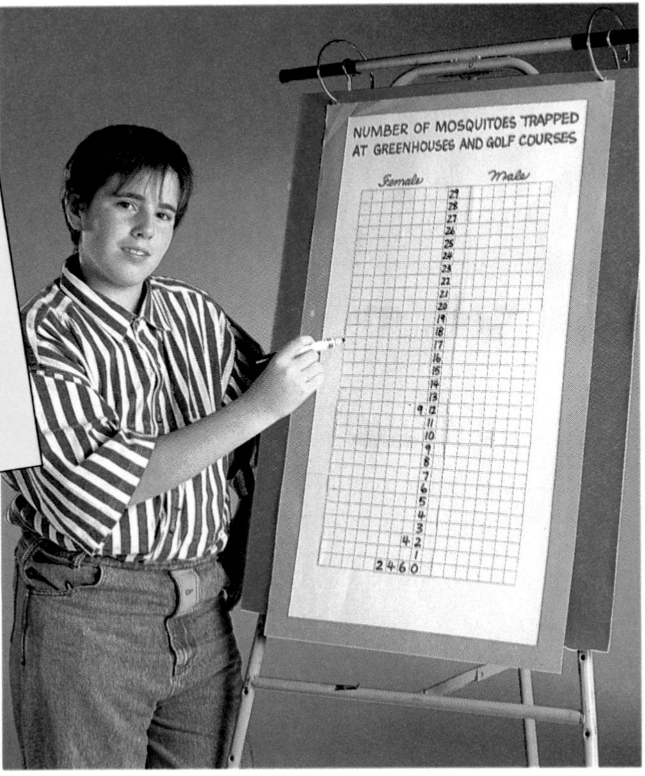

2. Tell three things you notice about the plot.

3. What is the middle number of females? males? About how many times as many females were trapped as males?

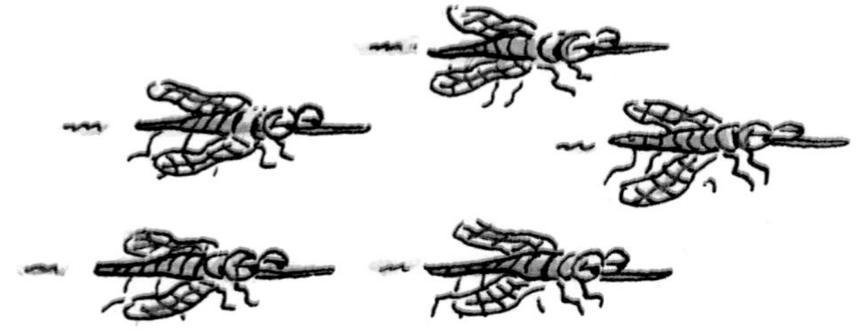

4. Would you want to show this data for the next four weeks on the stem-and-leaf plot you made?

Explain.

Number of Mosquitoes Trapped

Week of	Greenhouse Trap Female	Greenhouse Trap Male	Golf Course Trap Female	Golf Course Trap Male
July 30	1479	392	4060	478
Aug 6	994	228	6222	728
Aug 13	722	134	1873	178
Aug 20	1065	40	1446	83

5. What type of graph would show the change in numbers of mosquitoes over time? Find the total number of females and the total number of males for each week in Problem 4.

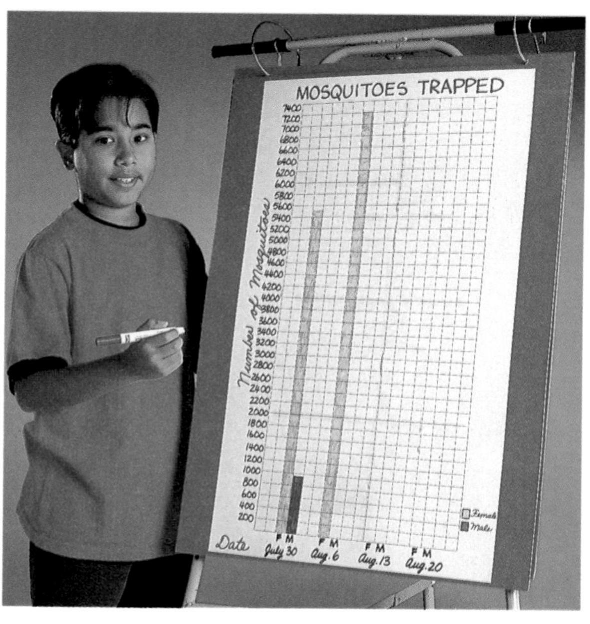

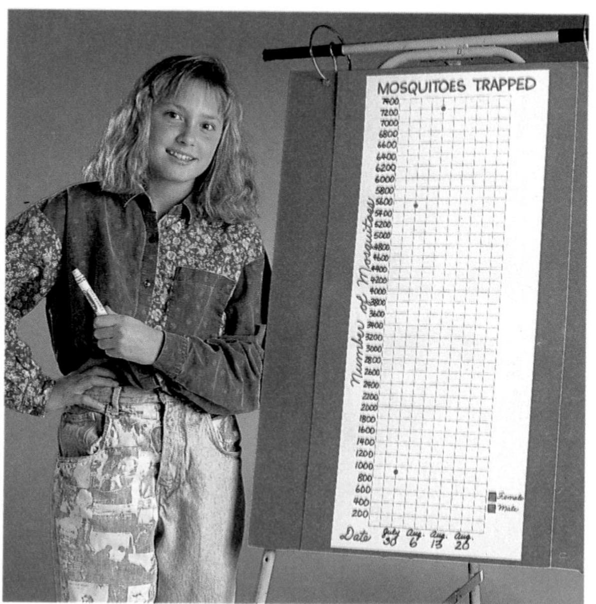

Make a graph using the totals. Use one color for female and another color for male. Why do you think the changes occur?

6. Female mosquitoes live up to 30 d and males live 10 d at most. How does this help explain the patterns in your graph?

7. The 423 female mosquitoes trapped the week of August 27 in the greenhouse trap were classified by species.

Estimate the percent of each species. Of which species could there have been 103 trapped? 76 trapped?

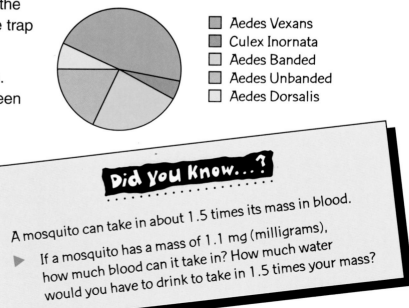

- Aedes Vexans
- Culex Inornata
- Aedes Banded
- Aedes Unbanded
- Aedes Dorsalis

8. Why do you think data is collected about mosquitoes?

A mosquito can take in about 1.5 times its mass in blood.

▶ If a mosquito has a mass of 1.1 mg (milligrams), how much blood can it take in? How much water would you have to drink to take in 1.5 times your mass?

WHAT'S Happening to Our Forests?

Canada has about 416.2 million ha (hectares) of forests.
1 ha = 10 000 m^2
What is the area of Canada's forests in square metres?

1. The non-forested land area of Canada is about 505.4 million ha. Which fraction most closely represents the fraction of Canada's land area that is forested? Explain.

   $\frac{4}{5}$ $\frac{5}{4}$ $\frac{4}{9}$

2. The world's forests are 10 times larger than those in Canada. About how many hectares of forests are there in the world?

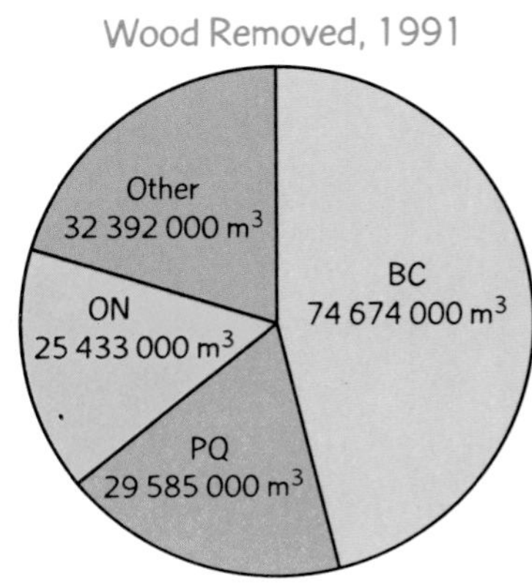

Forest Harvested, 1991

Other 229 174 ha

BC 193 654 ha

ON 199 719 ha

PQ 236 815 ha

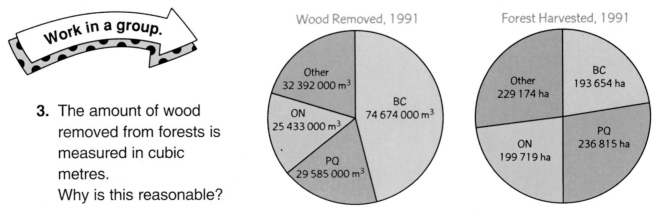

3. The amount of wood removed from forests is measured in cubic metres. Why is this reasonable?

   Approximately how many cubic metres of wood are removed per hectare of forest harvested for each part of Canada? Which part of Canada has the greatest rate? Why might this be?

4. At the 1991 rate of harvesting, about how long would it take to use up all of Canada's forests?

5. Find the missing entries in the table.

   Which provinces replace one-half or more of the trees they harvest?

Daily Forestry Activity in Canada

Province	Approximate Ratio of Area Harvested to Area Replanted	Approximate Hectares of Trees Harvested	Approximate Hectares of Trees Replanted
BC	1 : 1	?	525
AB	3 : 2	135	?
SK	?	50	15
MB	1 : 1	?	20
ON	5 : 2	550	?
PQ	9 : 2	650	?
NB	?	250	50
NS	?	100	20
PE	2 : 1	?	3
NF	7 : 1	60	?

6. It takes 1 ha of trees to absorb 6 t (tonnes) of carbon dioxide. That is about how much three automobiles emit in one year. There are over 13 million automobiles in Canada.
   About how many hectares of trees are needed to absorb their emissions?
   The total amount of the carbon dioxide produced in Canada is 4 times the amount produced by automobile emissions.
   Do we have enough forests to absorb our own carbon dioxide?
   Do you think other countries have enough to absorb their own? Explain.

7. What are some reasons why we use our forests? Why should we protect them?

Did You Know...?

Recycling one day's newspapers in Canada could save 40 000 trees.

▶ About how many trees could be saved in one year by recycling our newspapers?

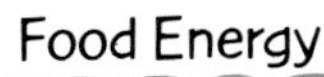

? I Wonder... ?

Food Energy

An average Canadian eats about 20 grocery carts of food in a year. Getting a cart of food to market uses the energy of about 25 L of gasoline. About how many litres of gasoline are used to get the food your family eats in a year to market? About how much would that cost at the gas pump?

Dumping Oil

Canadians dump about 300 million L of motor oil down sewers each year. If 1 L of oil can contaminate 200 million L of water, what effect does this disposal of oil have? If we continue to dispose of motor oil this way, how much of our lakes, rivers, and streams could potentially be contaminated over the next decade?

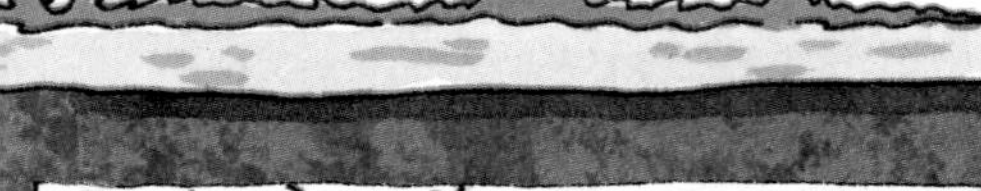

Car Pooling

To reduce air pollution, people are encouraged to car pool. To see people driving to or from work, count cars with 1, 2, 3, and 4 or more adults at an appropriate time and location. Display your results on a graph. What are other ways to minimize the number of cars on the roads?

Endangered Species

Each day 45 species of plants and animals disappear. At this rate, about how many fewer species of plants and animals will exist when you turn 18?

Investigate and report on an endangered species.

Population Explosion

Find out how the global population has grown over the past 100 years. How does this increase in population affect the environment?

Make up your OWN investigation. Then post it on the bulletin board for others to try.

Thinking Back . . .

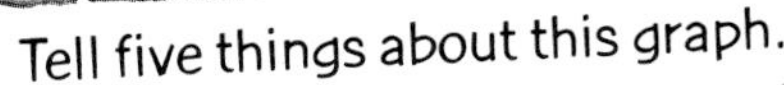

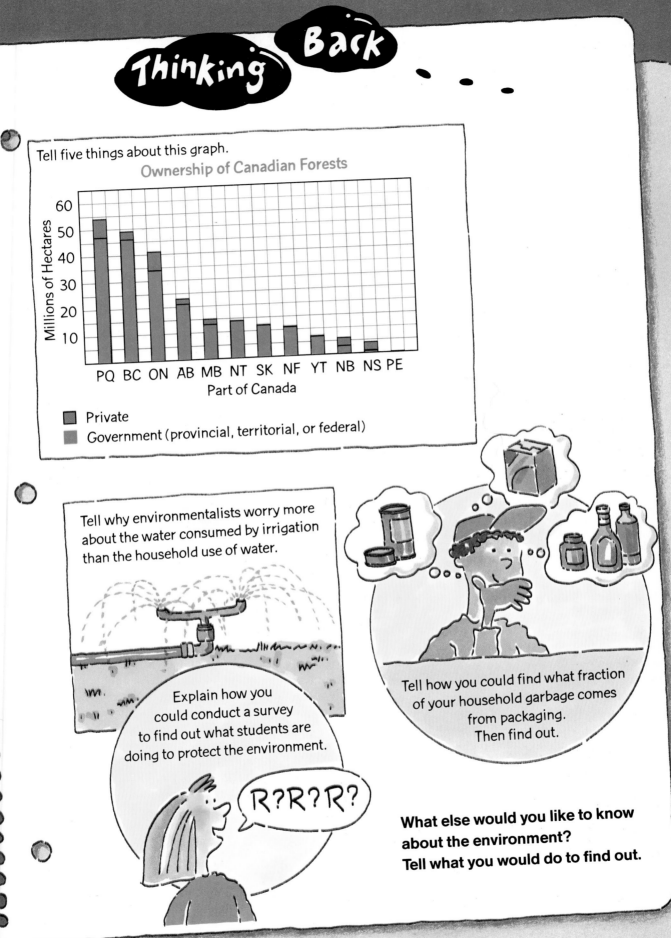

Tell five things about this graph.

Ownership of Canadian Forests

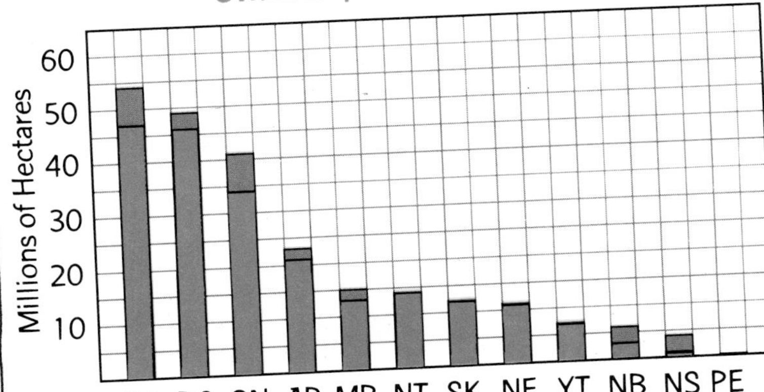

Tell why environmentalists worry more about the water consumed by irrigation than the household use of water.

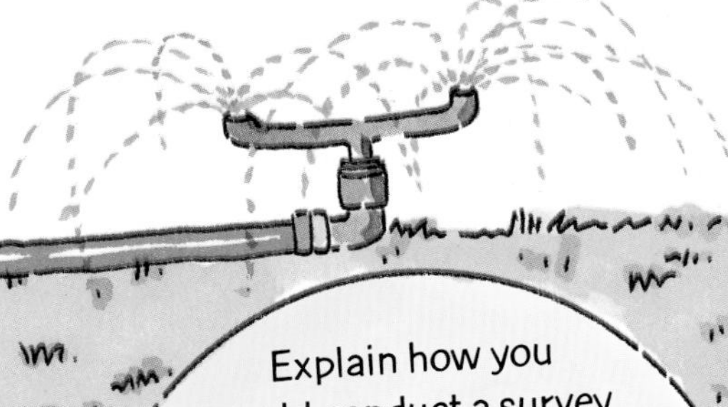

Tell how you could find what fraction of your household garbage comes from packaging. Then find out.

Explain how you could conduct a survey to find out what students are doing to protect the environment.

What else would you like to know about the environment? Tell what you would do to find out.

Index

A

Acute angles, 52-54, 56-58
Algebra, 154-167, 202-203, 206-207, 212-213
- equality, 156-159
- equations, 156-160, 202-203, 206-207, 212-213
- expressions, 154-155, 202-203, 206-207, 212-213

Angles, 44-65
- acute, 52-54, 56-58
- classifying, 50-54
- comparing, 46-51, 58
- drawing, 54
- estimating, 50-51, 53-54, 62
- in triangles, 56-58
- measuring, 52-58, 62
- obtuse, 52-54, 56-58, 62
- reflex, 53-54, 62
- right, 50-51, 52-53, 56-58
- straight, 50-51

Approximate numbers, 94-95
Area, 12-13, 137, 204-208, 217, 219, 228-229
- of a parallelogram, 207
- of a rectangle, 137, 204-208, 219
- of a triangle, 207
- surface area, 208

B

Bar graphs, 2-3, 7, 172-173, 178-179, 189, 227
- double bar graph, 178-179, 189

Broken-line graphs, 6-7, 178

C

Capacity, 84-85, 224-225
Circle graphs, 2-3, 74-75, 178-179, 183, 227-228
Composite numbers, 148-149, 164
Computer strategies, 3, 6-7, 178
- database, 6-7
- electronic network, 3
- graphing, 178

Congruence, 130-131
Coordinates, 132-133, 193

D

Data, 1-15, 74-75, 86-87, 90, 132-133, 170-171, 178-181, 183, 190-195, 226-229
- analysing, 2-3, 6-7, 10-11, 74-75, 178-181, 226-229
- bias, 4-5
- collecting, 4-5, 7, 75, 90, 181, 183
- comparing, 2-3, 6-7, 10-13, 74-75, 86-87, 178-181, 194-195, 226-229
- coordinates, 132-133, 193
- creating and solving problems, 190-191
- displaying, 6-7, 178-181, 226-227
- first-hand, 6-7
- general distribution, 6-7, 10-13, 170-171, 180-181, 190-191, 194-195, 226-229
- predicting, 192-193
- random sampling, 4-5
- schedules, 86-87
- second-hand, 6-7

Decimals, 10-11, 20-23, 28-29, 33, 36, 102-104, 110-112, 116
- division, 36, 110-112, 116
- multiplication, 33, 36, 102-104, 116
- number sense, 10-11, 20-23, 28-29
- ordering, 22-23, 28-29

Displacement, 214-215
Division, 33, 36, 40, 94-96, 106-112, 116, 142-143, 146, 150-151
- by powers of ten, 33, 36, 40
- decimal by a whole number, 110-112, 116
- decimal remainders, 108-109
- estimation, 36, 94-96, 106-107
- factors, 142-143, 146, 150-151

E

Equality, 156-159
Equations, 156-160, 202-203, 206-207, 212-213
Estimation, 36, 50-51, 53, 54, 62, 94-96, 192-193
- angles, 50-51, 53-54, 62
- large quantities, 36
- measurement, 192-193
- products, 94-96, 136
- quotients, 36, 94-96, 106-107

Expressions, 154-155, 202-203, 206-207, 212-213
- area, 206-207
- perimeter, 202-203

F

Factors, 142-143, 146, 150-151
Figurate numbers, 152
Flips, 126-129, 132-133, 135, 137
Fractions, 24-29
- equivalent, 26-29
- improper, 24-29
- ordering, 28-29

Frequency, 181

G

Geometry, 44-65, 84-85, 120-139, 200-215
- angles, 44-65
- congruence, 130-131
- flips, 126-129, 132-133, 137
- motions, 48-49, 120-139
- polygons, 56-57, 128-129, 200-208
- prisms, 124-125
- rectangles, 200-208
- slides, 122-125, 132-133, 137
- solids, 84-85, 124-125, 208, 210-216
- symmetry, 128-129
- triangles, 56-58, 203, 207

Graphs, 2-3, 6-7, 74-75, 132-133, 172, 178-179, 180-181, 183, 193-195, 226-228
- bar graphs, 2-3, 7, 172, 178-179, 227
- broken-line graphs, 6-7, 178
- circle graphs, 2-3, 74-75, 178-179, 227-228
- coordinates, 132-133, 193
- histograms, 2-3, 178-179
- percent graphs, 74-75, 178-179, 183, 194-195
- stem-and-leaf plots, 180-181, 226-227
- strip graphs, 2-3, 74-75

Greatest common factor (GCF), 146

H

Histograms, 2-3, 178-179
Hundred thousands, 8-9, 18-19, 40

I

Improper fractions, 24-29
Integers, 30-31
- comparing, 31

L

Least common multiple (LCM), 144-145
Length, 34-36, 192-193, 200-201

M

Mass, 84-85, 192-193
Measurement, 12-13, 20-21, 31, 33-36, 84-89, 137, 192-193, 198-222, 224-225, 228-229
- area, 12-13, 137, 204-209, 217, 228-229

capacity, 84-85, 224-225
estimation, 192-193
length, 34-36, 192-193, 200-201
mass, 84-85, 192-193
money, 20-21, 33, 88-89, 108-112
perimeter, 200-203
surface area, 208
temperature, 31
time, 86-89
unit conversion, 34-35
volume, 84-85, 210-215, 224-225
Millions, 8-9, 18-19, 36, 228-229
Mixed numbers, 24-29
Mode, 170-171, 180-181
Money, 20-21, 33, 88-89, 108-112
Motion geometry, 48-49, 120-139
combining motions, 132-133
slides, 122-125, 132-133, 135, 137
flips, 126-129, 132-133, 135, 137
Multiples, 144-145
Multiplication, 33, 36, 40, 92-104, 116, 144-145
algorithm, 100-101
by powers of ten, 33, 36, 40
decimal by a whole number, 33, 36, 102-104, 116
estimation, 36, 94-96
informal methods, 98-99
multiples, 144-145

N

Number, 8-11, 16-37, 148-149, 164
decimals, 10-11, 20-23, 28-29, 33, 36, 102-104, 110-112, 116
fractions, 24-29
hundred thousands, 8-9, 18-19, 40
integers, 30-31
millions, 8-9, 18-19, 36, 228-229
mixed numbers, 24-29
prime and composite, 148-149, 164
whole numbers, 8-10, 18-19
Number theory, 140-167
composite numbers, 148-149, 164
factors, 142-143, 146, 150-151
figurate numbers, 152
GCF, 146
LCM, 144-145
multiples, 144-145
prime factorization, 150-151
prime numbers, 148-149, 164

O

Obtuse angles, 52-54, 56-58, 62
Optical illusions, 130-131

P

Parallelograms, 200-203, 207
area of, 207
perimeter of, 200-203
Patterns, 152, 154-155, 162
Percent, 73-77, 79, 178-179, 183, 194-195, 224-225, 228-229
Perimeter, 200-203
Plots, 180-181
stem-and-leaf, 180-181
Populations, 4-5, 8-13
population density, 12-13
Powers of ten, 33, 36, 40
Prime factors, 150-151
Prime numbers, 148-149, 164
Prisms, 124-125
Probability, 168-188, 194-195
experimental, 174-177
sampling, 170-171
simulations, 172-173, 194-195
theoretical, 174-177
Problem solving, 38, 60, 77, 114, 135, 162, 183
doing an experiment, 77
drawing a diagram, 60
finding and extending a pattern, 162
finding relevant information, 183
guessing and testing, 114
making an organized list, 38
working backwards, 135

R

Random sampling, 4-5
Range, 180-181, 185
Rates, 88-89, 110-111
Ratios, 67-82, 178-179, 224-225
percent, 73-77, 79, 178-179, 224-225, 228-229
renaming, 70-71
Rectangles, 137, 200-208
area, 137, 204-208
perimeter, 200-203
Rectangular prism, 84-85, 208, 210-213
Reflections, 126-129, 132-133, 135, 137
Reflex angles, 53-54, 62
Relationships, 132-133, 152, 154-160, 162, 193, 202-203, 206-207, 212-213
Right angles, 50-53, 56-58
Rotations, 48-49
Rounding, 7-9, 18-23, 28-29, 108-109

S

Sampling, 4-5, 170-171
Schedules, 86-87
Simulations, 172-173, 194-195
Skeletons, 124-125
Slides, 122-125, 132-133, 135, 137
Solids, 84-85, 124-125, 208, 210-215
Statistics, 1-15, 168-188, 194-195
Stem-and-leaf plots, 180-181, 226-227
double stem-and-leaf plot, 226
Straight angles, 50-51
Strip graphs, 2-3, 74-75
Symmetry, 128-129

T

Temperature, 31
Thousandths, 10-11, 20-23, 36
Time, 86-89
24 h clock, 86-87
Translations, 122-125, 132-133, 135, 137
Triangle, 56-58, 203, 207
area of, 207
classifying, 56-58
perimeter of, 203
Triangular numbers, 152
Turns, 48-49

U

Unit price, 110-111

V

Volume, 84-85, 210-215, 224-225
and capacity, 224-225
by displacement, 214-215
of rectangular prisms, 84-85, 210-213
of irregular solids, 214-215

Credits

Acknowledgements

Acknowledgement is hereby made for kind permission to reprint the following material:
"If the World Were a Village of 1000 People" by Donella H. Meadows. From THE OLD FARMER'S ALMANAC 1992 by Yankee Publishing Inc. Copyright © 1992 by Yankee Publishing Inc. Reprinted by permission of Random House, Inc. "Germs" from AUNTIE'S KNITTING A BABY, © 1984 by Lois Simmie, reprinted with the permission of Douglas & McIntyre. "My Snake" from SOMETHING BIG HAS BEEN HERE by Jack Prelutsky, © 1990 by Jack Prelutsky, reprinted by Greenwillow Books, a division of William Morrow & Company, Inc. "Wink" from the KINGFISHER BOOK OF COMIC VERSE by Roger McGough, © 1986 by Roger McGough, reprinted by permission of the Peters Fraser and Dunlop Group Inc. "What's Cooking, Jenny Archer?" by Ellen Conford from WHAT'S COOKING, JENNY ARCHER? by Ellen Conford. Text copyright © 1989 Conford Enterprises Ltd.; illustrations copyright © 1989 by Diane Palmisciano. By permission of Little, Brown and Company. Extract and illustration from THROUGH THE MAGIC MIRROR by Anthony Browne, copyright © Anthony Browne, 1976. First published by Hamish Hamilton Children's Books in 1976. "The Sock Monster" from AN ARMADILLO IS NOT A PILLOW, poetry © 1986 by Lois Simmie, illustrations © 1986 by Anne Simmie, reprinted with the permission of Douglas & McIntyre. "Stone Soup" by John Warren Stewig. Text copyright © 1991 by John Warren Stewig. Illustrations copyright © 1991 by Margot Tomes. All rights reserved. Reprinted from STONE SOUP by permission of Holiday House.

Every reasonable precaution has been taken to trace the owners of copyright material and to make due acknowledgment. Any omission will be gladly rectified in future editions.

Photographs

page 8, Comstock/Malak; pages 22-23: Focus on Sports Inc.; page 74: Michael Ponzini/Focus on Sports Inc.; page 83; Stephen MacGillivray/A Thousand Words Photography, Fredricton, N.B.; page 85: Comstock/W. Griebeling; page 122: Clay Morehead/Cadcorp Systems; page 172: Maria Taglienti/The Image Bank; page 189: David Madison/Tony Stone Images; page 190: (top right) Greg Stott, (bottom) Canapress; page 191 (top and bottom) Canapress; page 194 (top right) Canapress; page 210: (top right) Peter Wilson, (top left and centre) E.G. Walker/University of Saskatchewan; page 223. Tom McCrae; page 224: (top) Greg Vaughn/Tom Stack & Assoc., (centre) Tom McCrae, (bottom) Kadir Kir/Southern Stock Photos; page 225: (top) Comstock/S. Feld, (bottom) Al Harvey/Masterfile; page 228. Yuri Dojc/The Image Bank: page 229: (top) Al Harvey/Masterfile, (bottom) Thomas Kitchin/Tom Stack & Assoc.
Product photos by Tom McCrae: pages 1, 19, 44, 67 (top), 71 (top), 84 (top, second last, bottom), 85 (top), 88 (top), 92 (top), 100 (bottom right and left), 101 (top), 120 (triangles), 125, 129, 199, 204, 208, 212, 215 (left and right), 226 (top)
All other photos by Ray Boudreau